The Guardian Year

'96

Introduction by **Nick Hornby**
Edited by **Georgina Henry**

FOURTH ESTATE • *London*

First published in Great Britain in 1996 by
Fourth Estate Limited
6 Salem Road
London W2 4BU

A catalogue record for this book is available from
the British Library

ISBN 1-85702-551-2

Typeset by Rowland Phototypesetting Ltd,
Bury St Edmunds, Suffolk
Printed in Great Britain by Bath Press

Contents

The state we're in
....

Family values
....

Contents

Mad cows and Englishmen

Foreign parts

Crime and punishment

Contents

Cultural matters
··························

Fond farewells
··················

Contents

Sporting life

Nick Hornby
Introduction

'**D**o you love England, lads? Do you really love England?'
Three of us, my brother, a friend and I, were dragging our feet
through the streets of Wembley, drained and a little dispirited after
the epic but ultimately fruitless Euro '96 semifinal against Germany; the last
thing we wanted was to have to engage in a debate about nationality with a
confrontational nutter – especially a nutter wrapped in the flag of St George, a
sartorial detail which suggested that through his own internal dialectic process
he had successfully managed to quell all those nagging little doubts many of
us have about patriotism.

I have to say, though, that at that precise moment – just 15 minutes or so
after our national team's dignified exit from a tournament to which they had
made a surprisingly stylish contribution – I found the nutter's question interesting. Do I really love England? Maybe this was the time to sort it out, once and
for all. (I should point out here that the nutter was, significantly, on his own,
as people like him so often are. There may be hundreds of thousands of Englishmen who are prepared to come up to you in the street and start spouting
gibberish at you, but at least none of them seem to have friends.) 'Well,' I
wanted to say, 'most of the time, I don't. Most of the time I'm embarrassed.
But just occasionally – when I'm watching a Mike Leigh film, say, or Vic and
Bob's *Shooting Stars*, or when I'm eating a delivery curry, or taking my son to
the GP – I get this little twinge of something or other that might, in a dim
light, pass as a love for my country. Do you know what I mean?'

But I feared, looking at his cloak, that he might not know what I mean, and
that in any case this was not the answer he was looking for. So the three of us
mumbled that we did love England – very, very much – and he nodded with
satisfaction and told us to 'fucking sing up for them', and then he wandered
off into the night, baying rabidly, and we plodded on.

1996 has been a year in which the flag-wearer's question seems to have been
asked – by John Major and Tony Blair and Gareth Southgate and Tim Henman
and the *Daily Mirror* and hundreds of others – over and over again, in precisely
the same tones. Do you love England? (Not Britain. Not this year. This year
the Scots and Welsh and the Irish have left the English to get on with it, and
very wisely too.) Then you must eat our diseased beef. Do you love England?
Then you must hate the Krauts, or the Frogs, or the Tories, or the Labour Party,
or Brussels, or some Swede with a big forehand of whom you had never even
heard a couple of weeks previously. When the pathetic, imbecilic editor of the
Daily Mirror declared war on Germany three days before the Euro '96 semifinal,

the temptation to take the usual liberal escape route, and express disgust with anything and everything that might provoke any kind of patriotic stirrings, became almost overwhelming.

The trouble with running away from it all is that the hole you create by your departure is (and has been) filled by the monsters, and no one has any kind of sensible debate about what it means to be English, or whether there is any pleasure to be taken from our nationality. There isn't a *Guardian* reader alive who has any truck with the versions of nationalism so crudely disseminated in other newspapers, not all of them tabloids; so what does it mean, then, when a great many of these same readers began to howl with a very real anguish at the television screen when Darren Anderton hit the post in extra time?

Englishness, pronounced Bernard Crick with great finality, is 'ironic tolerance, not vulgar self-assertion'; and yet it was not only the vulgarians who leapt to their feet when David Seaman saved the crucial Spanish penalty to win England's semifinal place, nor was it only the vulgarians whose hearts sank to their boots when Gareth Southgate missed his kick, thus costing his team an appearance in the final. Unless we are all vulgarians, of course, in which case Professor Crick has got it wrong: a definition of Englishness which takes no account of the way the majority of the English actually *are* (and there is no doubt that a majority of us wanted our national team to beat the Germans in the most vulgarly assertive fashion imaginable) isn't really worth very much. In any case, one suspects that Crick's definition of Englishness is now applicable to the male, white, middle-aged middle class – to Julian Critchley, say, but not to Benjamin Zephaniah, and to Sir Tim Rice, but probably not to Jo Brand.

Ironic tolerance doesn't really help when you sit down to watch a football match. Sport works best for the spectator when there is some kind of passionate involvement, and when England play Germany, the chances are that Englishmen and women are going to want to see England win. Is that a bad thing? Should we all be supporting Brotherhood of Man United, or is it OK to feel a kinship with David 'Bull' Seaman and Gazza? When passionate involvement leads to pictures of Stuart Pearce in a tin hat and riots in Trafalgar Square, one is bound to feel uneasy about it all; but I have to say that very little of the behaviour of the enormous, noisy, partisan crowd at Wembley for the semifinal struck me as unhealthy. There was a pained, dignified silence in the immediate aftermath of the defeat: warm applause for the losing team's lap of honour; slightly less warm applause, but applause none the less, for the winners as they left the field. We loved having a major sporting tournament in this country, and despite all the fears and dire predictions, we behaved as though we loved it, too.

Maybe the best thing about Euro '96 was that, for a brief period, all that Eng-er-land stuff wasn't left to the politicians and the boneheads; for once, Wembley was full of the right kind of football fans, the ones who don't make Nazi gestures during the National Anthem, and both players and coach expressed their impatience with the tabloids and their insistence on ersatz warfare. Just for a moment we looked like a happy, celebratory, sensible nation with a half-decent football team. (The following week, Cliff Richard sang unaccompanied in the rain at Wimbledon while a collection of Sloanes, suits and baffled tourists waved Union Jacks, and we went back to looking barking mad and pitiably useless once again.)

Why can't life be more like the best parts of those three weeks? Partly because sport can never really answer any questions – in fact, it simply poses more. English blacks, according to *The Voice*, were not supporting England at all; rather, such was their sense of alienation from a team that found room for only one black player that they were supporting England's opponents, whoever they were. (Presumably, the sinister link between a hard core of England fans and the far right hasn't helped persuade England's black community that this is their team too.) But news from elsewhere suggested that a healthy racial mix did not necessarily produce a healthier atmosphere: it emerged that the Dutch team, which was nearly half black, had split neatly along racial lines into two warring camps.

In the end, I suppose, anyone with any sense will always find more in their country that embarrasses them than fills them with pride, and England seems a more embarrassing country than many, especially this year, when being English seemed synonymous with being bumptious, arrogant, stupid, bellicose and puerile. (Hi, Piers!) So when something goes right, as Paul Simon observed, it's apt to confuse us, because it's such an unusual sight. When Alan Shearer scored England's fourth goal against the Dutch to cap a brilliant performance, full of flair and wit and guile, against one of the best teams in the world, I and many millions of others were very confused indeed.

I spent some of 1996 travelling in Europe to promote a book, feeling humbled by my hosts' familiarity with a literature other than their own, by their facility with the English language, by their obvious ease with the idea of a modern, cooperative Europe. It was difficult this year to look towards home for any similar sense of cosmopolitan comfort – or for any sense at all, half the time. The football helped, for the first time ever; so did this newspaper. Several times on these trips I was asked whether I ever wrote for the *Guardian*. 'I wish we had a paper like that,' they said when I replied that I had done on occasions. *The 'Grauniad'*? I thought. Surely *everyone's* got a paper like the 'Grauniad'? But of course that couldn't be true. The *Guardian*'s eccentric mix of right-on rage, sassiness, humanity, and, yes, ironic tolerance could surely only be possible in Britain. It's not much, but it's home.

The state we're in

25 *January 1996*
John Vidal
In the forest, in the dark

aynes Park, south London, 3.45pm, Sunday: 35 men wait at the station for the 'Nostalgia Tours' bus to Newbury. Six protesters have arrived, too, and are removed by the police. Ten days after a cursory interview, after three false starts and 20 phone calls to 'Howard' at Blue Arrow employment agency, I still have no assurance that I have work as a guard on the controversial bypass. Using my own name and national insurance number I have posed as a French carpenter with broken English and a theatrical accent looking for work in Tooting.

The only work offered was 'in security'. My job references (one fake, two half true) have not been taken up. I have been given no training, no physical or mental test. I was asked to bring two pieces of identification to the interview but have not been asked to show them. Blue Arrow has given me a piece of paper which explains how to lift objects. The hardest question I have been asked is to copy the number 54321. I am told only that the work is 40 miles outside London.

'You been watching television' – Howard.

'But *non*.'

'Well, the company, Reliance Security, will tell you everything when you get there. Don't worry, Frenchie. It's £4 an hour, less three quid a day food and board, less tax, less insurance, so you should clear £200 a week. Bring a thermos and a torch, kit for a week, OK?'

5pm. The bus leaves for Newbury. The former RAF, now occasionally used depot 10 miles north of the town is bleak, windswept. There are floodlights and security checks on one outer, one inner gate. 450 men – the majority new recruits aged 18–25 from all over south London, Kent and Hampshire – are billeted in hangars B and C. The beds are three feet apart, each 'dormitory' is 90 yards long and lit by 160 fluorescent tubes. I am in C block.

9pm. The queue for food stretches 100 yards. It takes three hours in the open to get served (warm) spaghetti bolognese and chips in the dark. There is one stove, two cooks, one microwave for 440 people.

'It's the f***ing army, innit?' – Steve, from Chatham.

'More like f***ing prison.' – Dick.

'F***ing Auschwitz. You can't even phone out. It's my wife's birthday tomorrow.' – Colin.

'Half the guards got food poisoning last week.'

'It was the f***ing chicken. It went off and they had to throw it out in the

Newbury bypass

morning. I reckon the caterers served it up in curry in the evening. They sent 100 of us home. It's f***ing chaos here.'

10.30pm. Queue for 50 minutes for boots, overalls, helmets, etc. Showers do not work; there's no lighting in the outside lavatories. 'This is heaven after last week, mate. We had a f***ing river running through our tent. Mud up to our ankles.' The camp is full of unskilled, uneducated, unemployed Britain. Plumbers, chefs, roofers, carpenters, labourers, drivers, factory workers. About 10 per cent are black; there are Algerians, Indians, a few students and about eight women. Two guards say they were homeless the previous night.

'This work is a godsend. It's the first I've had in two years. We should thank the protesters for it.' – Michael.

'I've been watching telly for two years. That's not a life, is it?' – Darryl of Dartford.

11pm. 'But who are zees 'ippies in ze trees? Zey are poor people, unemployed like you, *non?*'

'They're f***ing smellies.' – Jim.

'They spit at you, taunt you. Most of them are quite nice, but they're mental, aren't they?' – unidentified guard.

'They piss at you from the trees.'

'Anyone pisses on me from a tree and I'll sort them.'

'The women are f***ing ugly.'

'They plait their f***ing armpits.'

'They must f***ing love those trees. Love them to f***ing death.'

'But they are brave, *non?* They defend the beautiful Engleesh environment?'

'F*** the f***ing trees. They know their business. They're f***ing sharp.'

'Mental more like. You listen to them. They've got nice voices, but they live in f***ing holes. How can you talk like that and live like a f***ing animal?'

11.30pm. Briefing in Hangar A. 'Right, lads. We've had to organise this camp in three days so there are a few teething problems. What you need to know is yellow hats are management, team leaders wear red and you're all security officers, so you're white, right? All you've got to do is what you're told. It's 12 hours a day shifts. Seven days on, three off. We're here to allow the bypass to be built. So, all new guards over here. All without beds there. Those without kit here. Old guards with no bedding here. We'll sort out identity cards tomorrow.'

Chaos ensues. 'F***ing hell. Who are these gits?' – Steve, Chatham.

'Every red hat talks a right load of bollocks.' – Gerry.

1.30am. 'I look like a giant dick in a condom.' – Ray, jumping around in sleeping bag as the blacks turn up the rap music and whites retaliate with house. 'Turn it f***ing off.'

Shouts, cheers, jeers, etc.

4.30am. 'Morning, lads. The showers aren't working because the generator leaked diesel last night. So breakfast will be f***ing late.' We queue for two and a half hours for two warm sausages, beans, and cold eggs. There's no water. The milk is off. There is a three-feet-high pile of chips and last night's plates have not been cleared away. There are no clean cups and the Portaloos are squalid.

'This is bollocks.' – Jim, at end of queue for breakfast.

9am. On bus. Protesters locked themselves to the gates at dawn. They have delayed the work of 450 people for three hours and been freed by firemen coming to clear the spilt diesel. Paranoia and disinformation are rife. Coach talk is how the protesters are being paid £30 a day, tree climbers £500 a day by Greenpeace; how the leak in the generator was by saboteurs. 'Animal f***ing rights are coming up, and those heavy gits from Brixton. At least two protesters have mustard gas.'

10.30am. Still on bus. 'Most of the men here are OK. They're here just for the money. I'd say 5 per cent want trouble.' – Jim (red hat).

11am. 'I'm here for the action. It's like a hunt, innit, Frenchie? It's the adrenalin. You take out someone and you know you've got two men backing you up. You ask how you can take out someone twice your size. How the f*** do I do that, you say. You go over to someone. Hit him as you go past, step on him you know where. Then you say sorry.'

'But why must you say sorry?'

'This is f***ing Britain, innit?'

11.30am. Arrive at Penn Wood. One hundred and fifty guards run out of the three coaches screaming. The red hats try to make a square around an acre of trees. They are obsessed with the space between people: 'Three feet to the left, lads. No, six feet to the right. You, over there, five paces, quick. You join the line there. We want a strong taut line. Face outwards. Now. Now!'

'Why?'

'Cos the f***ing enemy is out there in the trees.' – Red hat.

The 'enemy' arrives in dribs and drabs, singing songs and playing the mandolin and pipes, laughing. Some protesters sit in the trees, hang upside down like howla monkeys. Some bellow insults. We guards are arm to arm, silent, sullen. More protesters walk around with drums, pipes, flutes. We are told to stare ahead. The rules of engagement are that the protesters can insult us. We are not allowed to accept anything from them (fear of poisoning?), to fraternise, or to discuss the rights and wrongs of the bypass (fear of argument, the press, etc).

'You. What you going to tell your children tonight?'

'What's it feel like to rape your mother? Your children won't be able to breathe. There'll be no air.' – protesters.

'How you feel when zey say this?'

'It makes me want to f***ing clock 'em. We'll get our turn, later, Frenchie. Just wait.' – John.

The security box unit moves slowly along the edge of an old railway embankment, ingesting anything over six feet high. It takes up to 20 seconds to fell a 30-foot tree. There are 10,000 trees to fell. Today perhaps 100 have been dropped. 'We're almost on target.' – Engineer with the road contractors, Mott McDonald.

A protester throws water up to a friend in a tree. It falls short and lies on the ground.

'Don't anyone give it to her.' – Red hat.

'Why not? She is human, *non*? It is a right to have water.'

I throw it up to her. It misses. A red hat takes me by the arm. 'That's it, mate. That's f***ing it, you're fired.' We go to a yellow hat. 'I told him three times,' he lies.

'Why you cannot give water?'

'OK. It's your first day. Don't do it again.'

2.45pm. Lunch, eaten standing up, 'on guard' against the quiet, empty wood. Two rounds of sandwiches ('This f***ing ham's thinner than a blue Rizla. Call this lunch?' – Dave), one can of Coke.

6.30pm. Back in camp. 'I've had enough of this bollocks. It's not a life. The work is cak, the food is cak, the pay is cak. I'm going back to Dartford. They can f***ing take me back.' – Derek.

8.30pm. Reliance has fired the catering company, found another. 'Real chefs don't cook chips,' says Mike. He serves bolognese and rice. Busloads of men have gone into the village to collect drink. They return with wine, beer. Wafts of marijuana in the recreation hall and C block. 'It's f***ing party time, Frenchie.'

11.20pm. Coaches arrive back from village with more drink. Rows started in the pub now spill into the dormitory. The noise of rap and house music in C block is deafening. A faction of young drunk whites has been taunting a group of 12 or more drunk blacks. There is sparring and shouting. Within 20 minutes it is more serious, beds are being overturned, there are running fights, screaming, and more than 50 people are involved. Red hat security guards restrain and lead away the (white) ringleader.

1am. C block begins to quieten, with sporadic eruptions. 'The police are coming. We'll deal with those people who need to be dealt with in the morning,' says a red hat. 'If we do it now, it's likely to incite more trouble. Three people are badly hurt. No one has been knifed. Get to bed.'

In B block the security guards are told the camp is burning. No one sleeps more than an hour.

4.30am. 'Right, lads. Time to get up. Breakfast is sausage, eggs, beans and bacon and it's ready and the buses are leaving on time.' – Red hat. Breakfast is eggs, beans and cold bacon. 'More crap.' – Steve.

'I wish I'd never heard of that interview. I'd rather do nothing than stay here. This is stupid. I'm going back and I know at least 20 who will come, too.' – Kevin.

6.30am. 'This is going to be one bitch of a day.' – Woman security guard on coach watching rain, sleet.

It is bitterly cold. The protesters are locked on to the gates again, and to one of the coaches. Work has been delayed. 'Of course a lot of what they say is right. In this country it's all about money and power. The politicians say there is too much congestion so the road is built at any price, no matter what the cost. We know it's wrong, but we need the money.' – Older guard.

8.30am. Arrive in lay-by near Newbury. Coach door opens. 'Keith', Reliance head of operations on Tuesday, enters. He wears a masonic ring and a helmet numbered 45064.

'Right, lads. Sorry about yesterday. No one had a fair crack. There's going to be no pratting about today. Anything in the trees today you whack, right? Anything hanging in a tree, f*** it off. Thwack it with your helmet. Anything. And don't get caught.' [Exit, to cheers.]

The bus is excited. 'Don't forget to say good morning as you break their fingers.' – Puffy-faced, rimless-spectacled Guard 1.

'I'd cut the trees down with the smellies in them. Do that once and you won't have this problem.' – Smaller spectacled Guard B.

'If you're up the tree you're coming down with it.' – Guard 3 (no identification).

'It's their own fault.' – Guard 1.

'Take no prisoners.' – Guard 2.

'Tell them to f*** off three times.' – Guard 3.

The coach stops. 'Can we go and kick crap out of them now?' – Guard 2.

'Remember, a kidney punch doesn't leave bruises, lads. That's a well-learned lesson. That's how I got away with bullying at school.' – Guard 1.

The pine woods are silent, eerie in the mist and the drizzle. As we file off the coach 20 protesters are hanging in trees. Some are pulled down, others arrested on the spot for aggravated trespass. The guards form a square around the trees. The chainsaw gangs move quickly to cut the ropes and then fell the trees. More protesters arrive, singing songs. An Oxford musicologist tells a story. 'You're the worst audience I've ever had.'

Two people with 'legal observer' jackets arrive. I am told by a red hat not to let them pass through to where people are being arrested.

'Why not?'

'They're protesters, that's why.'

'But who can you trust to see justice?'

'These people' [he motions to a group of green hatted men who work for the contractors, Mott McDonald]. 'Only them.'

'But they are *parti pris, non?*'

'Shut it, mate, or you'll get fired. Listen, most us are OK. We just want to work. We can't say anything or we lose our work. What can we do?' – Security guard.

12pm. Enter protester bearing water. [To me, in French.] 'Where are you from?'

'*Je viens de Paris.*'

'No you don't, I'm from Paris. Who are you?'

'*Merde alors.* Trust me. I am a journalist. Please don't tell anyone.'

Enter Keith. 'Monsieur, I do not understand. This morning you tell us to "thwack" ze protesters from the trees. But that is not the law. How can you explain thees? I have no training. I do not understand. How much force can I use?'

He is furious. 'You will go from here. I'm sending you away from the front line.'

'But what have I done? I am being puneeshed for 'aving no training, no identification. No one tells me anything. I 'ave no security number. Is this *la loi anglaise?*'

'You are not being fired. But if you have no training you cannot be on the front line. Take him away.' I am escorted 800 yards to the road, told to sit in a van. It is easy to get out, dodge the guards, use a mobile phone and summon a friend with a car.

One hour later the guards 'kick shit' (say the protesters) out of a pantomime horse which tries to make a dash to the trees. Ten minutes later one protester falls out of a tree. An ambulance takes him away. ●

Some names have been changed.

12 February 1996

Nancy Banks-Smith

Eyewitness

The solid body of Otis the dog, put down as a supposed pit bull, was lying on the pavement outside Limehouse police station. A small bunch of us had gathered in woolly hats and the darkening damp to make a fuss about this. There was a rather ragged chorus of 'Murderers!' A small crew from *London Tonight* were covering the story. It is the sort of job a junior reporter gets on a Friday night.

The police had been slow to produce Otis's body. They said there was a bomb scare. We said that was a likely story.

In retrospect everything – the body, the TV crew, the anger – seemed like a parody of what was to come.

Eric and I went home on the Docklands Light Railway. Eric is my dog. From the little train, which winds overhead, the lights of the glass palaces are reflected in the darkness of the water. Very like Disneyland, where monsters from the black lagoon raise snaky heads as your little train passes.

No monsters here.

At Canary Wharf station we were told there was a security alert and we should continue by bus.

Canary Wharf looks like the opening titles for *Dallas*: a fountain, a skyscraper. The bus stop is solid glass.

A dozen of us were waiting. There was a woman with a sheaf of Madonna lilies and a bunch of young lads trying to get to the Arena. They had tickets for a basketball match, which started at 7pm. It was 7pm. Now.

At 7.01pm there was a noise like the door of a padded cell slamming, soft and vast. I went deaf.

A woman fell flat on the pavement, her bags of shopping spread out on either side like plastic wings. Eric collapsed. A fleet of black cabs took off from their rank in perfect formation like bats out of hell. Their lights were on but they weren't picking up anybody.

Everyone started to run and, as they ran, they all turned their heads and looked back at Canary Wharf Tower.

I picked up Eric and ran after them.

There were fire engines, ambulances, police cars and a helicopter, but no buses. Mobile phones were out in force but public phones were dead. We all trudged like a column of refugees. It is about four miles round the Isle of Dogs.

On TV Richard Gaisford, the young reporter who had been doggedly covering Otis, was now covering the bomb. *London Tonight* said they were the first crew

West Belfast

on the spot. They didn't say why. My picture was full of snow because the cable company's dish had been knocked askew by the blast.

Eric? He has started to run away. I found him yesterday, after hours of searching among shattered glass, with a film crew who were shooting *Bugs*.

There is always a film crew shooting on the island. For one reason or another. ●

13 February 1996
Hugo Young
A Major mistake and chance lost for ever

There is not and never was a chance of the IRA's capacity for violence disappearing into history. Too much Semtex and too many guns are piled in the back roads of Cork and Armagh and, no doubt, the Home Counties. This would have continued to be the case, whatever terms of 'de-commissioning' had been agreed, and whatever undying promises had preceded the all-party talks. Violence was, is and always will be a potential condition of existence in and concerning Ireland, whether or not any given batch of leaders has agreed to end it.

In these circumstances, the British demand on de-commissioning and renunciation was always more totemic than substantive. If it had been satisfied, that wouldn't have removed the threat of violence. For ministers to talk about not negotiating 'when one party has a gun outside the door' may have sounded reasonable, but posed, in fact, an unreal hypothesis. The purpose was symbolic: to make the IRA eat dirt. That is a diet the IRA deserves to have stuffed down its throat, but it had almost nothing to do with effective peace-making. Unmentioned in the Downing Street Declaration, it was a way of belatedly recompensing the people most put out by both declaration and framework document, the Ulster Unionists.

However, the demand was inconsistent with the strategy Major had already adopted. This was, bravely and irregularly, to override the Unionist veto on political progress. Major's text was that Britain no longer entertained a 'selfish' interest in Northern Ireland. Deciding to devote himself to a new way of peace, he was prepared to shatter icons. He liberated himself from the past, and sought to bypass old entanglements. Ulster, he made plain, no longer had the same eternal place as Cornwall or Wales in British thinking. Its connection was contingent, and he would not strive to keep it alive against any majority inclination that disclosed itself in the future.

This was a remarkable shift. It was not, however, a betrayal of the Ulster majority. Behind it stood the unequivocal assertion that the majority would be defended. It proposed a new way forward whereby the mainland polity, entering an alliance with the Dublin government, simultaneously defended the status quo while acknowledging that, if the will of the people changed, it might not last for ever. The logic of this was that London would talk to Sinn Fein even though the IRA threat could plainly not be definitively written out of the script.

The point of the strategy was to create a new reality that might lead to a political settlement. It could never ordain that the threat of violence was wiped off the agenda, but it could make the cost of violence, to the IRA, ever more unsustainable. If all-party talks began, in parallel with rather than preceded by de-commissioning, they would be another step forward, a proof that the momentum of peace could be preserved, a way of further bedding down a new status quo. It is a great tragedy that they did not occur. If they had, there would have been no South Quay bomb. There might, it is true, have been a later bomb somewhere else. But if the logic of the Major strategy had been pursued, both to protect Unionist rights and to recognise Nationalist aspirations, it would have ended by marginalising the IRA.

So it is tragic that the logic was suspended. The South Quay bomb was an IRA obscenity. Nobody else takes a scintilla of the blame. By detonating it, moreover, the IRA has eliminated the chance of Major resuming the line he was pursuing. His own party and his own instincts, quite separate from the Unionists and their control over his parliamentary position, will now combine against permitting the kind of slow, slinky manoeuvres he seemed at one time to be constructively engaged in. For now that this appalling act of violence has been carried out, it is hard to see how any democratic politician could fail to demand from Sinn Fein, before resuming political dialogue, a more rigorous renunciation than they've ever made up to now. This must mean that the chances of resuming the peace process are slender. It seems most likely, long though it will be denied, that Mr Major's strategy has been destroyed, along with Gerry Adams, in whom lay the best hope of making it work.

If my analysis is correct, it says something grave about the British political process. If the de-commissioning demand was, in the real world, a chimera, then this whole political edifice Mr Major constructed was not well served by it. It was invented to satisfy the Unionists, who were thus able to impose their view on the entire negotiating procedure, and almost the entire House of Commons.

The House of Commons is important. It has been a place of reliable consensus from the beginning to the end of the peace process. But we begin to see the weaknesses of this. There was a huge majority for the process, and thus for the adventurous modifications it made on time-honoured British attitudes to Ulster. It is hard to believe, given the symbolic nature of the required de-commissioning, that the majority, given a free hand, would have allowed that to stop the process dead. If the Government had found another way of dealing with it, Mr Major would have secured the certain agreement of most MPs. But at the last, he ran away from his own logic. Instead of assembling a critical mass of British politicians behind a process that posed no genuine threat to the Unionist constituency, he let the Unionists draw their line in the sand.

We know one reason why this happened. The Tories feared for their position. Enjoying a vast majority for their Irish policy, they were and are vulnerable on every other policy. Such is the grim arithmetic of political priorities. But, over Northern Ireland, they had started something brilliant, and sustained it, on behalf of the people, against many malignities. Its enemies were denied their opportunity. But now that they have seized it, the moment may not recur for years. ●

....

3 April 1996
Martin Kettle
Cowardice in the face of the ruling class

A persuasive security briefing, especially ushering from the painted lips of Dame Stella Rimington, is a difficult thing for an impressionable chap to argue against. If an intelligent lay Health Secretary can find himself powerless to contradict his specialist medical advisers, then what chance is there that a jobbing politician could defy the advice of a security chief who speaks with sweet reason and whose information is, of its very nature, uncontradictable?

For Labour shadow ministers, who ache from lack of office, the pressure to agree is almost irresistible. The police are familiar with the psychology of such moments and how they fuel the longing to please. No one should imagine these things are easy. Which of us, beguilingly informed by Dame Stella that the IRA plans an Easter Rising 80th-anniversary bombfest over the Bank Holiday and that fresh powers are needed to prevent it, could deny her what she wants?

Certainly not Jack Straw, that's clear. Labour's shadow ministers may have played hard to get before Michael Howard called them in to announce his instant-whip anti-terrorism legislation. They may have been told something so horrendously shocking about an imminent IRA outrage and the capacity of fresh powers to prevent it. They may even have persuaded themselves that they forced Howard to accept some important concessions restricting the police's right to rummage unchallenged in our underwear.

But the reality is that they were taken for a ride. We know it. Most MPs know it. And deny it though they must, the shadows probably know it deep down too. Monday's Commons statement and yesterday's blink-and-you-missed-it legislative process were a revealing moment. Jack Straw is neither a fool nor a rogue, but this week he has been a sucker. And if he can be a sucker now, in opposition, then what will he be like in government?

The greatest fear that anyone can have about a future Labour government is not that they will do a silly thing, a wrong thing or an unsuccessful thing. Those we can take. The real fear is that they will do nothing. And this week's shabby little shocker, to purloin a phrase from an early review of *Tosca*, sends just such an awful shiver down the spine.

The first time I ever sat through a parliamentary debate was in November 1974 when the Wilson government rushed the first Prevention of Terrorism Act through the Commons. It was an evening which is hard to forget, especially for Roy Jenkins's speech in which he described the bill as draconian and unprecedented in peacetime. The whole debate, it is worth remembering, was predicated on the fact that the act would be strictly temporary, and that in no way was it the thin end of the legislative wedge.

Twenty-two years on, we know better. The PTA has become permanent. The powers of detention and questioning which were so unprecedented have now been written into the Police and Criminal Evidence Act. The accretion of powers – of which yesterday's package was the latest instalment – goes inexorably on. And in those 22 years has terrorism been prevented? Cue P O'Neill's latest bomb warning.

That debate in 1974 was full of warnings about the dangers of ill-considered emergency legislation. I was never a great personal fan of all the Labour MPs who uttered them, some of whom managed to combine their indignant concern for civil liberties in Britain with a lifelong blindness towards the achievements of the judicial system of the Soviet Union. But the fact remains that they were right on every count about the PTA. Like the equally quickly rushed Official Secrets Act of 1911, another supposedly temporary measure, the PTA was built to last. It was a political gesture, forced on a weak Labour government by the police and MI5 as part of a bigger agenda of their own devising – and it didn't prevent terrorism.

Police failure is frequently the midwife of fresh police powers, but unfortunately police powers are rarely the midwife of police success. This is not a complete argument against police powers, which self-evidently have a necessary place. But it ought to encourage an appropriate modesty and reflection among those who urge them as the answer to all societal ills. The IRA bomber who went to heaven on a 171 bus in London's Aldwych earlier this year, like the IRA bombers who did the same thing to themselves in the doorway of Barclays Bank in St Albans five years back, were what MI5 calls cleanskins – terrorists with no terrorist record, bombers who were only detected when they lit the touch paper by mistake. The Prevention of Terrorism Act failed to prevent their terrorism. That, above all, is what is wrong with it.

Such concerns, though, are far from Labour's mind these days. Tony Blair and Jack Straw were embarrassed by their party's latter-day opposition to the PTA because it was a hole in their otherwise tightly constructed defences. It enabled the Conservatives to paint Labour, scandalously, as soft on terrorism. Their conclusion, 30-something points ahead, was not to scorn such contemptible smears but to close the loophole. That was why they abstained on the PTA-renewal debate last month.

When they did that, Michael Howard had got them. When Labour had cringed once, they were committed to a policy of cringe. There was no way without humiliation that they could oppose Howard's bogus new bill even if it had proposed the precautionary culling of the first-born children of all Irish families. They have squandered a principled and distinctive position on the PTA for no reward, and have done it without a single whimper from the front bench. Don't tell me that it's only the old lefties who are disgusted by this retreat, because it simply isn't true.

Of course, the real villain in this story is not Jack Straw but Michael Howard. But we know about Howard. It was Straw who was being put to the test, and he failed. That's what sends the shiver down the spine. For it is the shiver of familiarity and recognition. Offered the warm embrace of the governing class, Labour fell into it. The same Old Labour which has found itself weak in the presence of duty so often before. Straw had something to prove this week. The great fear is that he proved it only too well. •

....

12 December 1995

Simon Hoggart
Putting the right spin on spin

The spin doctors have started spinning against each other, in a demented dance of the whirling dervishes.

This is how it works. In the old days, as long ago as last month, you'd be sitting in your office when some chap (or, occasionally, chapess) would come in and make a short, even runic remark, such as: 'I'm sure you'll agree we've got Brian Mawhinney on the run over this one . . .' This would be a Labour spin doctor. You might pay polite attention, then return to your work.

These days it's totally different. Instead, someone comes in and murmurs: 'I'm sure you'll agree we've got Brian Mawhinney on the run over this one,' and you know it's a Tory spin doctor.

No, they don't! Just my silly joke! Conservatives may be agreed by now that, as the new party chairman, Dr Mawhinney is a blustering, bullying disaster who makes everybody long for the return of Jeremy Hanley. But they do not yet pay people to go round saying it.

Instead what happens is that the Labour spin doctors come round and explain that the Tories are up against it because they have nobody with the same gyratory talent as themselves.

Then the Tories come along and say that the Labour people are terrified because they, the Tory spin doctors, are doing such a magnificent job at out-spinning them.

It doesn't seem to occur to any of them that we, the spinees, might have an opinion. Not only are we being told what we ought to think; we are now being told what we already think.

The gist of it is: 'I know you agree with me that I'm doing a wonderful job making sure you agree with me.' I don't know why they don't dispense with mere journalists altogether. No doubt they soon will.

The ludicrous situation came to a head yesterday when the Deputy Prime Minister was obliged to answer queries about Dr Mawhinney. Giving Michael Heseltine a question time all to himself has proved to be a mistake. It gives every Labour MP a chance to ask him about the speculation, coat-trailing and outright fabrications which fill the weekend press.

So yesterday they wanted to know about Dr Mawhinney's role in the great Lord Chancellor disaster and the alleged ill-feeling between him and Dr Mawhinney. A Central Office spin doctor had leaked to a newspaper a speech by Lord Mackay in which he appeared to criticise the judiciary for overturning Government policy.

It was an excellent story – or would have been if Lord Mackay had intended to make the speech, or even agreed with the sentiments it expressed.

Denis MacShane (Lab, Rotherham) asked for an explanation.

The Deputy Prime Minister rose majestically. Mr Heseltine is in himself the apotheosis of all spin physicians, the Sultan of Swirl, the Maestro of Maelstrom, a man who could turn a bagel into a Möbius strip. Naturally he blamed the other spin doctors.

'The leader of your party has unleashed in this country the most sophisticated misrepresentation of Government policy, by people who have learned transatlantic techniques of misinformation,' he said, or rather roared.

John Prescott tried again. Did Lord Mackay even think the non-existent thoughts which had been leaked on his behalf?

Mr Heseltine said scornfully: 'You have been listening to the spin doctors of the Labour Party. Matters have been fully explained!' Which of course they have not.

My new friend Michael Fabricant (did you read the charming letter he wrote in last Friday's *Guardian*?) sniffed the wind and denounced 'the sinister Labour spin doctors who compress everything into five words!'

Such as 'Michael Fabricant's wig is *weird*.' •

· ·

26 January 1996

Matthew Norman
Diary

I am astonished, and extremely distressed, by a clearly fictitious report by my so-called rival in the *Independent*. The downmarket rag's diarist describes a visit to Parliament in which he came upon the BBC's Huw Edwards being shouted and even sworn at by a mystery man. This enigma, it later transpired, was my old friend Mandy Mandelson, the avocado-fixated member for Hartlepool. Apparently, Mandy was screaming at Mr Edwards concerning the BBC's coverage of the Harriet Harman story. What nonsense. You may expect spin doctors to behave like thugs, but Mandy says he has moved on from that side of politicial life: the idea that Labour's spokesman on the Civil Service – not to mention a likely Cabinet minister of the future – would demean himself and his position so crassly is utterly preposterous. The *Independent* is lucky that Mandy is so sanguine about such matters, or the writ for libel would be a certainty.

31 January 1996

Signs of an unexpected crisis for Mr Tony Blair have been noted in Hemsworth. In the build-up to tomorrow's byelection, there have been attempts to remove posters bearing the slogan 'New Labour', on the ironic grounds that voters think they refer to Arthur Scargill's newly formed Socialist Labour party. This confusion gives Mr Blair, Mandy Mandelson and Alastair 'Bob's Boy' Campbell (the keeper of the Maxwell flame) a problem: what on earth is Labour to call itself now? Newish Labour? Quite Fresh Labour? Not So Old And Soiled Labour? All have their attractions, it's true, but the Diary's choice is Intermediate Labour. It gives the precise impression of middle-of-the-road harmlessness which Mr Blair is so eager to cultivate. 'So then, I say to you . . .' (Dramatic pause.) 'Intermediate Labour.' (Flashing eyes, man-of-destiny face.) 'Intermediate Labour . . . for an intermediate Britain.' (Standing ovation.) Yes, I think it might just work.

1 February 1996

There are signs that Mandy Mandelson, the MP for Hartlepool, is succeeding in training the town's Labour councillors to parliamentary levels of obedience. Asked by the *Hartlepool Mail* about Harriet Harman, eight Labour councillors refused to comment, while only one of the other 13 called for her to resign. Talent spotters among Labour whips should look closely at councillor Kevin Cranney, who announced that he knew nothing whatever of the St Olave's debate, and in fact had never heard of Harriet Harman at all.

25 June 1996

The Diary is also moved to weeping – in this case, by the saintly lack of self-regard of Mandy Mandelson MP. Interviewed on TV by Andrew Rawnsley, Mandy assured us that he and Gordon Brown are great friends (Gordon's jokes about him were 'a very effective way of putting aside all the gossip and tittle-tattle'). And yet, even more impressive than the deadpan wit, it was his utter lack of self regard that was so moving. 'To be perfectly honest, Andrew,' he said, 'at the end of the day, I don't really care what people say or write about me.' How true; how very, very true . . . No one is less inclined to complain to an editor. 'I think it might surprise you to know,' he added, 'that I'm not personally ambitious . . . I'm not in politics for self-promotion.' There really are no words. ●

17 *February 1996*

Hugo Young
Heavily armed against the truth

The emblematic character in the saga of the Scott Inquiry is not William Waldegrave but Geoffrey Howe. Sir Richard Scott had hardly begun his work before Lord Howe took it on himself to be the scourge and defamer of his work: prosecutor, judge and jury in the attack on what he was about to publish – traducer of his very existence.

Howe's contention was partly that Scott's procedure was unfair, and his inquiry 'not a tribunal upon whose judgement the reputation of anyone should be allowed to depend'. This perilous exaggeration did not deter the former foreign secretary yesterday from declaring that the report had vindicated ministers and government in all particulars. But it wasn't, in any case, the essence of his outrage. This was, rather, the 'gap of non-comprehension' existing between Scott's world and 'the real world', which rendered the judge incapable of engaging with what ministers had to do.

Howe offered this scathing opinion as an elder statesman, as if he were now above the battle which Scott so woefully failed to understand. But he was nothing of the sort. Reading the report, one is reminded not only that he, as Waldegrave's superior, presided with meticulous enthusiasm over every subterfuge by which Middle East arms sales were kept from public view, but that he exalts everything Scott, in his plump and half-mystified way, criticises about Whitehall life: its secrecies, its duplicities, its morass of unaccountable networks, its swift capacity to rationalise the misleading of Parliament as *raison d'état*.

The ministers involved in arms sales to Iraq have escaped any censure they're prepared to regard as such. They're satisfied that the sincerity of their errors protects them from any blame. In fact, they think they're heroes. Howe told Scott that the guidelines restraining arms sales to Iraq and Iran amounted, in contrast with the policies of other countries, to 'a huge national sacrifice'. Along with trying to put Robin Cook in the dock, this was also the distraction Ian Lang piously deployed on Thursday.

For in the world of Geoffrey Howe, not only do the ministers in this saga have nothing to be ashamed of, there isn't even a marginal case to answer. The national interest demands the sale of arms, lethal or non-lethal according to time and place. The rules are debated between honourable men, with conclusions, however, that must inevitably be kept quiet; and, if exposed, must be justified by the kind of casuistry which, in Howe's world, is second nature, but which, if admitted to Scott's world, requires to be taken apart. It is, above all, the act of taking apart that Howe resents as a grotesque intrusion on the public interest.

Reading the Scott Report, one can see why. It takes apart his world as never before.

Consider the single question of the guidelines. The question was: did Waldegrave knowingly deceive Parliament? Answer: no. He was not, says Scott, 'duplicitous'. Therefore he claims innocence. He says he sincerely didn't believe the guidelines had been changed. Yet behind this simple verdict lies a vast accumulation of evidence that they had changed, that officials and ministers thought they had changed, that ministers were aware how intensely embarrassing this might be, that 'the convenience of secrecy' – a phrase Scott proffered to Sir Robin Butler, the essence of which the Cabinet Secretary did not reject – prevailed whenever necessary.

The original guidelines, first of all, were not published. Howe, who framed them in 1984, thought they 'should be allowed to filter out'. It was 10 months before they became fully known. During the Iran–Iraq war, the restraints they were supposed to impose on lethal weaponry were even-handed but liberally interpreted – with full awareness, however, of how scandal might beckon. Of Matrix-Churchill machine tools, for example, one of Howe's officials wrote in January 1988: 'If it becomes public knowledge that the tools are to be used to make munitions, deliveries would have to stop at once.'

That the position altered when the war ended is attested to in numerous ways. Paul Channon, trade secretary at the time, told him: 'I think [ministers] changed the rules as they went on. In reality, if ministers decide to ignore the guidelines, they can be ignored.' Alan Clark, Channon's junior, ecstatically noted the 'brilliant' drafting that had exchanged a tight policy for a looser one – 'so obviously drafted with the object of flexibility in either direction'.

But we don't need to rely only on fringe players. Waldegrave and Howe both made things very clear. In September 1988, Howe remarked that 'it could look very cynical' if, shortly after he had condemned Iraq for using chemical warfare against Kurds, 'we adopt a more flexible approach to arms sales'. He wanted to encourage these. His officials should 'get moving down that path'. Asked by Scott to examine more closely why secrecy about the new policy must obtain, Howe alluded with a palpable shudder to 'the emotional way in which such debates are conducted in public'.

This was not a foreign secretary talking about a policy that did not change. Nor, obviously, was Waldegrave when his office wrote in February 1989 that he was 'content for us to implement a more liberal policy on defence sales without any public announcement'.

The civil servants who also knew this, acted on it and conspired to keep it quiet, litter the pages of Scott. Like the ministers, they became masters, at least in retrospect, of the linguistic trickery necessary to escape confessing that the policy had changed. Instead, the guidelines had been 'reformulated' (Gore-Booth of the FO), 'amended' (Goulden of the FO), were 'a form of interpretation' (Barrett of the MoD), subject to 'flexibility' (ministers and officials *passim*).

Asked why this flexibility itself could not have been admitted in simple terms, rather than concealed behind a succession of studiously misleading parliamentary answers, Waldegrave and Howe each supplied explanations that concede with utter starkness the priorities which they, in their heroic conduct of the public business, invite us to excuse.

'Because it was judged that there were overriding reasons for giving misleading information about tilts to one side or another,' said Waldegrave.

'If we were to lay specifically our thought processes before you,' said Howe, 'they are laid before a worldwide range of uncomprehending or malicious commentators.'

This is the moral quality of the world of Howe, Waldegrave, Major, Lang and every other minister who sees through one lens his own innocence, and through the other the naivety of Lord Justice Scott. It is not exactly an amoral world. It merely gives dissembling a higher priority than other worlds. But it countenances apologias which, I submit, would be intolerable in any other field of human conduct, culminating with the decisive *aperçu*, hitherto undiscovered even by Sir Humphrey, that, whatever new guidelines were manifestly being followed, policy hadn't changed because ministers said they hadn't changed it.

In the world of Sir Richard Scott, even after three years' exposure, it proved impossible to accommodate such linguistic relativism. In giving his account, Scott is not his own best ally. The report is absurdly long. Gigantism takes over his lordship as he journeys down every meandering and sometimes futile side-path of the arms export world, the licensing and concealment thereof, the 1939 statute that still governs it, etc. The limitless verbosity of the High Court bench, so ready to reach for double negatives where none would do much better, is rotundly on display. But in most ways, the judge lives up to Howe's worst expectations. More than anyone could see in the first few hours before yesterday's papers went to bed, he exposes and denounces the world Howe speaks for.

It is true that he acquits Waldegrave of knowingly misleading the Commons. The minister had no 'duplicitous intention'. On the other hand, his conduct and that of Howe and every other minister had duplicity about it. What remained 'duplicitous', was the 'nature of the flexibility claimed for the guidelines'. In any other context than one in which ministers were expecting to be hung, drawn and quartered, such a verdict would have been worth a resignation.

The panoply of linguistic game-playing may satisfy the world of Howe. The armies of Whitehall have rewritten the grammar of honest accountability. But the judge is not impressed. The contention that the guidelines were not changed, he said in a paragraph that somehow escaped Lang's attention, 'is so plainly inapposite as to be incapable of being sustained by serious argument'.

He saw what was up. The change was kept secret for a very old-fashioned reason, which he understands. 'It might legitimately have been feared that public knowledge of an intended relaxation of restrictions on the supply of defence equipment to Iraq would provoke such indignation in the media and among vociferous sections of the British public as to be politically damaging.'

What Scott won't accept is that commercial interests should override all other considerations. He calls public disclosure a 'constitutional' question, which should have been weighted better in the balance against political advantage and the intricacies of Middle East trade politics, real or imagined. His verdict on the world Howe defends is extraordinarily harsh. For six years, he finds, the Government consistently undervalued the public interest in Parliament being kept informed. 'Time and time again' ministers came down against full disclosure for no better reason than that this would be politically inconvenient.

Will the Scott Report redefine Howe's 'real world'? In one sense, the real world seems to be winning. Nobody is planning to resign. The linguistic conjurors think they've taken the big tricks. Besides, the judge did a lot to help them. His procedures, far from being unfair, went overboard to help the men in the dock. No fraudster is given the opportunity ministers have had to scrutinise the judgement and propose amendments to the counts against them.

Scott surrendered another point. On the last page of the report, he is meditating on questions of responsibility as against accountability. Should ministers be required to accept personal criticism for what goes wrong in their department? In the arms-to-Iraq affair, actually, ministers did a lot of the dirty work themselves. So the question is a trifle academic. The Scott doctrine, gratuitously, follows that of the high priest of the real world, Sir Robin Butler. He said government was now so complex that ministers shouldn't be obliged to take the blame, and the judge produces an acquiescent double negative: 'For my part, I find it difficult to disagree.'

The systemic indictment, however, stands. Ministers, clearly, intend to pay little attention. Having got the exonerations they wanted, they've made a few patronising references to Sir Richard's recommendations on export-licensing. For the rest, they have no shame. Their world is Howe's world, and the only reason this opportunity arose to expose it was a misbegotten prosecution of Matrix-Churchill executives that went wrong.

So the question is: would anyone else be different? The Labour Party has been in opposition so long it has forgotten what power is like. Its indignation at the dishonesty and parliamentary deception has the innocence of politicians who have seldom had to make hard decisions. It is committed to a Freedom of Information Act, but that hardly touches the point of commercial secrecies or the temptation to keep Parliament half-informed. Although led by Tony Blair, this was the party of Jim Callaghan and Harold Wilson when it last mattered.

The only weapon against such expectations is that the world of Richard Scott should capture the public mind as being ineffably superior to that of Geoffrey Howe. The ministers survive, to continue their heroic obfuscations. The judge, in his innocence, argues for something better. So should all who believe that these ministers, when put to the test, were serial defaulters against the truth. ●

Pass Notes

20 August 1996   Worcester Woman

So have you used an agency before, Mr ... er ... More-Weenie? It's Mawhinney. *Doctor* Mawhinney, if you don't mind. Yes. I usually go to Saatchi.

Very classy that. Mind you, they're always advertising themselves; you'll find we offer a much more discreet service. Anyway, you'd like to meet ladies of what sort of age? They can be up to 44, but I insist that they must be able to pass for 35.

And what sort of social background, if you'll pardon me using the jargon? I'd classify them as C1 and C2.

Oh my! I asked for that, didn't I. Anyway, it's not professional ladies you're interested in, even though you're a GP? I'm not that sort of doctor. I don't want career women; just women whose husbands are working – plumber, electrician, that sort of thing.

Ooooh, you naughty man; you just want to pop round while hubby's away, I suppose. I will ignore that degrading remark. I'll have you know I wish to meet ladies for strictly psephological and electoral purposes.

Well, I haven't heard it called that before! Still, what part of the country? The West Midlands. Specially Worcester.

But you're based in London, aren't you? I'd've thought you'd find Essex girls handier. I used to love them. But it got so I couldn't tell a Sharron from a Karen. Anyway, I get around.

You commercial gents! I suppose you're looking for a woman of experience. Well-travelled, been to Disney World and all that? Yes, well, there's nothing wrong with holidays in Florida – if you've got a couple of computer-crazed kids and an old man who doesn't earn more than £18,000 a year.

What sort of personality are you looking for? What sort of interests do you like your ladies to have? They must be easily manipulated; like dirty tricks; be easily frightened by stories about men in masks – that sort of thing. And be impressed by bullshit.

Anyway, it's definitely not a one-to-one relationship you're looking for? Certainly not. I'm a happily married man. I just want to invite lots and lots of women to my party.

Just how many do you have in mind? There are some 2.4 million in the West Midlands who fit the bill.

Sounds more like an orgy to me. What a disgusting suggestion. I want to save these women from the Smiler in the Mask.

Seriously, why have Tory election strategists decided to focus on Worcester Woman? Sheer panic. Dwindling popularity and re-drawn boundaries make it probable that they'll lose half a dozen seats in the region at the next general election.

Not to be confused with: Bob Worcester. Basildon Man. Essex Girl. Piltdown Man.

Let's hear the Worcester Wimmen's chant. 'Brian Mawhinney is a ninny. Time-share with Tony Blair.' ●

29 August 1996

David Ward

Labour leader in search of elusive Street-cred

The story so far: Jack and Vera Duckworth have come into money and bought the Rover's Return but keep dipping their hands in the till when the other isn't looking. Raquel has disappeared Down South, allegedly on an aromatherapy course.

Scene one: a minion sweeps away fag ends from the cobbles on the set of Coronation Street in Manchester while blazered minions pin the public behind iron barriers, except for a select group allowed to stand behind a red rope. Enter a stranger with a big grin and undemonic eyes. It is Tony Blair, who, arms outstretched, has come to embrace his people.

He claims he has come to sell the New Labour manifesto street by street, beginning with the thoroughfare he dubs the most famous in Britain. A voice in the crowd: 'Who's that shaking everyone's hand?' Second voice: 'I know I'm stupid but where is Tony Blair?' Third voice: 'He looks nicer than he does on telly.' Fourth voice: 'It's only that Tony Blair. I'm not standing here looking at him.'

Scene two: Enter a stage-hand with a tray bearing two pints of Newton and Ridleys and two port and lemons. [Looking at beer]: 'It's not real, you know.'

Tony Blair removes jacket in attempt to look like man of the people.

David Clarke, a voter [reaching for his camera]: 'It's not every day you bump into Tony Blair in the street. Who was that big bloke with the eyebrows? I met him in Leeds once.'

A reporter: 'Do you mean Denis Healey?'

Mr Clarke: 'That's him.'

Mr Clarke [reflecting on political realities]: 'Blair is being criticised for bending. But he has just accepted that the British people like a bit of Conservatism and a bit of Labour. Why not do what the people want for once?'

Enter Mr Clarke's wife Pauline. She ducks under the security barrier but is rapidly propelled back by a guard. 'I don't take any notice of this New Labour thing. I just vote Labour.'

Mr Clarke [fantasising]: 'I wish Blair could have met Bet Gilroy . . .'

Scene three: Mr Blair meets Raquel [wearing very short tartan skirt] and Jack and Vera.

A photographer: 'Go on Vera, give him a kiss.'

Vera obliges lubriciously.

Cut to crowd. Peter Somerville, a bystander [grumbling]: 'They should send flaming Tony Blair here at twelve o'clock at night when there's no one else here. This is ridiculous. I've come 200 miles to see Coronation Street, or at least my wife has. I've got a coach to catch at half past four. Ridiculous.'

Reporter (stupidly): 'Are you a Labour supporter?'

Mr Somerville: 'Only if the ship was sinking and he needed saving. True blue, me, Maggie and all . . . I went in that Rover's Return and they charged me £1 for a glass of yellow water. Put that in your notebook.'

Scene four: Mr Blair grins, meets the media. 'To go in the Rover's pub was absolutely fantastic. To see people you have seen for years and years on television was fantastic.'

A reporter (investigatively): 'Do you watch Corrie?'

Mr Blair (carefully): 'I was just saying to Vera, Liz I should say, that I usually don't get home in time to watch it. My kids actually watch it a lot.'

Reporters (hearing pledge that a Labour government will introduce a weekly nationwide Coronation Street omnibus): 'Gosh. That's not a bad line.'

Mr Blair (looking serious, containing grin): 'They are very typical English characters and the problems they describe are the difficulties ordinary families have.

'I guess we all sympathise with that. That's why it's so successful – it represents real life.'

Exit Mr Blair. Minions remove barriers. Families pose for pictures outside the Rover's Return.

Real life returns to Coronation Street. •

. . . .

4 June 1996

Larry Elliott

Labour's mean streets

N ew Labour loves flexing its muscles. It is tough on single mothers, it is tough on parents who let their children play truant, it is tough on noisy neighbours and, as we now know, it is tough on infants playing on the street after dusk. The only thing it is not tough on is the economy.

As far as the Opposition is concerned, the days when a national government could manage demand or ensure full employment are long gone. Globalised capital markets mean that all a 'centre-left' government can offer is some education, some training and a bit more research and development, then let the market get on with it.

But having decided that it can no longer regulate the economy, it is left with a bit of a vacuum. Governments have to do something. So Labour has a new idea. It will regulate the people instead, imposing a panoply of social controls to ensure that the problems caused by the uncontrollable deregulated economy –

crime, juvenile delinquency, family breakdown – don't threaten the comfortable lifestyles of its new middle-class constituency.

There is a rationale for this new approach. It is that Labour's core constituency, the traditional working class, is precisely that part of the electorate most affected by antisocial behaviour, and it will welcome a return to the social order that characterised the 1950s. After all, Clement Attlee was no soggy liberal when it came to social policy.

Actually, of course, the thing Labour's core constituency would most welcome would be a guaranteed job protected by decent employment rights and perhaps even defended by trade unions with some negotiating clout. But this is off the agenda.

Instead, New Labour's sales pitch at the next election looks like being the 1960s in reverse: instead of Harold Wilson's mixture of economic interventionism and social liberalism we will have economic liberalism and social authoritarianism.

Although some economists have worked out schemes for taxing foreign-exchange speculators, and a new computer is being introduced to clamp down on City insider-dealing, New Labour will take a hands-off approach to the markets. But there will be plenty of intervention when it comes to cutting out fatty foods, drinking less and installing surveillance cameras the length and breadth of the country. We will have all the pain of free-market capitalism, but with state-financed counselling to soften the blow.

The Wilson government of 1964–70 was interventionist in a different way. This was the heyday of Keynesianism, with George Brown's National Plan, Barbara Castle's super-ministry of Employment and Productivity, and an Industrial Reorganisation Corporation to create huge new conglomerates. The idea was that Labour would increase the growth rate to 3.8 per cent a year, guarantee full employment, improve living standards and be able to spend more on health, education, housing and pensions.

But at the same time the Wilson government saw no real reason why it should meddle needlessly in people's personal lives, so it eased up on censorship, made divorce easier and gave a fair wind to the private members' bills that abolished capital punishment and changed the abortion laws. It was not that the Wilson Cabinet was awash with kaftan-wearing members of the permissive society; merely that it was felt that these were matters best left to individuals.

Little remains of the Wilsonian approach. The 1964–70 administration is now seen as an example to avoid, even though in retrospect it delivered growth of around 3 per cent a year and kept unemployment below 500,000.

That New Labour has bought the Thatcherite idea that economics should be de-politicised was shown clearly by Tony Blair at last November's Confederation of British Industry conference. His speech was peppered with comments that reflected his conversion to the new orthodoxy, such as: 'The role of government is not to command but to facilitate', 'Government should not try to run business',

'Penal rates of taxation do not make economic or political sense. They are gone for good.' Hardly surprisingly, big business lapped it up.

New Labour economic policy now goes like this. Low inflation is the key to economic growth, and it must be maintained at all costs. Page one in Mrs Thatcher's primer for economic management says that interest rates have to be used to bear down on inflation. Page two says that budget deficits are another cause of inflation, so there can be no question of a return to Keynesian tax-and-spend policies.

The problem is that there is absolutely no evidence that low inflation and slashing budget deficits lead to higher growth. Indeed, the pursuit of them may lead to lower growth. This then leaves the question of where the money is to come from in order to finance improvements in training, education and investment allowances, and the rest of Labour's supply-side renaissance.

And, of course, for the extra police to impound those errant 10-year-olds. •

....

28 June 1996

Bel Littlejohn

To Ascot and the Tony Blair Handicap

Rush, rush, rush: believe me, it's been all rush. And in the mad rush, I haven't had time to tell you about our New Labour day trip to the races in Berks last week. Contrary to what the tabloids and the Murdoch press might have us believe, the Berks racecourse in question – popularly known as Ascot – is not remotely 'grand'. Far from it. In fact, it's filled with lots of ordinary, decent people of the sort we are hoping to attract into backing New Labour to romp home at the next election. I'm glad to report that by the end of the day quite a few of them were wearing our specially designed red-on-white BERKS FOR NEW LABOUR stickers on their top hats.

The lovely Robin Cook is himself a former jockey, having once ridden in the Derby. But half-way through, his donkey grew restless and threw him off. Ever since, Robin has been an enthusiastic spectator. In fact, his whole philosophy of New Labour has been formulated through binoculars in grandstands up and down the country. 'As each race comes to an end,' he once said in a moving speech at the Licensed Turf Accountants' Association Annual Dinner-Dance, 'I think to myself, in this day and age, why on earth can't we devise a system in which every horse wins? Why is it just one horse in every race that our society deems to be "the winner"? And – another thing – why the hell is it never my horse?'

It was Robin who organised last week's fact-finding mission to Ascot with a view to devising a fair and equitable policy for horse-racing under New Labour. Five senior figures – Harriet Harman, Peter Mandelson, John Prescott, Jack Straw and myself – joined Robin at Waterloo Station, Jack and Peter in light-weight lounge suits, John Prescott in tail-coat with full gold braid and captain's hat, Harriet and me in the specially designed New Labour Jasper Conran collection of floaty pastel synthetics with an emphasis on style.

'Of course, this event is traditionally known as Royal Ascot, but we in New Labour are set to change all that,' observed John Prescott as our train eased its way into the station.

'I agree with John,' purred Peter Mandelson. '"Royal Ascot" has a somewhat harsh, almost unwelcoming tone about it. "Royal Races" or "Royal Fun-Day" would be more in keeping, don't you think?'

Once inside the course, Peter sped off to sound out ordinary folk about their hopes and dreams for the new millennium. Peter is a great believer in the representative views of ordinary folk, as is evidenced in the case histories detailed so lovingly in his recent book, *The Blair Revulsion* (Faber, £9.99). He reappeared at our picnic, thrilled with his vox-pop findings from old people nearby.

'Philip and Elizabeth have been married nearly 50 years,' he began. 'Elizabeth's elderly mum, 95, lives on the same inner-city street but finds it hard to get around much these days. Their eldest son, Charles, separated with two kids, has always found it hard to settle down. Seventeen years under this Tory government has taken its toll on this family unit. Understandably, they desperately want to know what New Labour can offer them.

'So let's take a closer look at their future under Tony Blair. A freshly motivated Social Services sees to it that Elizabeth's old mum gets out to the races twice a week. Philip and Elizabeth may once again bask in the respect of the entire community. And Charles can face the future confident that his talents will be developed under New Labour. Yes – everyone profits under Tony Blair.'

Flushed with enthusiasm, we made our way to the paddock. 'It's an utter disgrace that those horses should be permitted to flout all hygiene regulations by walking around in circles so close to human beings,' barked Jack, his spectacles steaming over in exasperation. 'A New Labour government will call a halt to these geegee merchants!' Then he went on to survey the race-track with mounting concern. 'This wicked Tory government has callously allowed this paving to grass over,' he said, 'making it wholly unfit for the elderly and infirm.'

But Robin was far away in another world, sizing up the likely winner. 'A little tip in your ear, Bel,' he said to me conspiratorially. 'Always place the same amount of money on every horse in the race – that way you're absolutely bound to win something.' But Harriet was having none of it. Looking around anxiously, she said, 'I'm not being élitist, but surely in our position we can pay just a little bit extra to someone and they'll tell us which horse is going to come first. Surely that's what true democracy is all about.'

After a lunch of New Labour lobster, a great day's racing was crowned by the Tony Blair Handicap, the winner being the horse that smiled the most and made the sweetest noises. Yes, guys, with New Labour we're all on to a whinny! ●

....

25 January 1996

Suzanne Moore
Just do as I say, not as I do

J oe Dromey is obviously a bright little boy who should do well at whatever school he goes to. His parents (Harriet Harman and Jack Dromey) want the best for him. Wanting the best for one's children is not a middle-class prerogative, although to read some editorials this week one would be forgiven for thinking that the country was divided into anxious middle-class parents willing to sell their souls for the sake of a few GCSEs for their offspring and the rest of us, who are so stupid, so poor, so unambitious, that we end up sending our children to any old school. Even worse, some of us are willing to send our children to the local comprehensive in the name of some vague political principle about equality of opportunity for everyone. To do this is somehow equivalent to sacrificing your children's future. One may as well slaughter them in cold blood as let them go to a school where they don't have to wear a uniform.

Having recently made such a decision about my daughter's secondary school, I am afraid that I cannot support Harriet Harman, just as I couldn't support Tony Blair's decision to send poor Euan trudging across London on a cold and frosty morning. I realise, of course, that Euan's journey will be made shorter when he lives in Number 10, but that is not the point. I cannot support these decisions largely because I cannot support the increasingly narrow definition of the education that these controversial choices assume is always the best. If education is to be reduced to O-levels, A-levels, S-levels and league tables, to entry into the right kind of university, then unquestionably the old-fashioned grammar schools produce the required results.

Yet in my naivety I still think that education is about more than what you know and who you know; it's about being able to get on with all kinds of people in all kinds of situations. It is about learning to be at ease in society, rather than only being able to function when one is surrounded by those who have the same experiences as you. When I saw some of the boys of St Olave's interviewed on the news, I was struck by their cocky self-assurance. 'If he is intelligent enough to go here, he should be allowed to,' said one little boy, already assured of his right to rule the world. Quite frankly, I wouldn't want a child of mine mixing with such children. They are a bad influence.

I may be out of step here. You get what you pay for and many parents are willing to pay the price. They will take on bigger mortgages and move to areas precisely so that their children can go to schools like this. This is selection as it is already practised. Middle-class parents talk euphemistically of better schools meaning whiter schools, free of 'ethnic' children who might contaminate their little ones. They wish it wasn't like that but it is. Those who support Harman say that she is only making the best of a bad job. The Tories have mucked up the schools, not Labour. Why should her son be penalised for 16 years of Tory mismanagement?

Would Joe Dromey be penalised by going to any other school? Would he fail to keep up the good work, fall in with a bad crowd and end up failing to fulfil his potential? This seems unlikely, especially with the parental pressure that he is under. What may happen is that in any other school he may not be pushed hard enough. This, incidentally, is one of the main complaints that the middle classes have about many state schools – that both the weakest and the brightest children are left to drift somewhat. This was certainly a consideration when I had to choose a school for my daughter.

My main concern, though, was that she was happy, that she went where she wanted to go – which was where her friends were. I also wanted her to go to a school that she could walk to because a) I am lazy, b) I wanted her to be independent, and c) I wanted her to be part of what goes on where we live. Before you all write in and say that it's all right for me because I live in an ivory tower in Hampstead, let me just point out that I live in Hackney – hardly famous for being the pinnacle of academic achievement. It's all very well Blair blathering on about community, but how can you be part of a local community when you are being bussed 12 miles away from where you live? How can the Labour Party lecture the rest of us about cutting down on car use when it has to ferry its own children half-way across the city day in, day out?

When Harman says that she was making a choice that any other parent could have made, she is being disingenuous . . . One needs certain means to be able to trek around even looking at schools that far away. Let's not pretend that we all start on a level playing field, because we don't. This little boy's education has now become a political hot potato because Blair, having done so much to woo the aspirant middle-class vote, cannot be seen to return to the class consciousness of Old Labour. He and Harman are appealing over the heads of many in their party by saying: 'Look, I'm just like you, we both know what really matters here. Individual choice comes before collective principle.' This does appeal to lots of people, especially the leader writers on many of the newspapers who have made the same choices that Harman and Blair have made.

What it does not do, however, is make clear what education policy is or will be under a Labour government. Parents are totally confused. Having been promised more power and more choice, they find they have less. We are told that selection is a thing of the past when it is clearly visible in many schools. We cannot believe that Labour will abolish selection because we know in our hearts that there will always be a kind of self-selection in operation. Roy Hattersley told a story at the Labour Party conference where one of the questions asked in the interview of prospective parents at an over-subscribed school was 'Is the father tattooed?'

The schools that run themselves on traditional models are the most popular, yet we know that overall results in the comprehensive system are better than they were 20 years ago. Nearly all parents support streaming as long as their children are not in the bottom stream.

The old system, that divided the population into the academic ones and the factory fodder, can hardly be reactivated at a time when the factories have closed down. Instead, the expertise required for the future – self-sufficiency, transferable skills, adaptability – are all best learned in less traditional environments. The new vocational education being talked of for less able children recognises that education has to be opened up instead of closed down.

Harman's resignation is not the answer, not because, as is claimed, it would send a signal that parents are not expected to do the best they can for their children, but because it would still not make clear what Labour's policy is. It cannot claim to be the party of aspiration when those aspirations cannot be met. It is easy enough to blame it all on the Tories, but a Labour government would not change the system overnight. There is no point in having the right to choose without the means to choose. This is not real choice. If Labour is in business to extend choice, then instead of saying that it is going to abolish selection it would surely be better off being honest. This is where not only hypocrisy but self-delusion comes in.

Selection exists in the state system and will continue to exist wherever a school has more applicants than places. Read my lips. If schools are encouraged to be entirely open about what selection methods they are using, parents would start on a more equal footing. The likes of Harman can play the system because they know how the system operates. For most parents the system is thoroughly confusing and full of underhand hints and suggestions as to how to get your child into the right school. No wonder, then, that what is described as middle-class aspiration is really a sort of angst that somehow their precious progeny will be left behind in the modern world. Class will out after all.

The tragedy is that we have so little faith in our children and fear they will turn into junkie monsters if they do not get taught the right things in the right way. We are more concerned for their future than we are for their present. Such angst produces a return to the symbolic order of uniforms and Saturday-morning detentions. Through such order children will learn their place in the world. We force our children to repeat what we ourselves hated. Teach them that education is something that only goes on within classrooms. For what? I don't call this aspiration. I call it despair.

Blair must come out of hiding. I would have more sympathy if he and Harman supported selection in public as they appear to do in private. An advert for army officers placed next to the Harman interview in yesterday's *Guardian* asked 'Could you be a more inspiring leader?' Good leaders, it told us, 'lead by example, never asking people to do things they wouldn't do themselves'. Indeed. Editorial duckers and divers have managed to blame the Tories for what they insist is a private and parental decision. Harman's choice is either beyond the bounds of politics or it is not. You can't have it both ways, something that for all Blair's expensive education he doesn't appear to have grasped. •

* * *

30 January 1996

Leader

Responding in the vernacular

Former Chancellor Norman Lamont, newly adopted as prospective Conservative candidate for Harrogate, yesterday dismissed allegations that he might be ousted by a grass-roots revolt because he was not a local man. 'Both intellectually and, if I may say so, spiritually, I have long considered myself a Yorkshireman, tha daft hap'porth,' he told a reporter.

Mr Lamont, who arrived in the constituency wearing a cap and leading a small whippet, declared himself utterly loyal to the Prime Minister. Asked if he stood by the complaint he had made shortly after his dismissal as Chancellor that Mr Major was 'in office but not in power', he told journalists: '*Je ne regrette* nowt. There are them as says our John ought to be waited on by Tory grandees after the next local elections, and instructed to resign in the interests of the party. But that might open the way for some right mithering tussock like Heseltine, sithee.' The former Chancellor, who during the interview unbuttoned his jacket to reveal a silk T-shirt inscribed 'Boycott for Pope', was asked if he thought Mr Major was likely to be replaced after the next election. He said he was 'too topfull o'throng' to waste his time on such speculation. Probed about his own leadership ambitions, Mr Lamont replied: 'I've never thowt owt o' that, you girt bugger.' But suppose – reporters persisted – John Major were to resign after the next election, and the party's right-wingers proved hopelessly torn between Michael Portillo and John Redwood, could the former Chancellor yet emerge, *faute de mieux* as it were, as a dark horse candidate? Downing his pint of Tetley's in a single gulp, Mr Lamont buttoned his jacket, placed his cap on his head, fastened the lead on his whippet, and smiled an inscrutable smile. 'Happen,' he said. •

....

9 *January 1996*

Will Hutton

Stake that claim

The snap reaction of the left to the idea of the stakeholder economy and society is that it is little more than Thatcherism in drag, just another way of talking about popular capitalism or the enterprise culture. The right is no more forgiving. The dynamics of capitalism are immutable and brook no reform. Tony Blair will find that championing stakeholding is no easy ride; he has entered the political battle of ideas with a vengeance.

But the stock criticisms are wrong. Like it or hate it, stakeholding does represent a different political economy of capitalism with profound implications for economic, social and political organisation. It stresses that workers should be seen as members of firms rather than locked into an antagonistic confrontation between capital and labour. In this world view, firms are social organisations embedded in a complex skein of rights and moral obligations, and if they are reduced to commodities bought and sold on the stock market, that undermines the trust and reciprocity of obligation on which long-termism and productivity thrive.

Too much fracturing and tiering of society in the quest for simple economic efficiencies are ultimately socially unsustainable – and that spills over into the sustainability of economic growth. Social citizenship and economic membership are interdependent – but this links up with political citizenship. An active participative democracy goes hand in hand with underpinning social cohesion and promoting stakeholder firms.

These are no platitudes. A different vocabulary opens up – social inclusion, membership, trust, cooperation, long-termism, equality of opportunity, participation, active citizenship, rights and obligations – in sharp contrast to the right's language of opting-out, privatisation, the primacy of individual choice, maximisation of shareholder value and the 'burden' of welfare and social costs. Behind the vocabulary lies a different value system, a different view of what makes a successful market economy tick – and a dramatically different approach to economic and social policy.

Corporate law, the organisation of pensions, systems of training, company decision-making, the behaviour of the Stock Exchange and the role of education are markedly different in a stakeholder world. The international evidence, as Blair said in Singapore, is that this approach delivers social cohesion and economic growth; the two feed off each other. By pinning his colours to the stakeholder mast, Blair has taken a decisive political step. New Labour has now enlisted a substantial and novel body of ideas: it stands in sharp opposition to the *laissez-faire*, financially driven model of capitalism promoted by the right.

This may have been good enough to beat its ideological rival, communism, and even good enough to take on and beat British collectivism – but as a model for the good society or efficient economy it falls far short of any decent yardstick. It is characterised by endemic short-termism, economic volatility and social divisiveness – and, when married to the top-down centralised nature of British government, has delivered a society in which civic duty and public service have become progressively emasculated.

It was exactly against this kind of *laissez-faire* capitalism that the stakeholder idea was first developed – by the American left during the sixties. The word derived from the way US settlers staked their claim in virgin territory. Business strategists in the late fifties and early sixties used it to rethink the idea of a company as a network of reciprocal *claims* between shareholders, employees, bankers, suppliers and managers. Large industrial organisations were bureaucracies which arbitrated between these rival claims – a necessary function in any industrial economy, market capitalist or market socialist.

But it was when J K Galbraith picked up the idea in *The New Industrial State*, published in 1967, aided and abetted by Robin Marris, author of *The Theory of Managerial Capitalism*, that the idea first gained economic and political currency. During the seventies, American corporate raiders complained that companies were cynically appealing to stakeholder interests to obstruct takeovers and limit shareholders' rights (a complaint they still make). But as no US politician has attempted to organise the ideas into a legislative programme, stakeholding has not progressed much beyond encouraging worker share ownership through Employee Stock Ownership Plans.

In Germany, the social market ideas developed by left theorists in opposition to fascism and communism had similar roots – they thought of the firm as a social organisation with long-term stakeholders which operated in highly competitive markets. The welfare state was seen as a protective social instrument to promote social inclusion, and allow capitalism its much-needed flexibility to build up and run down industries without worrying about the social consequences. The political purpose was the same as Galbraith's: to secure the fecundity of capitalism whilst humanising it – and defending it from authoritarianism of the left and right.

In Britain the whole debate has never taken off before. The post-war settlement was a compromise, allowing the left to achieve its social goals through raising public spending and extending public ownership, but leaving the right to protect City freedoms and the ancient notion that the firm represented no more than the shareholders' interests. The case for stakeholding was left to fringe groups campaigning for worker participation and cooperatives. But with the instruments of Old Labour collapsing, and the right building on the *laissez-faire* model, the most promising avenue for the left is stakeholding.

The TUC has recognised this for some time, and General-Secretary John Monks has established a task force to suggest legislative proposals and ways the unions might profit. The Dahrendorf Commission on Wealth Creation and Social Cohesion came out firmly in favour of stakeholding last summer. Tony Blair has been tantalisingly slow to adopt it publicly but the Singapore speech is a watershed.

It establishes authentically left credentials, blindsides his opponents and has a reforming sting. Witness just one passage. 'It is surely time,' he said, 'to assess how we shift the emphasis in corporate ethos – from the company being a mere vehicle for the capital market to be traded, bought and sold as a commodity – towards a vision of the company as a community or partnership in which each employee has a stake, and where the company's responsibilities are more clearly delineated.'

Michael Portillo immediately attacked this as a straight copy of long-standing Conservative policy – but it is difficult to recall a Conservative politician ever indicting the operation of stock-market capitalism for *commoditising* companies and workers, or proposing a clear delineation of corporate rights and obligations. Isn't the Conservative idea to promote deregulation and to regard stock-market freedoms as sacred?

But Blair's advocacy of what he calls the Stakeholder Welfare System may arouse more concern. There is a clear accent on social cohesion and the necessity to recast the welfare state so it ceases to offer an obstacle to training or self-employment; and it is equally attractive to open up collective means of self-insurance to allow individuals to produce pensions or sickness benefit above the basic levels. The danger, though, is also clear: Singapore-type provident funds could be progressively used to replace existing welfare structures, with their accompanying need for a redistributive tax system.

Yet in sum the commitment to a stakeholder economy and society is a key moment – a way of binding the centre and left together in common cause while providing the ideological impetus for important economic and social return. Blair went to Australia this Christmas with no advisers and a suitcase of books. On this evidence he should go again. ●

Pass Notes

11 June 1996

The feelgood factor

Age: First spotted under President Reagan but imported to Britain to describe the turnaround in Mrs Thatcher's fortunes after the war in the Falkland Islands.

Appearance: 1,318 times on the *Guardian* database (and here we go again). Often accompanied by champagne, and free spending in the High Street.

What is it? Long before the phrase turned up in leader columns, Mori and Gallup had been asking voters how they thought the financial situation of their household would change over the next 12 months and turning the results into an index of the public mood. Generally, how people are feeling about the state of the country.

Reasons to be cheerful: Unemployment is down, the mortgage rate has been cut, interest rates have been cut again, inflation is low, people are shopping more (car sales are up more than 10 per cent), house prices are rising, the London *Evening Standard* says, 'Suddenly, Britain really is feeling good', building societies are soon to create millions of new shareholders, Wimbledon, sunshine, Tony Blair.

Reasons to be miserable: Tony Blair, you are unemployed or about to be made unemployed, they've repossessed your house, you haven't got any money, you are buying a house, England can't beat Switzerland let alone the rest of Europe, you can't eat beef any more, what is being done to the NHS, the BBC, the railways, etc.; John Major.

Great Feelgood Moments: Mrs Thatcher saying 'Rejoice, Rejoice' after the Falklands war (but not if your son died in the fighting); Mrs Thatcher's defeat; Oasis playing 'Don't Look Back in Anger' at the end of *Our Friends in the North*; winning the World Cup in 1966 (the Germans were robbed, which is a bonus to Feelgooders); IRA ceasefires.

Great Feelbad Moments: Spare us, please.

The World Cup won Harold Wilson a landslide feelgood election victory. No, it didn't. Harold won the election four months before England beat Germany 4–2, by which time Harold's popularity had suffered a nasty dip.

So feelgood and football is a myth? Don't boot it out of the stadium altogether. Some claim that England's 1970 World Cup defeat in Mexico helped Ted Heath unseat Harold Wilson.

But if England won Euro '96 John Major would be swept back to power in a snap election? Feel good but vote sensibly.

But if voters feel good they'll vote for the party in power. Once that was probably true. Now the link between the feelgood factor and voters' intentions seems to have broken down. England can score loads of goals, the economy can improve but voters, it seems, are going to vote the Tories out.

Not to be confused with: The Mori Mood of the Nation Index, Dr Feelgood, the good feel factor – the high you get if you go jogging a lot, an orgasm.

Most likely to say: 'Rejoice, rejoice.'

Least likely to say: 'I think the government is doing a wonderful job.' ●

....

11 April 1996
Linda Grant
Knee-benders for the truth

When you were at school, doubtless some know-it-all told you that the longest word in the English language was antidisestablishmentarianism; so you went and looked it up in the dictionary and discovered that it meant being against the movement for state recognition of the Church, and you thought, well, a fat lot of good that's going to do me in after-dinner party conversation. But you'd be wrong. After 17 years of Tory government, the Labour Party looks as if it might win the next election, it's odds against the monarchy lasting into the next century, and even the Prince of Wales is musing that if he does manage to clamber on to the throne, he might be defender of faiths rather than *the* faith.

In other words, a minor revolution could take place in Britain, usurping or radicalising key social institutions, clearing the way for the development of a post-industrial, multi-ethnic country which would need to find some use for its scrapped, unskilled, male proletariat. So what are the chattering classes chatting about? God.

Ian Hislop, Melvyn Bragg and Tony Parsons are all discovered to be regular knee-benders in the Church of England. At one's most cynical, it feels not all that surprising that the middle-aged and middle class are returning to church attendance. Anglican churches are, after all, often buildings constructed by the great artists and craftsmen of their day; they are like National Trust properties in which we all have a non-entrance-fee-paying stake. Anglicanism is about all that's left of our sense of what it is to be British.

But the fashion for religion may also indicate a yearning for ethical values and meaning after the longest experiment with amoral materialism Britain has ever known.

In his interview with the *Sunday Telegraph* last weekend, Tony Blair tells us he 'can't stand politicians who wear God on their sleeves'. If he is our next prime minister, however, Britain will be run by a man whose political ideology is inseparable from his religious faith. 'It is from a sense of individual duty that we connect the greater good and the interests of the community – a principle the Church celebrates in the sacrament of communion,' he says. I have read that sentence over and over again and I still don't have a clue what it means. The problem is not just its vagueness, but that I have only the dimmest notion of what occurs during communion. Despite the continued institutionalisation of faith through the political system, which gives the Anglican clergy seats in the legislature, Britain is no longer a Christian country in anything but name. Only 7.7 per cent of the population attend any religious worship on a regular basis;

of those, 2 per cent are Roman Catholic, and a further 1.2 per cent are Muslim.

Last year, during the commemorations to mark the liberation of Auschwitz, a recurrent query emanated from the lips of broadcasters: after 50 years, was it not time for Jews to forgive? This was greeted with some amusement in Jewish circles. The Old Testament makes no mention of forgiveness; it is an innovation that arrived with Christianity, the notion that Christ died for one's sins, that God is full of loving kindness, and that, through confession, one can obtain absolution and the slate can be wiped clean. The historian David Cesarani remarked at that time that Christians, in asking the Jews to forgive the sins of fascism, did so because they could not bear it if there was no happy ending. They did not understand that the meaning of Auschwitz was, in Eli Wiesel's words, that it remains on earth 'the place of endless night'.

In Blair's version of Christianity, people 'are more likely to act well and improve themselves in a society where opportunities are offered to them to do so; which strives to be cohesive and treats people as of equal worth'. This is an admirable notion but only part of the story. America, founded on equality and opportunity (for whites) and a cohesive sense of nationhood, produced spectacular examples of people behaving badly and discrepancies between rich and poor. Christian socialists have always been strong on heaven but poorer on hell. They are part of a movement from the 18th century onwards which believes that wrong can be socially engineered out of existence by sheer niceness. Have they learned nothing at all from the history of the 20th century, which teaches us that virtue and innocence are frequently punished and sadism rewarded?

Theo Richmond, author of *Konin*, a remarkable attempt to re-create in language the Jewish population of a small Polish town before the war, routinely asked all the survivors he could find about their religious beliefs. He discovered that some thought their survival could only be explained by the existence of God, while others were of the view that if there was a God at all, in saving them and not others more worthy than themselves, he must be a shockingly unpleasant individual.

Primo Levi concluded that the fact that he was alive at the end of the war, rather than up in smoke along with almost everyone else with whom he had been transported to Auschwitz, was based almost entirely on luck. He did, however, mention one other factor: 'And finally,' he wrote, 'I was also helped by the determination, which I stubbornly preserved, to recognise always, even in the darkest days, in my companions and myself, men, not things, and thus to avoid that total humiliation and demoralisation which led so many to spiritual shipwreck.' What we need in Britain is a wholesome dose of humanism, the belief that each other is all we have. This view is less prevalent than one might think: in one of the most egregious sentences ever written in a newspaper, last year Carla Lane, describing her experiences at Shoreham, said that it was only the animals now who were pure, presumably because they are the bearers of such virtues as loyalty, good nature and, in the case of many, vegetarianism. Whenever I hear the word purity I reach for my passport.

Christianity (and indeed all religious belief) has a tendency to write off anything it cannot understand as evil and hence not part of humanity: Thomas Hamilton was evil; the children who murdered Jamie Bulger were evil. Then, having done that, it injuncts us to 'love the sinner' (though not the sin, as if the latter were something that had been visited on the subject and was somehow separable). Humanism, on the other hand, does not write off misconduct as spawn from hell; it seeks explanations for our total identity. It is prepared to investigate humanity's darkest places; it acknowledges greed, rage and lust as well as condemning the deprivation and loneliness and poverty that wrong inflicts, for these are all part of our nature.

When man does his absolute worst and others are the victims of his actions, humanists do not wave their hands about as if indicating the mysterious ways in which God moves. Levi, when asked if he could forgive, said no, he could not. But nor did he want revenge. He asked for justice, the greatest of human inventions. It is entirely possible for people to build a moral code without having had it written down for us by God. And when Christians ask me how I can bear the idea of a world that is not suffused with the love of Jesus and the hope of everlasting life, I want to say, between gritted teeth, 'Oh, grow up.' To believe, as Levi did, in man is to build a world out of what we've got.

Two thousand years after the birth of Christ we are no longer drifting in a supernatural fog but have moved clear away from such explanations for the universe. The removal of God has not diminished it; rather, the huge shadow his presence casts over understanding no longer blocks out its true immensity and wonder. Do we really want, to lead us into the next millennium, a man who believes that the world was created by a deity who takes a personal interest in whether he breaks down over Lent and sips a quick whisky? To build a world based on human ethics and human values, rather than materialism and religion, is the coming task. •

. . . .

8 May 1996

George Monbiot
Living on this land of ours

Sitting in the lee of a flapping tarpaulin, coughing on sawdust and dandelion seed, is not the easiest situation in which to write a column. All around me, nails are being levered out of reclaimed timber, concrete rubble is being stacked into garden walls and unearthly sculptures are rising from the wastes. Every couple of minutes, a helicopter on its way down the Thames passes over our makeshift village.

It's difficult, too, to pull myself back from my surroundings far enough to make sense of them. As both *Guardian* columnist and participant, observer and observed, I feel a little fraudulent, as if I can't be true to both stations at once. But most taxing is the difficulty of relating the dynamics of the weird little settlement we have built on the land we occupied on Sunday to anything that lies beyond it.

We have no rules, no rulers and no representatives. Every morning, anyone who wants to be heard chalks his or her request on a blackboard. At 11 o'clock it is carried into our meeting place and someone is chosen to facilitate. All the chalked-up issues – and any more that need discussing – are raised and debated until we reach consensus. The decisions we make must be respected until another meeting changes them.

The process sounds, I know, hopelessly idealistic – a bunch of dreamy anarchists sitting together and planning their Utopia. It looks dangerous as well: consensus is notoriously easy to manipulate. Yet both the subjects discussed and the conclusions reached are anything but dreamy. Someone has rung in with a yard full of topsoil that needs shifting. Does anyone want it? How can we get it here? Guinness, the owner of the site, has its AGM this month. Should we buy shares?

Local residents at the meetings say they're delighted that the land has been opened up and is being used intelligently; but they are worried about the sort of people who might want to live here. 'We want written guarantees,' one man demands. 'No theft and no crossing the road to piss in the stairwells.'

This is the first time that anyone other than the owners of the site has been asked to make a positive choice about it. One unpopular proposal after another has been presented to local people. On each occasion both they and – uncharacteristically – the council have rejected them. But, unless they have a serious ambition to buy and develop the site themselves, the planning process provides no room for their own ideas.

They have been left, as a result, with bitterness and a sense of alienation and rejection. The new flats being built on the neighbouring site, they complain, are too expensive. The prospect of yet another new supermarket here is even less appealing than leaving this land derelict.

Trying simultaneously to restore both the land and the decision-making process that governs it is wildly ambitious, and not helped by tempers frayed by the exhaustion of months of frantic planning. But, even under these fraught circumstances, it seems to work, and no one has yet complained of being frozen out. Creative ideas – such as applying for a grant from the Guinness Housing Trust – emerge from people who have never been called on before.

It is true, of course, that we've only been here for three days, and frustrations and factionalisation might take longer than that to emerge. But elsewhere in the world, decision-making like this has been taking place for centuries. The Turkana nomads of northern Kenya lead lives far more complicated than our own, sharing resources among people scattered across thousands of square miles. But, through constant negotiation, sitting in a circle and beating the matter out as equals rather than petitioners and representatives, they have sustained a labile economy and a fragile ecosystem since they arrived in the 18th century. In more fertile parts of Kenya, it took the British decades of imposed leadership to usurp and destroy consensus politics.

It is an insult to our intelligence to insist, as Wandsworth Borough Council does, that decision-making about matters like this should be left entirely to our representatives. The disastrous developments which litter both sides of this part of the Thames are eloquent testimony to the inefficacy of representation. It is simply too blunt an instrument for tackling the diverse and hoary questions that planning throws up. A fraud has been perpetrated upon us. The powers that should have resided in our hands have been enclosed.

It's impossible to say what will happen here; whether we will break up or be broken or stay on and make development work for us. But whatever happens to the land, none of us will ever be the same again. Having once tasted real participatory decision-making, nothing else will do. ●

Family values

22 November 1995
Suzanne Moore
The new model goddess

First I was afraid. I was petrified.
Kept thinking I could never live
Without you by my side . . .

And now she's back, she walked through that door and straight into our living rooms. She has walked among us, this goddess. Diana – part-time saint and supermodel, a sexed-up Mother Teresa – chose to reveal all, and then some, and we were hooked. She looked strained, older. 'Too much sun, too many holidays,' said my friend. 'Pass the fruit and nut.' And there we sat bingeing while she purged herself before us.

'Stitched him like a kipper,' was Lorraine's verdict. 'I'd vote for her,' I said. And Tony Benn, who is after an elected monarchy, can put that in his pipe and smoke it.

While Charles chose, for some misconceived reason, to be filmed in breeches (no, not the Darcy kind), shooting deer in his little interview, Diana as always opted merely to look like one. Understated suit and overstated eyes, she looked . . . well, stately. A real pro. While he twiddled and twitched, she sat still except for the famous head tilt. While he was vague, she was direct. While you wished he would just shut up, she did what all true stars do: she left you wanting more. She was telling you, she indicated, as much as she could, as much, in fact, as she could get away with.

So can she get away with admitting to an affair, to feeling like an outcast, a 'non-starter' in the royal household? Can she get away with talking freely about her bulimia, her post-natal depression, her self-mutilation? Can she get away with hinting that Charles might not be a happy king? Can she get away with carving a role for herself as a roving ambassador with special responsibility for 'battered this' and 'battered that'?

If anyone can, she can. As she made clear, she has paid her dues. She has had 15 years' experience of the royal firm, 15 years' experience of being followed and photographed everywhere she goes. She has changed. She has to use that horrible word 'grown'. But she can only get away with it if we want her to.

Maybe we want her to because she has the ability that all great stars have of asking us to make it happen for them, of asking us to fill up their emptiness. Just like Marilyn Monroe, these women who have everything feel as if they are nothing and so we the public, the audience, the punters must make full this emptiness. It gives us something to do. It makes us feel special, needed even, and Diana's gift — as anyone who has seen her in action will tell you — is that she does make those she meets feel special.

> *But then I spent so many nights*
> *Thinking how you did me wrong,*
> *I grew strong, I learned how*
> *To get along.*

The circle of unappealing men who surround Charles may dismiss her as 'barmy' because in their world it is simply insane to be this emotional. It is to be weak. The world in which they operate and expect everyone else to is delineated into fixed categories of private life and public duty and they are horrified that Diana should rupture this divine order. They do not see that what Diana does, that what she embodies, in a way that Charles never can, is modernity itself. She is a modern woman, with the aspirations and problems that face many women today.

While Charles waffles on about his right to be king in quasi-spiritual terms, Diana is applying for the job of monarch on the grounds of experience and ability. She can reach out and touch somebody's hand not because she was born to do it but because she is good at doing it. There is a world of difference here. While Charles builds his model villages and rails against modern architecture, Diana speaks another language altogether — a private, innately personal discourse of pain and love and affection and distress and the need for human contact.

She knows what it is like to suffer. She has been there. And the promise is that she will be there for you too. She understands how in trying to cope we may destroy ourselves. She remembers what it is like to have cries for help dismissed as mere attention-seeking. Such private language is, of course, laughed off as psycho-babble, as somehow inappropriate, as a further sign that she is out of control. Too many shrinks have spoiled the broth. For this language is coded as feminine, as inferior, and it finds little respect in buttoned-up public life.

What is radical is that Diana is insisting on speaking this language as well as insisting on a place in public life. Women particularly will identify with her honesty about post-natal depression and eating disorders. They will understand what it is like when you can't get out of bed in the morning and face the world. They will understand what it is like to be rejected by one man and then fall for another cad. They will understand Diana's wry little smile when she says she might be better off to derive her satisfaction from her job and her children rather than from a man. She is resigned to not having it all. She is a nineties woman with nineties conflicts. There are a lot of us out there.

> *It's a promise that I had*
> *Not to fall apart,*
> *Kept trying hard to mend the*
> *Pieces of my broken heart.*

What she did so effectively was to oscillate between being a victim and being powerful, but she made it clear that she had empowered herself. Yes, she had been weak but, yes, she had found inner strength. She had sought help and there is nothing wrong with seeking help. She may have been classified as unstable, as hysterical, as selfish, yet what she represents more than anything is the current instability of the institutions she is required to function in. Her critics would have preferred that she did the right thing, that she put up and shut up, that she allowed her husband a mistress, that she kept quiet. They would prefer it if we were all quiet.

In the old days women did this. In return, if they were lucky, they got financial security. But Diana screwed up the deal. Diana wanted a husband, a partner, someone to share her life with. She wanted, in other words, a modern marriage, not the arranged marriage of so many of her class.

She wanted romance, silly girl, and perhaps for a while she had it. Is that so wrong? When she came to realise that this was not in fact what she had at all she blamed herself, hated what she was. Now she has turned that disappointment outwards. She is angry with those who would constrain her, who see her as a manipulative child in a household full of dutifully repressed grown-ups.

When women start to understand that their situation is not entirely their own fault but the result of far greater forces, they become a threat. Diana is not, she told us, a political animal but it is inevitably a political act to start seeing one's life defined by circumstances outside one's control.

Diana has seen the light. This light may not be the burning flame of holier-than-thou feminism but there is something alight none the less and she is canny enough to know that it can never be named. Even women of her background have felt its heat from a distance.

> *And you see me, somebody new.*
> *I'm not that chained up little person*
> *Still in love with you.*

Her discourse, like that of Thatcher's, who at times she reminded me of, must be full of a more acceptable image of female strength. This is the maternal feminine which has been employed throughout history and is less threatening to the establishment. She is a tigress fighting for her children, she is a mother to all she meets, she has a woman's instinct, she just knows, as women do, certain things that cannot be put into words.

Just as Maggie pretended to be a housewife while she invaded another country, so Diana speaks of her inner strength and in those sad eyes we see the ghosts of other brave women, from Elizabeth I to Florence Nightingale. This is manipulation of the highest order but how else is she to conjure an image of strength that is not driven by lust for power but is combined with duty, duty to her children, to her country?

She is not mad but she is dangerous to know because of what she now knows. Media fixers from Max Clifford to Madonna could learn a trick or two from the pop princess. She embodies the instability of the changing relationships not only between men and women but also between the monarchy and its subjects. The royals do not need to get on their bikes to be in touch with common people, they just need to be more like her. She is the new model and she knows in her heart that they cannot be like her. They have their pomp and circumstance she instead offers her heart and she would be the queen of ours too.

In this she is a greater threat to republicanism than a hundred debates on the immorality of hereditary privilege would be to the monarchy, because the great majority of people have let her into their hearts, understanding that she is flawed just like them. She offers a vision of the monarchy that is not simply about automatic deference and god-given rights but something altogether different and if she was acting, if she was insincere, then this is what happens in job interviews – and believe me this was a job interview. She can earn her keep better than any of the others. New Britain. New Monarchy. Young Country. Young King, as some might say.

What became clear as the interview progressed was that the narrative she has invented for herself is one of the most popular. Di, queen of all soap queens, plays the victimised woman who finds herself and goes on to win.

Romance has let her down so now she wants power, to be not the wife of the king but the mother of the king.

She has not given up. She will not go quietly. In her way she cheers us on as we cheer her. Go for it, Di. Go down screaming. We already know the words to the tune she is humming, for we have been singing it for a long time now. It's just a little weird to think that a supposedly shy and immensely privileged Sloane would be the one to get up on the dance floor with us. But there she is shaking it up, shaking it down.

> *I've got all my life to live,*
> *I've got so much love to give.*
> *I'll survive. I will survive.*

Song lyrics from Gloria Gaynor's 'I Will Survive', written by D Fekaris and F Perrin.

. . . .

22 December 1995

Leader

The Windsors: a doctor writes . . .

Memo from a marriage guidance counsellor: The Windsors, like most separated couples, are still suffering much pain and anger over their separation. They are locked in a struggle to win public loyalty, which must be excruciatingly painful for their children. The father is now ready for divorce but the mother is refusing to be bounced and has not yet replied to her mother-in-law's letter until she has had time to talk to her lawyers. The mother-in-law is a problem. With apparent disregard for the feelings of her grandchildren she wrote the letters suggesting divorce in the run-up to Christmas. This will have been particularly painful to the grandchildren, who, like most children of relatively recently separated parents, must still be hoping that their parents will get together again. It was only on 9 December 1992 that the parents were legally separated. Christmas is an important time for children. It is awaited with much anticipation. A sensitive grandmother might have waited until after the celebration before sending her letters. There was always the risk of a leak. The grandchildren had a right to a Christmas which was not dominated by a public debate over the divorce of their parents.

There is something wrong with a man of 47 waiting until he receives a letter from his mother before declaring that he is ready for divorce, although divorce is clearly the obvious and sensible next step. Both sides agreed to the legal separation. Now that they have been separated for more than two years, they can proceed under the dignified consent process using their separation as proof of irretrievable breakdown.

Both would benefit from the use of a mediator for the most important issue facing the family: not the crown but the future of the children. To their credit, both parents have worked hard to allow each to maintain a relationship with the children. They seem to have already taken on board the most crucial message from mediators: 'The best thing a separated parent can give a child is loving permission to spend time with the other parent.' It should not be necessary for Charles to join Fathers Need Families.

The focus needs to be on the future, not the past. Both parents have a duty under the Children Act to sort out arrangements about the children.

Grandparents should keep out. The children should be involved in the discussions on residence and contact (the old custody and access issues) but not required to carry the burden of making the decisions. Spending alternate Christmases with each parent, for example, might seem sensible. The court will require a statement of arrangements before agreeing to a divorce but will prefer not to make an order concerning the children if the parents can reach a joint agreement. The Windsors have a chance to demonstrate that family life need not end with divorce, even though it needs careful restructuring. •

· ·

28 August 1996

Leader

Long to reign over us?

Is there a more exquisite form of modern torture imaginable than that involved in waiting to be our King? Every dawn brings a fresh assault by headline. No private whisper goes unbugged or unpublished. No fleeting glance goes unsnatched. No week passes without a tabloid poll shrieking intrusive verdicts on the supposed intimacies of your failed marriage and future relationships. There is no suffragan bishop or prebendary too insignificant to be sought out for spiritual authority. If your subjects are not calling Nick Ross about Camilla, they're devouring the latest outpourings of Lynda Lee-Potter. *Sun* readers urge you to 'Bed her, don't wed her.' *Daily Telegraph* leader-writers furrow their undergraduate brows before loftily advising abstinence. *Mirror* readers, having yesterday ruled out Camilla as your future wife (a whopping 88 per cent against), are today asked whether they would object to you marrying someone else. And this, in Bagehot's exhausted adage, is supposed to be the dignified part of our constitution! This is the part which 'excites and preserves the reverence of the population'.

But where is the dignity in being the Prince of Wales today and what prospect is there of salvaging any dignity in the foreseeable future? The ending of his unhappy marriage has closed off one source of prurient speculation and intrusion only to open several more. Rupert Murdoch may or may not be a closet republican, but he has a shrewd nose for a commercial storyline or six. If Charles does indeed love Camilla Parker Bowles it is a love which will have to survive persecution and humiliation on a bleak and epic scale.

We have it on no less an authority than Jonathan Dimbleby that not once, even in his darkest moments, has the Prince of Wales ever seriously contemplated the surrender of what he has always thought to be an inescapable duty. Mr Dimbleby tells us that the word 'abdication' is anathema to the royal family. 'It not only reeks of crisis and failure,' he writes in his door-stopper biography of Charles, 'but it denies the fundamental assumption of an hereditary institution.' Yet who could seriously condemn the Prince if he were eventually to come to the conclusion that the game is not worth the candle? He may indeed fear the perception of 'failure', but what, in the context of a modern constitutional monarchy, is 'success' – and how might Charles be deemed to have achieved it unless by following the moral dictats of assorted telephone polls, focus groups and minor clerics? If stepping down involved a denial of the fundamental assumptions of an hereditary institution, would that be such an unthinkable thing? Even Tony Blair has difficulty with hereditary institutions nowadays (though he, in common with his party, has stopped short of tackling the fundamental assumptions of monarchy; the subject has not been discussed at conference since 1923 – and then in a debate lasting all of 15 minutes). There is no doubting the Prince's sincerity when he speaks of his sense of duty. Yet, in his conversations with Mr Dimbleby, Charles can offer only painfully stumbling clues as to what he thinks might be involved beyond a mere sense of duty. 'If, at some stage in the distant future, I was to succeed my mama, then obviously I would do my best to fulfil that next role,' he told his amanuensis. 'But it's very difficult to speculate myself about how I would function in that role . . . Sometimes, you daydream about the sort of things you might do.' In the absence of dignity, not to mention more conviction, might not the kindest course for the Prince of Wales be if it were all to remain just that – a daydream? •

11 September 1996

Catherine Bennett

A few top tips from Norma and Cherie

Cheese, as Sandy Carr writes in her lyrical pocket guide to coagulated milk, is all things to all men. 'It can be robust or delicate,' she notes, 'strong or soothing, an abundant meal in itself, or a rare and delicate morsel to be savoured, cosseted, and treated with the reverence afforded all great miracles of art or nature.'

It goes without saying that cheese should not be frozen. But Carr says it anyway: 'Never put cheese in the freezer. It is one sure way of destroying its flavour and texture irretrievably.' Until last weekend, it seemed that this simple precept – *never* put cheese in the freezer – would remain for ever unchallenged, a steadfast beacon in this uncertain world. Then Norma Major gave one of her rare interviews, speaking with all the authority of a career housewife. 'Oh yes,' she insisted, 'cheese freezes wonderfully. If you have any grotty bits left, you grate them and put them in a box in the freezer.'

Those women who have never maintained a cheese-freezing box could only reflect on the mountains of unpromising cheese casually jettisoned over the years. It was a moment charged with a sense of waste, of loss, even of shame. Nor was cheese-paring the only chastening top tip to emerge from this brief interview. 'On my own, I will use the same tea-bag more than once,' Ms Major revealed.

Here again, her teaching is revolutionary. In the 1970s it was not unusual for girls to spend a double domestic-science lesson learning the correct brewing of tea, from pot-warming, to measuring the leaves, to tray-setting technique. But Ms Major's authority cannot be in doubt. She, herself, once worked as a domestic-science teacher, before willingly sacrificing herself to husband and family. 'Domestic life suits me,' she says. In her current role as the Tory Party's secret weapon, she is tormented by one urgent desire: to get home where 'there are some cupboards that need cleaning'.

It has long been said that Norma Major is an undervalued ornament to the Tory party. 'In reality she is an intelligent, humorous, cultivated person,' the commentator Edward Pearce claimed recently. 'Certainly Norma has none of that commanding, iridescent, hard-surfaced quality which marks the career-woman wife.' Now that Norma has offered a sample of her charms, careert women clearly have some hard thinking to do. If a housewife with a cupboard-cleaning habit is now considered, as *The Times* reported, 'a huge electoral asset', working women must accept that they have got their priorities all wrong. Instead of earning a living, thereby acquiring qualities which so alarm the iridescent Pearce, they should perfect the arts of the scullion, procreate, and embrace a lifetime of dependency.

This toppest of tips was confirmed by Cherie Booth's decision to guest-edit *Prima*, a magazine whose obsession with domestic chores makes it about as appealing to most 'career women' as *Angler's Mail*, *Railway Modeller*, and *Cage and Aviary Birds*. *Prima* is a magazine for women who have time not only to batch-bake but to embroider childish samplers ('simply send off for our embroidery kit'), to knit horrible throws ('to snuggle under while you're watching TV') and to deface the walls and furniture with stencilled flowers ('simply stamp the design on to a piece of paper. Then repeat . . .').

In her editorial, Booth describes herself as a 'keen knitter', who has always been 'a fan of *Prima*'. As this cannot possibly be a cynical, barefaced lie, it suggests that hard-surfaced career women have been typically misguided in admiring Booth for her intelligence, application and success; quite wrong to consider her the most impressive aspect of Tony Blair.

For if Booth had wanted to identify herself with working women, she could have guest-edited any number of women's magazines which presuppose a productive life outside, as well as inside, the home. Instead, she has submerged herself in the world of handy hints, allowed herself to be presented as 'mum to three school-age kids', and participated in a question-and-answer session with *Prima* readers, featuring such posers as 'How old are your children?', 'Do you like gardening?', and 'Why have you retained your maiden name?' The one vaguely political question, 'Would you try to persuade your husband to help working mothers?', elicits the doting response: 'As a working father, Tony knows about these things.' Top tip: When you're asked something you don't want to answer, simply change the subject!

Women are familiar with having their intelligence insulted, whether it is by advertisers, or by male politicians such as the uxorious Steven Norris: 'I suspect that we're more at home with spouses who are supportive and loyal.' It is new, however, to find able women colluding in the enterprise. Norma Major, for example, uses the interview promoting her new book on Chequers to admit that she regrets writing it, when she could have been out supporting her husband. But Norma, at least, appears genuinely to enjoy her submission. Cherie Booth's justification by knitting is less convincing, and more depressing.

Perhaps, in her frenzy of autumnal housewifery, baking conkers and carving pumpkin lanterns ('use the leftovers to make soup'), Booth has missed the new Fawcett report, Winning Women's Votes? Although it is unable to correlate keen knitting or cheese-storing preference with voting patterns, the study does reveal that women have recently acquired interests beyond children, church and kitchen. Only 9 per cent, for example, consider being 'mainly a home-maker' – or, as it might be, a *Prima* reader – to be an ideal lifestyle for women; 82 per cent believe women should combine home and work. Only 11 per cent agree that family values means 'having children'. A 'huge majority' do not feel that the political parties will pay enough attention to issues that are important to them (health, education, unemployment, cheese).

In conclusion, the report says, female voters would like some respect: 'Women want more than just lip service.' If this election campaign is to become the duel of the wives, women will demand more than words. Let us see some specimens of Cherie's knitting, and Norma's curtains. Or – top tip! – why not simply get the pair of them to run a race? In *Prima*, young Cherie reveals herself to be in prime condition, after making regular visits to the gym. Norma, by contrast, is barely able to swim . . . ●

● ●

20 December 1995
Joanna Coles
Estranged bedfellows

And so it was over . . . Silvana Ashby reached for her Marlboro Lights, she picked up her brown fur shapka and trotted across the courtroom, her noisy little heels breaking the terrible silence which had just descended upon Court 13. 'I'm *zo zorry* David,' she whispered in her thick Turin accent, kissing the top of her husband's bald head. Then she started to cry.

She cried even more as her husband, who had just started weeping himself, shrugged her away. '*Oh leeeave meee aloooone,*' he hissed in his misery. And so she trotted back to the safety of the *Sunday Times* lawyers. David Glynn Ashby, barrister and Conservative member for North West Leicestershire, took a long breath and swayed to his feet in disbelief at the verdict and, no doubt, the prospect of £400,000 costs. Still crying, he staggered out of court, an utterly broken man.

There was only one question remaining: what on earth made him do it? Of all men, a criminal barrister with 32 years' experience at the bar might have guessed at the gamble he was taking. That the evidence amassed by the *Sunday Times* was so comprehensive he couldn't possibly persuade a jury otherwise. *On the balance of probability* . . . True, in its second article stating Ashby was homosexual, the newspaper had been wrong to suggest the MP had spent a week on holiday with one Dr Ciaran Kilduff in Goa. In fact, Ashby had gone on his own. But it turned out to be the paper's only mistake. They had everything else. And much, much more.

They had rummaged through Kilduff's rubbish bags and found the receipt for the *gastronomique* weekend the two men had enjoyed together in northern France. One room, one bed! They had the manager of the hotel, Château Tilques, saying there had been plenty of rooms available that night, they hadn't *needed* to share at all! They had the dimensions of the bed, 1.5 metres wide! As Richard Hartley observed: 'That's hardly very big, is it?' They had the vendor who sold Ashby his flat, who told the court that the MP had been so desperate to buy the apartment above Dr Kilduff that he had ended up paying over the odds. They had private detectives who produced videotapes of Ashby entering Kilduff's flat at 5.30pm and leaving at 8.30am the following day. They even had a gay *Times* reporter who swore he had seen Ashby loitering in London's oldest gay pub. But, best of all, *they had the wife*. A wife prepared to testify against her husband of 28 years. And, by God, what a testimony that turned out to be.

In the end it was the details which made it so poignant. The snatches of ordinary conversation which must have reverberated around every household in the country. There was Ashby's plaintive cry about supper after he's washed too much lettuce: 'Bloody hell, who's going to eat all this salad?' That was just before the row on Christmas Eve 1993 when his wife arrived and started chanting 'Poofters, poofters!' through his letter box. The couple then wrestled each other to the ground, she stripped his study wallpaper with her bare nails and Dr Kilduff had to call the police to break them apart. 'I'll kick you in the bollocks so you can't fuck any more,' Silvana shouted, later claiming she had learned her bad language from Channel 4. When the police arrived to take her away she set about them with the same obsessive fury.

The ordinary details which turned out to have such extraordinary consequences . . . The small box of silver fruit knives given to Ashby as a present from a pupil which triggered Silvana's jealousy. The time she asked David what he wanted for supper and he wrote a note to the butcher demanding 'Pig's arse and cabbage'. The occasion she demanded David spend more time with her. 'No,' he replied. 'I will buy you a dog instead.'

Though much of the time the jury looked bored, they did manage to perk up when Silvana recalled her husband's delight at being elected. Alas, he did not plan to share his new life with her. 'We were on the Embankment and he said: "Remember, Silvana, from now on for you I am dead. I don't exist for you any more. I will dedicate myself to my work. Don't count on me. I can have whatever I want now."'

Then, of course, there was the remarkable insight into the Ashby family business, about which Ashby was at least frank. 'I'm afraid we're a blackmailing family,' he told the court, admitting he had yelled at his sister: 'You shit, you shit, you shit. You bastard. You are a nasty little girl. Now fuck off.'

It was, it transpired, his sister, Lynne Garling, who had initially tipped the *Sunday Times* off, by phoning them to tell them that her brother's marriage had broken up and he was now living with a male friend. She then tried to get him out of the family firm by threatening to tell everyone he was gay. 'She hates me,' said Mr Ashby. 'She was determined to get me, she was coming in for the kill.' She even drew doodles of him hanging from a gibbet. Whatever his election leaflet promised, David Ashby's family was not as other families.

Though who, outside the immediate family, would have guessed it? On the surface, Ashby appeared to be a Whip's dream. As an MP, he rarely said anything out of place, he never said anything memorable – in fact, he hardly said anything at all. His only recorded ticking off was for writing Christmas cards during a Commons Committee Session. 'I was doing important constituency business,' he blustered. 'Anyway, I was just trying to spread a little cheer at Christmas.'

Elected in 1982, he didn't put a foot wrong, plodding obediently through the division lobbies. After the first gruelling week of the trial, his constituency chairman even threw a small party to demonstrate local support. The word among the ladies of North West Leics was that this was a personal matter, and probably Silvana's fault. She was, well, difficult, 'volatile', you know, at *that time* of her life.

In the witness box, it was true that Silvana, who is 53, looked like an exotic bird who had gradually lost her plumage. Her nose, strangely bent, bears the unfortunate result of an accident in 1984 when she was hit in the face by a golf ball – prompting her husband to call for a golfing ban on Wimbledon Common.

Defying all logic, the Ashbys still professed to care for each other, sometimes greeting in the court corridor with a kiss, at other times ignoring each other. Occasionally, provoked by the other's evidence, they would stalk out of court and sit smoking voraciously, until they had calmed down. Fiction was never this strange. Even Richard Hartley, QC, for the *Sunday Times*, sometimes lost his way, occasionally referring to Dr Kilduff as Kildare.

It's an easy cliché to say that the only winners in cases like these are the lawyers, but even they didn't appear to be enjoying themselves. There was none of the normal barristerial badinage, none of the fun. During one legal tussle the judge suggested the two opposing counsel might iron out their differences over a cup of tea or 'something stronger'. Richard Hartley sniffed and said he thought it unlikely.

Hartley, in particular, had a trying time cross-examining the plaintiff, which lasted almost a week. Ashby is used to asking, not answering, questions and he resolutely refused to be intimidated. In his closing speech Hartley could not hide his distaste. 'You may think he is *pompous, arrogant and easily hurt* . . . ' he spat at the jury. 'A Jekyll and Hyde character. Sometimes he bursts out crying, next minute he starts laughing . . . Can you really believe a word he says?' The difficulty was that at times it was hard to believe what anybody said.

Ashby's counsel, Geoffrey Shaw QC, didn't look that comfortable either. Ashby was constantly chivvying him along, passing him notes, tugging at his gown, whispering directions and demanding he ask extra, often superfluous, questions. At times Shaw could barely look in Ashby's direction, flinching as his client hissed yet another instruction.

In the end, of course, it was all to no avail. How much better if Ashby had dropped the case at the start. How much better if neither husband nor wife had forced their daughter to take sides in this grotesque family saga. What must she have thought, as she stood there in the witness box recounting the terrible time her mother had taunted her in front of her friends by claiming she was a lesbian. Alexandra, now safely working for S G Warburg in Milan, told the court that her mother was always accusing her father of affairs with both men and women. Then there were the devious ways her mother tried to stop Alexandra seeing her father on his own.

'There was competition for my father's attention. The three of us together were quite an explosive mix,' she told the court, shaking her brown bob. Her mother was possessive, spiteful and had a tendency to make things up. 'She reinvents things,' she said sadly, as her mother tore into another packet of Trebor Softmints.

In legal terms, the case highlighted the difficulties of defining homosexuality. At what point, for example, does male friendship develop into homosexuality? Does there have to be full sex? Does there have to be any sex at all? Though the two men admitted sharing a room in France, did that alone constitute a gay liaison? The jury decided it did, ignoring Mr Justice Morland's interjection that surely Mr Ashby's impotence made it less likely that sexual intercourse had taken place.

Supposing Ashby and Kilduff cuddled but did not have sex, was that enough to declare gayness? Given the balance of probabilities, the jury decided the MP and the doctor did have an affair, but does that mean the MP should be newly redefined as gay or bisexual? At the last count, he voted for the age of homosexual consent to be reduced to 16. Is his heterosexuality – in evidence during much of his marriage – now compromised, even negated?

But it was not these finer points of the law which interested the spectators who gathered in Court 13 every day. It was the same instinct which draws crowds to a bullfight, to witness the toppling of a once confident, nay magnificent, beast, in the form of a Tory MP. Day after day they came. The students who sniggered as Ashby wept. The dapper man 'in fashion' who dispensed Fox's Glacier Fruits to the regulars. The odd woman in the purple checked coat who, at 3pm on the dot, would rifle through a plastic bag and produce a scone which she then smuggled to her lips. This week, as a seasonal gesture, she had replaced the scone with mince pies.

Then there was Ernest Swithins, retired, who daily recommended Joshua Rosenberg's latest book on the law to anyone who would listen. 'I've met Mr Rosenberg and I've told him it's a very absorbing book,' he muttered to the stranger sitting next to him yesterday. 'I see the houses in Cromwell Street have dropped in value,' the stranger retorted.

After the incident with the golf ball, Silvana Ashby won substantial damages. She won again yesterday too, though her husband will pick up the costs. The true cost, of course, is incalculable. The *Sunday Times* never dreamt that Ashby would put his sexuality to the test. Ashby was convinced the *Sunday Times* wouldn't ask him. He was wrong. He was after damages, but succeeded only in inflicting damage, gross damage, on both his family and himself. •

5 June 1996
Catherine Bennett
Love and death in an impure world

L ess than a week since her conviction for manslaughter and subsequent release were extensively reported, Sara Thornton has returned to public notice – as cover-girl in the *Independent* newspaper. Her familiar features, graced with her now equally celebrated 'goddess stone', introduce two instalments of love letters which Thornton wrote from prison to a man called George Delf. The pen-pals are pictured grinning in a tree and posing in a park. And the letters? They illustrate what we already know: that Thornton is intelligent, articulate and convinced that her husband's death was not her fault.

The only surprise here is Mr Delf, who wrote to Thornton in August 1990 and offered to help her, if he could. Within a month or so, we discover, the two were on mole-kissing terms. 'Darling,' Sara writes, 'when I get out, you can kiss all my other moles!' Other comments relate to her case. 'I am not nuts, and I never was,' she writes – an assertion which sounds a little strange after her recent defence of diminished responsibility on account of a personality disorder called 'dissociation'. Thornton was unable to give evidence at her retrial, it was explained by her counsel, because of this very disorder.

Dissociation has not, however, prevented Sara Thornton from informing the *Independent* that 'Malcolm and I were a disaster waiting to happen.' Clearly concerned that four pages of letters might not be enough for Sara Thornton, the *Independent* cleared more space for an interview in which she is introduced as 'a tortured soul in search of peace'. Here, Thornton's explanation for not giving evidence is that she had talked about the killing so much, that 'I honestly do not think I could have given a true account'. Her interviewer is sympathetic: 'She is someone who needs a hug.' Lest her huggability be in any doubt, the interview is illustrated by yet another picture of Ms Thornton, looking forlorn in her 'Victims of Injustice' T-shirt.

The Thornton–Delf correspondence, which will shortly be published by Penguin as *Love on the Wing: Letters of Hope from Prison*, is just the start of a bumper Thornton season, also featuring 'Provocation', a *Cutting Edge Special* (filmed before the retrial), in which she will tell her side of things to Channel 4 viewers, and a BBC drama (completed before the retrial) on which Thornton had script approval. The BBC says the play, entitled *Killing Me Softly*, will tell 'Sara's story' while 'tackling the issues of provocation and domestic violence'. Later, we are promised a book about Thornton's time in prison. After that, who knows – a chat show? A recipe book?

It is nothing new, of course, for someone who has killed to become a celebrity. The demand for documentation of true-life bloodshed is such that killers cannot keep up the supply; a shortage which explains the regular recyclings of Jack the Ripper theories, and the annual output of murder anthologies which rely on breadth, rather than depth, for reader stimulation. For all their authors' protestations that slaughter studies are a respectable branch of psychology, most books and articles about killers are simply literary freak shows, produced with varying degrees of polish and gloat. The biographies fascinate precisely because their subjects are so grotesquely different from ourselves.

Sara Thornton, on the other hand, has long been introduced to the public as someone we can readily comprehend; an abused woman first, and a killer second. Her case was adopted and publicised by the pressure group Justice for Women, in its mission to make the defence of 'slow burn' provocation available to battered women who face a murder charge. In the cases of Emma Humphreys, who had been repeatedly brutalised and raped by a vicious pimp, and of Kiranjit Ahluwalia, who endured a decade of assaults and rapes by her husband, the JFW campaign was well supported by the evidence. It was clear that both women had been abominably treated by a judicial system which has been consistently harsher to provoked women than to provoked men.

But Thornton's story is too ambiguous to bolster the defence of cumulative provocation; indeed, the retrial judge sentenced her on the basis that 'abnormality of mind', rather than provocation, had diminished her responsibility. So what can we learn from the case of Sara Thornton? Not much, except that a pair of unpredictable, occasionally violent, heavy drinkers should avoid living together. Or, more importantly, that the mandatory life sentence for murder is absurd, taking no account of the fact that every murder is different, and that not all murderers deserve lengthy incarceration.

But this cannot satisfy Sara Thornton's supporters. 'As far as we are concerned, it's still a major victory,' said a representative of Justice for Women last week. In other words, because their campaign for a retrial was based on provocation, and because Sara Thornton won her retrial, her case is still to be claimed as a victory for women victims of male battering, and thus for women in general, oppressed as we all must be by institutionalised male violence.

If it helps Sara Thornton privately to believe that she stabbed her comatose husband under provocation, one can hardly object; she needs, as the *Independent* says, to find peace. For newspapers and programme-makers to endorse this interpretation is a different matter. Already, regardless of the judge's comments, she is beginning to acquire martyr status; becoming, to paraphrase Brigitte Bardot, the Jeanne d'Arc of provocation. The beatific impression is enhanced by Thornton's 'goddess stone' head-dress, a symbol, she says, of her 'right as a woman to be who I am'.

Like Princess Diana's revelation of self-mutilation and bulimia, Thornton's claim to representative victimhood is now being allowed to eclipse the larger factors which differentiate her from most women: one is royal, and the other a killer who suffers from a personality disorder. To claim, as the BBC does, that the dramatisation of Thornton's story 'serves a wide public interest' is either to misrepresent her case or to suggest that such mental abnormalities are a female commonplace.

One can only hope that *Killing Me Softly* makes it clear that the real victim in the Thornton case remains the alcoholic, sporadically violent and now dead Malcolm Thornton. Judging by the title, it seems unlikely. •

••

12 April 1996

Ros Coward
Make the father figure

Feminists may not agree about much these days. But one subject is guaranteed to revive the old alliances: the importance of fatherhood. Most feminists still think this subject is taboo, and raising it an act of treason. Yet keeping the gag on will be increasingly difficult. Currently a stream of books about fatherhood is flowing across the Atlantic and at the end of this month we will get the first UK conference on the subject. The media are already pouncing on some of the promised themes, paternal 'role strain' attracting early attention.

The IPPR, organisers of the conference (in Westminster on 30 April), are probably emboldened, not just because masculinity is now a more fashionable subject but also because fathers have recently been much more aggressive in standing up to feminism. In the UK the fathers' lobby, including groups like Families Need Fathers, have become much more organised, and vituperative, around divorce-law reforms. The journal *Male View* bitterly describes no-fault divorces as pandering to the feminist lobby by allowing 'the wife to off-load her legally defenceless husband, but keep his home, money and children whenever she fancies a lifestyle change'.

This sounds like the paranoia of a few bitter individuals blaming feminism for the loss of their actual families. And certainly reports from Families Need Fathers meetings suggest they would be more aptly named Families Need Therapists. But just because they may be paranoid doesn't mean that feminists *aren't* out to get them. Some time ago feminists stopped talking about getting men to care and share more and started wondering, as Yvonne Roberts put it in a *She* article, 'exactly what, in the 1990s, is a father for'. Now there's scarcely a leading feminist who hasn't added her own thoughts about the redundancy of fathers.

Bea Campbell, explaining hostility to single mothers in her book *Goliath*, writes: 'To reveal the redundancy of the men is the real crime of the mothers.' Sue Slipman, then director of the National Council for One-Parent Families, was even more contemptuous when she replied to the complaint by right-wing theorist Charles Murray that the increase in single motherhood has cast men loose as uncivilised rabble: 'He cannot explain why any woman in her right mind should want to take one of his "new rabble" home.' Suzanne Moore has also joined in, stating: 'It remains unclear what fathers do that is so important.'

The defensive tone is not surprising. Social theorists of all political persuasions have blamed fatherless families (i.e. single mothers) for the social disintegration of the 1990s. John Redwood, Peter Lilley and more recently John Bowis in the adoption discussions all make fatherless families synonymous with crime and inadequacy. Even a pamphlet from the Institute of Economic Affairs warned Labour supporters of the problems of 'Families without Fathers'. In America such views are commonplace. Robert Bly's new book *Sibling Society* explains escalating violence and gangs as initiation rites of boys desperately lacking a paternal authority figure. Another, *Life Without Father*, published this week, lists 'compelling evidence' that fatherhood is indispensable for the good of children and society.

The right have had a major success in their attack on single mothers as the root of all social evils. But feminists often get bogged down in their response. Sometimes they rightly insist that social unrest has other causes. Sometimes they challenge the centrality attributed to feminism in causing these family changes. It was the men who left the women. But mostly they accuse anyone who wants to discuss fathering as suffering from nostalgia for the patriarchal authoritarian family. Men who value egalitarian sexual relationships shy away from discussing the positive role of the father in case they undermine single mothers. This becomes part of a damaging cycle. If men feel they have no role other than to support the greater bond of mother and children, no wonder it is so easy for them to leave.

There have been real losses for fathers in the contemporary family and to say so does not involve harking back to outdated ideas of the father's role. Fathering has changed fundamentally in the past 30 years. The first change happened in the 1960s, with the emergence of the modern egalitarian family emphasising equal partners and the welfare of children. But even that model still assumed the father would provide for the family, gaining a certain moral authority and status as a result. So long as he provided for his family he could call himself a good father, however little he involved himself emotionally. More recently, increased economic uncertainty for men and women's challenge to the authoritarianism inherent in the provider role have undermined the breadwinner role. Fathering has changed, but no new ideals have emerged to take account of those changes.

When a relationship is working well the gains of greater intimacy far outweigh the losses and few men stop to question what paternal identity should be. Most have evolved new roles without looking for labels. But when relationships break down some men realise they have played a marginal role, a walk-on part to the central drama. Women may have been working but few have given up their central role with the child or fully delegated primary care of their children to their partners.

Fathers suddenly find themselves without any automatic role and seeking a language to embody what has been positive, and what they want to protect, in their relationship with their children. The only place to articulate this is the right-wing, pro-family lobby.

One or two pro-feminist men have risked discussing what fathers bring to the family. Sebastian Kraemer, a psychotherapist, addressed a Demos seminar on fatherhood last year. He made it clear he had no nostalgia for the authoritarian family but argued that children from families in which the parents have separated are over-represented in child mental-health clinics. He went on to cite evidence that children of fathers who share more than 40 per cent of their care 'demonstrate more cognitive competence, increased empathy, less sex-stereotyped beliefs and a more internal locus of control'. With two parents involved, children also experience a greater richness of caretaking, and a greater depth of understanding relationships, being exposed to the full complexity of an adult relationship.

Another psychotherapist, Andrew Samuels, goes even further. An active and physically affectionate father can make many positive contributions. He can bring to a son a feeling of 'homosociality', an ability to relate to other men affectionately and communally, as women often relate. A father's affection for his daughter can also break up an identification with motherhood, introducing other sources of identification. Radically, he talks about the affirmation which a father can give to his daughter as an evolving sexual being.

Samuels feels compelled to entitle his paper on this subject 'The good enough father of either sex', understandably reluctant to draw feminist wrath by suggesting that only biological men could play the roles. Yet the time has surely passed for this tentativeness, this reluctance to unleash feminist contempt. The feminist resistance to any discussion of fatherhood has been defensive, and sometimes downright offensive when it shades into virgin-birth fantasies about the total redundancy of men. And by making it taboo for liberals to evolve a positive discourse a vacuum has been created for right-wing misogynists. •

....

31 May 1996

Susie Orbach

The dangerous aesthetic of thinness

Wow. Such are dreams made of. Omega cancels its ads in *Vogue* as a protest against the use of skeletal models in the June edition.

Twenty-six years ago a group of women concerned about how the uniformly skinny physical representation of females in advertisements and fashion magazines found its way into the consciousness of young girls and women had the glimmer of an idea (now taken for granted) that there was a relationship between eating problems and the image of womanhood portrayed on billboards and in magazines.

Each year as the mannequins got thinner, young women struggled to find a way to mimic those images by transforming their own bodies.

The group of concerned women dreamed of boycotts. They would use their economic power to force manufacturers to present women in all their variety and to extend the range of what might be considered beautiful.

They knew that thinness was just the latest construction. After all, just a generation before, Sophia Loren's voluptuousness had reigned, bringing with it the same kind of distress to women who failed to meet that kind of curvaciousness. But this new aesthetic of thinness was particularly dangerous.

It just happened to coincide with that moment in history when women were beginning to demand that they take up more not less space in the world, when women attempted to be seen as more than (sexual) objects.

The campaigners were ineffectual. Bulimia, compulsive eating, anorexia entered the vocabulary. We learned what torture such experiences were. Responsible citizens shook their heads and felt helpless about the pull of the thin imagery on their daughters.

The surprise on looking at the June *Vogue* is how familiar it all is. The thinness of the models is not new or dramatic, but its effect is shocking all the same.

It is the pictures of prepubescent bodies dressed up to look like sexually available women that magnetise us. The pictures combine vulnerability with an aggressive edge. They invite, magnetise and bewilder all at the same time.

But Omega has withdrawn and hopefully this will set a trend. The work of countless women and men who have campaigned against the destructive power of such images of women could receive no greater reward than to have a younger generation see pictures of beautiful women in all shapes and sizes representing the full glory of femininity. •

. . . .

4 December 1995
Nick Hornby
The Great British Male (aged 10)

The day starts for Nicky Glancy shortly after eight o'clock; he emerges from his bedroom wearing a pair of Hi-tec trainers, a pair of Arsenal socks, a pair of Arsenal shorts and an Arsenal shirt. He's a big Arsenal fan. The shirt is brand new. Nicky and his dad, Nick, queued up to buy it on the day the redesigned away strip was launched – and the lettering on the back indicates that Nicky's favourite player is Dennis Bergkamp, Arsenal's £7.5 million summer signing.

It is a pre-season Tuesday morning so Bergkamp has not yet played for the team (and has not, therefore, done an awful lot to inspire this kind of devotion, apart from cost an awful lot of money) but already the 'B' is peeling away from the Nike shirt. This shoddiness, sadly typical of big football clubs, peeves Nicky. These things matter, especially when you are 10.

Nicky doesn't eat breakfast straight away –'I feel a bit funny in the mornings' – and watches *The Big Breakfast* intently while he gets his bearings. 'This lady left 10p in the phone box round the corner so I nicked it,' he tells me gleefully and suddenly, apropos of nothing much. (Later on, this 10p will become, in the retelling of the story, £1.20.)

'You didn't really nick it, did you?' his mum says deflatingly. 'You found it.'

Nicky concedes the point with a shrug, his bravado shrivelled by his mother's common sense, and goes to the kitchen to make some toast and pour himself a glass of milk.

Nicky, his mother, his father and his three sisters live in a large top-floor flat on a pleasant street in Highbury, just up the road from the entrance to the

Arsenal ground. Nicky's parents own and run a newsagent's kiosk just outside the local tube station; they work Mediterranean hours, with a break after lunch while the station is quiet. The kids hang out at the kiosk at odd periods throughout the day, and Nicky in particular loves it there. In fact, taking over the kiosk is his number two career choice, right after becoming a professional footballer. 'I'd play for Tottenham if Arsenal didn't want me.'

The Big Breakfast has finished; now Nicky and two of his three sisters, Lisa (aged 14) and Sarah (eight), are watching the dismal American teen sitcom *Saved by the Bell*, although their view of the screen is somewhat obscured by the third sister, Samantha (six), who is demonstrating her considerable skill with a hula-hoop. None of them mind; on the contrary, they are all extremely proud of her talent and roar her on. 'She can do much better than that,' Nicky assures me after an early failure — Samantha seems to be exempted from all sibling rivalry on account of her age, and is in any case cute beyond all resentment.

Saved by the Bell is replaced by *Batman*, but, by this stage, Nicky and the girls have come to resemble one of those research projects examining what people get up to while they are supposed to be watching TV. Samantha is still hula-hooping frantically, Sarah is drawing, and Nicky gets out his Gameboy. He's playing a basketball game, All-Star Challenge 2; I have a go, but fail miserably. 'I wasn't very good at it at first either,' Nicky reassures me sweetly.

He finds a copy of an Arsenal magazine and talks me through it patiently, as if I was newly arrived on the planet. 'That's another advert. That's Alan Smith. He's had to pack it up because of injury. I had him on my shirt and all.' Then it's on to a puzzle book, and we do a wordsearch game. We are looking for words containing the letters 'arm' — ptarmigan, marmalade, pharmacist and so on. Nicky becomes fixated on the quest for the word Marmite and becomes extremely agitated when we can't find it. 'Oh, God. Oh, God. Marmite. Oh no. Oooooh, owwww. Marmite . . .' These are the only signs of distress he shows all morning.

What's it like being a 10-year-old boy? The worst thing, Nicky thinks, is that sometimes you are bad without meaning to be. 'I got in trouble for saying the F word at school. It just slipped out. This kid was messing me about in the playground and I said F you. He never told on me though. It was his brother. I got a detention.'

The best thing about being 10 is having a good time, but the best age to be is Lisa's age, 14, when you get to hang out more. Nicky wants to get married, to 'someone nice and kind'; the best thing about being married will be the honeymoon — because you get to go somewhere 'nice and hot, like Hawaii'. The best place he has ever been so far is Pontin's Holiday Camp, Camber Sands. He wants two children, a boy and a girl.

The best thing about being grown-up will be having a job and getting paid. 'If you do a good job, you get paid well. If you only do quite a good job, you get paid about half, probably.' I am glad that I won't be around to see his face when he finds out about water company chairmen, or Michael Fish or Jeffrey Archer.

There are other great things about being 10, too, things that Nicky doesn't mention. You can say whatever comes into your head, in any order, without having to bother with expressions like 'By the way' or 'A complete change of subject . . .'; in a brilliant stroke that left me gasping with admiration and envy, Nicky managed to leap from the topic of summer holidays to the far more fruitful subject of European football simply by spotting a resonant car number plate: 'Look – EWC. That's like ECWC. European Cup-Winners' Cup. Did you go to that game? We should never have lost . . .'

And you can be as self-pitying or as mercenary as you want, simply because you have no suspicion that the articulation of these feelings is ever regarded as regrettable. 'Sarah's not bothered about me at all. I say hello and she just goes "Huh!"' He makes a face intended to illustrate a grumpy lack of interest. 'And I bought her a Scrunchy for her birthday, and that's £1.75.' Which of us hasn't felt exactly like this, probably within the last couple of weeks? And which of us has had the courage to own up? Not me, although I am sorely tempted to sit down and trade horror stories.

If being 10 means sitcoms, Gameboys, grudges and stream of football consciousness, it is also a time of deep, dark, barely grasped fears, many of them revolving around the topic of death. During *Batman*, Nicky wanders over to the family video shelf and talks me through his favourites: he expresses particular enthusiasm for *Hook*. 'Have you seen it? Wo!' ('Wo!' is used to express excitement or approval.) He points to the cover. 'See him? He dies. He's a kid and all.' That 'and all' speaks volumes about what is fair and unfair, right and wrong; he knows that children die, but also that in a just world they shouldn't. Later on, a discussion of the merits of *Casper* gives rise to similar sentiments. 'Great film!' And then, more soberly: 'Two people died in it.'

I ask him if he worries about death and he starts to nod even before I have finished the question. 'If I was asleep in my room and I had my bedroom window wide open 'cos it's hot like now, and someone dropped a bomb through it . . . I'd be killed, wouldn't I?' I have to concede that, in this particular set of circumstances, his chances of survival would indeed be slim. But who would want to drop a bomb on him? 'The Germans. 'Cos we beat them 50 years ago.' This is an unlooked-for effect of the VE Day celebrations: it has probably been decades since little boys last worried about being blown to bits by the Germans.

One suspects, though, that the Germans are simply more prosaic, more threatening nightmares dressed up in uniform. A family conversation about Cheryl from *Neighbours*, who has recently had a baby at an advanced age, draws from Nicky the observation that 'she'll be dead before that little baby grows up'. It gets a laugh from his sisters, but later it becomes clear that Nicky is at an age when parental mortality is preying on his mind. He hates it, he tells me, when his mum and dad become ill; he says that his parents are the most important thing in the world. He's right, of course. For now and for the foreseeable future, there isn't really much else that matters.

Today Nicky's dad is taking him and big sister Lisa to Wembley for a guided tour of the stadium. Nicky has been looking forward to this – indeed, he wasn't able to get to sleep last night because he was so excited. This excitement manifests itself only in a solemn, wide-eyed silence for the duration of the tour, which turns out to be a mixture of the thrilling (the walk up the tunnel, a bath that takes three hours to fill), the peculiar (we get to see the actual crossbar that Geoff Hurst may or may not have scored off in the 1966 World Cup final, although there is, we find, a limit to the amount of fascination one can lavish on a 30-year-old piece of wood), and the tacky: the tour guide spends a lot of time boasting about how expensive it is to watch events from certain positions in the stadium, as if Wembley ticket prices were a natural, rather than a very recently manufactured, wonder of the world. Nicky drinks it all in, and when we get to the Royal Box, where we must all lift a dummy cup towards the imaginary fans behind the goal, he does so with a reverence that the rest of us cannot manage.

What's it like being a 10-year-old boy in 1995? Not so different from how it was 30 years ago, I reckon. Nicky doesn't talk about drugs or sex – even his future honeymoon he regards simply as a chance to go somewhere exotic; he doesn't surf the Net, he does not seem to have a taste for outrageous, life-threatening acts of vandalism, he doesn't use a mobile phone in or out of the classroom. No parts of his body are pierced, as far as I can tell. He doesn't even come from a one-parent family. He has models of Thunderbirds 2 and 3. He warmly recommends the new film version of *Black Beauty* because – giggles from everyone – 'Black Beauty blows off in it.' I haven't heard that particular phrasal verb since 1972.

He watches more TV than my generation ever did, simply because there is more TV to watch; there is no doubt that he has less autonomy than I was granted, although it is unclear whether this is due to the climate of the times. I wasn't brought up in the inner city, and have no idea what the boundaries for a 10-year-old were back then. He is probably more aware of gender issues than I was. When I ask him if he knows the name of the previous prime minister (he remembered, after some prompting), he said that she was 'the only woman prime minister he'd ever heard of', and wondered whether that was fair.

'They should do it 50–50. Take turns.' I reckon he's an all-woman shortlist kind of guy. If you're looking for a moral panic, look elsewhere.

On the way home, we stop at a chip shop for a late take-away lunch. Nicky has a sausage and chips, but he doesn't eat the sausage. Back at the flat there is a game of marbles ('Mark down he's a cheat,' Sarah instructs me after she has been beaten by her brother); then it's Connect 4, then water pistols, which degenerates into water without the pistol, and tears from Sarah after an unfortunate hair-wetting incident; and then – I'm sure there's a technical term for this, but it escapes me – there is some painting with pieces of potato. As the afternoon wears on, activities have lost their ability to stick – each is exhausted in seconds. I had forgotten just how long childhood lasts, and how little there is to fill it up with. Nicky has another 1,200-odd days to dispose of before he gets to the magic age of 14, and even then, if memory serves me, he might find himself wishing some of his life away. •

. . . .

6 January 1996
Linda Grant
Children of the eighties

The selected 10 come into the classroom and ask urgently, 'Miss, miss, is it all right to sit on the desks?' From time immemorial this has been the true cool way for a schoolchild to demonstrate her or his sophistication, by breaking ranks from the orderly rows of daily school life. I say yes, it's OK, and they sit on the desks, dead grown up. Feet dangling, nine pairs of trainers and one set of Doc Martens wave about before my eyes. The girl in the clodhoppers is not a lone individualist; her parents have never allowed her to wear trainers and, as a result, she moves in her own, externally enforced world of old-for-her-age hipness. On their chests are 10 'tops' (that's the right word), each bearing a logo: Blue Jeans, Giorgio, Levi, Timberland, Aramis, Official Bison. What would happen if you didn't have a logo on your clothes? Don't ask. And if it was the wrong logo? Well, there are worse things that could happen to you. Like what? You could have Fred and Rosemary West for your mum and dad.

Here are 10 12- and 13-year-olds at Highgate Wood Comprehensive in north London. They come from Finsbury Park and Hornsey and Crouch End and Wood Green. The word Highgate may be in the school's name but Highgate residents don't, on the whole, send their children to the local state comprehensives. I ask them what they wanted for Christmas. These are their lists: 1. Leather jacket, Sony Playstation, money. 2. Bike, Sony Playstation. 3. Money, clothes. 4. 'Just money because then you can get what you want.' 5. Jewellery, money, clothes. 6. Money, camera with a zoom lens. 7. Clothes. 8. Jewellery, clothes. 9. Money, a computer. 10. Music, tapes, CDs.

They like: swing, jungle, hip-hop, soul, indie, garage, house, socca and Brit pop. Someone tentatively suggests that he likes Oasis but is barracked. You aren't allowed to like Oasis. This, I am later told, is because the majority of kids in the class are Rudes. You can be a Rude or a Grunge or an Independent in-betweeny. Their pocket money runs at between £2.50 and £5 a week. They read the *Sun*, the *Express*, the *Mirror* and *Melody Maker*. They watch on TV: *The X Files*, *Fresh Prince of Bel Air*, *Heartbreak High*, *Beverly Hills 90210* and *East-Enders*. The average age at which they first knew about sex was six; about Aids, a couple of years later. Tactfully, I don't ask them if they have taken drugs, just if they would know where to get hold of them. 'Ye-es,' they cry in derision.

We move on down through my list of questions. What foreign holidays have you had? 1. France, Belgium, USA. 2. South Africa. 3. Cyprus and Spain. 4. Trinidad. 5. Canada, Canaries, USA, Lanzarote, Majorca, Turkey. 6. USA, Spain, France, Italy, Greece, Ireland. 7. Greece, Cyprus, USA, France. 8. Trinidad and Canada. 9. Cyprus, France, Germany, Italy. (Their teacher, Karen Field, will later listen in awe as I read this list. 'When I was a child,' she says, 'holidays were a caravan in Devon.') Five have their own PCs, four have divorced or separated parents. All of them have seen some kind of pornography.

When I was their age, back during the Palaeo-lithic era, a group of us gathered at a bus stop and a girl said: 'Only six months ago I still thought that a girl just had to sleep in the same bed as a boy and she'd get pregnant.' So we all laughed. Nervously. And went home and went to bed and stared out into the darkness, never connecting those dutifully copied anatomical diagrams of the reproductive cycles of fruit flies with our own flushed faces as we watched the Rolling Stones on *Top of the Pops*. I had been abroad once, to Ostend, had never heard of drugs or pornography or the word fuck, and I did not know anyone whose parents were divorced. I wanted a framed ballet picture for Christmas to hang on my bedroom wall.

We have never seen anything like them before, the teens and pre-teens of today, if that's what they still are. If the fifties created the teenager, the nineties seems to have destroyed that infant phenomenon. A spokesman at Sony confirms that, apart from computer games, it does not create and market electronic products specifically for teenagers. Teenagers want what their parents have, at prices that have nothing to do with what their pocket money can buy – or even within the long-term range of pocket money to save for – and they make their choices with advanced adult consumer skills. You can barely distinguish their Christmas lists from those of their 20-something older brothers and sisters. Every year the ad agency J Walter Thompson interviews a panel of children aged between four and 13. For the first time this year clothes topped the Christmas present list for all ages and both sexes.

Whatever happened to Just William, school tie askew, lover of dirt, free roamer on the dusty highways of middle-class England, in flight from Violet Elizabeth Bott? 'Boys of around 10 to 13 are increasingly interested in fashion,' the agency's report concludes, 'and are perhaps more pressured to have the right labels and the specific design than their female counterparts.' The girls at

Highgate Wood explain that with the boys, if two pairs of trainers are more or less identical, they will want the more expensive ones. Label, price, those are the main things when it comes to boys and trainers. The pair with the biggest price tag worn in the group were on the feet of a boy and they cost £100. 'From a catalogue,' he says.

What did William worry about? Being forced to bathe and dress up for company. It is the absence of anxiety and the freedom to grow up largely without interference from adults or their peculiar concerns which demarcate previous generations from this one.

At Highgate Wood a huge sign announces the activities for World Aids Day. The children bear an adult burden of worry and gloom – about drugs, unsafe sex, playground violence and the future of the planet. A study carried out at Exeter University showed that teenagers believe that Aids is the most common sexually transmitted disease.

In one week last spring, elsewhere in the country, a 13-year-old girl killed herself with her mother's antidepressants and a 13-year-old boy shot a pensioner with an air pistol after she told him off for swearing.

Thirty-two per cent of 14-year-olds have tried cannabis and nearly 60 per cent have been offered drugs, according to a report by the Institute for the Study of Drug Dependency. The youngest teenager to have died as a consequence of using Ecstasy was 14. Two years ago a pair of 10-year-olds were convicted of the murder of the toddler James Bulger.

And, as we know, last month a head teacher in London, Philip Lawrence, was murdered by a teenage gang as he tried to prevent them from attacking a 13-year-old.

A recent survey carried out by the National Association of Schoolmasters and Union of Women Teachers shows that serious assaults on teachers by children are up by 37 per cent on the previous year. For some months early last year, many children at Highgate Wood were not allowed to play in Priory Park in nearby Hornsey because a gang from a neighbouring school had stabbed a boy there in what was said to be a racial attack by Afro-Caribbeans on Asians. For the whole of the autumn term of last year Warwick Park School in Peckham offered children between the ages of 11 and 16 on-site counselling, in a project sponsored by the Children's Society. During that period a 14-year-old attending the school was stabbed (outside school time) and 14 pupils sought bereavement counselling. Ominously, another 26 looked for help with bullying.

Does that mean then, that the age of the onset of adolescence is dropping and dropping with each year? Does childhood unofficially end at 10 now? So it would seem, except that many of today's 10- to 14-year-olds have less personal freedom than a five-year-old in 1936.

'My mum could do anything she wanted when she was my age,' one Highgate Wood girl says. 'But I can hardly walk out the door. My dad still thinks I'm a little girl.'

Each generation is supposed to deride the one that went before, but here is a 13-year-old dreaming of a golden age of youth: 'I wish I was around in the sixties. It seemed so free, you could do what you wanted, everyone was protesting and they weren't scared of saying what they thought and making sure you got your rights. You could smoke and no one knew it was bad for you.'

Sixty years ago, the oldest of this group would be leaving school at the end of the summer, getting jobs and drawing a pay packet. At 14 in 1996 you have another two years before further education or a YTS placement. If you don't get a job as a school-leaver (and only 9 per cent do) you have no chance of leaving home until you are eligible for housing benefit at 18, unless you move on to the streets and grow up very fast indeed.

After Christmas the *Guardian*'s Mark Lawson wrote of the urgency in learning to drive now he had become a parent, and Suzanne Moore noted people's disbelief that she was a mother and a non-driver. Among the myriad ways in which the middle classes believe the working class is unsuited for parenthood, one of them is not owning a car and subjecting the kids to the dangers of public transport, or, worse, the streets. So how do today's children become adults when all their lives they have been ferried back and forth in cars by parents; when they only learn how to use a bus when they go to secondary school; when their waking lives are supervised at every moment by adults taking them to after-school ballet classes and playgroups and go-kart racing?

They may be independent of their parents in thought, but they are entering their teens and hence early adulthood with only the most rudimentary skills in how to negotiate independent action.

When I was about six or seven in suburban Liverpool, a friend and I used to dress up in our mothers' clothes and board a bus three or four stops to the local shops to buy sweets and comics with our pocket money. Our parents did not know where we were, except with each other.

Last summer, a little girl sleeping in a tent in her back garden in Wales was abducted and murdered. The same weekend, two boys fishing near their home in Cheshire were also killed. And every child in Britain lost a bit more freedom.

The known world, according to anxious parents, is full of paedophiles and child-murderers. It isn't, of course, but it seems that way. Between 1983 and 1993 on average 86 children under the age of 16 were murdered every year in England and Wales, but the vast majority were killed by their parents or people acting in *loco parentis*. In those same 10 years only 27 children between the ages of 10 and 14 were murdered by strangers.

But as all parents know, the facts don't matter. If only a handful of children are out playing without supervision, these will be the ones targeted for abduction, not the ones safely at home in front of the TV or the computer games console. So how can any parent stick their neck out and say, my child will be as free as I was? There are no more places left for children to play safely alone or with each other.

A Barnados survey last year showed that out of a sample of 94 parents only two rated their neighbourhoods as 'very safe' for their children to play in. Only 14 parents thought it would be safe for a child under the age of 10 to walk to school unaccompanied, though 65 had done so when they were children.

Violent crime creates its own climate of fear and its culture becomes our own. Since the mid-sixties there have been three criminal cases which have served to tell parents that their children are not safe out alone: the first was, of course, the Moors murders, which fixed child abduction and murder into the collective conscious mind of Britain. When Myra Hindley considers the effect of her crimes on her victims' families, she might also take into account the millions of children who lost some of their freedom after 1966. Parents used to say, if you're lost, find a nice lady to take care of you. Hindley put an end to that.

Throughout the eighties a series of paedophile murders were committed for which Leslie 'Catweazle' Bailey was convicted, though he was only one member of an east London paedophile ring. The three victims were boys aged six, seven and 14, two of whom were abducted. In his cell, before he was murdered by a fellow inmate in 1993, Bailey 'confessed' to 20 other killings.

In 1994, after little coverage of the trial itself, Robert Black was convicted of the abduction, rape and murder of several little girls. When asked what parents could do to protect children from killers like himself, Black replied: 'Never take their eyes off them.'

We also became aware in the eighties of the enormous submerged mass of child abuse; that it happened so frequently in families made parents even more cautious of Uncle Bob and Grandpa, and the nuclear family tightened around children even further.

We have indicated to them that the world is full of monsters we are not prepared to name: the 'bad men' (and women, too) who do things we're not prepared to talk about. My nephew, aged around eight at the time, was caught short in Piccadilly Circus tube station and insisted that he was old enough to go into the gents on his own and not be escorted by his aunt into the sissy ladies. So how do you tell an eight-year-old that the gents at Piccadilly Circus is a focus for the burgeoning trade in under-age male flesh known as the meat rack? More importantly, how, a year or so later, did one explain exactly what it was his idol Michael Jackson was accused of?

The ironic effect of our fear for our children's safety is to make the world more dangerous in a different way. The streets are dangerous because they are far fuller with traffic as a result of all those parents ferrying their children around.

Last year, the Royal Society for the Prevention of Accidents noted that traffic accidents account for a quarter of all child deaths in the UK. Five child pedestrians die every week, and one child in 15 can expect to be injured in a road accident before they leave school.

'We have infantilised children,' says Gerison Lansdowne, director of the Children's Rights Development Unit. 'I grew up in the fifties and a lot of my play was with other children with no adult supervision for hours on end. The loss of freedom and autonomy has been substituted by higher levels of out-of-school, adult-focused activities and by consumer goods. So there's a division between an apparent street-wise ability, together with far less access to the world. There's a huge amount of access via the media but little direct access. From a very early age they are exposed to the complexity and horrendous nature of so much experience that there's no protective barrier and, consequently, there's anxiety and stress but no capacity to influence or inform.

'At the same time, they can't develop their capacity for negotiating peer relationships, building up the confidence to negotiate the external world, and that has profound implications for this generation. I would like to see children as actors in their own lives rather than recipients of what others do to or give them. If they can't develop their lives as actors we may lose out on them as potential contributors to the democratic process.'

So children grow up dragging the load of their parents' fears for them and not only for their safety. 'We worry because our parents want us to do well,' one Highgate Wood girl said.

Mothers used to fret that their daughters would get pregnant before they were married, and that their sons would be doing the getting pregnant and having to do the marrying. Beyond brooding about whether their children would pass the 11-plus and worrying about whether they would get a good job, that was more or less it.

The worries that emerged during the Second World War were of a different order. You worried about your evacuated children, you worried about the ones with you, whether the air-raid shelter would stand the bombing. You worried that they would get called up and be killed. Yet you believed that if the war was won, the world would be a better place, that there would be bluebirds over the white cliffs of Dover and Johnny would go to sleep in his own little room again. That is, the world would be like it was before, but better. And, as it turned out, it was.

Today's parents should be so lucky. Almost two out of three adults believe that today's children have a worse deal than when they were children, according to a Mori poll commissioned by Barnardos last summer. Seven out of 10 grown-ups believe children are more aware of issues such as poverty and homelessness and nine out of 10 believe they will witness more crime and violence than a generation ago. It is not only the middle classes who worry about their children's future, but the more widely you read, the more you know to be worried about.

'I have a hunch that the national curriculum and SATS have created a pressure we never had,' one parent of an 11-year-old told me. 'If you're a child of middle-class parents constantly poring over the school league tables, some of that must rub off. My son is part of the first group to be tested at seven and again at 11. Children today have been under the educational microscope more than ever before.

'I'm slightly frightened about Aids on his behalf because it's not that difficult to forget to use a condom when you're drunk at a party, but mostly I'm afraid of him being on the streets. I know that the next stage is him going places by himself on buses, but to me he looks vulnerable and I'm not that convinced he's good at crossing roads. Then, because technology is speeding up so quickly, I have this fear that Tony Blair's super-information highway will get installed in the schools and that he will be one of the generation that was all huddled over one computer and he didn't get educated in the right way for the future.' One could go on finding things to worry about indefinitely.

What children themselves worry about is the one issue that parents have been trained not to worry about at all, on their behalf. Repeat after me: 'It is better for parents to part than for children to live with a mum and dad who are arguing all the time.'

We have wallowed in this for a quarter of a century; almost everyone agrees, except the Catholic Church, *Observer* columnist Melanie Phillips and children themselves. I asked the kids of Highgate Wood School what was the thing that scared them most and they said, something happening to my mum and dad. My parents splitting up. What was the most important thing in their lives? 'My parents. Family. Being wanted. Family.'

One of the most extraordinary aspects of the West trial was the mapping of a legacy of abuse down the generations that could not eradicate the bonds of love: 'Part of me still loves my father despite what happened to me and what I know now,' Anne Marie West has written in her ghosted autobiography, *Out of the Shadows.* 'I can't help it — he was my dad and that's that. It doesn't mean I approved of or condoned anything he did, just that I can't separate myself from him entirely.'

They understood that at Highgate Wood: 'If they were my parents I wouldn't forgive them, but I'd still love them,' a girl remarked.

We are, apparently, not very good at listening to what children feel and think and it seems we are unaware of a radical shift that is taking place among them in which issues of independence and dependency, maturity and immaturity, are much more complicated than they look.

Another message is slowly creeping into the debate about divorce, away from the capacity of single mothers to cope and the need for boys to have role models towards a more informed, less theoretical understanding of what the effects are on the children.

One of the most disturbing chronicles of how we treat children is Lloyd de Mause's *A History of Childhood: The Untold Story of Child Abuse.* De Mause's argument is that adults believe that children cannot feel pain, either physiological or emotional, and that any disagreeable experiences they encounter are quickly forgotten, which was indeed one of the contentions of Fred West, according to his daughter Anne Marie.

A century ago, according to Martin Richards of Cambridge University's Centre for Family Studies, the chance of a child aged 16 living with both parents was about the same as it is today, but the absent parent would have been taken by death rather than divorce. Paradoxically, though the trauma of the death of a parent is assumed to be greater, this does not seem to be the case.

'On the whole, children cope better with death than divorce because it's far better socially supported,' Richards argues. 'There's the ritual of the funeral and grandparents gather round.

'Most children don't want their parents to split up. They like to think that their parents would have their greatest interests at heart and then they do something very damaging to you. The sense of betrayal is very hard to cope with. So the child is very angry but anger is hard to express because they are afraid that anger will drive the parent away.'

We are, then, requiring quite young children with little emotional maturity to cope with extremely complex adult emotions. An apparently high level of emotional literacy, of being able to talk about their feelings, often seems to be borrowed from *Neighbours*' daily television diet of ready solutions to the problems of relationships. A child said to his mother when she told him his parents were splitting up: 'The important thing is that you're happy.' But a child couldn't care less about his parents' happiness. He wants to be happy.

'He was saying what he thought the adults wanted to hear,' argues Vivien Gross, clinical director of the Institute of Family Therapy. Martin Richards sees in his Cambridge students a theoretical knowledge about life coupled with naivety: 'The soaps have an extraordinary importance for young people,' he says. 'They provide a model of doing divorce which is helpful but also unreal. You have to experience those emotions yourself sooner or later.'

When every human dilemma, from divorce to abortion, from death to teen pregnancy is already processed for you by television, with the approved message of dealing with it attached, children are growing up like so many junior psycho-therapists. When a real-life trauma hits, they are terrified of responding with what *Neighbours* has told them is the wrong line in the big script.

To be against the effects of divorce on children is to feel that one is automatic-ally complicit in the generalised assault on single parents. But we may be deluding ourselves if we continue to believe what makes adults happy also makes children happy.

Last year the Exeter Family Study on children in 're-ordered families' – those with step-parents and possible step-siblings – concluded that a raft of difficulties were opened up by divorce and remarriage. Monica Cockett, of Exeter Univer-sity's Department of Child Health, one of the report's authors, thinks that children are the ones who get left out when a decision is made to separate.

'We've tended to view divorce as an adult process. The message has been that divorce removes children from conflict, but it plunges them into a different set of conflicts, such as access. Divorce is a choice that is made by the parents, but not by the child. We have an end-of-the-20th-century dilemma about personal happiness and commitment, but if you have children, can you be as free as you want? Adult freedoms don't always make the world better for children.

'Why our study was an uncomfortable message was that we don't listen to what children say they want. To a child, the family is still total security. To a child, the natural parents are still the real and closest members of the family, and that's why we don't have closed adoption any longer. Biological ties are so strong that it's hard for the children of Fred and Rosemary West to accept the full evil of someone who is supposed to care for you, and it's very hard for a child who has had a wonderful father who has walked away to reconcile those two things. It's an awful lot to take on board and we're asking children to function like adults without the adult sense of internal security. They grow up with their emotional world unattended to and hollow.'

So we have these apparently grown-up children, struggling with adult emotions when their own emotional development is only partially complete. The real meaning of their consumerism may be a striving for choice and freedom in lives which have increasingly little.

Today, an 11-year-old boy can choose with fine distinction between 40 different kinds of trainers, but, though he may be consulted over whether Mum's new boyfriend should move in with them, he was given no choice at all about whether his father would leave in the first place. He has no power to prevent his world being detonated by an adult sex drive.

And this is why the trainers are so important. Where do you find an apparent stability and an apparent freedom? From your peer group, Vivien Gross argues: 'That sort of social pressure and worry about not being in the right group is part of the move they are making away from family towards independence. Being a real individual is scary, so your peers become an alternative family, a middle space where you have a bedrock, the new source of approval.'

Caught up in their own small world of this right label and that wrong group, children seem far, far away from us.

'Parents often feel they have nothing to offer their kids, that their message will go unheard,' Gross suggests. 'They need to be reminded that they have a contribution.'

Whenever one generation writes about another, the older ones are in danger of lapsing into laughable fallacies. The literature of the youth of the sixties written by the men and women of the thirties and forties, especially when larded earnestly with the 'with-it' expressions of the era, in almost all cases missed its mark.

The best we can say is that, along with most parents, we don't understand what's going on, and, to some extent, that is right and proper as a new generation struggles to define itself in opposition to the nearest models it can find of what went before. Next month's British Social Attitudes Survey will include, for the first time, a parallel survey of the opinions of young people, commissioned by Barnardos. For the first time we may be in a position to view the world through our children's eyes.

When I went into Highgate Wood School, as one bell rang for the end of class and hundreds of children hit the halls, I felt that I had walked into a wall of sound. As Dickens described schoolchildren more than 100 years ago, 'Instead of 40 children behaving as one, one child behaved as 40.'

En masse, they were scary. Individually, with their endless wants, they're scary.

But inside, one suspects, they're just scared: frightened of the disapproval of their friends, frightened that they might join the ranks of those with divorced parents, frightened of the bullies, frightened of exams and frightened of the demands their frightened parents place on them. Dreaming of more freedom than they are allowed, they know deep down that no one can ever be free.

'Everyone in this school's got such an attitude problem,' a girl says, belligerently. I don't honestly know what she's talking about. When I was 12, what everyone in the school had was spots. •

. . . .

1 May 1996

Francis Wheen
Family men on their high horses

Those jaded citizens who complain that Parliament is incapable of sustaining intelligent life are often advised to come along and watch a debate on an issue of 'conscience', where no three-line whips apply and MPs are able to discuss an issue purely on its merits. Then, we are told, you will see the House of Commons at its best.

There was just such an occasion last week, on back-bench amendments to Lord Mackay's Family Law Bill. Having studied a Hansard transcript of the entire six-hour debate, I have only one conclusion: if this is really the best the House can offer, God preserve us from its worst. Swarms of *non sequiturs* flapped and buzzed through the chamber as self-righteous politicians boasted of their unswerving commitment to the sanctity of marriage. At the end of the evening, they voted to extend the 'cooling-off period' for parting couples from 12 months to 18 months, and more than 100 of them supported an unsuccessful amendment challenging the main point of the bill – the 'no-fault' divorce.

The *Daily Mail*, which has run a ceaseless and increasingly deranged campaign on this subject in recent months, was delighted. 'The very concept of "no-fault" divorce devalues marriage,' it thundered, 'reducing it to the status of a temporary arrangement, breakable on a whim. The pity is that the Lord Chancellor seems uncritically to have swallowed the liberal arguments peddled by that unelected and unrepresentative quango, the Law Commission.' Unlike the heroic Tory dissidents, of course, who swallowed the arguments of the unelected and unrepresentative *Daily Mail*.

The ghastliness of last week's debate was, however, relieved by occasional flashes of sanity and common sense. Interestingly enough, almost all of them came from MPs who have worked as divorce lawyers and have seen for themselves how much misery is caused by the quest for 'blame' in broken marriages. 'My experience is that in very few marriages is the fault wholly on one side,' the Labour MP Donald Anderson observed. 'In connection with one or two well-publicised difficulties of some of the senior members of the royal family, it is certain that both the parties could, if they were so minded, rely on various faults in a divorce petition.' Even the *Mail* seems to admit as much: one day it denounces Prince Charles for his adultery; the next it damns Princess Diana for the same offence. No human being is faultless – not even, dare I say, the editor of the *Mail* – yet we are asked to believe that either a husband or a wife must always be the sole culprit.

The Tory MP Patrick Nicholls was magnificently incredulous at the idea that 'by encouraging bitterness and mud-throwing we shall protect the institution of marriage'. Having dealt with countless divorce cases during his career as a solicitor, Nicholls demolished the *Mail*'s moralistic blatherings with one well-chosen example: 'What about the situation in which a wife deserts her husband and commits an act of adultery? That is a bad enough fault, but wait a moment. She may claim that she was driven out by a hard and domineering husband, so perhaps the fault was his. But hold on another moment – the husband may claim that he had to control and direct his wife because she was a rotten housekeeper, was getting the finances wrong and the children were suffering. Then the wife might say: "Come off it, I married at 18. I didn't know enough, so obviously I was going to get it wrong." What is the answer?' Answer came there none.

The sabotaging of the bill was greeted in the *Mail* as a victory for the moral majority. 'A study of the 171 Tory rebels reveals it was the night when the family men from "Middle England" came out in force,' it reported. 'The rebels represent a class who believe that marriage is for life.'

Oh, really? Here are a few of them: Vivian Bendall, Stephen Day, David Faber, Sir Peter Fry, Roger Gale, Sir George Gardiner, John Horam, Toby Jessel, Michael Mates, Sir Nicholas Scott, Richard Spring, Sir Malcolm Thornton, Nigel Waterson, John Wilkinson. What do these men have in common, apart from finding themselves in the same division lobby last week? They have all been divorced at least once, and in some cases more than once: Roger Galt is currently on wife number three.

True, some of the rebels have stayed clear of the divorce courts. Tim Yeo is still married to his first wife in spite of having fathered a child by a different woman. Tony Marlow was so keen on the family that he maintained two of them: a wife and five children in his constituency; a lover and four children in London. Another uxorious Tory, Hartley Booth, sent drippy love letters and poems to a female student. Yet another, Robert Hughes, resigned as a minister when his jilted 'mistress', Janet Oates, revealed all to the *News of the World* ('My Great Sex with Tory Who Wanted All-night Sessions').

It is unpleasant to exhume all these foibles and infidelities – but not half as unpleasant as the sight of a posse of maritally challenged Conservative MPs leading a crusade against divorce. How do they explain the contradiction? Most were unwilling to try. 'I don't have anything to do with the *Guardian*,' Roger Gale informed me. 'When you've settled your case against my colleague Jonathan Aitken I might consider talking to the *Guardian* again. Until then, forget it.' (Actually, the *Guardian* has no lawsuits outstanding against Jonathan Aitken; quite the reverse. But Roger Gale is a former producer of *Blue Peter* rather than a lawyer, so I suppose he can be forgiven his ignorance.)

One Tory rebel, who was quite chatty at first, became distinctly frosty when I asked if either he or his wife had been 'at fault' in their divorce. 'As a matter of fact she was; she went off with a colleague. But you can't print that.'

Toby Jessel was slightly more cooperative. 'I believe in the ideal of happy marriage,' he cooed. 'I've been very happily married since October 1980. I had an early unhappy marriage which took place in 1967.' Was he humbled by the experience? Apparently not. 'However much the experts may say there is often if not always fault on both sides, people at large do believe "it was his fault" or "it was her fault".' Maybe so; but how can 'people at large' ever comprehend what goes on inside other people's marriages?

John Wilkinson, the twice-wed MP for Ruislip, supported the extension of the cooling-off period but missed the previous vote because he had to attend a constituency surgery. 'Abstention was probably the best thing for me,' he admitted, 'as I should be reluctant to cast the first stone.' Nevertheless, he would have voted against the principle of 'no-fault' divorce. 'Fault does lie at the heart of divorce,' he told me, without revealing who had been the transgressor in his case. 'Having gone through this traumatic experience, one may be better qualified to deliberate on these matters. But that is not in any sense to adopt a high moral posture – that's the last thing one wants to do.'

Well, you could have fooled me. Perhaps Wilkinson should have a word with his preening, sanctimonious colleagues on the Tory benches, and with the nanny-state enthusiasts at the *Mail* – a paper whose proprietor, Lord Rothermere, is such a devoted 'family man' that for many years he commuted between a wife in London and a mistress in Paris. With such an exhausting domestic routine, I'm surprised he never felt the need for a 'cooling-off' period himself. •

Smithfield

Tom Jenkins

Mad cows and Englishmen

....

23 *May 1996*

Martin Kettle

Frogs and Krauts fill heads with hate

I t comes as a shock to be reminded just how easily the British can don the mantle of a nation at war. You spoke for Britain, Nicholas Winterton told John Major in the Commons on Tuesday, consciously repeating the resonant words which Leo Amery uttered during the real crisis of 1940. Many who listened to Major's statement also caught echoes of Neville Chamberlain's broadcast of September 1939. 'Major Goes to War at Last' said the front-page headline in the *Daily Mail*. The *Sun* adorned its beef coverage with a picture of Churchill. And yesterday morning the Press Association was even reporting the formation of a War Cabinet.

Of course it is not war *really*. No one is actually going to get killed in this battle with our foes across the main – unless you count several thousand dumb and perhaps infected cattle who will be clubbed senseless and incinerated in the cause over the coming weeks. But the spirit of something very similar to war is on the march and we must all decide whether we will join its ranks or not.

Among the European nations this could probably only happen in Britain and Greece, though conceivably also in Russia. For among the EU nations it is only in Britain that there is this genuine and deep cultural yearning to relive the last war, and for the nation to stand historically apart from its neighbours. Anyone who thought that this instinct was dead, laid gently to rest in the long prosperous European reconciliations of the second half of the 20th century, must think again.

The pent-up resentments of British nationalism have found another cause to rally for. By threatening non-cooperation with Europe, John Major has not just made the latest tactical manoeuvre in the long struggle to control the Conservative Party. He has let a nationalist genie out of the bottle which he will find it hard to put back. Note the *Mail*'s 'war *at last*'. These are happy, fulfilled people. This is finally a part of the nation at ease with itself. A nation at war. Or playing at being at war.

If nothing else, the last 48 hours offer a very salutary reminder of the grip in which the Second World War still holds large and influential sections of the British nation. To those who grew up in the 1950s and 1960s, the war seemed to be parental business, not ours. Yet we have turned out to be carriers too. Fourteen years ago, many were surprised by the capacity of the Falklands crisis to reawaken a bastard version of the wartime spirit. Now, fully 51 years after the end of the last European war, an even more bizarre mutation of the bulldog spirit is on view in the battle for British beef.

In some ways the true emotional parallel this week is not the grim determination of September 1939, when there was an overwhelming sense that the nation was embarking on a hazardous and perhaps terminal war against a ruthless, evil and powerful enemy. Nor is it the summer of 1940, when Britain genuinely stood alone in the cause of the peoples of Europe. A much more real parallel is surely with the glad confident morning of August 1914. The truly striking characteristic of the Conservative Party this week has been its cathartic *delight*. One recognises in the Tories a version, albeit a degenerate one, of 'Now God be thanked Who has matched us with His hour/And caught our youth, and wakened us from sleeping.' We are heading back into the world of *Oh! What a Lovely War*.

This is not an entirely fanciful parallel, though it actually leads towards a conclusion which the Europhobes will not like. In earlier times, the struggle for international markets was a cause of real wars. If this was 1896 not 1996, the fleet would almost certainly be steaming for Wilhelmshaven and we would be flooding the Channel Tunnel. The fact that no British lives are likely to be lost in this latest conflict is due to the success, not the failure, of the European Union.

The Europhobes cannot see this. For the more cerebral among them, the argument about beef is simply a surrogate for an almost sacred and mystical cause, the reawakening of British nationhood. For those with the light of martyrdom in their eyes this promises to be a truly purgative moment, just as 1914 was for Rupert Brooke, in which the folly and the humiliations of the European ensnarement can be expunged in a moment of national purification.

Not everyone who rallies to the sound of the drum thinks this way, of course. There is none of the high-minded classical Powellism of the Europhobe commentators in the instinctual xenophobia which sustains the foot-soldiers of this army. When John Townend says that Germans only understand the language of force, when Teresa Gorman says she wants to stuff British beef into German sausages, or when the *Sun* offers you 20 ways to be rude to the Germans, then we are witnessing something far nastier, far cruder and far more dangerous in our politics than anything we have witnessed in our public life for decades.

The surreal qualities of the beef crisis ought not to blind us to its deeply serious consequences. Since we cannot go to real war, we can only go to pretend war. And since we will never win – and indeed have never fought – a real war against the combined forces of Germany and France, there can be no real victory or real defeat.

This presents us, nevertheless, with a very real choice. Do we continue to live in the fantasy world of Hun-bashing or do we try, at last, to set ourselves free from these harmful and dead-end delusions? Do we, in other words, work with the other European nations in the only kind of international alliance which makes sense for a nation in this part of the globe at this time, or do we set ourselves against it?

The entire logic – if that word can be used in this context – of the Conservative Party's position is that we can never make the European choice. The Conservative Party can go to Europe, but it cannot be European. Instead, as this week's events have proved and others may shortly emphasise, it is rapidly becoming the British, or even the English, nationalist party.

The choice for the opposition parties is whether to be dragged along or to stand up. Me Too or Not Us. Whatever the reservations about particular aspects of the European project, such as the single currency, there is now something much more fundamental at stake. A phoney war is almost as destructive of Britain's long-term interests as a real war. If the Conservative Party insists that all must choose over Europe, then there is only one serious answer. •

• •

26 March 1996
Simon Hoggart
Tory petulance leaves bad taste

The Government yesterday produced tough new measures to fight the panic over mad cow disease. Ministers decided to go back to bed and pull up the covers.

It was weirdly reminiscent of that moment which helped destroy the last Labour government, when Jim Callaghan returned home amid corpses and garbage in the streets, and declared: 'I see no sign of mounting crisis.'

As the world bans British beef, as ancient British firms such as Wimpy ban British beef, as the beef industry faces final collapse, the Government's rallying call to public confidence is: 'Trust us, we're politicians.'

It seems the folks who gave us Black Wednesday, the doubled crime rate and Yorkshire Water, have come up with their masterpiece: an incurable illness which turns your brain to sponge.

Yet the only glimmer of emotion any of them showed yesterday was when they furiously accused Labour of making party political capital from the crisis.

The Health Secretary, Stephen Dorrell, in a statement both peevish and complacent, denounced Labour MPs for 'the worst kind of scaremongering – ferreting around in the sewer of party political advantage'.

You'd think that BSE was some terrible act of God which had nothing to do with them, like the harsh winter, or the Duchess of York. But why should Labour not take advantage from their dithering, their cowardice, their arrogant dishonesty? What else is an Opposition for?

(The really odious thing about the former agriculture minister John Gummer feeding a hamburger to his daughter in 1990 was the way it reflected their Saatchi & Saatchi culture, the way they believe there is no problem so serious that it can't be solved by a PR man and a photo opportunity.)

Peter Mandelson made a rare on-the-record intervention, and he must have startled some of his multitudinous enemies with a question of real anger and passion. (He blamed the crisis on obsessional deregulation. The term 'real anger' may be an exaggeration, but it was certainly a good vegetable oil version of real anger.)

Michael Heseltine replied that the question was 'contemptible, even by his standards' – proof once again that ministers just don't understand what is happening to them or to us.

Mr Dorrell's oddest contribution was a petulant remark that 'it is no good saying that it is unnatural for one species to eat the remains of another; that is what the meat industry is all about'.

No, minister: the objection is that cattle are vegetarian by nature. You might as well use the same argument to feed your children hay.

Bizarrely, he and his colleagues persistently repeated that all human activities include a measure of risk, as if eating beef were on a par with bungee jumping.

Angela Eagle (Labour, Wallasey) was told scornfully that Mr Dorrell would rather take advice from Sir Richard Southwood, who wrote the first BSE report, than from her. Could this be the same Sir Richard Southwood who has accused the Government of allowing, through its complacency, the 'nightmare scenario' to occur?

Tory MPs lined up like diseased sheep behind their masters. One accused Labour of 'hypochondriacal hysteria'; let's hope he never gets into the food chain. Another said McDonald's was endangering the public by importing dangerous Continental beef. Harriet Harman was called a 'stupid cow' by Tony 'Von' Marlow – so performing the miracle of making some Labour MPs feel almost sympathetic to her.

Douglas Hogg, the Agriculture Minister, was little better. The thought of him elbow deep in a cow's backside is a pleasing one, though not at all convincing.

The real problem is that we just don't think that these people are on our side. ●

Pass Notes

3 April 1996 Douglas Hogg

Age: Over 30 months. But no swine fever jokes please.

Occupation: Still Minister of Agriculture at the time of writing.

Appearance: Frequently in Brussels, Luxemburg and any other forum where BSE-inflamed foreigners are demanding mass slaughter of our bovine friends.

That's hardly Douglas's fault, is it? BSE was around long before he was. Quite so, but he's unpopular enough with the colleagues to make a tempting scapegoat.

Can scapegoats transmit scrapie to humans? Ho, ho. It's no laughing matter, there are 650,000 jobs and £5 billion at stake here. Or is it *steak*?

Hold it a minute. Why is Hogg unpopular? He was the first minister to say we might have to engage in mass moo slaughter before squaring the colleagues and Europe. Big PR gaffe. Apart from that he's bombastic, juvenile and erratic. Wears that bloody silly fedora. And another thing, he's clever.

What sort of clever? Well, you wouldn't send him out to post a letter or persuade the EU not to ban British beef exports to Argentina. But he was a scholar at Eton, at Oxford and at Lincoln's Inn.

Wow, a really clever little Hogg. That's nothing. His father and grandfather were both regarded as seriously brilliant, both Lord Chancellors. Both called Quintin too. So is Hogg's son, heir to the Hailsham peerage.

So Douglas had it easy then? Not at all. Rejected for lots of seats before landing Grantham in 1979. As a liberal old school sort of Tory he crawled very slowly up the ministerial ladder under the Leaderene. Refused to be reshuffled while wearing silly hat in 1989. Caused a log jam.

Didn't he do better under Johnny Major? Er, um, tricky that one. He couldn't get an important job because his wife, Sarah, already had one. Wouldn't be fair if they Hogged all the acorns.

You mean that Sarah, thrusting daughter of ex-cabinet minister, thrusting journalist turned thrusting head of Downing Street policy unit (1990–95), now thrusting peeress and mother of two? The same. She's reckoned to be the seriously ambitious one.

Douglas must be so proud of her. Very probably. It's a close family. But her pro-ERM stance and other 'Bolshevist' views enraged the Tory right. He got blamed too. Should have kept the wife in order.

Least likely to say: 'Where's the beef?'

Most likely to say: 'Help.' ●

26 June 1996

Catherine Bennett

Continuing scandal of the food we eat

You cannot play games with people's health, Jacques Santer warned Britain last week. Most of Europe seems to agree with him. Half of Germany will not eat beef from anywhere; French farmers are still rampaging about, in protest at a drastic fall in domestic beef consumption.

And here? In Britain, we are meant to have stronger stomachs. Those of us who actually share the German fear of what we might have eaten and disgust for those who produced it; those who believe that French farmers are right to be outraged by the export of banned feed, are expected, instead, to side with the guilty farmers and exporters, and approve what appears to be the end of beef hostilities. From the Government, there is still neither shame nor apology.

It is almost as if the BSE announcement and ensuing scare in March had never been. It has been rewritten, rejected, dismissed as a moment of hysteria.

John Major has just described as 'nonsense' a convincing *Panorama* exposé of a decade of Maff's dilatoriness, guile and bombast. Maff refused to answer for its actions on that programme, yet no assault followed in the press, or from the Opposition. On the contrary, Tony Blair was reported at the weekend cracking 'woof woof' jokes about beef-eating. In Britain, it appears, Maff will happily play games with people's health, and – better still – neither the people nor their representatives will protest. Only the farmers are to be pitied. If Maff hoped that British apathy about food would finally triumph over fear, its plans have been well justified.

Overall, beef consumption is back at around 85 per cent of the level before the BSE announcement. Put calves in lorries, and angry calf-lovers will shriek at every port; put potentially infected meat in pies, and the public will shudder for a while, then start eating pies again. No incensed matrons will wave banners outside Maff's headquarters, or hurl themselves against the car bearing Stephen 'no conceivable risk' Dorrell to the Department of Health.

Perhaps the most remarkable aspect of the British beef scare, is how quickly it has become unscary. Although the Government regularly berated the media for spreading hysteria, it was a matter of weeks before fearful headlines gave way to pitiful announcements about the cattle cull, 'It's Mass Moo-der', and then, inexorably, to attacks on foreigners: 'Germans Sabotage our Hopes for Beef'.

This campaign could hardly have been conducted if the British public had cared deeply about the dangers, real or imagined, of BSE. But public confidence, at first said to be so comprehensively dashed, was rapidly restored. At Sainsbury's sales fell significantly. 'Then,' says a spokeswoman, 'we had a four-day, half-price sale, and most of our stores sold out. Since then, they've been generally creeping back up.' Surveys may suggest a widespread lack of confidence, but shopping habits reveal blank indifference.

'With some notable exceptions, British consumers are more concerned about price than quality,' says Francis Blake of the Soil Association. 'Whereas the French and Germans and other European countries are more concerned about quality.' But he still professes surprise that the public's appetite could be so quickly restored. 'After a scare lasting three months, it's still not having the dramatic impact that it has elsewhere.' This is possibly because British super-markets are stacked with soothing leaflets, reassuring buyers that they should have no fear – their packages of beef only originate from animals under 30 months old. But this is hardly a generous gesture, being enforced by law, and neither is it wholly reassuring. Scientists still do not know whether BSE could be passed on by maternal transmission, and a Government trial investigating this possibility will not be completed until November.

If, as everyone hopes, British beef is eventually confirmed to be safe, the way we have responded to the scare remains an alarming illustration of our debased eating habits. It shows that the oft-announced food revolution has yet to touch most of the population, who remain addicted to cheap food, at whatever cost to livestock, the environment and their own health. As Joanna Blythman says, in her splendid book *The Food We Eat*, 'The consequences of the UK's love affair with cheap food can be seen all around us, in items like spindly, tasteless chickens, bland Golden Delicious apples, watery tomatoes and breads of such staggering uniformity of character that they are hardly worth eating.' Not to mention crippled turkeys and battery eggs which now contain more salmonella than they did in the days of Edwina.

British indifference to food quality is usually attributed to rationing, then to a post-war food policy which put quantity and cheapness before all other considerations, but the decline in taste probably started far earlier.

'English domestic cooking has never stood in high repute,' wrote J C Drummond, in *The Englishman's Food*, a book which records centuries of food adultera-tion. 'Its reputation appears to have declined during the 19th century, probably because when we acquired from the Continent the knowledge to grow garden vegetables we did not trouble to learn how to cook them properly. It is one of the major tragedies of English domestic life.' Today, that domestic tragedy has its wider consequences, including hideous conditions for farm animals and poultry, and a generation of food retailers who compete on price before everything. 'Loyalty cards', rather than food quality, are now the favoured marketing tool of rival supermarkets; before long, it is predicted, they will be competing with banks, as they already compete with dry cleaners, chemists and newsagents.

In the absence of any powerful food consumers' body, we are left in the hands of Maff, which as everyone knows, exists to protect the food industry, not food consumers. As the BSE scare proved, and a recent Consumers' Association paper pointed out, Maff actually works to keep consumers in ignorance. Earlier this year it congratulated itself on removing 'unjustified food labelling rules', in particular on having 'done away with rules for fish cakes altogether'. But then the British don't want to know what they themselves are eating, do they? So who can expect them to care about what the cows have been given? •

23 March 1996

Matthew Fort

Household fetish turns into Trojan horse

Will we ever be able to look on its like again with an easy mind? The majestic hill of beef, a rib on the bone, like the rock of Gibraltar, with its crust of creamy, golden fat cascading down its flank?

Will we be bug-eyed in anticipation, watching the flaccid slice, scarlet as a guardsman's tunic, slide away from the edge of the carver's knife, salivate as it is laid gently, reverently, on the plate, keeping its place alongside the roast potatoes, the Yorkshire pudding, the searing mustard and creamy horseradish sauce?

When politicians cry 'where's the beef?', future generations will stare at them with blank incomprehension. There will be no jolly sing-alongs to the old music hall standard 'Boiled Beef and Carrots'.

Let us ignore for a moment the fact that most of us are more likely to die of heart disease, suicide, motor accident, motor neurone disease or multiple sclerosis than of Creutzfeldt-Jakob disease. The thought of being susceptible to an unspeakably unpleasant degenerative disease is disturbing enough, but beyond all this we mourn something deeper, more instinctive. Had BSE cropped up in pigs or chickens or tomatoes, would we have been so horrified? I think not. It is the fact that it is beef that shakes us so deeply. Beef has a symbolic importance that far outweighs its dietary importance. Beef is one of the great unifying symbols of our culture.

The Roast Beef of Old England is a fetish, a household god, which has been suddenly revealed as being a Trojan horse for our destruction. To have one of the mythic foundations of Our Island Race so traduced and demeaned strikes at the very heart of our sense of identity.

After all, beef, in all its forms, is an epitome of our class structure. At the top end, so to speak, is the rib, majestic, magnificent and expensive. In the middle we order the brisket and rump steaks on special occasions. At the bottom are the burgers, pies and sausages formed out of the odds and sods that do not find their way on to the butcher's slab.

Of course, few of us now consume it in forms we can readily associate with the 'gigantic round of cold roast beef' beloved of Mr Pickwick, but we still feel betrayed by its treachery, and we turn with anger on the keepers of the fetish.

But it is too easy to blame the farmers. The fault does not simply lie with them. It lies with the policies of successive governments, whose single aim was to produce as much food as cheaply as possible whatever the ecological cost. It lies with the agro-chemical companies who saw the opportunity to ruthlessly exploit the situation for commercial purposes. And it lies with us, the consumers, who turned a blind eye to what was being done in our name. ●

· ·

4 April 1996
Simon Hoggart
Big beef by gaucho from the Groucho

We had to wait a fortnight, but yesterday Douglas Hogg, the world's rudest legislator, finally lost it. Off his bike. Out of his pram. Swinging from imaginary chandeliers.

It would be tempting to make cheap jokes about all those fillets, sirloins, steak and kidney pies, hamburgers, topside roasts and corned beef hashs the poor fellow has had to cram down his face every day since the crisis began. He must be one of the few Tory MPs from whom the phrase 'a nice bit of skirt, sir?' evinces groans of despair.

No, it's all those meetings with European ministers, their wearisome sense of moral rectitude, their plump self-satisfaction – them droning on until six o'clock yesterday morning.

No wonder that his press conference afterwards lasted 22 seconds. (A colleague tells me this is unfair; it actually lasted 23 seconds. Apologies. I would hate to suggest that Mr Hogg was ever curt.)

And all this happening to a man who suffers the worst burden which anyone can bear – the absolute certainty that he is right.

There's a line in *Broadcast News* when someone says sarcastically to Holly Hunter: 'It must be great looking round a room and knowing you're the only person there who's right.' She replies: 'No, it's not, it's horrible.' Mr Hogg must feel the same way.

And of course there's that ridiculous wide-brimmed hat, which comes from some hinterland between trendy metropolitan London and the rich cattle lands of the Argentine pampas. He is a gaucho from the Groucho.

Yesterday the jet-lagged Mr Hogg made a statement about the European Union talks in Luxemburg. These were a complete failure for Britain, in that nothing we were prepared to offer would make our European 'partners' lift the ban on British beef.

Naturally none of this was the Government's fault. Indeed, you would imagine from Mr Hogg's statement that the crisis was almost over. With his staccato speech, in which exclamation marks appear in quite unlikely places, he declared: 'There are encouraging! signs that confidence! is returning. Retailers! say their customers are! looking for beef again.

'So! Those with! cattle to send to market should! know there are buyers for British! beef! The whole trade is beginning! to return . . . beef is! for all practical purposes safe to eat – safer than it has ever been!' he raved.

Gavin Strang, his Labour opposite number, felt this Bovril-fuelled machismo did not quite meet the occasion. He wanted to know, reasonably enough, how many cattle would have to be slaughtered. And when might the ban be lifted?

It was at this moment that Mr Hogg suddenly decomposed in front of our eyes. His body flopped against the dispatch box, his feet twisted round each other, and he gripped his hands together, as if afraid they might fall off.

He started slowly, menacingly, in the manner of a TV barrister who has suddenly got his hands on the crucial piece of evidence. ('Begging your pardon, sir, but I found this letter in the lodger's jacket. D'yer think it might be important?' 'Mrs Bottomley, this letter might! just save a man's! life.')

'Let me make this first point,' he said. Then he got louder: 'So that the House can hear! it! very! clearly! The honourable gentleman did! NOT! condemn! the! ban! He has expressed his *understanding* of the ban!' The voice went higher. You could hear the larynx twang. 'Those who have heard the [drop to low sneery voice] honourable gentleman! will take *comfort*!'

Mere typography cannot convey the controlled hysteria, the dampened dementia. The Chief Whip held his hand in front of his face. Messrs Major and Heseltine took deep calming breaths. The Opposition roared. The moment for which they had waited so long had come. ●

....

29 May 1996

Leader

Xenophobic? That's them not us

The notion has got about that some sections of the British people, and especially of the British media, aren't all that keen on foreigners. Goodness knows why. Maybe it's the way the *Sun* talks about giving the Germans a boot up the Bach-side. Or the *Daily Express* proclaiming that it's 'time to repel the Euro-invaders'. Or Gillian Shephard, no less, joining the clamour against the choice of Beethoven's 'Ode to Joy' as a theme for the Euro '96 championships because some German wrote it.

But there's no excuse from now on for talk of xenophobia. For yesterday the *Express* produced an 'easy cut-out-and-keep guide' designed, it explained, to help intellectuals, 'like most BBC interviewers or the Tory MP George Walden' to distinguish between defending one's national interest and xenophobia. On the one hand, there is patriotism: 'In Britain, it unites all classes, ever since the battles of Agincourt, Poitiers and Crécy, where English peasants fought with Norman noblemen against a common foe.' On the other, there's naughty old xenophobia – 'hatred or fear of foreigners or strangers or of their politics or culture'.

Happily, we don't have that sort of thing here. Outside Northern Ireland, where the conflict is 'almost incomprehensible to most Britons', xenophobia 'has been almost unknown'. Europe, however, emerges with much less credit. In Belgium, for instance, heart of the 'internationalist' European Union, there are bitter divisions between Flemings and Walloons, though fortunately these have stopped short of major violence.

So at last the distinction is clear. It's not that true Brits don't like foreigners *per se*: it's just that they can't stand foreigners who don't like other foreigners. Xenophobia, it now appears, starts not at Dover but at Calais. ●

25 June 1996

Matthew Engel

A coarse and demented newspaper

Fourteen summers ago, in the midst of the Falklands War, the *Sun* was fomenting hatred against Argentina. The *Daily Mirror* called the *Sun* a 'coarse and demented newspaper', and quite right too.

Among the headlines and captions on the first three pages of yesterday's *Mirror* were 'Achtung! Surrender', '*Mirror* Declares Football War on Germany', 'The *Mirror* Invades Berlin' and 'Filthy Hun', plus, of course, the expected collection of cod-Teutonic phrases, stale jokes about sun-loungers and even staler puns on the word '*Herr*'.

The tone throughout was that this match was not a re-run of the World Cup final but of the Second World War. Maybe it was intended to be funny. Only the humourless could believe that. It was coarse and demented journalism. Britain has not been at war with Germany for 51 years. The two countries are about to meet each other in a football match. Under the Public Order Act 1986, incitement to racial hatred is a criminal offence. There is a strong case for saying the *Mirror* should be prosecuted.

Everyone expected the tabloids to go a little berserk faced with the prospect of a semifinal between England and Germany, a fixture that has exceptional sporting resonance, relating to 1966 and 1990, even if any connection with 1914 and 1939 is forgotten. And it was hard to know where the line might be drawn in a week when the lines 'IN BED WITH ELTON: His boyfriend tells of tears, tantrums and tenderness' appeared on the cover of the colour magazine produced by, believe it or not, *The Times*.

However, the other tabloids have proved surprisingly mild thus far. Perhaps the *Mirror* thought the other papers would pile on the hatred much more strongly, and panicked, as newspapers sometimes do.

There are three aspects of this to be considered. The Germans can probably take it. They will assume this is yet another manifestation of the British tragedy: the fact that we have achieved so little since 1945 and have to hark back for solace.

The hooligans may not be so relaxed. English football is not yet so free of the disease that nearly killed it to make this kind of provocation necessarily cost-free. It is obscenely irresponsible journalism.

To those of us who care about newspapers, there is something else. It was the Second World War that raised the *Daily Mirror* to greatness. It saw the reality of Hitler very fast and warned repeatedly of what was to come. During hostilities its mixture of lightness of heart and seriousness of purpose made it the favourite of the troops and the embodiment of the ordinary Briton's determination.

If the *Mirror* is articulating the nation's attitude now, this is a very sick country. I hope and trust, though, that all we have is a sick, failing and desperate newspaper. •

. . . .

25 June 1996

Matthew Norman
Diary

From the Column That Supports Our Boys (hilarious catchphrase: 'Kraut of the tournament you go, *mein Herren*!!!') comes this statement: on the eve of the semifinal with Germany, the Diary dissociates itself from any mealy-mouthed, pinko talk of appeasement to be found elsewhere in the *Guardian*. Captain Mainwaring wouldn't tolerate it, and nor would Vera Lynn. So then, taking care not to overdo the war allegory, and pausing only for a nourishing mouthful of powdered egg, we come to our Book of the Week – *Biggles Defies the Swastika*. With 'his jaw set in true Prussian fashion', squadron leader James Bigglesworth has joined the Gestapo, escaping certain doom only by stealing a plane and flying to neutral territory. There, however, he learns that his pal Ginger has flown off to rescue him. 'When he finds you're not at Boda,' says Ginger, 'he may be able to grab a machine and fly here.' Biggles snorted. 'Suffering crocodiles! Is he daft enough to think that the Boche leave their machines lying about for anybody to pick up?' When Biggles counsels inaction, Ginger reluctantly accepts it. 'OK,' agreed Ginger. 'But I'm bound to say it sounds a sticky business to me,' he added glumly. 'All war is sticky business,' Biggles reminded him. It is a reminder upon which Lord Haw-Haws everywhere might do well to reflect. •

. . . .

26 June 1996

Matthew Norman
Diary

Only hours before the balloon goes up, the Column That Supports Our Boys has obtained a document of potentially unimaginable import. *The Vogts Diaries*, which were discovered only yesterday in the dungeon of a spooky Bavarian castle, purport to be the secret thoughts of morose German coach Bertie Vogts in recent weeks. Early entries – written in a sinister Gothic hand – show signs of paranoia ('9 June: Zey keep zaying zat I – alone of all German coaches – have von nussink. *Schvein! Schvein!!*'); however, a note of calm later appears. '22 June: Ze lads done vell first half, ven ze Croats come at us early doors.' The final entry, dated yesterday, betrays a confidence bordering on arrogance. 'Ze only team zat vorries me is ze French, who believe zey have an excellent defence,' it reads. 'Mind you, zey thought that in 1940. Ha ha. No, just my little joke!' Naturally, question marks are raised (why, for example, does Vogts write as though applying to be a scriptwriter on *Allo, Allo*?). However, *Daily Mail* editor Paul Dacre, a leading expert on everything, is categorical. 'There can be no *possible* doubt about their authenticity,' said the former Paul Trevor-Roper yesterday. ●

* * *

16 December 1995

Michael White
The ins, outs and pre-ins of coining the right name

British diplomacy clocked up another triumph in Europe yesterday when the heads of government agreed to call the new-fangled single currency the Euro. The decision came shortly after John Major had denounced the name as 'fairly uninspiring'. And he should know.

Eurosceptics were predictably negative. The Euro doesn't even have a smaller denomination – (the Eurine?) – they whinged. It isn't even a prefix, so we can say Euro-pound or (strictly hypothetical, this one) Euro-lira.

But these people have no vision. The decision was the climax of a brilliant plot hatched in Whitehall to discredit the whole idea by landing the currency with a real plonker of a name. Only the ever enthusiastic Kenneth Clarke was not let in on the secret.

Plonker was one of the options rejected by the Euro leaders who turned up in the Spanish capital, those not at death's door like Andreas Papandreou, the Greek prime minister, or helping police with their inquiries. Fortunately Felipe Gonzalez was the host and therefore did not need his passport.

Other suggestions failing the consensus test included dago and portillo (both cunningly proposed by the Foreign Office) and the florin, shilling, crown and ecu. The latter was particularly unacceptable to Chancellor Helmut Kohl because its linguistic origins can be traced to the homeland of his dear friend and ally President Jacques Chirac.

What little hope exists that the Euro public will take the Euro to its heaving bosom may well be extinguished by a huge advertising campaign being planned in Brussels to make the plucky little currency as popular as BSE, Yorkshire Water and asylum seekers from Romania.

Comforting slogans, such as 'the Euro in your pocket will not be devalued', are being market-tested alongside, 'I can remember the time when you could buy a round of drinks and a Chinese take-away and still get change from a Euro.'

British spin doctors reported that the 'little countries' had nodded approvingly while Mr Major made the case for Euro caution. But it was not a day of unqualified triumph for the British bulldogs as snow fell on the summit's venue, a municipal conference building which could have been in the suburbs of Coventry, Copenhagen or Koblenz.

Basically what happened was that Messrs Major, Clarke and Rifkind urged their colleagues to think before rushing into a single currency which could topple the entire European project. Then their colleagues told them to take a running jump in all 11 EU languages, including English.

It is hard to understate the enthusiasm for a single currency among the governing élites across the Channel. At one point yesterday, Antonio Guterres, the prime minister of Portugal, was moved to compare the occasion to Christ's injunction to St Peter: to be the rock on which he would build his church. 'The Euro is the rock on which we will build Europe,' he predicted.

As a symbol of Catholic universalism, the image was wholly appropriate to the Euro federal project. It would take a churlish northern Protestant to point out that St Peter was subsequently crucified upside down. Whether that happens to the Euro is a matter that governments feel should properly be left to George Soros and the gentlemen in red braces who speculate in Wonga.

Such is the enthusiasm here that, strictly speaking, there are three prospective categories: ins, outs and 'pre-ins'. These are countries which want to be in but will not qualify. Some are bankrupt or have banks run by the Mafia and their television stations by Silvio Berlusconi, Europe's answer to You Know Who.

Come to think of it, ins, outs and pre-ins sound like some of those late-night smut shows which are Mr Berlusconi's contribution to the New Europe.

The day's momentous decisions took place before the heads of government trooped off to the royal palace to greet their newly allied Latin-American associates, who are also itching to bring their hallowed traditions of currency stability to the new project. The ceremonies were followed by a long lunch before Euro hostilities resumed. The harmonised Euro siesta is surely something we could all agree on. ●

796·4·7·96   ~©Steve Bell 1996~

Foreign parts

....

23 May 1996

Matthew Engel

Bible or burger?

The moment a Jew first sets foot in the Promised Land is supposed to be revelatory and unforgettable, even if one happens to arrive after five hours on British Airways rather than an improbable passage through the Red Sea and 40 years in the desert.

This was as true for me as for my forefathers, though the manner of it was not necessarily the same. Before I had even passed Customs at Ben-Gurion Airport, something happened that was so totally *Israeli* that it became a sort of motif for my entire trip.

It happened at the money-changer's, a place that does have a certain biblical resonance. I had spoken to no one, except to say '*Shalom*' to the immigration officer, but I was in my usual traveller's tizz and when the clerk handed back my passport I wandered off without waiting to be given any shekels. He called me back, smiled patronisingly and passed over the money. At that moment the large Israeli behind me in the queue called out: 'You *see*. Honest people.'

It is difficult to convey in print the emphatic mixture of defensiveness, aggression, triumphalism and national self-absorption contained in those four words. Indeed, the clerk was honest and I was grateful. But even an obvious *noodnik* like me was bound to notice a complete absence of local currency sooner rather than later and would have been back to argue. The bank's procedures would have proved me right. Dishonesty was not an option, here or at any other airport in the world. But only in Israel would a third party have tried to make this trivial incident part of a patriotic advertising campaign.

It was an early introduction to something fundamental. To a Briton, Jewish or not, Israel is in many ways superficially familiar: a country with Marmite, HP Sauce, Marks & Spencer, cricket on cable TV, even pork and bacon (sometimes euphemistically known as 'white steak' or 'low cow'). English is spoken everywhere and it is possible to get by for years without even knowing the Hebrew for 'please' and 'thank you'. Most Israelis seem to.

But, in every important respect, Israel is Britain's cultural antipodes. If the British are formal, civil, phlegmatic, pacific and furtive, Israelis are unstuffy, rude, argumentative and open. Britain is ashamed of its flag; Israelis tie theirs to their car aerials. On the outside of the Prime Minister's office, I counted 107.

In Britain 'immigration' is the foulest word in the political lexicon; in Israel it would be equally unthinkable to restrict it. Many Britons never see a soldier; Israeli men serve three years, women two, and the men are called up again one month a year until their 55th birthday. The British are alienated; the Israelis suffer from an advanced case of collective narcissism. It is a country so busy looking in the mirror it sometimes forgets to clean itself up.

Israel's enemies have often likened it to apartheid South Africa. There are similarities, but the comparison is not quite apt. White South Africa used to trawl the world for compliments and a kindly word from a London newspaper or an obscure MP would be transformed into a big local story. Israeli news often sounds like 'Your Slights Tonight'. On a quiet day last week the headline event on the radio was one inflammatory pamphlet produced by an obscure group in East Jerusalem. Army spokesmen will call in erring journalists and say: 'You are not very fair to us. We are very nice really.'

There is, I think, a reason for this difference. Apartheid was wicked and its perpetrators knew it. Zionism is a just cause but it has brought with it much injustice and suffering to other people, suffering that Israel has never recognised, still less understood.

Until, perhaps, now. Next Wednesday Israel goes to the polls in an election that will decide the future of far more than one country. Its 4 million voters will either decide to retain Shimon Peres as Prime Minister and continue along the boulder-strewn road towards peace in the Middle East or will elect Benyamin Netanyahu, who has specifically repudiated the idea that alongside Israel there can be a state called Palestine.

And here is another difference with Britain, where politics seem ever more trivial and fatuous. Six months after the assassination of Yitzhak Rabin by a right-wing fanatic, three months after the suicide bombings in Israel's main cities, the country has to make a dramatic decision. It is hard to remember when a democracy can ever have faced a more stark or serious choice. And no one is sure who will win.

Overtly, the choice is not that simple. Peres is, after all, the man who last month ordered the bombing of Lebanon, largely for political reasons. As the combatants grapple for the middle ground, Peres's posters emphasise the word 'strong' while Netanyahu's talk of 'peace'. Spokesmen for his Likud Party often say he will merely be a tougher negotiator. 'We will get a better peace because he will compromise less,' in the words of one candidate, Danny Danon. But peace and Palestine are not alternatives. Either Israelis will recognise that other people have the right to the national redemption they themselves have achieved or the state's second half-century will be much like the first.

Yet already the country is moving into a new phase. Three years after Prime Minister Rabin stood on the White House lawn and shook hands with Yasser Arafat with the air of a man obliged to accept a stinking fish, Israel feels like a place intrigued by the possibilities of a peace it has never known.

It spent 19 years, from 1948 to 1967, struggling even to exist. It got through by the hard work of its pioneers and the courage of its soldiers, very often the same people. It has spent the last 29 years as an imperialist power, securing its survival by bullying, sometimes tyrannising, those it conquered. Now at last Israel has the chance to move on.

This cannot be an entirely dispassionate piece. I had, in a sense, spent my own 40 years in the wilderness. It was not an act of omission that I had never been to Israel before. Fed what I regarded as absurdly one-sided propaganda as part of my Jewish education in the 1960s, I sullenly sabotaged the Hebrew lessons and turned my back not merely on the place but on the whole idea. As a journalist I went everywhere but.

I now wonder, had I followed some of my Jewish contemporaries and been attracted by the glamour of the Six Day War, what effect the Israeli army and I might have had on each other. I regret missing out for so many years on a place of glorious intellectual ferment and disputation.

Most people see the Middle East as a region split between Jew and Arab. But in these parts you cannot get away with anything as simple as that. Every orthodox Jewish household requires at least two sets of crockery: milk and meat. The Israeli electorate can be bisected in an infinite number of ways: left and right; hawk and dove; Ashkenazi (Jews from the north European tradition) and Sephardi (from further south); religious and secular. The religious community itself splits into 'modern orthodox' and extremists, who then divide into the followers of the Hasidic and Lithuanian traditions. And, of course, this is to over-simplify horribly.

Political science here is more like geology, the study of the fissures in a huge piece of rock. But it comes down to one major split. The Jewish-Arab confrontation, in the Holy Land's infinite timescale, is the brief aberration of a century or so. The real split here is between old and new.

Modern Israel was originally a place where people did without, and where 30 per cent of the budget went on defence. In 1981 Menachem Begin's Likud government won re-election after lowering the burdensome tax on cars and TV sets. In 1985 the Labour–Likud coalition began to dismantle the apparatus of state socialism. In the 1990s – mostly under Labour, though the change arguably predated their election win of 1992 – the economy has exploded.

Since the collapse of communism, Israel has absorbed 600,000 migrants from the old Soviet Union, yet unemployment has halved. The per capita GDP is rapidly chasing the British level. Overseas travel, once heavily taxed, is now the norm: there are people who regularly pop to Britain for weekends to watch soccer. Nowhere is more besotted by mobile phones. I saw one orthodox Jew carrying two: milk and meat, probably.

'Ten years ago you had to wait five years for a phone unless you were a journalist, a doctor or a party official,' recalled Hirsh Goodman, editor of the *Jerusalem Report*. 'Now there's five companies trying to shove one down my throat. Four years ago you couldn't get a decent cup of espresso anywhere in Jerusalem. Now there are dozens of places.'

There is a new tower block complex in Tel Aviv called Einstein-by-the-Sea.

But the whole country could be called that. This is a place where if you shouted: 'Let me through, I'm a doctor' you would probably get the reply: 'So who isn't?' There used to be great excitement in Israel when *Moby Dick* or *Ulysses* was first translated into Hebrew. Now the big news is the Hebrew version of Windows 95.

With a population that is both highly motivated and highly educated, this is probably going to be the most potent of all the Asian business tigers; indeed it may be Israel's forthcoming economic domination of the region that will be the prime cause for conflict in the 21st century. Some day an Israeli may even invent a computer sophisticated enough to define the mini-micro-second between the moment a Tel Aviv traffic light turns green and the driver behind you hoots – though in truth most Israeli drivers, mixing Levantine impatience and Western efficiency, usually save time by hooting while it is still red.

Since its foundation, Israel has rarely stopped to think, and the pace of development has left little time to contemplate modern Western preoccupations, like public health or road safety or the environment. The ancient landmarks are hardly threatened, though the most striking message of the Western Wall, repeated on the back of every single plastic chair, is that the chairs were donated by the Zakheim family of Brooklyn. Modern landmarks attract little sentiment. The Atara Café in Jerusalem, a Mittel Europa-style centre famous for coffee, cakes and argument since the days of the Mandate, is scheduled to close, to be replaced by a Pizza Hut.

On the outskirts of Jerusalem there is a junction. One turning points to Jericho and the Dead Sea. The other points to Burger House. And that is one aspect of the choice Israel now has to make. Back to the Bible or straight to the Burger House?

The country's attitude to religion is the biggest shock of all to a Diaspora Jew. Outside Israel a Jew defines himself through various forms of ritual observance. Here, confident in their Jewishness, people can afford to ignore their Judaism. The pioneers were militant secularists by temperament, so Israel has never been in real danger from theocrats. But part of the nation's tradition of hardship – now starting to change – has been the six-day week, so Saturday has had to encompass, for instance, soccer as well as synagogue – a combination that is anathema to the orthodox.

Maybe a sixth of the country count as 'ultras' – the black-hat, black-coat, black-beard Jews; maybe another sixth are what they call the 'knitted kipa' class, who cover their heads and observe kashrut and the Sabbath without entirely retreating from the 20th century. Indeed, this group has replaced the kibbutzniks in the forefront of the Israeli armed forces.

The rest of the country fall into various degrees of disdain and contempt. Nearly all will have a family dinner at Passover, just as all Britons will have Christmas Dinner, and most will fast on Yom Kippur, a day whose solemnity was given a modern dimension by the Arab invasion of 1973 – but they will do little else. It is widely held that the ultras are gaining ground, partly because they breed as zealously as they pray, partly because most new Western migrants belong in their camp and partly because Israel's quirky PR electoral system has given their mullah-like rabbis inordinate power and suffocated the emergence of a more liberal Judaism.

It is perhaps more accurate to say that the country is becoming more polarised. 'In our community,' said a civil servant who comes from a family of Moroccan migrants, 'it used to be traditional to go to synagogue on Saturday morning, have lunch at home and then go for a drive in the afternoon. Now people tend to be in one camp or the other.'

The civil servant in question is Yakov Azuelos, the head of Jewish Enrichment at the Education Ministry. He is not very observant himself – a splendidly Israeli quirk. He cares passionately that people should be able to make an informed choice: 'I want a new Jew who knows his sources. Then it's up to him. The problem now is ignorance.' Eighty-eight per cent of Israelis, according to a recent survey, do not know all the Ten Commandments; and two in five cannot name the Five Books of Moses.

The ministry runs a programme in which Jewish and Arab Israeli children get together. These meetings tend to be stilted before the participants discover they are interested in the same things. A private organisation known as 'Bridge' has the far harder job of bringing secular and religious teenagers together. 'The secular see the religious as narrow, bigoted, anti-democratic demagogues,' says Bridge's director, Danny Tropper. 'The religious see the secular as fun-loving, valueless, discothèque dancers. This is one of the tragedies of Israel today. The great irony of the country is that the Jewish tradition, which should have helped unite Israel, is in fact the great factor dividing it.' Modern indifference may be winning but the determined anti-religion of the kibbutz is in retreat. The pioneer with gun and hoe seems irrelevant to the burger-eating classes. And even the concept of making the desert bloom, which first won Israel global admiration, now seems like a waste of precious water.

Most of the kibbutzim ran into financial trouble in the 1980s. Kibbutz Yizreel, in the Jezreel Valley, came through because, among the almond groves and the cotton fields, it now runs a factory building advanced machines to clean swimming pools. Its central beliefs remain intact; everyone is still paid the same. 'With respect,' said Yossi Piekarski, one of the managers, when I expressed surprise, 'Margaret Thatcher's beliefs have not weathered very well.' But the ancillary aspects of kibbutz-socialism have been swept away. Last year Yizreel members finally voted to allow everyone to have private cars; a decade ago they were not even allowed air conditioning, on the grounds that it was unfair for some to have what others could not afford. No longer do children sleep away from families in dormitories. 'Does everyone still spend their evenings dancing the hora round the camp fire?' I inquired. 'You must be joking,' said one kibbutznik. 'They all go back home and watch their videos.' For what they are worth – 3 per cent of the votes – the kibbutzniks will still choose, near-unanimously, Shimon Peres. But three hours' drive from them, and just an hour plus roadblocks from the nightclubs of the new Jerusalem, is Hebron, the last major town on the West Bank (Jerusalem excepted), where the forces of Arafat's incipient statelet have yet to take charge.

Here are perhaps the most exposed of all the Israeli settlers on the West Bank, a few dozen families who have re-colonised a town where what they claim was a 3,700-year-old Jewish tradition, dating back to Abraham, was ended in 1929 when the Arabs massacred the Jewish community, killing 66 people.

It was Sunday morning and blazingly hot. From down the hill, the bedlam-noise of an Arab market day wafted fitfully. Most of the settlers had gone to work but a few Israeli servicemen stood on guard, their boredom contending with the ever-present fear of some further terrorist lunacy; their hunger, as they grumbled about the absence of lunch, at that moment surpassing everything.

Suddenly a siren started, and came closer. An armoured car appeared and behind it a coach. Inside was a group from the Tel Aviv suburb of Ra'anana.

Religious zealots themselves, they come to Hebron every New Moon to express their solidarity with the settlers. Among them was Shlomo Slonim, who as a baby survived the 1929 slaughter when his family were killed. 'This was the house of my parents and my grandparents,' he said. 'I was the fifth generation born in Hebron.' There was really no need to ask: these were Netanyahu voters. But I felt obliged to try. Did he think this should be Israel or Palestine? Mr Slonim was too staggered by the question to reply. From behind me a woman with an American accent almost spat: 'There is no such thing as Palestine.' Will these people win next Wednesday? Will Israel's voters insist that the battles of the Bible, 1929, 1939–45, 1948, 1956, 1967, 1973 and so on be continued unto the thousandth generation? Or will they decide that Hitler is dead and that it is possible that good and evil are not always the exclusive properties of different sides in a conflict? Philip Roth wrote that Zionism sprang not only from the urge to escape persecution but came 'out of a highly conscious desire to be divested of everything that had come to seem . . . distinctively Jewish behaviour – to reverse the very form of Jewish existence. The construction of a counterlife that is one's own anti-myth was at its very core.' A few days ago an Israeli was telling me about a friend of his, an accountant or something, and an army reservist who, as part of his annual stint, found himself in Gaza at three in the morning hauling terrorist suspects out of bed at gunpoint. 'You know,' he told his friend, 'I'm beginning to think this isn't really a job for a nice Jewish boy.' Maybe the time has come to counter the counterlife – if, as the man at the airport said, the Israelis are truly honest people. •

. . . .

1 June 1996

Derek Brown

An ego rises in the land of fear

The next Prime Minister of Israel, as a profound admirer of Winston Churchill, is doubtless familiar with the great man's celebrated description of Soviet policy in 1939: 'It is a riddle wrapped in a mystery inside an enigma.'

There could be no fitter description of Benyamin 'Bibi' Netanyahu, both the best-known and least-known political leader in Israel. Everyone knows Bibi: he's the one with the face that launched a thousand quips. The sound-bite king; the great performer; the man who illustrated his country's peril during Desert Storm by wearing a gas mask on CNN, and who shocked Israel into fits of giggles by confessing, live on prime-time TV, that he had had an extramarital affair.

But then again, nobody knows Bibi. Not even those who work with him. One former member of his staff enthusiastically described his qualities: hard-working, a stern but fair taskmaster, easy to approach, a good listener, and so on. But what was he really like? 'You know, I really have no idea,' she said. 'I never learned anything about him.'

When Israelis talk about Bibi, two words invariably pop up: 'shallow' and 'superficial'. Such is the flattening effect of television on image. In reality, he is a great deal more complex than the usual Israeli leaders: the grizzled veterans, marinaded for generations in their own clichéd slogans, and open books to their followers.

Bibi is a closed book, which just happens to have a shiny bonkbuster cover hinting at the story within – enshrined as Bibigate, featuring sex, lies and maybe a raunchy videotape. Of which more later.

The dizzying rise of Netanyahu is not so much mysterious as chilling. Astute, articulate, and, when need be, utterly ruthless, he carved his way past the sagging old guard of the Likud movement, and the 'party princes' – the rising and middle generations with more experience. Bibi is, by common consent, a driven man. He is consumed by personal ambition, but there are other, higher gods in his pantheon. One is the survival of the Zionist state; another is the elimination of 'terrorism'.

Obsessiveness is part of his inheritance. Born in Tel Aviv in 1949, he is the son of Benzion Netanyahu, renowned scholar and arch-nationalist. Part of Netanyahu senior's life's work, *The Origins of the Inquisition in Fifteenth-century Spain*, was published last year. The other part is his austere dedication to revisionist Zionism, the cause of his idol and mentor, Ze'ev Jabotinsky. This is a hard, uncompromising view of Zionism; that the Arabs were the implacable foes of the Jews, and that Israel should be established on both sides of the Jordan, whatever the cost.

There is no evidence that the reclusive Benzion Netanyahu, now 87, has retreated an inch from this view, and considerable evidence that his second son, the new Prime Minister, has absorbed much of it. The other great formative influence in Bibi's life is the United States. He went to live there aged 14, when his father, embittered by modern Israel, took up an academic job in Philadelphia. Bibi was apparently devastated by the move, but adapted so readily that when he returned to Israel for army service, he had difficulty fitting in with the egalitarian informality of his native land.

He had a distinguished military career, rising to captain and serving in the dangerous, daredevil border reconnaissance unit. He was wounded in the face while helping to rescue hijacked passengers from a Sabena aircraft in 1972.

Later that year, he returned to the US to study at the Massachusetts Institute of Technology. He graduated in architecture, took a master's degree in business administration, and honed his political skills by defending Israel in public meetings. Whatever doubts he may have had – he simplified his name by deed poll to Benjamin Nitay – were swept aside by possibly the defining event in his life: the death of his brother, Yonatan.

Yoni Netanyahu was the only Israeli soldier killed in the sensational commando raid on Entebbe, which rescued 106 hijacked hostages from under Idi Amin's nose. Bibi was devastated and hurled himself into the national movement, which elevated Yoni to icon status. In 1980 Bibi set up and directed the Yonatan Institute, dedicated to the study of terrorism and how to combat it. The work crystallised his passionate conviction that terror is ultimately a weapon of states and can be successfully countered.

By this time, the singular pattern of Bibi's personal life had been set. In 1978, while working in a swank business consultancy in Boston, he married Micky, a postgraduate student. They had a daughter, Noa, but the marriage foundered when Micky learned of Bibi's affair with Fleur Cates, an English graduate of the Harvard Business School. The soap opera switched to Israel, where Bibi was briefly employed as a furniture company manager. He married Fleur in 1981, but Bibi's political career started to soar and again the marriage imploded. There was speculation about infidelity, incompatibility and Fleur's politically embarrassing lack of fluency in Hebrew. They divorced in 1988.

Bibi's first public job came at the request of Moshe Arens, a leading Likudnik and newly appointed ambassador to the US, to join him in Washington as number two – a dream job for the young, articulate, American-accented Netanyahu. He dazzled diplomatic correspondents with his silky smooth, deeply sincere advocacy of his country. Israel's blood-soaked invasion of Lebanon in 1982 could probably have been defended, but not as effectively as Bibi did it. Soon he found himself in the high-profile role of Israel's ambassador to the United Nations.

Lionised by New York society, he honed and buffed his US-Israeli composite image. It did him no harm in his first, successful, tilt at the Knesset (parliament) in 1988, and a great deal of good when he became deputy foreign minister – to Arens again.

The Gulf War brought truly international fame. Bibi's mastery of the sound-bite may have cemented his two-dimensional image, but it gave him a persona and a priceless weapon in the campaign for the next target: leadership of the Likud.

In 1991, Bibi was married for the third time, to Sara, an El Al stewardess. He also found time to embark on an affair with a PR consultant; the affair that led to Bibigate. Sara was tipped off in an anonymous phone call in January 1993, two months before the crucial leadership election. What occurred between the Netanyahus may never be known. What is known is that Bibi headed immediately for the place he knows best: the television studio. He confessed, almost tearfully, that he had been unfaithful. The nation was convulsed – by laughter.

Marital infidelity is just as hurtful, just as seamy, in Israel as anywhere else. But it is also a good deal more common. That a politician should think it worthy of prime-time was bizarre to most Israelis.

But Bibi had more spice to offer. A political rival, he claimed, was threatening to release a videotape showing him 'in compromising romantic situations' unless he dropped out of the leadership race. It was, he intoned, 'the worst political crime in Israeli history, perhaps in the history of democracy'. Phew!

The clear target of this remarkable charge, though unnamed, was the man who, before and since Bibigate, loathes Netanyahu more than any other: former foreign minister and thwarted would-be Likud leader David Levy. Levy threw a fit and extracted an apology from Bibi. The police were called in and found no evidence of a video or a plot. But the damage was done: in March 1993, Netanyahu swept to victory in the party convention.

When they had finished laughing, many Israelis found the extraordinary episode disturbing. Who is this man? Which planet is he from? they asked.

And some are asking still. As opposition leader, Bibi has had to endure a government which was seemingly unstoppable; a government which made all the running. As the peace process unfolded, to incredulous Israeli gasps, Bibi was reduced to impotence on the sidelines. He could fulminate about the deal with Yasser Arafat, but he had no solid alternative.

The opinion polls swung back and forth with every new atrocity and every new breakthrough. Israel's peace deal with Jordan was hugely popular, and Bibi could only trail over to Amman in the wake of Yitzhak Rabin and Shimon Peres. The bombings and shootings were more to his advantage, but still the question remained – and remains – what would Likud do?

Last year, opposition to the Oslo accords with the PLO became more ugly. Posters appeared of Prime Minister Rabin in SS uniform. Slogans against 'traitors' were shouted at Likud and other right-wing rallies. On 4 November, Bibi's worst nightmare was acted out in a Tel Aviv square. Yitzhak Rabin was gunned down by a young Jewish zealot, an ardent opponent of the peace accords, Yigal Amir.

In an instant the nation was plunged into cathartic grief and an orgy of remorse. Young people poured on to the streets to light candles for the man whom Bibi had reviled. Endless queues wound past Rabin's grave. The politics of hatred was excoriated. Leah, the widow of the murdered leader, accused Bibi of incitement.

In vain he blustered and indignantly denied the charge. The opinion polls slipped from crisis to calamity. The new Prime Minister, Shimon Peres, had a 20-point lead. The story of how that unprecedented advantage was squandered is not Bibi's story. He was not consulted when Peres ordered the assassination of Hamas master bomb-maker Yahya Ayyash, sparking the inevitable vengeance. Nor could Bibi do more than look on when the bombers struck back, taking 63 lives in less than two weeks.

Even when the election was called, the Likud leader's hands were, to an extent, tied. He did not dare unleash the fire and brimstone fervour of the old campaign against Rabin. He could not criticise too loudly the government's disastrous adventure in attacking Lebanon.

What he could do, and nobody could have done it better, was to drive home, with deadly drumming persistence, the single point that the peace has not brought security. At the climax of the election campaign, last Sunday's television debate, he did not have to be glib or clever or inventive. He just had to say the word 'fear'. He said it 14 times, because that's the way the message gets over. And it did. ●

· ·

14 August 1996

Peter Preston

Mr Bean sugars Republican hopes

Would you like a jelly bean? Every time I pass the Ronald Reagan Library stand in the convention emporium, a nice lady gives me another packet. And I keep passing the stand, because it is fascinating. There is every autobiography (his and hers) on sale. There are pictures of Ronnie with Gorby and King Hussein and, right at the back, Margaret Thatcher. But the videos draw the crowd. The old wizard telling his Irish visit joke, or his golfer and anthill joke, or his priest who got into bed with the wrong woman joke. And the Republican delegates clustered round the screen, hour after hour, laugh along, moist-eyed.

A few years ago, I was wandering through the Army and Navy store in Victoria. Shuffling by the shirt counter went an elderly couple: she holding his arm, he slow and tottery and staring. Nobody helped them. Nobody opened doors. Nobody paid a moment's court, or even notice. Exit Harold Wilson, four times prime minister of Great Britain, and his Mary of better or worse. America may be a rougher, tougher society, but they sure treat their retired politicians well. When you win an election, you keep its title for ever. Once a governor always a governor. When you lose or fade, a sweet cloud of cloying benediction drops on your head.

At the Richard Nixon Library stand, there are no videos, but you can get your photograph taken between cardboard cut-outs of Nixon and Elvis at their 'world famous meeting'.

Would the Tories allow a Neville Chamberlain ('Smile over Adolf's shoulder and wave that famous letter in a timeless photo of your own') or Anthony Eden stand within a hundred miles of Bournemouth, Brighton or Blackpool? Do they, indeed, want to see any of their erstwhile best-beloved ever again? Gerald Ford not only looks like Jack Benny, but sounds like him. 'We don't have a Ford or a Lincoln in the White House today. What we have is a convertible Dodge.' George Bush flaps and whines, but they roar when he introduces 'the most popular woman in America'. Enter Barbara Bush, dressed like the Queen Mum and walking like John Wayne.

They're not very tactile in the Bush family: George senior handles his wife like a fragile chamber pot, and when George junior introduces his wife, Laura, they shake hands.

But jelly bean-loving Ronnie is the big one. He was, they keep saying, the American Dream. He ran the Republican's Camelot saloon. He is, when you read the script of 'honesty' and 'integrity', their Back to the Future. He has tragically forgotten them, but they will not forget him.

Jack Kemp, on soft-centre video, calls Reagan 'the last lion of the twentieth century'. Billy Graham calls him 'a national grandfather'. We're invited to weep a little as he and Nancy amble away into the sunset. And Nancy arrives in person, with more tears, to tell us he is still the eternal optimist. 'He still sees that shining city on the hill.'

Ronald Reagan is different. He is Californian gold. But deference and the appearance of love follow all of them. The goofy ones, the crooked ones, the ones who had trouble thinking and chewing gum at the same time. They become monuments.

The real difficulty here, perhaps, is making sure Bob Dole doesn't turn Memorial Library before he is elected. Bush looks sprauncier. Ford looks quite as awake.

'My name,' says an unprepossessing voice from the podium, 'is Sam Brownback. I'm a farm boy from Parker, Kansas, and I'm running for Bob

Dole's seat in the US Senate. These are mighty big shoes to fill. They're size 25 shoes even Michael Jordan couldn't fill.'

Apparently 'Kansans, like Dwight Eisenhower and Bob Dole, embody the spirit of Kansas.' Now that would be a ticket. •

....

15 June 1996
Ed Vulliamy
Testimony for the terrorised

In the event, despite months of preparation, it was a scramble to get into court on time. 'Brace yourself,' said the attorney from out of the blue, 'you're on in five minutes.'

The previous witness had concluded 24 hours ahead of schedule. So I exchange a pair of jeans for the attorney's Armani suit. He is American and works out; waist 30 inches. I'm not and don't; waist 32 inches.

'How's it feel, at such a moment in history?' he asks.

'Not comfortable,' I reply, before being ushered through a security door into the witness box, in front of a bulletproof glass screen, in the first international war crimes trial since Nuremberg.

Opposite the witnesses' entrance, between two police officers, sits Bosnian Serb Dusko Tadic, accused of murder, torture and rape in the Omarska concentration camp and others of its kind, and of a pivotal role in the 'ethnic cleansing' of Muslims from his home region of Prijedor.

To the right are the prosecution, by whom I am called. To the left, Tadic's defence. This trial – like arguments over intervention in the war itself – is a tussle between the New World and the Old. The prosecution is by three Americans and an Australian. Defending are two British barristers, and a Dutch-Russian.

In front are the judges, a former governor-general of Australia, Sir Ninian Stephen, the Malaysian Lal Chand Vohrah, and the forthright African-American chairwoman of the bench, Gabrielle Kirk McDonald.

The Hague tribunal is a vast, more complex phenomenon than it appears from the formalities. The investigating teams have been brought in from such fields as the US Marines, the Lancashire Constabulary and the federal prosecution team that put away the police officer who beat up Rodney King in Los Angeles.

The gathering of the witnesses is an extraordinary scene. For the first time in the history of international justice, former camp inmates are due in court to see if they can identify their alleged torturer. At a hotel on one of The Hague's arterial roads, they assemble from across the wretched diaspora scattered by Omarska and the other camps in Serbia's gulag.

Many have not met since their days of incarceration, when as captives they suffered conditions of ferocity and abject terror that boggle the mind. Now they greet each other, and exchange tidings, over breakfasts of fruit and cheese.

There, sipping on coffee, is Dr Azra Blazevic. We last met in the Trnopolje concentration camp, where she was helping out in the pathetic medical centre. She and another doctor handed us an undeveloped film which, once processed, revealed the savage beating of prisoners. Now, the doctor and I can talk generalities, but not about the case.

It is for the terrified, emaciated prisoners, of whom we saw but a few on that putrid day in August 1992, when we stumbled into Omarska and Trnopolje, that I am here to testify.

The attorney leading my evidence is Major Michael Keegan of the US Marines. His purpose is to show that the persecution of Muslims around Prijedor was part of an international conflict – not a civil war – so that the charge 'Grave breaches of the Geneva Convention' apply. The second is to show the pogrom as 'widespread and systematic', not some isolated incident, so that 'Crimes against humanity' applies.

We conclude the first day's evidence with recollections of a convoy of 1,600 Muslims herded over the mountains by Serbian gunmen. The second day begins with a round-robin of similar pogroms: Bosanska Krupa, Bihac, Jajce, Zepa, Visegrad and Sarajevo. Five years' work, several narrow escapes, experiences as epic as they were terrifying, condensed into a morning. Afraid of guilding the lily, I was apparently playing things down too much, the lawyers said.

Our tortuous journey to Omarska between 28 July and 5 August, 1992 became court record. Meeting Dr Karadzic; a 'briefing' in Prijedor with those who ran Omarska and tried to suggest alternative destinations; a mock gun battle faked by our Serbian escort to put us off proceeding; and our final arrival at the back gates of Omarska mine.

I had not seen ITN's 'rushes' – the untransmitted footage – of that day, with which the court accompanied my account. I have described the scene a thousand times but it never fades and here it was in vivid detail. The yard drill, the canteen, those spindly fingers, lantern jaws and burning eyes, the guards swinging their guns.

By the time we got to a now infamous shot of the barbed wire at Trnopolje, and the emaciated ribcages behind it, I asked if I could switch off my monitor and refer to memory only – those skeletal corpses, talk of massacres at other camps.

The last tranche of the direct examination concerned a return visit to Omarska earlier this year, in search of those who ran the camp. Guards had said no camp existed there but had declined to give their names because 'look what happened to Dule Tadic'. At that moment in my evidence the defendant abandoned his usual nonchalance and picked up his headphones.

Tadic and I had eyeballed each other twice in court. His eyes are dark, sharp, hard and rodent-like. On the first occasion, I turned my gaze away. Second time, more in my stride, I outstared him.

Many colleagues think that to have given evidence is bad professional ethics. Only two journalists have come forward to testify at The Hague. Both are British: Martin Bell of the BBC and myself.

Bell says that the question of whether or not journalists should testify in the war crimes trial is 'an argument that can be made convincingly either way – it's purely subjective'. I agree.

At The Hague one is simply offering the facts at one's disposal to the court. It is for the judges to decide whether those facts favour the prosecution by which one is called, or indeed the defence, or are of no consequence.

That would be the case in any trial. But at The Hague there is an extra dimension which concerns the difference between 'objectivity' and 'neutrality', in both journalism and civilised life.

If 'objective' is to mean that our writing must be fact-specific, then of course we must be objective. But 'neutrality' is not the same thing.

At a certain point, the perpetration of atrocity crosses a line, and breaches not only international law but the bases of civilisation. I believe that at Omarska (and elsewhere in Bosnia), that line was crossed, and that to remain 'neutral' was not neutrality at all – but rather, complicity.

This is not a matter of being 'anti-Serb' or 'pro-Muslim'; it is a judgement about where one stands between camp guard and inmate, persecutor and persecuted.

The international community has largely chosen to accept the argument that because atrocities have been committed by all sides in Bosnia, then 'neutrality' is acceptable. But this takes no account of the relative scale of atrocities, that the vast majority have been committed by Serbs against Muslims. The CIA puts the percentage ratio at 90 per cent Serbian perpetrators; 8 per cent Croat; 2 per cent Muslim.

The Hague is trying alleged criminals from all three groups, but appropriately the majority of the accused are Serbs. The fact that the tribunal is doing this, in the wake of the cowardice of the rest of the world, makes The Hague the West's last chance to display any credibility.

Prosecuting at Nuremberg, Sir Hartley Shawcross said the purpose of those trials in 1945 was that such things would never be heard again. He was, as he wrote recently, disappointed. I would have been as proud to testify for Sir Hartley against the Nazis as I am to do so at The Hague against those who echoed them with a pale but unmistakable imitation. ●

11 March 1996

Ed Vulliamy

Bloody trail of butchery at the bridge

The bridge that spans the River Drina's lusty current at Visegrad is a Bosnian emblem. *Bridge on the Drina* is the title of a great work of literature by the country's most celebrated author, Ivo Andric, a Nobel Prize-winner. In Andric's book, the bridge is at once backdrop and silent witness to Bosnia's history.

It is a mighty and glorious structure spanning the river at a point where savage, precipitous rocks briefly part, giving way to a verdant valley. The water flowing through its elegant arches is a luminous blend of turquoise and jade.

The bridge was built, as the carved inscription proudly declares, in 1571 by order of the Ottoman Grand Vezir Mehmet Pasha, of robust pumice stone hewn by Rade the Mason. 'Of all the things that life drives man to shape and build,' wrote Andric, 'none, I think, is as precious as bridges . . . They serve no arcane or evil purpose.'

Andric, who died in 1975, once complained that a house newly built in Visegrad obscured the view of the bridge from his home. Had the author lived into the 1990s, he might have been grateful for the obstruction. For in the hidden history of Bosnia's war, the bridge on the Drina was bloodily defiled.

It was turned into a slaughterhouse – a place of serial public execution – by a man we now reveal as one of the most brutal mass killers of the war. Virtually unknown, not indicted by the war crimes tribunal, this monster turned the Drina red with the blood of hundreds – maybe thousands – of Muslims murdered on the bridge, whose corpses the bold current swept downriver.

A few of the bodies were rescued from the waters by a teenager whose quiet testimony begins the unveiling of butchery at the bridge.

Jasmin R's fresh face belies what he knows. Jasmin was evacuated to Dublin last Christmas from a prison camp in Serbia, to which he had fled from the crushed Muslim enclave of Zepa, to which he had fled from Visegrad in 1992.

During his three years at Zepa, Jasmin, aged 14 on arrival, was considered too young to fight. Instead, he was assigned to a hamlet called Slap, a lonely junction between the Drina and Zepa rivers. There his job was to haul bloated corpses out of the Drina's current as it flowed from Visegrad, bring them ashore in a small boat, often under Serbian fire, and give them a proper burial.

'We dug the graves,' he says calmly, 'and buried 180 people. Some I knew personally, they had been my neighbours in Visegrad.' The Bosnian government calculates that probably about one in 20 bodies was salvaged.

Jasmin's companion in this work was Mersud C, now based in a barracks for exiled Zepa soldiers up a front-line mountain in central Bosnia.

'The bodies came,' says Mersud, 'almost every day. Men and women, old and young. They had been beaten and tortured, they were black and blue, and some had been decapitated. Yes, and there were children. Mostly 10 or 12, and two infants of about 18 months.'

Eighty-two corpses were identified. The graves were dug for one, three or five at a time, named or numbered, and ringed by a low fence.

Before the war, Mersud had spent summer evenings with friends on the bridge. 'It was the place to meet before going for coffee. I read the Andric book, it was compulsory at school.'

The Serbian slaughter of Muslims in eastern Bosnia at the war's inception was largely hidden from prying eyes.

Unknown to the outside world, on 5 August 1994 a Serbian soldier from Visegrad called Milomir Obradovic, held prisoner in Muslim Gorazde, told his captors the story of one man: Milan Lukic. A UN policeman, Sergeant T Cameron, took notes.

Obradovic told how Lukic paraded around Visegrad with a megaphone, shrieking: 'Brother Serbs, it's time to finish off the Muslims' and how Lukic set about achieving this goal.

Lukic, he said, locked men, women and children in houses and incinerated them. He arrived at factories, took employees out and shot them – for a while he kept the wife of one such victim, Igbala Raferovic, as a captive sexual partner.

Lukic tied a man to his car with a tow-rope and dragged him round town until he was dead. One member of Lukic's gang, 'The Wolf', raped one of the girls they kept prisoner for the purpose at the Vilina Vlas spa hotel so violently that when the rest demanded their turn the girl, Jasna Ahmedspahic, jumped out of a window to her death.

There were two massacres in May 1992, said Obradovic. At a village called Prelevo, Lukic took men off buses shipping Muslims out of Visegrad, laid them face down and shot them. 'There is,' confessed Obradovic, 'a mass grave at Prelevo.'

Another convoy of refugees was stopped by Lukic at Dragomilje, the men again taken and shot. Obradovic told of mass murder on Visegrad's bridge, adding that the killing was sanctioned by the Yugoslav army.

By a cruel twist, Obradovic's captors exchanged him, apparently unaware of his value. The witness was lost. Obradovic has not been heard of since, and any investigator might wonder whether he met the same fate as another Serb official who objected to Lukic's mass murder, Stanko Petcikoza. Obradovic said Lukic murdered him.

But, following the trail of Lukic's bloodlust, the *Guardian* has reconstructed the case, and found other witnesses to the Visegrad carnage scattered across Bosnia and Europe. Their testimonies interweave like threads in a tapestry.

There is no Muslim from Visegrad who does not know what Milan Lukic did on their bridge, and there are very few who do not mourn in his wake.

Mersud the gravedigger knew the man whose victims he pulled from the river; they had been neighbours. Lukic, now about 30, was born in the village of Rujiste, said Mersud, and 'seemed a good guy'. Another neighbour called Omer, now in Sarajevo, said that Lukic's family had been 'fervent Chetniks in the Second World War'. Lukic moved to Serbia after leaving high school to keep a café in Obrenovac, near Belgrade, but returned as the clouds of war gathered in spring 1992.

Lukic assembled a gang of 15 braves, including his brother Milos, cousin Sredoje, a chum from Belgrade called Deyan Jeftic and a waiter, Mitar Vasiljevic. Before long Lukic committed the first murder in Visegrad's war.

Mirsada K. was at home when she heard a shot next door. The little girl from the household came running to Mirsada's house, saying her mother, Bakha Zukic, was dead, shot in the back, and her father, Dzemo, taken. The man who had fired the shot was Milan Lukic: he had taken a fancy to Dzemo's new red Volkswagen Passat, and had made off with both man and car.

Dzemo Zukic was never seen again, but the car became omnipresent. From that day hence – as another witness, Fehima D, said: 'If the red Passat arrived at your house, you knew something terrible was about to happen to you.' Thus Milan Lukic sparked an orgy of violence which emptied Visegrad of 14,500 Muslims.

The bridge was not the only killing field. Women have survived to bear witness to Lukic's house-burnings. Her hands and face deformed by fire, Zehra T was the sole survivor of an inferno at Bakovica, above the bridge, on 27 June, in which 71 people were incinerated.

Esma K was herded into a stadium and thence to a house with 60 others. The Passat arrived at 5pm. Within four hours, she said, 'the sky was light because the house was in flames'. Esma escaped through a window.

A man called Hasan Ajanovic survived a cull of men in the house of a waiter called Meho. Meho had worked alongside Lukic's waiter-henchman Vasiljevic at the Panos restaurant. Six men, including Meho and his son Ekhem, were driven to the river bank in a convoy led by Lukic and Vasiljevic, where they were lined up and shot. Hasan jumped into the water before he was hit, and was shielded by Meho's floating corpse.

But the bloodiest arena was the bridge itself. The structure is visible from almost every balcony and window in Visegrad, which climbs both sides of the valley. Its cobblestones are a stage at the foot of an amphitheatre; the executions were intended to be as public as possible.

From her balcony, Fehida D watched. She saw 'Lukic, in his Passat, and the trucks behind, arriving on the bridge each evening'. The gang would unload their human cargo and the killing began. 'We saw them by day or by the city lights, whether they were killing men that time, women or children. It took half an hour, sometimes more.'

The Serbs usually stabbed people into various states between life and death before throwing them into the water below. 'Sometimes they would throw people off alive,' Fehida recalled, 'shooting at the same time. Sometimes they would make them swim a bit, then shoot.'

One witness, Admir H, recalled Lukic enjoying music from the Passat's radio while throwing two men into the river. 'I can't swim!' protested one of them, Samir, as Lukic fired into the water.

At the end of June a Visegrad police inspector, Milan Josipovic, received a macabre complaint from downriver, from the management of Bajina Basta hydroelectric plant across the Serbian border. The plant director said could whoever was responsible please slow the flow of corpses down the Drina. They were clogging up the culverts in his dam at such a rate that he could not assemble sufficient staff to remove them. The dam is well downriver from Jasmin's and Mersud's Zepa graveyard – their 180 bodies were a small fraction of the total.

Hasena M lived in a first-floor flat, 150 yards from the river bank in Visegrad. By 15 July she had spent 12 days wondering whether her husband, Nusret, was alive. He had been taken by a Serbian neighbour he had known well, Dragan Tomic, and disappeared.

Hasena set off for work at 6.30, across the bridge as usual, to find Lukic already busy at that unusual hour. 'Two young men with their hands tied behind their backs' were being executed to the sound of his car radio.

At lunch time, Lukic came by Hasena's factory to promise that the time had come to 'finish off the Muslims' remaining in Visegrad. Hasena and her three Muslim workmates left early, electing to take another route home. Looking upriver at the old bridge, they saw 15 men lined up and killed. Terrified, Hasena hid at home for four days with her daughters, Nusreta and Nermina, aged eight and six.

In the afternoon of 19 July, the red Passat pulled up outside Hasena's flat, into which her elderly parents and sister had moved. Milan and Milos Lukic, armed with machine-guns, kicked the door open. Hasena's children were playing outside. Their turn had come.

'Milan Lukic said that in the next 15 minutes he would kill us all,' recalled Hasena. She was sent outside to fetch the little girls, but implored her Serbian neighbours to hide them; the neighbours refused. So Hasena and her girls slipped unheard past her own front door to an empty flat on the third floor.

From there Hasena heard Lukic ask: 'Where's the third woman?' She heard her mother, Ramiza, call for her but waited. From a window she saw Lukic march her mother and sister Asima out into the Passat, and drive towards the bridge. Hasena followed, to a vantage point near a school.

Half-way across the river, the bridge widens to form a lovely overhang above the current called the Sofa, a Turkish word. Here is a bench of fine flagstones where people can sit comfortably, leaning back against the parapet, which reclines. This was where Hasena used to chat with her friends. But not on 19 July.

'I watched them put my mother and sister astride the parapet, like on a horse,' Hasena said. 'I could hear both women screaming, until they were shot in the stomach. They fell into the water. The men laughing as they watched. The water went red.'

This was the beginning of Hasena's calvary. She hid overnight in an empty house with the children, returning home at dawn to seek out her invalid father, who was unable to walk.

'My father said: "Go. Take the girls, run away. You obviously can't take me. I'll wait here until they come for me. Go." I looked at him, and then at my girls. I made him some breakfast and he said: "Come here, my daughter, so I can kiss you the last time." He kissed me and the girls, and we left him sitting there, alone.'

When the Serbs caught up with Hasena, they took her and the girls to a house full of other Muslim women, where they were held captive for two months. Many women from Visegrad say they 'shared a house with other women' during that summer. That is all. Some details, if spoken, can destroy any attempt to rebuild life.

On 13 September, Hasena was moved. And now her story adds another, fresh name to the grisly list of Serbian concentration camps in Bosnia: Uzamnica.

Hasena was kept in a crowded hangar of this disused barracks for three years, while her daughters lost their childhood. 'I used to look at them in the morning, asleep, locked in while the sun was shining outside, and cry.'

Uzamnica was a forced labour camp, so that when they were outside Hasena and her girls were working, even six-year-old Nermina. It was hard labour, dawn to dusk, planting tomatoes or feeding cattle. The only food the Serbs provided for their Muslim prisoners was forbidden pork.

Lukic was a regular visitor to Uzamnica. 'He came every day, wild, saying "I'll kill you filthy gypsies" ' – beating and abusing prisoners at will.

The screams of pain, said Hasena, came mainly from the men's quarters. Each week, convoys of male prisoners would leave the camp, heading into Serbia, never to be seen again. Last October Hasena and her girls were exchanged, and made it to Sarajevo.

Visegrad is now a baleful, watchful town. It is awful to look down at the vigorous current gliding beneath the Sofa and its parapet, and to wonder that this was the last thing those terrified, mutilated people saw as they plunged.

But Visegrad is still home to the Ivo Andric library, the finest collection of his books in the world. The librarian, Stojka Mijatovic, offered us a volume, a gift. 'We have taken so many books from Muslim houses we hardly know what to do with them,' she said.

Mrs Mijatovic had once presented this very edition of Andric to the library's most regular and best-loved client. Now she had it back, looted from the dead man's house.

'Would you like me to cross out this Muslim name?' she offered. 'No, thank you.' The dedication from the library was to Emir Ajanovic, a relative of the witness to the murder of Osman's father and brother.

Would you ever want to see the bridge again? Osman and Fehida shuddered. 'Never.'

And Hasena? She shivered. 'Never. Not if I lived a thousand years. I wish I could drive that bridge from my mind, but I see it as though I were there now. That bridge will drive me mad.'

Looking for Milan Lukic is a dangerous pastime. The bush telegraph informs us that he is now back in Obrenovac, Serbia, and a wealthy man.

It is a drab, faceless town and the glass-fronted Viski Bar he is said to have managed is a comfortless place, scantily patronised and blaring out Montenegrin folk music. An inquiry as to Mr Lukic's whereabouts is met with a stony glare charged with menace, and not sensibly challenged.

But there was one, ominous, recent sighting. A Muslim soldier from Zepa, present at the fall of the enclave in 1995, said he saw Lukic with the Serbian army patrolling the columns of Muslim fighters as they lined up to surrender. He was looking for anyone he recognised, and shouting: 'Anyone from Visegrad step out of the line! Anyone from Visegrad!' Even then, it seemed, Lukic's work at the bridge on the Drina was unfinished. ●

. . . .

18 March 1996
Suzanne Goldenberg
Families enslaved by a life of casual brutality

Like his grandfather and father before him, Rupo Koli was born a slave, and all his days were the same: long, hard hours in sugar-cane fields, with a coil of rope hissing through the air towards his shoulders when he faltered under the burning sun.

Life was bearable until four years ago when Rupo, his wife and eight children were sold for 50,000 rupees (£1,000) to Ali Baksh Leghari of Batin district, a landlord whose cruelty still makes them shiver with fear.

They wore leg-irons in the field and were made to squat at wooden posts before they were chained for the night. They were beaten when the landlord was drunk or had guests to entertain, and were paid only in flour, in such miserly quantities that for several days every month they ate grass.

'If we even took an onion from the field, the landlord used to beat us,' Rupo said. Otherwise, they survived by gulping down a paste of uncooked flour and water and the occasional chilli; the landlord wouldn't spare the cooking fuel.

Forty-eight hours after human rights activists and police led Rupo out of bondage, the bazaar in this nondescript town remains a source of wonder for him. Rupo has walked into town three times this afternoon, a slow shuffle in phantom chains.

Neither Rupo, aged about 40, nor his father can remember the original debt that reduced the family from free men to bonded labourers, but after years of back-breaking and unpaid labour on sugar-cane plantations it had unaccountably grown to 118,000 rupees (£2,360).

Although his story is horrifying, Rupo recounts it as if it were completely normal – and in this part of Pakistan it is. Here in the southern province of Sind, feudal landlords rule as they have always done: with casual brutality.

Bonded labour was outlawed only in 1992. Shakeel Ahmed Pathan, the Sind representative of the Human Rights Commission of Pakistan, argues that officials are reluctant to enforce the law, partly because they are themselves from landed families, and partly for fear of offending the most powerful people in the land.

Many of Pakistan's leading politicians are landlords, including the Prime Minister, Benazir Bhutto, and demands for agricultural reform in the past have met with fierce resistance.

Sind's agricultural wealth depends on bonded labour, mostly tribal (meaning indigenous) or so-called untouchable Hindus, called *haris*, for labour-intensive and highly profitable cash crops like sugar cane which are replacing traditional agriculture.

For the *haris* living on vast banana or sugar estates, the landlords are akin to God: quick to anger, slow to forgive and answerable to no one. They rule unencumbered by such modern niceties as land reform, taxation, trade unions or rights legislation.

'All landlords think that *haris* are their property,' Mr Pathan said.

So much so that landlord Ibrahim Mangrio did not worry about witnesses when he grabbed Meran Devi by the hair and dragged her into a field. 'He would rape me in front of my mother, he would rape me in front of the entire world,' Meran said.

Hanif, the bewildered-looking eight-year-old burrowed into her side, is the living proof of her shame. She said his father's only concern for his future was that Hanif bear a Muslim name.

The original debts often forgotten, unscrupulous landlords take advantage of the *haris*' illiteracy to ensure they can never be free. Often, the accounts are just scribbled in a child's notebook. The *haris* spend their lives on the estates in conditions the Human Rights Commission describes as private jails.

There was no question of escape, said Meran's mother, Jhema Devi. The estate was patrolled by armed guards. 'We died there; we were born and married there. We didn't leave his land for 22 years.'

But, with the intervention of human rights activists who bombard officials with complaints about bonded labour or sometimes raid estates to liberate *haris*, about 1,000 peasants have been freed.

For their pains, Mr Pathan said, the activists have been beaten and threatened with reprisals; several landlords have turned up at his office in Hyderabad demanding that he pay for the *haris* he has taken away. Despite an encampment of freed *haris* a mile from the Matli police station, the local police chief denies all knowledge of bonded labour in his district.

The rude shelters of thatch and wood where Rupo and Jhema Devi live with 400 to 500 other recently freed *haris* are the local equivalent of the 'underground railway' in the southern US states before the civil war.

The *haris* remain desperately poor. Most have only one set of clothes and a few battered kitchen utensils. But they are beginning to find work as paid farm labourers, taking home 80 rupees a day. As the fear of being recaptured by their landlords lessens, the *haris* chart their own physical transformation. They stand straighter, and learn to speak above a whisper.

'Now I am becoming less and less black,' Jhema Devi said. She had never been able to wash properly before.

The *haris* have a temporary protector in the local church, but the Irish priest in Matli, Father Tomas King, originally from Galway, describes their freedom as tenuous. The *haris* are too unused to independence to know how to avoid falling into debt. Some of them have become trapped again.

'In the bonded system you have nothing, but at least the landlord looks after you, you have security. Even if you are a slave you belong to someone,' he said. ●

. . . .

4 March 1996

Andrew Higgins
Up, up and away

O n the 25th floor of the knife-edged Bank of China skyscraper, icon of Hong Kong's new establishment, Michael Heseltine is still hanging on, albeit banished to a corner behind the door. Slightly more visible is Margaret Thatcher, though even she seems diffident and on the defensive, her photograph dwarfed by large portraits of Deng Xiaoping and Zhou Enlai, Mao Zedong's premier for 27 years, at the far end of the executive suite. Such are the eclectic but unambiguous mementoes of power and money in the final days of the British Empire.

The pictures – as well as a superb collection of Chinese antiques worth many tens of millions of pounds – belong to T T Tsui, Hong Kong tycoon, patron of the arts, friend to the Victoria and Albert Museum, keen-eyed connoisseur of politics and porcelain, professional schmoozer *sans pareil*. He is chairman of Citybus, which runs buses in London as well as Hong Kong, and a string of other firms. Most important, though, is the nexus of political and economic clout represented by his newest endeavour, New China Hong Kong Group.

When John Major made his first trip to Hong Kong as Prime Minister in September 1991, Tsui counted himself among a select group of local millionaires ready to prove their allegiance with more than mere words. He is said to have donated £100,000, small change for a man who can drop millions in an afternoon at an antique auction. (He does not deny the payments, but will not discuss them either: 'I am unable to answer.')

The Conservative Party, eager to keep such funds flowing, set up an offshore bank account in Jersey to funnel donations from sympathetic overseas moguls. To show his appreciation – and encourage further largesse ahead of the 1992 general election – Major slipped away from an official reception during his 1991 Hong Kong trip to spend one of only two evenings in the colony cloistered with friendly tycoons.

Major is again in Hong Kong now. But with only 484 days left before the five-starred red flag of the People's Republic of China ousts the Union Jack, most magnates have found more fruitful ways to spend both their time and their money. Invited to meet Major this weekend, T T Tsui sent his regrets: 'I've got a meeting in Beijing,' he explained before his departure for the Chinese capital. 'I won't be back in time.'

Also out of town – in Cuba, on business – is David Tang, flamboyant founder of the China Club, an upstart rival to the venerable, musty and increasingly marginal colonial-era Hong Kong Club. 'British politicians are probably irrelevant as far as the majority of the people in Hong Kong are concerned,' he said.

Instead of the Conservative Party, it is the Communist Party in Beijing that can now enjoin displays of devotion. From an ox-blood leather armchair commanding a master-of-the-universe view of Hong Kong, Tsui offered this advice to the Prime Minister: 'Whether or not he wants to hand over sovereignty to China, this is going to happen. Just as the British left India, Singapore and Malaysia, they must leave Hong Kong. The return of Hong Kong to China is 100 per cent certain. Whether Britain cooperates or not, it will happen. China will rule Hong Kong after 1997. Britain is leaving. That is the reality.'

Change may be unavoidable, but this does not make it easy. Revealing of the emotion underlying what the more pragmatic accept as a *fait accompli* is a stubborn last stand being staged along the waterfront of Victoria Harbour. On Kellett Island – long since joined to the shore by landfill and shadowed by skyscrapers but still known by the name left by a vanished past – the Royal Hong Kong Yacht Club wrestles with the question of how to accommodate the inevitable. 'Hong Kong is going to change. Fine, let it change. Great, take down all the flags and go for new flags. Put bauhinia flowers on all the mail boxes. Let's do it,' says Ian Dubin, a royalist civil servant with the Hong Kong government. 'But how far are we going to take it? Is it going to be an offence to sing "Rule Britannia" in Wanchai, or to wear Union Jack boxer shorts?'

For government institutions such as the Royal Hong Kong Police Force and the Royal Observatory, a change of nomenclature has always been just a matter of time. Both will drop their 'royal' at the stroke of midnight on 30 June 1997. Already designed for this moment is a new police emblem. The 19th-century opium-trading junk will be replaced by an image of Hong Kong's business district skyline, a motif dominated by the Bank of China.

One by one, bastions of colonial society have judged it wise in recent months to sever their connection with the British monarchy ahead of Britain's formal retreat next year. The Royal Hong Kong Jockey Club, holder of a horse-racing franchise worth more than £6 billion a year, has proved itself more than worthy of the new, rapidly approaching order. Among local brahmins holding the coveted rank of steward is Larry Yung, the son of China's pre-eminent 'red capitalist' vice-president, Rong Yiren, and the chairman of CITIC-Pacific, China's biggest state conglomerate in the colony.

The Jockey Club's governing council not only voted to drop its royal appellation but did so with lock-step unanimity, a display of discipline that will have comforted even the most hard-headed practitioner of democratic centralism in Beijing. The Hong Kong chapter of the RSPCA is following suit, as will the Royal Hong Kong Golf Club.

On Kellett Island, though, the R-word has proved more resilient: against all expectations, a recent general meeting of members fell just short of the 75 per cent majority needed to drop the royal tag first granted by Queen Victoria in 1895.

In an emotional debate preceding the ballot, a Shanghai-raised British lawyer offered the mocking suggestion that the club name be changed to 'Humble People's Sampan Club'. Most urged pragmatism, pointing out that the People's Liberation Army will soon take over control of Hong Kong's waters from the Royal Navy. One member explained that, as someone who had seen the PLA in action in Tiananmen Square, he thought it unwise to retain the royal.

Leading the campaign for change is the yacht club's commodore, Tony Scott, a colonial policeman with the Independent Commission Against Corruption. Retaining the royal, he says, would be a 'dubious and hollow distinction' after 1997. 'It would be extremely unwise to keep it. These people are in denial of reality. The royal is an expensive anachronism. Change is inevitable. There is no point trying to block it . . . Everyone can go off chuckling to the bar, but what worries me is that we will end up with this bloody royal albatross hanging around our neck.'

Those demanding change plan to hold a second vote in coming weeks. Dubin, the royalist, has written to Buckingham Palace pleading for help. He received a polite reply but no promise of redcoats to the rescue: the Queen had 'taken careful note' but 'would not become involved directly in a matter such as this.'

Undeterred, he proposes that Deng Xiaoping be made joint patron and get his portrait put on the wall next to the Queen. 'The Pax Britannica stood for 200 years. You've got 500 million people in the Commonwealth who owe a large part of whatever veneer of civilisation is upon them now to British culture,' said the Canadian-born Dubin. 'That is what royalty is about. It is that history, that tie. As we move into a brave new world, should we not try to keep a bit of the history? Not a lot, but just enough so as not to forget the lessons of history?'

The problem is that Beijing draws very different lessons from the same history. Britain's capture of Hong Kong in 1841 marked the start of what, from the perspective of the Chinese Communist Party, was a century of weakness and shame.

Whatever China's promise to leave Hong Kong's way of life intact for at least 50 years, past dishonour must be expurgated. For the tycoons, it means another chance to cash in. 'For more than 100 years the Chinese had no equality here. For more than 100 years the English had privileges in every area,' says Tsui. 'The changes under way now are entirely natural.'

Central to such changes are companies like his own New China Hong Kong Group, a well-connected investment fund, and the emergence of a new comprador class serving Chinese, rather than British, interests. With projects ranging from property in Beijing to a toll road in Sichuan, Tsui makes no apologies for cosying up to Hong Kong's future sovereign. As well as having a seat on the standing committee of the People's Political Consultative Congress and a slot on the Hong Kong preparatory committee, he counts a dozen government agencies and ministries as partners.

For the moment, the Communist Party, much like the Conservative Party, does its best to nurture and reward the loyalty of the rich. It may sometimes fulminate against 'money worship' and 'bourgeois liberalisation', but embraces Hong Kong tycoons with gusto. 'This is only natural. Hong Kong is a society where the most important thing is business,' says Tsui. 'This is an economic society. Without business, Hong Kong has nothing.'

Early in December he crossed the border into China for a meeting in Shenzhen with the party's general-secretary, Jiang Zemin. The occasion amounted to an investiture of Hong Kong's future power élite – a final confirmation of the alliance of interests that will dominate Hong Kong after 1997. Also invited to Shenzhen were a dozen other moguls, including other erstwhile friends of the Conservatives, such as multi-billionaire Li Ka-shing and shipping magnate Tung Chee-hwa, front-runner for the post of post-1997 chief executive.

The balance of loyalty, stacked so decisively in London's favour for more than a century, began to shift the moment Britain and China signed their 1984 joint declaration. For a while, London could still claim to matter. No longer. The game is up. Adding piquant irony to this final chapter of Britain's imperial history is the role of Chris Patten. As MP for Bath, he chaired the Conservative Party at a time when Hong Kong tycoons were still shovelling cash into the coffers. As governor of Hong Kong and author of modest democratic reforms, he is stigmatised by the same tycoons as a menace to society, though the wealthier among them refrain from the pitbull polemics proffered by China's more crassly opportunistic cheerleaders in Hong Kong.

An invitation to Government House, Patten's residence since his electoral defeat at Bath, is now more a liability than an honour. A recent guide to 'what's hot and what's not' in Hong Kong *Tatler*, bible to local high society, advised against dining there. The hot hosts, it decreed, are people like Zhou Nan, the choleric head of China's *de facto* embassy, the Xinhua News Agency.

'Some people have not come to terms with reality. Individuals and organisations must all come to terms with this reality,' warns Nellie Fong, a leading member of a Beijing-appointed preparatory committee and head of the Better Hong Kong Foundation, set up by a group of millionaires last year to improve Hong Kong's image. (Each founder member contributed a start-up fee of more than £400,000.) 'The reality is that the British administration ends in Hong Kong on 30 June 1997. Hong Kong becomes part of China. If they cannot come to terms with this, they may just have to leave.'

Another reality, however, is that Beijing frequently turns on its friends. In 1949, the Communist Party devoted one of five stars on a new national flag to patriotic capitalists and spent the next three decades persecuting them. Few can now remember what the fifth star stands for.

Ms Fong has a British passport. ●

· ·

11 July 1996
Jonathan Freedland
Aliens are coming home

D ialogue doesn't get much of a look-in in *Independence Day*, the sci-fi blockbuster now blowing US box-office records out of the sky like so many enemy alien spaceships. What with the hi-tech crushing of New York, Los Angeles, Washington, London and Moscow, the movie has little room for words. But one short sentence squeaks through: an incredulous child, gazing at the city-size saucer in the heavens above gasps: 'It's just unreal.'

Snarly critics might well say the same of the film, whose dialogue flips between B-movie tacky and disaster-movie cheesy. But they'd be wrong. *Independence Day* is very real, and not just because it's the monster hit of 1996 and possibly of all time: on Monday it became the fastest-earning film ever, bagging $100 million in six-and-a-half days (*Jurassic Park* took nine).

Independence Day has grabbed attention for reasons beyond its phenomenal commercial success – fuelled by the Americans who have queued round the block to get to screenings at one, four and seven o'clock in the morning. The film has been hailed as a cultural snapshot, capturing much of what's going on in Hollywood and in America itself.

It makes perfect sense that *Independence Day* is seen as a handy summary of the state of the US movie business. It is a virtual amalgam of every film currently churned out by Hollywood. The story of a world laid siege by hostile spacecraft has a US leader modelled on Michael Douglas's *American President*: young, handsome and vaguely Clintonian (the White House scenes were filmed on the same set). The sky-high terror causes havoc, throwing trucks and tankers around like children's toys – just like the upcoming *Twister*. Only computer wizardry can confound the forces of evil, as audiences have already learned in *Mission: Impossible*. There's even an exotic dancer, who performs solely to support her child – the shaky premise of Demi Moore's summer flop *Striptease*.

Independence Day stands above them all because it has dared to take to a logical extreme the current direction in Hollywood movies: films as rides, more appropriate to a theme park than a cinema.

Sean Connery's *The Rock* and Arnold Schwarzenegger's *Eraser*, along with *Twister* and *Mission: Impossible*, have packed the multiplexes this summer with films that make your chair vibrate, and where the only emoting comes from the enhanced Dolby sound system. These thrill-a-minute spectaculars take as their inspiration the attractions at the Universal Studios Tour, rather than old-fashioned drama.

That's why, even though Americans said they couldn't follow the plot of *Mission: Impossible*, most didn't care. It's the same with *Independence Day*. Even if you accept its far-out premise, the plot is so riddled with holes it's a hunk of Emmental (Man has to search entire United States to find girl, does it within minutes).

Steven Spielberg spots a trend: 'If the seventies and eighties were the era of the What If? movie, then the nineties are the era of the What the Heck! movie,' he told *Time* magazine. 'We say, "Hey, this is so beyond our logical grasp, so out of this world, that we're just going along for the ride." In this, *Independence Day* is the model of the form. It doesn't worry that its characters are utterly one-dimensional – Jeff Goldblum as clever Jewish scientist-geek, Will Smith as cocky *Top Gun* pilot, Vivica Fox as tart with a heart, Margaret Colin as cold career woman – just as it didn't bother to recruit any really big-name actors. It knows its true star is the special effects department and that in the business of spaceships, laserfights and sheer spectacle, size is all that matters.

Industry analysts are already venerating Fox's marketing strategy as the textbook for other studios to follow. They built up the hype for six months with teasing trailers and a 30-second TV ad during the mass-audience Superbowl in January. That was what created *Independence Day*'s status as an event movie – a must-see that would make those left behind feel like they'd been living on Mars.

The film is set over the July 4 weekend, so that's when it opened – with the added gimmick of all-night screenings. And Fox also practised neat synergy: the fictitious reports shown in the movie all come courtesy of Sky News which – like Fox – is owned by Rupert Murdoch. Still, *Independence Day*'s real interest lies in what it reveals about America. 'The US is desperately in search of an enemy,' says Paul Verhoeven, who directed *Robocop* and *Total Recall*. In the post-cold war world, communists will no longer do. Middle Eastern terror is already passé and it offends Arab-Americans. The Rock tried the enemy within – with a disaffected right-wing US general – but that gets messy and can alienate a chunk of the audience.

Extraterrestrials are the perfect solution. 'They're bad. They're evil. And they're not even human,' says Verhoeven.

Mind you, alien flicks are always really about life on earth. One critic has noted the link between the screen depiction of aliens and American attitudes to their own government. When Eisenhower was in the White House, people trusted Washington to fight the little green men. Witness *It Came From Outer Space* and *Invasion of the Body Snatchers*.

But by the seventies – after Vietnam and Watergate had broken that public trust – it was the celestial visitors from outer space who offered goodness and salvation, the government that was standing in their way. *Close Encounters of the Third Kind* was the definitive post-Watergate space movie, with its cousin *ET* not far behind.

Independence Day straddles the two eras. The President is now on the people's side – he leads his fellow fighter pilots into battle following a St Crispin's Day-style pep talk to the troops – a sign, perhaps, that Americans trust their government once more (or that Hollywood likes the Oval Office again, now that a Democrat is sitting in it).

But the film also features the now-standard secretive, shadow government. Feds have shielded from the Prez the existence – touted as fact by real-life conspiracy theorists – of Area 51, the secret airbase where an alien has allegedly been studied since it fell to earth in New Mexico in 1947. The film's ambivalence toward government is expressed in its hallmark scene, the detonation of the White House. Right-wingers and militia-types can cheer, liberals can wince.

Independence Day exposes several American traits with no such uncertainty. America sees itself as the last superpower, so it's left to the US to fend off the aliens. In one scene, a British commander is shown standing around until he hears the Americans are launching a counter attack. 'About bloody time,' he says.

America wants to be a place where all the races get along. So *Independence Day* has a WASP president, surrounded by Jews, blacks and Hispanics who join together to save the day. Americans love family values, so Will Smith's pilot makes sure he ties the knot before flying off to 'whoop *ET*'s ass'. Which leaves the small matter of what the aliens themselves represent. Historians say Orson

Welles's radio version of *The War of the Worlds* struck such a chord because the Germans were on the march. The fifties crop of space-invader flicks were all veiled allegories playing on American fears that the Russians were coming. Some critics suspect the patriotism of *Independence Day* might be a coded cry of panic over aliens of another kind: illegal immigrants heading for America's southern border.

Either way, *Independence Day* is a film of its time. Americans are obsessed by the paranormal – scan the bestsellers' lists or the ratings for the *X-Files*. Tim Burton's *Mars Attacks!* is coming this Christmas, along with *Contact*, *Starship Troopers* and Michael Crichton's *Sphere*. When it comes to America's appetite for tales from space, there's indeed something out there. ●

. . . .

4 May 1996

John Pilger
In a land of fear

At dawn, in Burma's ancient capital of Pagan, crows glide without a quiver among the temples in the desert. In Ananda, the most celebrated of these great cathedrals, there are four colossal standing Buddhas. As the light catches one of them, it is smiling. As you get closer the smile becomes enigmatic, then it fades. As you walk to one side and look back, the Buddha's expression is melancholy. Walk on and it becomes fear veiled in pride. I have not seen anything quite like it. For the devout, no doubt, it symbolises Buddha's timeless wisdom. For me it is the face of modern Burma.

Six years ago, more than 4,000 people lived in Pagan, a city which stands as one of the last wonders of the ancient world. They were given two weeks to leave, some only a few days. The city was being opened to mass tourism and only guides and the staff of a planned strip of hotels were permitted to stay. The people's homes were bulldozed and they were marched at gunpoint to a shadeless, waterless stubble that is a dustbowl in the dry season and runs with mud during the monsoon. Their new houses are of straw and poor-quality bamboo and stand mostly out of sight of the tour buses that come down the new and empty dual carriageway. Those villagers who objected were sent out on to the barren plain, or beaten, or taken away in the night.

The dispossession was mild by the standards of the dictator Ne Win and the generals who have ruled Burma since a military coup in 1962 crushed the democratically elected government. Last year the International Confederation of Free Trade Unions reported that a million people had been forced from their homes in Rangoon alone, in preparation for tourism and foreign investment. Throughout Burma perhaps 3 million have been brutally swept up and exiled to 'satellite zones' where they are compelled silently to serve Burma's new façade of 'economic growth'.

Arriving in Rangoon on a Sunday afternoon, there is a veneer of normality. Frangipani perfumes the air and incense fills the covered bridges that lead to the stupas surrounding the great golden pagoda of Shwedagon. Families seek the intonements of a passing monk, though there is a furtiveness about them all. Rowers glide on Inya Lake. Behind them, work on high-rise tourist hotels proceeds at a frenzied pace. There are surreal touches. A billboard advertising Lucky Strike cigarettes has 'Welcome to Yangon' in the space otherwise allotted to a cancer warning. 'Yangon' is the name the military regime has given Rangoon; Burma is 'Myanmar', which is the equivalent of the German government insisting that the rest of the world call their country Deutschland. A billboard near the airport announces 'Visit Myanmar Year 1996' beneath a cartoon picture of a Burmese Betty Boop. In the next street is the headquarters of Military Intelligence, known to the Burmese as 'Em-eye'. It is Burma's KGB and, alongside the old tyrant Ne Win and the army, it is the power in the land and the source of what the United Nations special rapporteur has described as 'an atmosphere of pervasive fear'.

For arriving foreign tourists and businessmen the drive to their hotel inevitably includes a short detour along University Avenue. To the uninitiated, this has a frisson of the forbidden and seditious. Number 54 is the home of the 1991 Nobel Peace Prize winner and leader of the Burmese democracy movement, Aung San Suu Kyi. Here, she spent six years under house arrest until her release last July. Now, every Saturday and Sunday, she is allowed to speak from over her garden gate to several thousand supporters corralled behind barbed-wire barriers. This is not so much a concession by the regime as a showcase for the new 'openness' of 'Visit Myanmar 1996'. A coachload of Taiwanese tourists was just ahead of me, snapping through the tinted glass. What struck me was the extraordinary courage of the Burmese who came to listen to her – in doing so they branded themselves as opponents of the regime – and the Kafka-like absurdity of the country's elected leader having to address people standing on a platform behind her garden fence.

Since her 'unconditional' release, Aung San Suu Kyi has been denied freedom of movement. On a recent attempt to leave Rangoon she tried to catch a train to Mandalay, only to find her carriage adrift at the station as the train pulled out. She cannot freely associate with anyone. Those Burmese who pass through her gate take a risk: their names are noted and they can expect a call in the night. Shortly before I interviewed her, eight members of a dance troupe who had celebrated Independence Day with her 'disappeared'. They include the popular comedians U Pa Pa Lay and Lu Zaw, who are said to have made a joke about the generals. Each has since been sentenced to seven years' hard labour.

Aung San Suu Kyi lived in Britain for many years before she returned to Burma, and her family live here still. A few weeks ago her husband, the Oxford

Tibetologist Michael Aris, was once again refused permission to visit her. The ban also applies to their two sons, whose Burmese nationality has long been withdrawn. The official newspaper, the *New Light of Myanmar*, attacks her regularly and with mounting viciousness. She is 'obsessed by lust and superstition'; she 'swings around a bamboo pole brushed with cess'; she is 'drowning in conceit'; and 'it is pitiable and at once disgusting to see a person (like her) suffering from insanity . . . now at a demented stage'. Aung San Suu Kyi dismisses all this with a laugh that is brave though difficult to share.

Of course, the reason for such intimidation is her popularity, which could not be greater, it seemed to me. At the mention of her name, the contrived neutrality of faces, by which people survive, breaks into smiles. People whisper her name as you brush them in a market, then turn and put a finger to their lips. And if you are able to speak and disclose that you have been to see her, all caution is discarded and questions pour forth as to her well-being. But with expressions of admiration, affection and solidarity are fears for her safety and the recognition that she, and the democracy movement, may be trapped. 'She is a Mandela without a De Klerk,' a close friend of hers told me. 'Unless pressure comes from the very governments that the regime is now courting in Asia and the West, nothing will change for a long time.'

Aung San Suu Kyi herself told me that foreign investment and tourism were shoring up the power of the junta, and that the world must realise the scale of Burma's human rights abuses, particularly forced labour. 'News comes and goes like fashion,' she said. 'After the people rose up in 1988 and paid the price in bloodshed, we slipped from the headlines. It will be a pity if we slip again.'

In February the UN Commission on Human Rights reported, as it does every year, that the following violations were commonplace in Burma: 'Torture, summary and arbitrary executions, forced labour, abuse of women, politically motivated arrests and detention, forced displacement, important restrictions on the freedoms of expression and association and oppression of ethnic and religious minorities . . .'

Take at random any of the reports by Amnesty International and what distinguishes the Burmese junta from other modern tyrannies is slave labour. 'Conditions in the labour camps,' says one study, 'are so harsh that hundreds of prisoners have died as a result . . . Military Intelligence personnel regularly interrogate prisoners to the point of unconsciousness. Even the possession of almost any reading material is punishable. Elderly, sick and even handicapped people are placed in leg-irons and forced to work.'

Pick up a travel brochure these days from any of the famous names in British tourism – British Airways, Orient Express, Kuoni – and there is no problem. Indeed, to British Airways Burma offers 'the ultimate in luxury' and a 'fabulous prize' for its Executive Club members. 'To find an unspoilt country today may seem impossible,' says the Orient Express brochure, 'but Burma is such a place. It has retained its charm, its fascinating traditions . . . its easygoing ways are a tonic to the Western traveller.' Moreover, this 'truly unique experience' includes a 'free lecture on Burma's history and culture'. I inquired about this lecture. It makes no mention of the momentous events of 1988.

In 1988, the year before the democracy movement in China was destroyed so publicly in Tiananmen Square, the people of Burma rose up and as many as 10,000 were killed by the army. Unlike the Chinese leadership, the generals in Rangoon moved quickly to curtail foreign media coverage. Although there was eyewitness reporting, there were no professional TV cameras and no satellite images to shock the world. Troops had orders to shoot on sight anyone with a camera. On one tape smuggled out of Rangoon, the voices of two amateur Burmese cameramen are caught at the moment they were spotted by soldiers. 'What shall we do?' asks one of them. His friend replies: 'Keep on filming until they shoot us.'

It was in April 1988 that Suu Kyi returned from England to take care of her dying mother. Her father was Aung San, the revered national hero, whose guerrillas were trained by the Japanese, then turned against them during the occupation of the Second World War. Having laid the foundations of a demo-cratic state, and negotiated independence from Britain, he was assassinated in 1947. More than 40 years later, his daughter agreed to take on leadership of a renewed democracy movement. It was her demand for the restoration of demo-cracy that led to her house arrest in 1989. However, the generals did hold elections. Having banned canvassing, threatened the electorate and disbarred and silenced Aung San Suu Kyi, they were confident they had fragmented her party, the National League for Democracy, and that their own front would gain the largest bloc of seats. The opposite happened. The NLD won 82 per cent of seats in the new parliament. Stunned, the junta responded by arresting 3,000 NLD workers and handing out prison sentences of up to 25 years to those of the new MPs who tried to establish the government.

The euphemism for oppression was now 'economic stability'. Having rein-vented themselves as the State Law and Order Council, which goes by the fine Orwellian acronym, Slorc, the generals declared Burma 'open to free enterprise'. At the same time, in order to rebuild the crumbling infrastructure – roads, bridges, airports, railways – they set about turning the country into a vast labour camp. Last year the moat around the imperial palace in Mandalay was excavated and restored almost entirely by forced labour, including chain gangs guarded by troops. When photographic evidence of this was produced, the regime claimed that 'contributing labour' was 'a noble Burmese tradition' and, anyway, many of the workers were convicted criminals who had 'volunteered to work in the open air'. In totalitarian Burma the term 'convicted criminal' can embrace someone guilty of having been elected to office or of handing out leaflets calling for democracy (five years' hard labour), or of singing a song the generals don't like (seven years' hard labour).

This has thrown up a terrible irony. Alongside the 16,000 British and Allied soldiers who died as slaves on the Japanese 'death railway' that linked Burma with Thailand during the Second World War were some 100,000 Burmese and other Asian dead. Outside the gates of the Commonwealth war cemetery at Thanbyuzayat in the south of Burma, the death railway is still there. The same rusted lines rest on the same sleepers: a life was lost for every sleeper laid, one survivor calculated. A Japanese locomotive stands as it was abandoned on the day the horror ended. It is jet black and on the track in front of it is a square of barbed wire enclosing three figures rendered in cement – a Japanese guard with a rifle and two emaciated, shaven-headed PoWs working with pickaxes.

Now history is repeating itself. An extension of this line is being built in Mon State, between the towns of Ye and Tavoy on the Andaman Sea. This is Burma's great secret. Although human rights organisations have documented the testimonies of the slave workers on the new death railway, few outsiders have seen it and the slave camps along the route. This is because much of Mon State is closed to foreigners. It is Burma's gulag.

In making our forthcoming ITV documentary, my film-making partner David Munro and I entered the country under the subterfuge of travel consultants. We headed south, leaving Rangoon well before dawn, travelling over spine-gutting roads, often without headlights. We passed watchtowers and groups of prisoners in chains, quarrying rock. Those guards at roadblocks were junior, asleep or uninterested; money fluttered across to them.

The towns in this remote part of the country are a step back in time, as if the British Raj were temporarily away at the hill stations. Ancient sewing machines whirred on balconies; the roads were filled with bicycles not cars; carbon paper, radiograms and sleeveless sweaters were for sale. Tavoy has streets of decorous teak houses, the biggest with lace iron balconies. Others are dungeon-like, with iron bars and damp trickling over torn posters of coy women holding parasols.

People considered us with due curiosity; a whole generation here has seldom laid eyes on Europeans. To talk openly to anyone is to beckon interrogation and worse. Hotels must copy guest registration forms to as many as 14 different authorities. On the day we arrived in Tavoy all 'independent travellers' were told they had to leave. Fortunately all the roads out were now closed, and the ancient Fokkers of Myanmar Airways had been commandeered by a general. We calculated that we had about a day and a night to find the railway before we were caught. Following the line of embankments north into the jungle, we succeeded in getting lost, then by chance came upon a clearing that presented what might have been a tableau of Victorian England. Scores of people were building embankments and a bridge across a dry riverbed that is now, with the arrival of the monsoon, an ochre-coloured torrent. From out of jungle so dense that its bamboo and foliage formed great wickerwork screens, they were carving the railway. A 20-foot-high embankment had been built with earth dug by hoe and hand from huge holes. The skilled were paid about 30 pence a day. The majority were slave labourers, of whom many were children. Laboriously and clumsily the child workers wrested clay from the excavations, sharing a hoe between three. One little girl in a long blue dress struggled to wield a hoe taller than herself, then fell back exhausted and, with a wince, held her aching shoulder.

The children carried heavy loads of mud mixed with straw in baskets and dishes on their heads and clearly agonised under the weight of it. They poured it into a vat and grinder, turned by two tethered oxen. The sticky clay, now almost as hard as rock, was gathered by two small children, one of them small enough to fit up to his shoulders in a hole directly beneath the grinder. Horrified, I watched a load of clay, like fresh cement, tip over him, almost burying him. I reached under his arms and pulled him out. The others laughed, as if this was normal. How many children are trapped and injured and die like that? As many as 300 adults and children have been killed or have died from disease and exhaustion, according to one estimate. There were at least 20 other bridges in the vicinity and children were working on all of them.

Every village along the way must give its labour 'voluntarily' regardless of age or the state of people's health. Advanced pregnancy is no excuse. If people protest that, as peasant farmers, their labour is all they have to keep them and their families alive, they are fined and their possessions confiscated. If a whole village objects, the head man is beaten or killed and all the houses razed.

'I saw one old man accidentally drop his load into the river,' a former civil servant told me in a nearby safe area controlled by the Karen National Union. 'As he tried to retrieve it, the soldiers shot him in the head. I could see the water turn red with his blood, then the river carried him away.'

A man who escaped with his wife told me: 'I saw people dying because of landslides or fever. Some of the bodies were never found, only the head or a foot. They didn't bother to bury the bodies properly, with a funeral. They just dug a hole and left them there.'

His wife, Min, said: 'I feel for the children. They are too young to anticipate danger, so they are vulnerable. They are the ones who die first.'

I asked her if she knew why she was being forced to work in this way. 'We were told nothing,' she said. 'We overheard we were building a railway so that a French oil company could run a pipeline through, and foreigners came to look over the site.'

The oil company is Total, which is part-owned by the French government. In partnership with the American Unocal company, Total is building a $1-billion pipeline that will carry Burma's natural gas into Thailand. The deal will give the Rangoon generals about $400 million a year over 30 years. Since they put an end to democracy in 1990, it is estimated that the Slorc have received 65 per cent of their financial backing from foreign oil companies, including Britain's Premier Oil.

In its 1993 report on human rights abuses throughout the world, the US

State Department says the Slorc 'routinely' uses slave labour and 'will use the new railway to transport soldiers and construction supplies into the pipeline area'. Unocal says reports of slave labour are a 'fabrication' and both the oil companies deny the railway is linked to the pipeline project. But more than 5,000 troops have already been shipped to the pipeline area and army patrols protect Total personnel. Although taken aback by the sudden arrival of two Europeans on the embankments, the chief engineer admitted to me that the railway was being built mainly with 'volunteers'. He said that the children made bricks for the army, which sold them to the construction company. As we talked, soldiers guarding the 'volunteers' began to emerge from their tent. We left expeditiously.

In 1993 the British trade minister Richard Needham told Parliament: 'The Government's policy is to provide no specific encouragement to British firms to trade or invest in Burma in view of the current political and economic situation there.' In the same breath he said: 'British business visitors to Rangoon can of course look to our embassy there for advice and support.' Last year most veils had dropped. The Department of Trade funded a seminar in London called 'An Introduction to Burma – The Latest Tiger Cub?' The organiser was Peter Godwin, a merchant banker and Government adviser on trade in South-East Asia. 'To be a Briton in Burma,' he told the delegates, 'is a privilege.' Godwin said he had been assured by the senior general in Slorc 'openly and categorically' that Burma's 'socialism' had been 'a mistake' and that this mistake had caused the upheavals in 1988. He made no reference to the generals murdering thousands of unarmed civilians, then throwing most of the elected government into prison. The 'good news', he said, 'is that economic growth is picking up'.

A few Western businessmen operating in Burma claim that foreign investment in the country has multiplied tenfold since 1992. 'It's not so much a gradual pick-up,' said Pat James, a Texan entrepreneur, 'as a skyrocket.' This is disputed by, among others, a recent report in *The Economist*. The World Bank and the IMF have yet to lend the generals a penny. However, what has begun in Burma is a familiar process in which a dictatorship's crimes against its people are obscured and 'forgotten' as foreign businessmen seek to justify what the East Asian governments call 'positive engagement' and the Europeans and Australians call 'critical dialogue'. The prize is a cheap labour colony that promises to undercut even China and Vietnam.

Peter Godwin had just returned from leading a Government-backed trade mission to Burma when I met him in March. Companies of the size and import-ance of GEC, Powergen and Rolls-Royce were represented. I pointed out that there was documented evidence that some 2 million people were being forced to build the infrastructure of Burma in brutal conditions so that foreign invest-ment might get off the ground. 'Isn't that a factor to you and your business colleagues?' I asked.

'I suppose it is,' he replied, 'but the involvement of foreign companies is going to improve conditions quite substantially. No foreign company is likely to employ labour under those terms.'

'But you've got to use the roads and railways.'

'Indeed.'

In spite of a certain sound and fury aimed at the regime by Madeline Albright, the US Representative at the UN, US policy is 'not to encourage or discourage' business with Burma. The EU countries have followed a similar double-faced policy. While most Western aid remains suspended, the Japanese government gives $48.7 million a year and the great *zaibatsu*, Mitsui, Mitsubishi, Honda and Nippon Steel, have offices in Rangoon. By far the biggest investor is Singapore, whose state arms company came to the Slorc's rescue in 1988 at the height of the demonstrations when troops were running out of bullets.

Burma's most profitable export is illegal. More than half the heroin reaching the streets of American and Australian cities originates in the 'golden triangle' where the borders of Burma, Laos and Thailand meet. Under the Slorc, heroin production has doubled. Two researchers, Dr Chris Beyrer and Faith Doherty, conclude from a long investigation for the South-East Asian Information Network that the Slorc have allowed heroin to circulate freely and cheaply in Burma in the hope that it 'pacifies' the rebellious young.

'At last the doors to Myanmar, the magic golden land, are open,' waxes Dr Naw Angelene, the Director of Tourism, in an official handout. 'Roads will be wider, lights will be brighter, tours will be cleaner, grass will be greener and, with more job opportunities, people will be happier.' One of the biggest foreign tour operators in Burma is the Orient Express Group, which operates 'The Road to Mandalay', a 'champagne-style cruise' between Mandalay and Pagan in a converted Rhine cruiser. The cabins, says the brochure, 'are not simply luxurious'; there is a Kipling Bar and a swimming pool.

When I found her at anchor in the heat and mosquitoes, *The Road to Mandalay* looked squat and sturdy rather than luxurious. Once on board, however, it seemed the perfect vehicle for pampering tourists in one of the world's 10 poorest countries. Like an air-conditioned bubble, it is constantly cleansed of the smells and noise and dust of the land through which it glides. In the 'staterooms' the television rises at the foot of the bed and, hey presto, there is Rupert Murdoch's satellite TV. In February, the captain of *The Road to Mandalay* welcomed his inaugural guests. 'They might have been,' wrote the *Times* travel writer Peter Hughes, 'the cast from an Edwardian novel: a prince and two princesses from the Endsleigh League of European Royalty, our own Princess Michael of Kent among them; a duke; a marche and marchese; a film star, Helena Bonham-Carter; and assorted lords and ladies whose names tended to be the same as their addresses. Those without titles merely had money.' The actual road to Mandalay has recently been converted into an expressway for tourists. For the local people forced to work on it, it is known as 'the road of no return'. According to Amnesty, two workers who tried to escape were executed by soldiers on the spot. Another eight were beaten until they were severely injured; one was hacked to death with a hoe.

Aung San Suu Kyi was two years old when her father was murdered. What distinguished the movement he founded was its complex attempt to apply a blend of Buddhism, socialism and democracy to the freely elected governments that followed. The ideas of Nehru, Sun Yat Sen, Manzini and Voltaire were adapted. Marx was virtually reinvented as a disciple of Buddha. But this flowering coincided with a period of turmoil as the ethnic peoples demanded autonomy. In March 1962 the army stepped in and seized power. Its leader, Ne Win, became Burma's Stalin. He displaced whole populations, built labour camps and filled the prisons with his enemies, real and imagined. His wars against the ethnic peoples were unrelenting and vengeful. He abolished Burma's lively free press; and along the way he made himself extremely rich. In 1984 the *Far Eastern Economic Review* reported that the privately chartered jet taking him to a Swiss health clinic 'was delayed because chests of jade and precious stones carried on board had been stacked incorrectly and had to be reloaded'. Three years later Burma ignominiously applied for Least Developed Country status so that it might seek relief on its massive foreign debt.

In 1987 the man who called himself 'Brilliant as the Sun' produced his *coup de grâce*. Without warning, he withdrew most of the country's banknotes, replacing them with new denominations that included or added up to the number nine. According to his chief astrologer, nine was his lucky number. The people of Burma did not share his luck. As most of them kept their savings in cash, most were ruined.

In a nation now so impoverished the touchpaper was lit. By March 1988 the regime was at war with the students at Rangoon University. The moment of uprising came precisely at eight minutes past eight on the morning of the eighth month of 1988. This was the auspicious time the dock workers, the 'first wave', chose to strike. Other workers followed in succession; and in subsequent days and weeks almost everyone in the cities and towns, it seemed, showed a courage equal to those who stormed the Berlin Wall the following year. Without guns, ordinary people began to reclaim their country.

Then the slaughter began. The army fired point blank at the crowds and bayoneted those who fell. In Thailand and Norway, I have interviewed the exiled witnesses to these epic events, most of them speaking publicly for the first time. 'One of my friends was shot in the head right there, in front of me,' said Ko Htun Oo, a former student. 'Two girls and a monk were shot next to him.' Another student, Aye Chan, said: 'A lot of flame was coming out of the crematorium which was surrounded by troops. They weren't even identifying bodies, so the parents would never know. The dead and wounded were all mixed up. They just burned them alive.' Another spoke of hearing a wounded schoolboy cry out for his mother as he was buried alive in the cemetery: 'The caretaker didn't want to do it,' he said, 'but the soldiers had guns pointed at him.'

Now well into his eighties, Ne Win remains the centre of the Slorc's power. His former aide, the secret police chief, General Khin Nyunt, is 'Secretary One'. Behind sunglasses Khin Nyunt's pudgy face appears at least five times a day in the *New Light of Myanmar*. His seminal work goes under the catchy title *The Conspiracy of Treasonous Minions within the Myanmar Naing-Ngan and Traitorous Cohorts Abroad*. One wonders how many of the gallery of faces in its pages are dead. Pol Pot and his gang turned out similar tracts. This is the man whose job is the silencing of 'heretics': those like the lawyer Nay Min, serving 14 years for 'spreading rumours' to the BBC, and the Unicef researcher Khin Zaw Win, serving 15 years for sending 'fabricated news' to the UN, and the writer San San Nwe, sentenced to 10 years for 'spreading false information injurious to the state'. Last year the general subjected a US senator, John McCain, to an hour-long harangue about how the Slorc were holding back the 'red tide', then played him a videotape showing 'communists' beheading villagers with machetes: footage so sickening that McCain's wife had to leave the room. The aim was to convince the senator that Aung San Suu Kyi was a front for 'red subversives'.

The taxi dropped us far from the long green fence of number 54 University Avenue. Our cameras were concealed in shoulder bags; a figure in sunglasses stood up to watch us. We peered through a hole in the corrugated-iron gate and a face asked our names. Inside, another sunglasses told us to write down our names and occupations. We then crossed an imaginary line into friendly territory and were greeted warmly by Suu Kyi's assistant, U Win Htein, who was arrested with her and spent six years in prison, mostly in solitary confinement. He led us into the house, a stately pile fallen on hard times, overlooking a garden that tumbles down to Inya Lake and to a trip-wire, a reminder that this was one woman's prison.

Aung San Suu Kyi wore silk and orchids in her hair. She is a striking, glamorous figure who looks much younger than her 50 years and appears at first to carry her suffering lightly. Only in repose does her face offer a glimpse of the cost and the grit that has seen her through, though when she laughs this vanishes; it is like a blind closed and open.

We talked in a room dominated by a huge portrait of the father she barely knew, painted in the style of Andy Warhol by the artist Soe Moe at the height of the 1988 uprising. I asked her if her release from house arrest was a cynical exercise by the regime to give itself a human face. 'I think they also miscalculated,' she replied, 'that the National League for Democracy was a spent force and that releasing me was not going to make any difference . . .'

'But with such a brute force confronting you, how do you reclaim the power you won at the ballot box?'

'We are not the first people to face this dilemma. In Buddhism we are taught the four basic ingredients for success: first, you must have the will to want it;

then you must have the right kind of attitude; then you must have the persever-
ance; then wisdom . . .'

What struck me was her extraordinary optimism, fuelled, it seemed, by her
Buddhist principles that draw a stark contrast with the realities outside. This
changed when I mentioned foreign investment. I said that the Foreign Office
minister Jeremy Hanley had told Parliament that 'through commercial contacts
with democratic nations such as Britain, the Burmese people will gain experience
of democratic principles'.

She laughed. 'Not in the least bit, because the so-called market economy is
only open to some. Investors will help only a small élite to get richer and richer.
This works against the very idea of democracy because the gap between rich
and poor is growing all the time. The same applies to tourism. They should
stay away until we are a democracy. Look at the forced labour that is going on
all over the country. A lot of it is aimed at the tourist trade. It's very painful.
Roads and bridges are built at the expense of the people. If you cannot provide
one labourer you are fined. If you cannot afford the fine, the children are forced
to labour.'

In his moving introduction to *Freedom from Fear*, a collection of essays by and
about Aung San Suu Kyi, Michael Aris quotes from a letter she wrote him
shortly before they married: 'I only ask one thing: that should my people need
me, you would help me to do my duty by them . . . if we love and cherish each
other as much as we can while we can, I am sure love and compassion will
triumph in the end.'

I reminded her about this. 'I asked him,' she said, 'to be sympathetic when
the time came . . . and he said, "yes" . . . During my house arrest the longest
period we were out of touch was two years and four or five months. I missed
my family, and I worried about my sons very much because the young one was
only 12, and he had to be put into boarding school. But then I'd remind myself
that the families of my colleagues in prison were far worse off.'

She revealed that in her isolation she had difficulty breathing and would lie
awake listening to the thump-thump of her heart, wondering if it would fail.
There were times when she did not get enough to eat and her weight fell to
90 pounds.

'Weren't you terrified?' I asked.

'When I was small,' she said, 'it was in this house that I conquered my fear
of the dark. I just wandered around in the darkness and by the end, I knew all
the demons weren't there.'

During the first years of her house arrest soldiers were ordered to lie with
their ears to the ground so as to detect her 'tunnelling' to the house next door.
They failed to grasp that she had no intention of escaping, or seeking exile.
Outside, her name became a byword; and people would pass her house just to
be reassured by the sound of her playing her piano. When it stopped there were
rumours that she was dead. 'That was when the string broke,' she said. 'I was

pumping too hard. I have a hot temper, so I took it out on the piano!'

'Will Burma be free in the foreseeable future?'

'Yes!' she replied unhesitatingly.

'That's not just a dream?'

'No, I calculate it from the will of the people and the current of world opinion
. . . I knew I'd be free . . . some day.'

The next day I joined the crowd outside her gate waiting for her to speak.
The people were different from any I had seen; they were smiling, talking freely
with each other, as if waiting for a gig to start. There were betel-nut sellers
and cheroot sellers and a man with a block of ice ingeniously balanced in a red
sock, selling cups of cold water. With the grace and courtesy that is never
deferential and is so much part of the Burmese character, people made way for
the foreign Gulliver, offering a cushion for me to sit on.

When Aung San Suu Kyi appeared she was flanked by two other figures of
principle and courage: General Tin Oo and U Kyi Maung, a former colonel,
the vice-chairmen of the NLD, both of whom have spent years in prison. The
clapping and whooping lasted minutes. She now looked grey and drawn. Yet
she had people in stitches as she carefully mocked the dictatorship, using irony
and parable (so I was told; she spoke only in Burmese). As they laughed I
counted the spooks in sunglasses, filming, photographing, watching. Their arbitrary power was like a presence. Recently a young man tried to ease the crush
by moving the barrier and was bundled away and given a two-year sentence.

At the end of her speech people asked questions. She leaned over the spikes
in the fence and listened intently, replying expressively. An old monk pushed
through and asked her if she would join him in prayer; and she did. Most did
not linger. A man told me he never went straight home after a meeting. 'If
they follow you,' he said, 'things start to happen. The power goes off; the kids
are sent home crying from school.'

When I asked him if 1988 could happen again, this time successfully, he
said: 'Imagine a zebra crossing. The traffic never seems to stop for the pedestrians.
One or two dart across. The majority wait impatiently at the kerb, then they
surge across, until the traffic has lost all its power. Well, we are all back at the
kerb now, waiting impatiently.' At that, he looked over my shoulder and walked
quickly away.

Desmond Tutu – like Aung San Suu Kyi, a Nobel Peace Prize-winner – said
recently: 'International pressure can change the situation in Burma. Tough
sanctions, not constructive engagement, finally brought about a new South
Africa. This is the only language that tyrants understand.'

What is hopeful is that there is the promise of sanctions in a remarkable
disinvestment campaign already well under way in America. Based on the boycott
of apartheid South Africa, selective purchasing laws have been enacted by a
growing number of US cities, including San Francisco. These make illegal
municipal contracts with companies that trade with or invest in Burma. Last

week New York State was considering similar legislation; and one of the biggest investors in Burma, Pepsi Cola, with its headquarters in upstate New York, has withdrawn.

A Massachusetts Representative, Byron Rushing, who has written a selective purchasing law for his own state, told me: 'In the case of South Africa, we were able to put pressure on a whole range of companies, like General Motors, Coca-Cola, Pepsi Cola, and most eventually withdrew. And that really added to the pressure on the white government. That was a victory. As for Burma, it's not going to happen overnight, but we have started. The civilised world should follow.' ●

Dunblane

Crime and punishment

25 November 1995

Duncan Campbell

Nightmares on Cromwell Street

I n the early seventies, I used to go down with a group of friends to a cottage in the Forest of Dean in Gloucestershire most summer weekends. I'm sure we were fairly insensitive towards the locals and I'm sure they regarded us as middle-class London hippies up to no good. But sometimes, late on Saturday nights, a group of lads from places like Littledean and Mitcheldean and Cinderford, fortified by a few flagons of cider, would knock on the cottage door.

They would have sideburns as thick as their West Country accents and it was always quite clear what they were after. They knew that women with long hair were staying there, women who would sunbathe without their clothes on. They knew about these hippie girls and had read about 'free love' in the papers. They would ask nudging questions about where people slept, clearly hoping that one of the women would toss her long hair back, stop listening to the Incredible String Band and take them by the hand upstairs. I went abroad, the cottage was sold and I never really thought of the Forest of Dean or Littledean, Mitcheldean and Cinderford again.

That was until two months ago, when the Forest of Dean and those long-forgotten places cropped up time and again in the trial of Rosemary West. Girls had hitchhiked from Mitcheldean, girls had run away from Cinderford, relatives had moved to the Forest of Dean. Then the image returned of those young men with their Fred West sideburns and their desperate desire to be part of a sexual revolution that was being waved in their faces in every newspaper and every record store. At the same time those young men were stumbling optimistically up the hill to the cottage, Fred and Rosemary West were opening the door of their Ford Popular and beckoning girls inside.

What we learned during the trial was that Fred West fantasised about young women at the same time and in the same way: they were all interested in sex, these girls, they forced themselves on him, he told the police in the tape-recorded interviews, they wanted it so bad. Poor Fred, he was saying about himself, they grabbed his flies and he swatted them away and killed them by mistake. They were horrible lies told about girls who must have struggled frantically to escape from him, but they fitted his fantasy of a world where every woman was grateful for the attentions of a sturdy country lad.

Perhaps the Wests are our Mansons, turning what was happening sexually in the country at the time into a distorted image of itself. In the same way that Manson manipulated foolish women, so Fred did with the sad succession of women who married or wanted to marry him and whom he despised or killed. Every generation has its demonic figures and Fred and Rose may now be ours, our Mansons from the Forest of Dean, where Dennis Potter always hinted they might be lurking.

As each witness in the trial appeared, I would make a brief note beside their names in my notebook so that I could recall them after their evidence. Most notes just indicated 'fair hair/ponytail/leather jacket' or 'smart/black hair/fringe/Welsh'. But flipping through seven books' worth of trial, I noticed how often the phrase 'dead eyes' cropped up. So many of the people who had survived, the 'lucky' ones – if it is lucky to escape with just a few years of sexual abuse or with only being tied up, gagged and raped rather than murdered and beheaded – were clearly deadened by their experience.

So does it deaden everyone who touches it or reads about it? The jurors were offered counselling at the end of the case and I imagine some will take it, for they looked weary. We are not allowed to interview them and we know them only by the nicknames we gave them –'Julie Andrews', 'the old codgers' and so on. Relatives of the victims and police officers have also been given help. Even the journalists covering the case were offered it, though there were no takers.

But of course, the case invades the brain. On a mundane level, I can't now dissociate masking tape from the masks that gagged the murdered girls, see a DIY sign without thinking of Fred, the DIY king of Cromwell Street, or spot a hitchhiker without a thought of the cheery bell-bottomed teenagers in their maxi-coats and platform shoes who disappeared. Of course, it invades dreams: one of the few women reporters who covered the whole trial dreamt of leaving a supermarket with bags of shopping and being approached by Fred West with an offer of help. I dreamt of sifting through earth and finding fingers buried in it while a little girl sat beside me and wept. We have heard horrible things but there are horrible things all around us and to hear them is not to suffer them or to love someone who has suffered them.

So I feel a terrible irritation when I turn on the late-night television and see the commentators – for some strange reason in this secular society they tend to be chaps with their collars on back to front – who have been wheeled on to talk about the Moral Issues, and hear those phrases rolling off the conveyor belt. The Heart of Darkness, the Nature of Evil, the Loss of Innocence. For this was not a case which can be simply placed in a little box labelled 'evil' that can then be closed and locked away.

And I feel the same sense of irritation with all those other commentators who are magically able to read the soul of the Princess of Wales one day and the mind of Rosemary West the next. These are the people who fix the blame on the sixties or the social workers or whatever dusty prejudice they keep at their elbow for such occasions. (One columnist blamed the 'sixties generation' in one sentence and in the next wrote: 'They wanted to be free. They thought the family was tyranny.' Do these people read what they write? For every West child, murdered or living, tyranny was *exactly* what the family was.)

It may seem shocking to say, but there was quite a lot of laughter during the case. When the Wests' son-in-law, Chris Davis, was talking about Heather West's disappearance he said he had been told that she would phone home 'well lubricated'. Could he explain to the jury what that phrase meant, asked Brian Leveson, the crown counsel. 'Pissed,' he replied. When the lodgers, who had been young men in Cromwell Street in the seventies and now looked like Joe Cocker, told how Mrs West had visited each in their beds on their first night in their new lodgings, there were suppressed chuckles at the notion. Here was male fantasy made flesh.

But coverage of the case has brought disapproval from many quarters. It has been suggested that we have heard too much of it, that what happened was a one-off, and to cover it in such detail can serve only to distress or even provoke imitations. The argument goes that there has been voyeurism in the elaboration of what the Wests did and that the press has fallen victim to it.

People who argue this have no difficulty about the coverage of the atrocities in Bosnia – although Bosnians would say that there has not been enough of this in the British press – or cruelties committed abroad in civil wars or revolutions. But there is a feeling that the West case was low-rent, sordid, best passed over as the aberration of two wicked, ill-educated people, unlikely to happen again.

The Wests may indeed be a one-off 'earthquake' but many of the fault lines around which they operated still exist. No, there may not be any other couple routinely murdering young girls and burying them beneath their barbecue, but there are thousands of children still being regularly abused by their parents – parents who, like Fred and Rose, disapproved of drugs. Parents who tell their daughters, as Fred did: 'Dads do it best.'

No, there may not be many couples who cruise the back roads looking for runaways to abduct, but the ripples of the case wash over into almost every part of our public life. One of the Wests' surviving victims, Miss A, explained that she did not bother reporting the attack to the police at the time because girls in care were held in such low regard. Within a week of her giving this evidence a strange alliance had ambushed the Domestic Violence Bill and ensured that girls in care may continue to see themselves as worthless because they are so far outside the family.

It is not only in the issues of child abuse, of runaways and children in care that the case has resonances, however minor. The day after we heard the evidence of a frightened 16-year-old, who spoke about Fred West pursuing her in his van and trying to look up her skirt as she cycled home from school, two newspapers – one broadsheet, one tabloid – showed photographs of Hillary Clinton and a *Brookside* actress which showed their knickers with a suitably sniggering caption attached, the message being that it's clever to look up girls' skirts.

. They were human beings, the Wests – Fred fixed people's gutters, Rose rang her son's girlfriend's mother to complain about him being out late when he had school the next morning – yet they carried out the sort of atrocities that, as Brian Leveson put it, were 'beyond words'.

It is only in the detail that we can decode their lives: that Fred and Rose signed letters to each other with the words 'ever-worshipping'; that she kept in her attic for more than 20 years a newspaper cutting of their sexual assault on a girl; that runaway girls in care regarded Rose as 'a big sister'; that the abused and raped daughter Anne Marie saw herself as a 'daddy's girl'. It is perfectly understandable that people do not wish to read some of these details – and I have never had more people tell me that they *haven't* read what I've written – but to ascribe base motives to everyone who is curious about them seems patronising.

The Wests were not 'loners', those people like Dennis Nilsen, Peter Sutcliffe, Colin Ireland, Hindley and Brady, whom normally we find reassuring to blame for our darkest crimes. They were jolly, married family folk building extensions, installing avocado-coloured bathroom suites and living a stroll away from the centre of one of our cathedral cities. One of the reasons they survived undetected for so long, one of the reasons for all those pale women with 'dead eyes' in the witness box was because hardly anyone, over the 20 years they plundered and tortured and killed, was very curious about them until the digging started.

The moment before a jury returns their verdict is a strange one, like waiting for a hanging. The words that spring to mind are mostly clichés: silences are 'eerie', moods are 'sombre', faces of defendants are 'impassive'. I have seen – and felt – great elation at a murder conviction. I can remember being delighted when two young East Enders were recently jailed for life for putting an Asian cab driver in the boot of his car and pushing it into the Thames for no other reason than that he was Asian. But after the eight weeks of the horrors there seemed little real relish in the court as Mrs West's chest heaved with the realisation that someone had removed her free will in a less painful but almost as permanent a way as so many of those girls had lost theirs.

The first person I bumped into when I left court after the final verdicts had been delivered was Kathryn Halliday, one of the chief prosecution witnesses against Mrs West. She had had a consenting affair with Mrs West – 'see my missus, she'll sort you out', Fred had told her when they first met, words that became a catchphrase for reporters covering the trial. It was that kind of trial.

She had arrived too late for the verdicts so I told her of the convictions and asked her reaction. Which paper was I from? The *Guardian*. 'I'll give you a reaction for £200,' she said before retreating into the arms of a minder. A few minutes later she was indeed giving her reaction: tears, offers to pull the rope if capital punishment was restored.

Yet this was a woman who had had an affair with Rosemary West over a period of months. Her willingness to 'pull the rope', like her willingness to squeeze the last few bob from her story, is an indication of how the Wests have confused so many people.

'All those concerned in the case of Rosemary West . . .' was the phrase that got us to our feet in the cafeteria of the court as we stumbled back in to hear our daily dose of pornography. We can now say goodbye to the night porter in the Winchester hotel and walk away from it, but that is no reason why we should not all still, in many different ways, be concerned. •

. . . .

18 May 1996

Marian Partington
Salvaging the sacred

Lucy Partington was my sister, four years younger than me. On 27 December 1973, she left a friend's house in time to walk to the bus stop in Evesham Road, Cheltenham, intending to catch the 10.15pm bus back to our home in Gretton. She didn't catch the bus. She was 21 years old and in her final year of an English degree at Exeter University. She was reported missing and a national search was launched. She became one of thousands of 'missing people' for 20 years.

On 4 March 1994 – her birthday – Frederick West told the investigation team in Gloucester that there were more bodies in the basement of 25 Cromwell Street, and that one of them was Lucy's. The details about the criminals and the crime have been on general release in the media for several months at a time over the past two years. They warranted a 'V chip' or at least an 18 certificate. Or will the 'V chip' apply only to fiction?

The grotesque details surrounding Lucy's death are part of my life. I can't pretend it didn't happen. I work hard to understand. I remind myself that we can never know exactly what went on. But there is something about trying to get the measure of it before I can let go of it. It is vast and slippery. It is sticky and staining.

Most of Lucy's bones, her poetry and her soul, have survived. We will never know how she coped with what must be one of the worst possible ways to die. But let us not forget that many women, children and men are violently abused and killed in war, domestic violence and random murder every day.

There are many theories about the short-term and long-term effects of trauma, and many of them are pessimistic. Yet the Chinese word for 'crisis' has two meanings: 'danger' and 'opportunity for change'. I feel it is time to speak about my way through all this. I have been given a valuable chance to deepen my powers of compassion by facing the reality of my deepest fears. I am offering my attempt to find words and images to describe significant moments in my grapplings as I struggle to come to terms with what is essentially beyond reason and in many ways beyond words.

But words must be found. There must be something for all of us to learn

Marian and Lucy Partington

from this profoundly shocking profanity before it gets buried under the concrete of fear, prejudice or, even worse, indifference. I am offering you where I have got to so far in all this. It is speaking about Lucy's truth, in her life and in her death. It is about poetry and transformation. It is about my quest to find meaning by trying to remain open to the pain, the joy, the rage, the grief and what lies beyond. It is about living with the reality of violence, rape, torture and murder, trying to face up to it and trying to transform it. It is not always rational. I have followed my heart. It is a rite of passage. It is purgatorial. It is about time. It is about salvaging the sacred.

When I say, 'My sister was murdered; she was one of the Wests' victims,' it makes my throat ache. It was easier to say, 'My sister disappeared,' but more difficult to live with that sense of unresolved loss.

Lucy was lucky to come from a family who loved her. We are led to believe that the majority of the young women in this case were not so fortunate. 'They' managed to get lost without many people noticing or searching. 'They' did not have much of a sense of purpose or direction in their lives. 'They' have been labelled as 'natural victims'. If someone chooses to hitchhike, does that mean that she is more deserving of a terrible end to her life than someone like Lucy, who had strong opinions about not hitchhiking? Every one of the girls and young women in 'the West case' had a right to live. Heather, Charmaine, Lynda, Juanita, Therese, Shirley, Carol, Alison, Shirley Ann. Their lives had equal value. It seems important to remember this.

When Lucy 'disappeared', the dilemma caused by the huge sense of loss with no opportunity to grieve properly didn't fade as the years went by. On an emotional level I hardly dared to imagine that she had been murdered, and sometimes I hoped she was still alive. For a while I wondered if she had gone off to join a nunnery . . . or committed suicide. One of the most painful aspects of her disappearance was the feeling that we had never paid tribute, as a family, to her life. The subject almost became taboo. Part of me was stuck in the past. Part of me was terrified of us all dying and never knowing what had happened to her; no chance to honour her life. Eventually, 20 years after her disappearance, most of our family gathered together to plant a special tree in memory of Lucy.

This is how my daughter Marigold described it two years ago when she was 16: 'Although it seemed like a good idea to put Lucy to rest, the atmosphere felt really uncomfortable. Something wasn't quite right, because everyone found it really difficult to talk about her. This made me realise how painful the situation was and how devastating it was for them not knowing what had happened to her, and perhaps never knowing.'

It is very difficult to find the words or an image to describe the pain and disorientation of one's sister simply disappearing without trace, for 20 years. It's a bit like trying to search for a body that is trapped somewhere beneath the frozen Arctic Ocean, as the freeze continues and the ice thickens and there is no sign of a thaw, no sign of a seal hole. The features of that world become distorted as the seasons pass and the ice builds up, and you have to go inside to get warm if you want to survive and carry on. But you have to be ready for the thaw, for the rescue. Somewhere inside I became disconnected from the past and disabled by the future.

However, two months after our tree-planting ceremony we began to find out what had happened to her. I kept a diary at that time. Here are a few jottings. The only words that came to me at that time are mostly brief and factual, the result of a state of shock and a certain amount of denial.

Tuesday 1 March 1994 Phone call from Mum warning me that the press are suggesting that the third unidentified body that has been dug up at 25 Cromwell Street might be Lucy. They have been hassling her about it. The police haven't been in touch.

Wednesday 2 March Came across a paper at work and read about the three bodies. Date of unidentified body. Female in late twenties. That evening phoned Mum and said I felt we should contact the police.

Thursday 3 March Contacted the police in Gloucester. They said that they were following a line of inquiry and that they were almost certain that it was not Lucy. Because it's Lucy's birthday tomorrow and because the press speculation and horror of it all is stirring up our pain and anxiety, I decide to go and spend the day with Mum.

Friday 4 March Lucy's birthday. Radio news before I set off has put the dates back on the third body (now died any time after 1972, body in early twenties). Mention that West lived in Bishop's Cleeve, which is on the bus route to Gretton from Cheltenham, is making me sure that this must be to do with Lucy. Spent the day keeping busy but feeling a terrible sense of unease and dread.

Saturday 5 March 10.15am phone call from the police saying that they would like to come over to talk to us. They have some 'news' for us. That half-hour of waiting for them to arrive was full of a terrible restlessness and anxiety . . . palpitations and nausea. The numbness and muteness of shock began to invade. Two youngish plainclothes policemen arrived. They introduce themselves as Brian Smith ('Smudger') and Russell Williams. I notice Brian's polished brown shoes and his red tie and the scar on Russell's face. There is a pause. Then Russell confirms our worst fears. Fred West has been talking to the police and has told them that there are more bodies in the basement and that one of them is called Lucy. They have begun to dig. It was a lovely sunny afternoon and I felt like going for a walk up Gretton Hill. However, we went shopping. Denial was setting in. Numerous messages on the answering machine on our return. The Pain Vultures sounding as if it's unquestionable that we should call them back (TV and tabloids). We don't. By now they know that three more bodies have been recovered and that two families in Gloucestershire have been informed. Talk to Dad; he will come by train on Monday. Phoned Nick to say what has happened and that I must stay longer. I hardly slept that night. I felt a paralysing feeling of weight, fear and a pain in my heart. This is enormous. Shock brings you into the present like giving birth. All your energy goes into focusing on surviving. Some people die of it.

The parents of the 'other student', Therese Siegenthaler, died of grief before they knew what had happened to their beloved daughter.

Sunday 6 March Decide to go to Gloucester police station. Spent two hours with John Bennett as he tried to explain the complexity of the case, especially in relation to police competition with cheque-book journalists.

We carried on south to break the news to two of my children who were boarding at a Quaker school. I was very anxious that they might find out by watching the six o'clock news. We had to get there before it broke. By the time we had arrived they had already found out by phoning their stepfather. It was hard to leave them there, but we agreed that it would be the best solution for all of us. I also realised that their main concern was for my well-being. I have to find a way through that is positive but honest, for their sakes too. That has been one of the biggest challenges.

That night I lit a candle and prayed. I didn't watch the news.

My daughter has described her experience of this in a very moving speech that she composed and read out for the Annual Dymond Speech Competition. It said a lot to me about her bravery and the caring atmosphere of her school. It nurtures pupils, encourages them to question social and spiritual issues. The reality of Lucy's death has presented us all with huge questions about life and death.

Tuesday 8 March Back in Wales. Went to have my hair cut. I wanted to have it shaved off as a gesture to the world that I was grieving, that something huge had happened and that I wasn't the same as I was before it happened. I am beginning to understand how ill-equipped we are as a society for coping with mourning. It would be helpful to bring back some external sign that someone is grieving. Black clothing has lost its significance since the Goths' fashion. While my hair was being cut (very short but not shaved) the news about Cromwell Street came on in the background. My hairdresser asked me what I thought about the awful goings-on in Gloucester. I gulped and said something inane, thinking: 'Does she really want to know?'

Friday 11 March From the depth of suffering comes a release and a purification. The reality of Lucy's death rather than the imaginings of 20 years brings a renewal of the preciousness of each moment of life. I must find the courage to go on and face the worst kind of death imaginable and somehow try to understand it.

For the past two years we have all been plunged into the powerful rapids of the thaw, each of us finding a way to stay afloat. However, under the turbulence was a wonderful surprise: a huge lake of warmth and compassion, glowing, lapping, gently sustaining. It has been there throughout, sometimes in the material form of letters, phone calls, conversations, hugs. Sometimes it is less tangible but is to do with the best in humanity, the choice to send love in thoughts and prayers. Some of the communications were from people we hadn't heard from for 20 years. We feel so deeply grateful for that demonstration of support. It made a huge difference.

The closer I get to accepting Lucy's death, the more I can remember about our childhood. Images come floating back. We grew up in a converted cider-mill in the middle of a Cotswold village. Our bedrooms were once storerooms for the apples, small with thick walls and tiny windows. Sometimes we would roast a few of the windfalls from the orchard on sticks, watching the juice spit in the flames and the skins bubble and blacken. Sometimes we would crush the apples in one of the cider presses, making the juice trickle around the stone groove, which was patterned with yellow lichens. This brew was known as Black Lady, and we would take it in turns to sip the sour, gritty liquid, pretending it was a rare elixir. We often played games to do with getting around the 'big room' without touching the ground. We had the freedom to explore the hill, making slides in the woods and swinging off creepers. We skidded around the 'courtyard' on tricycles, veering on to two wheels around the sharpest corner past the lavender bush. There was a perfume of lavender and wallflowers in the summer, and the sound of the pressure cooker hissing with soup or stew.

I remember a massacre of guinea pigs by a fox. Lucy carefully buried each mauled corpse. A close childhood friend told us about another incident with a dead guinea pig. 'I was scared to kiss him as he was dead. Lucy was very angry with me. She told me fiercely that just because something dies, it doesn't mean that you should stop loving it, and that everyone deserves to be kissed before going to Heaven.'

We had a raft made of oil cans and planks of wood from the farm, which provided endless entertainment on the pond – ranging from timeless contemplation of newts, lying on our fronts gazing into the still water, to rougher battles that usually ended up with someone falling in. I can still remember the smell of that muddy, weedy water.

In teenage years we spent less time doing things together.

Murder in the Dark and Postman's Knock with our cousins and local village friends were always popular games as we moved into adolescence. I was always off riding our pony. I remember that Lucy always seemed to be copying what I was doing (like learning the viola), which was irritating. Actually she was going her own way and writing sophisticated poetry. I was not kind to my younger sister at times. I don't feel guilty now, just sad that we didn't share more time, express more love.

By the time that Lucy was 21 years old, we were both studying English at university (I'd had a few diversions on the way . . . well, it was the late sixties!), both in our final year. I was in London and she was in Exeter. We enjoyed reading and discussing T S Eliot together because we loved the concept of 'the still point of the turning world' (*The Four Quartets*). We were fascinated by the exploration of the intersection of time with eternity. Lucy's focus was on truth and beauty. She was single-mindedly and passionately exploring the deeper meaning of life; immersed in art, literature and religion. Somehow she was untouched by the impact of the sixties and yet very much in touch with deeper values, which she expressed in a way that was 'indelible' (to use a word chosen by one of her friends). She was emerging into adulthood with a powerful inquiring mind and a sense of vision.

During her last free evening, 27 December 1973, Lucy visited a friend in Cheltenham. She left in time to catch the 10.15 bus back to Gretton. Her satchel contained my last present to her. It was a Victorian cut-glass jar, just the right size to hold a nightlight candle. It was the colour of amethyst, and could be hung on a Christmas tree or in a window by its wire handle, casting a soothing, pale-purple glow resonant of sunlight shining through stained glass in a place of worship – meditative, or maybe the colour of the air at dawn, just before the sun appears. Lucy had been delighted with it, and talked of using it as her nightlight when she was back in her hall of residence after the Christmas holiday.

Also in her bag was a book called *Pearl* (this medieval allegory is about the premature death of a pure maiden or a young child and explores her father's grief and his journey towards consolation).

Finally, there was the letter of application to the Courtauld Institute of Art to do a postgraduate course in medieval art. It was never posted.

This is where, for me, it all goes into slow motion. The moment when Lucy, satchel swinging on her shoulder, hurried through the darkest of nights – there was a national power cut due to the fuel crisis – intending to post the letter before the bus came. The moment when Lucy's life met its opposite.

The gargoyles came to life and destroyed her.

Euphemisms serve to numb the senses and present the unpresentable. Maybe that is the best I can do. No, try again. I am avoiding it. Put it into words.

It is medieval hell. It smacks of concentration camps and nuclear bombs.

I am trying to imagine the moment when she was abducted from her own direction in life and debased into a physical object to be treated as mere flesh and bones for the gratification of some other human beings whose quest was the opposite to hers. They stole her, gagged her, tied her up, toyed with her, raped her, tortured her and, at some unknown time, killed her.

They didn't know the beauty of her soul.

They caused her unimaginable physical and emotional suffering. How long was she kept alive, unable to scream or struggle? I pray that her recent conversion to Roman Catholicism gave her some moments of strength. They beheaded and dismembered her and stuffed her into a small hole, surrounded by leaking sewage pipes – head first, face down, still gagged. Her flesh decomposed into a tarry black slime that stained the clay walls of the hole and coated the bones. The rope that held her in bondage, two hairgrips, a few strands of hair and the masking-tape gag survived, with most of her bones. Who knows what happened to her missing bones?

Did the Wests read the newspaper reports during the national search, and see her photograph stuck to trees and walls? We searched for her, desperately.

We lost her for 20 years. How many people knew she was there but didn't say anything?

I am speaking from my heart about what we lost. Lucy had kindness, sensitivity, humour, warmth. The photograph that you see (page 141) was taken in the summer of 1973 by my father during a visit to him in Yorkshire. We were at Fountains Abbey. It was the last time we spent together on our own. Lucy had me labelled as an incorrigible Romantic. The underlying implication was that I was a bit undisciplined and prone to Flights of Fancy and Imagination. I gently teased her for being a bit on the Classical side, preferring a Clear Structure and Lots of Discipline. We talked a lot about our parents and tried to understand why they had got divorced. We were beginning to re-form and deepen our relationship. I was the one who hitchhiked everywhere, explored flower power and fashion, lived with my boyfriend. Lucy claimed to 'do the opposite' of those around her. She was renowned for being 'sensible'. She protected her vulnerability with an acerbic wit and an ability to be witheringly critical. Her attitude towards me seemed to be a mixture of disapproval and admiration. I was beginning to appreciate her company and develop a great respect for her.

In a letter written to a friend, dated 1 June 1973, from Upton Pyne, Exeter, she wrote: 'I think I have changed quite a lot in the last few months, not fundamentally, but in the way of a general softening-up of sharp edges, and being more accepting.' She spoke about her conversion to Roman Catholicism: 'Although I still can't bear the idea of being a convert, I'm extremely happy about it and can't think why I didn't do something about it sooner.' In the same letter she spoke of one of her tutors. 'One of his poems, which for some reason incorporates a lot of American jazz idiom, ends:

> stick around, puss-cats
> we're all in this together

and has almost become the motto of the medieval department. I frequently mutter it to myself as I bicycle dangerously along the New North Road.' Later in the letter she refers to the 'medieval group', which 'has, from being such unpromising material, as I thought, turned into a very friendly company'.

She wrote about the impending finals (which she never had the opportunity to take): 'Just wait until the finals. Everyone will have forgotten about this year and no one will credit my predictions. It's sheer waste of time and crying in the wilderness to tell all these clever people that they're going to bluff their way through some more exams just like they have and always will do.'

Talking more of the course, she said: 'The most enjoyable literature studies have been the lyric and the romance, and almost all the art has been good. We went on a field trip to the Gloucester area for a weekend, and I was amazed how much we had absorbed and could apply.'

Crime and punishment

June 1994

The 'remains' have not been released for burial. The careful plans for the funeral have been put on hold. So Lizzie (another close friend of Lucy), Chloe (my dear friend), my mother and I decided to go ahead with our memorial gathering to celebrate Lucy's life, even though we had intended it to be after the funeral. On a hot afternoon in July, 130 people gathered together at the Friends' Meeting House in Cheltenham. My mother, in her introduction to Lucy's poems, said: 'Members of our family, childhood friends, school friends, university friends and teachers spoke eloquently and beautifully about their memories of Lucy, touching on every facet of her complex character. She lived again for us and we all came away feeling truly uplifted.'

Thank you, everyone, for that display of love. It was truly inspiring and a great moment of healing for all of us. As my daughter reminded us in her speech, quoting from the Quaker Peace Testimony: 'All the darkness in the world cannot put out the light of one candle.'

A friend of mine who also became one of Lucy's friends said this about her: 'She was like a flame and implacably true. There was no place in her life for convenient compromise. I think we should see her life as a life completed, short though it was, not as a life disrupted and cut off too soon. She had, in a way, reached a culminating point where her early life was complete, leaving her ready for something quite new. The gifts she brought with her and which she gave to us, as well as her example, will stay with us, and no one who knew her will ever forget her nor remain untouched by her.'

The significance of the trip to Gloucester that Lucy mentioned in her letter was not lost on those who attended the memorial gathering. One friend said: 'A few weeks ago my eye was caught by an article in one of the papers. It related a visit that the author had made to a number of medieval churches in the Hereford and Gloucestershire area. And it took me back on a journey that we had made 21 years ago this summer to see those very same churches, Kilpeck, Much Marcle – I'm sure you are familiar with this area. It was a field trip for the medieval group; we went around and looked at the churches and enjoyed the things that Lucy liked very much. Looking back on it now, it seemed very much a time of innocence. The sort of purity and innocence that has been mentioned already today, very much captures how it feels to me as I look back on it. It was much more related to the end of our childhood than to the beginning of adulthood and what went after it. I think maybe for us Lucy's disappearance marked the first rumblings, if you like, from the other world, or the underworld of uncertainty and suffering and loss and grief – and maybe even death, we had not encountered until then.'

May 1994

The legal process that we were trapped in moved slowly, beyond our control. I arranged to go to Cardiff with two close friends to perform another ritual. It was time to rescue and protect, in some way, Lucy's physical remains. We went in the spirit of love with a need to make the experience more real and personal. We had waited 20 years to know where Lucy was and we still couldn't have a funeral. The investigation team at Gloucester kindly made the practical arrangements.

I would like to thank the dear man who allowed us to go beyond merely sitting in a chapel of rest next to a full-sized coffin covered with a purple cloth fringed with gold tassels. I will never forget the look of understanding that came into his eyes when I emphasised that I wanted to place some special objects in with Lucy's bones. I know that some people might not understand my need to do this, but I have been pleasantly surprised by the number of people who did. It was a chance to love and cherish what was left of her. It was a chance to act in a situation that was still out of our hands. It was a chance to reclaim her from her murderers and the hugely disrespectful, wretched hole in the cellar of 25 Cromwell Street.

The mortician unscrewed the coffin to reveal two cardboard boxes. The larger of the two was exactly like the boxes I keep my A4 files in, pale-grey do-it-yourself 'archive system', about 12 inches deep, 15 inches wide and 20 inches long. I felt a moment of panic. I pointed to the smaller of the two boxes, which was plain brown with a hinged lid, and asked: 'Is her skull in there?' As he nodded and began to lift the lid, I was filled with the knowledge of what to do. A feeling of strength came over me.

As we drew nearer, I gasped at the beauty of her skull. It was like burnished gold and it was a part of Lucy that had survived to tell the tale. At that moment I was full of the joy of finding something that had been a part of Lucy after all these years. Not a glimmer of fear, not a morbid thought entered the experience. I lifted her skull with great care and tenderness. I marvelled at the sense of recognition in its curves and proportion. I wrapped it, like I have wrapped my babies, in Lucy's 'soft brown blanket', her snuggler. I pressed her to my heart. Before I placed her skull back, I laid a branch of heather entwined with sheep's wool from the top of Plynlimon in the bottom of the box. I visualised the space and beauty of that wild mountain top on a summer's day: the brown peat, the sheep, the warm wind, the distant range of receding mountains, close to the sky. A place Lucy would have loved; a place that feels close to our Welsh roots; a place of freedom. I offered it with so much love.

When Lucy was 11, she gave me a little woven woollen bag. It says a lot to me about her qualities then. In order to make the bag, she collected pieces of stray sheep's wool from the fences and hedges, probably from a field known as 'the top ground' where we kept our pony. Then she made the carders to tease out the wool by breaking off individual thorns from rose bushes and pushing them through two rectangles of cardboard. Next she spun the wool with a spindle made from a pencil and a cotton reel. Finally, she made a small loom and wove the spun wool into my much-treasured bag. The whole process must have taken days of intense concentration, patience and a determination to follow an idea through in practice. It speaks of her gentleness and her generosity and her desire to get back to first principles. The bag is one of my most treasured possessions. I keep my embroidery threads in it.

Beryl (one of Lucy's childhood friends) placed Chocka (a much-loved, very worn toy lion stuffed with straw) and One-Eyed Bunny, dressed in his smart velvet trousers, to sit either side of her wrapped skull, tucking a posy of primroses under Bunny's arm. These toys had been involved in endless games with us all as we grew up. Now they had the important job of guarding this physical presence of Lucy until we could have her back for the funeral.

The mortician stood throughout this ceremony holding the lid of the larger box, nodding with approval. At one point he said: 'I wish more people could be doing this.' When we had finally finished, he screwed down the lid of the coffin. We asked for some time to ourselves, turned the fluorescent light off, lit a candle, and stood in silence holding hands. I found myself thinking of every member of my family as if they were gathered there too. I was in another dimension, as if time had been transcended. Somehow we were united again within the 'still point of the turning world'. Something had been shifted. A step towards peace had been made.

For the rest of the time that Lucy's bones were still an 'exhibit' for the defence, I chuckled at the thought of a pathologist grumbling about interfering relatives, knowing that we had done the right thing. Through that experience I had the opportunity to transform the language from the crude butchery of the basement towards a poetry that we shared in our childhood. This was real and tangible evidence of her death.

Sometimes I return to the image of her skull as a way to release my grief. The orifices of the eye sockets remind me of the delicacy of her eyes that are no longer here, and never will be. They are empty holes, graves, the difference between being alive and being dead. The passing of time is reflected in the bones. The wonder at the durability of their substance and the beauty of their form increases my own sense of being alive. They remind me of my mortality and my physical structure. I feel deeply grateful for that unique, very intimate experience, an opportunity to pay tribute to Lucy in my own way, to begin to say goodbye, for real.

- -

October 1994

Frederick West's solicitor insisted on keeping the 'remains' as his 'exhibits', despite the fact that they had been well documented by the police. The coroner wrote to him threatening to seek a judicial review of the situation.

- -

12 December 1994

The coroner wrote to my parents again. 'I have reluctantly to write to tell you and all other relatives and next of kin of the victims concerned in the Frederick West inquiry, to say that, despite repeated attempts to reach agreement for the release of the remains, I have so far been unsuccessful . . . Unfortunately, I shall have to leave the matter over the Christmas period in view of the contentions put forward by those acting for Mr West, but you may rest assured that I will reconsider the position early in the new year and may well take further advice as to whether, notwithstanding the lack of agreement, in view of my duty to all the relatives and indeed, of course, to the public at large, grounds may exist for me to release the remains irrespective of the wishes of those defending Mr West.'

Twenty days later, Frederick West solved this problem by killing himself.

- -

6 February 1995

The committal trial for Rosemary West began. Carol, who has been my mother's friend since they were both eight years old, attended it with me. It was very comforting to be able to share this torturous experience. We both felt the need to find out as much as we could about the reality of Lucy's death, before it became public knowledge. During my attendance at the trial I felt truly supported by the investigation team in a way that went beyond the job description. My only complaint was the dinners. (But not the puddings!)

I found it almost impossible to match the figure of Rosemary West, sitting in the dock, with the endless graphic details of sexual depravities and brutality that were read out hour after hour for five days by the barrister. He spoke with an impeccable Queen's English accent and no emotion. The rigid structure of the court proceedings had the effect of modifying the impact of the grotesque details of the case.

It was when I heard Rosemary West's voice on the tape-recorded police interviews about her relationship with her daughter Heather that I began to have some insight into her mind. I soon got the feeling that her deviant ignorance sprang from the fact that she had rarely known beauty, truth or love. I tried to imagine growing up in an environment where fear and abuse were the main components. Her most common epithet was predictable but disturbingly accurate in the context of her world: 'bloody'.

To her, education was a 'bloody load of rubbish'. And yet she managed to keep up appearances. About her children, she said: 'I kept them clean, fit, walked them to school . . . they never wanted for nothing.' Heather 'gave us a load of hassle when she grew up . . . they just do what they likes'. 'When she left school she just sat in the chair . . .' 'Almost as if she didn't want to know me any more.' 'Once a child does cut you off, there is not a lot you can do.'

Rosemary West's extreme frustration about Heather was crystallised for me when she said: 'You can take a horse to water but you can't make him drink.'

I began to get the picture of the power struggle that led to Heather's death (and that of Rosemary West's stepdaughter, Charmaine). I began to understand her need to have absolute control, to cause pain and ultimately death, that she acted out in the night life at 25 Cromwell Street: the deep violent rage of impotence and ignorance that led to such terrible cruelty; the impoverishment of a soul that knew no other way to live.

Her behaviour was bestial and brutal in its attempt to make her victims experience a feeling of extreme pain, humiliation and impotence. (All of which, can one presume, she was made to feel in some way during her own childhood?)

There was one little glimmer of insight into Rosemary West's imagination that both touched my heart and disturbed me. It was the only reference to beauty during a week full of endless statements of explicit, crude sexual detail, which were expanded upon in the recent trial. It was her attempt to lure Alison Chambers to come and live in Cromwell Street by promising her a life in the country at the weekends on 'their farm' where she would be able 'to ride horses and *write poetry*'.

The image conjured up Lucy's world (Lucy spent a lot of her childhood involved in both activities). I began to sweat. Had Lucy had a chance to speak to them, or had they read about her life in the media shortly after they killed her, when we were desperately searching for her? Or was it simply unrelated, but one little moment when the world of the Wests brushed against Lucy's world on a more subtle level? That detail was used to lure another victim to their lair. There was something about the use of the word 'poetry' that leapt out of the general mire of blasphemy and made my stomach churn.

Another such moment was when we heard that their last child was called Lucyanna . . . a strange coincidence? Rosemary West was two years younger than Lucy.

. . . .

14 February 1995

Nine months after our first visit to Cardiff and a week after the committal proceedings for Rosemary West, Beryl and I returned there. Frederick West's death meant that at last we were free to proceed with the funeral.

We had arranged to meet the undertaker from Exeter. She had also been a student at Exeter University and was entirely supportive of any way that we chose to deal with what was a momentous occasion, charged with a huge need to express our love and our grief. Nick, my partner, had made a simple box for Lucy's bones. It looked like a medieval chest and was made from seasoned Welsh oak (kindly donated by another friend). The handles were made of thick rope. My boyfriend at the time of Lucy's 'disappearance', who now lives in Houston, Texas, sent a plaque of antique oak into which he had carved Lucy's name and dates: LUCY KATHERINE PARTINGTON 1952–73.

Nick had carefully mounted this with pegs on to the end of the box. This end became the 'head end' for the purpose of carrying the coffin in and out of the church.

This time we had to go to the mortuary. The porter took a while to understand why we were there. He had to lock up at 4pm. It was already 2.45pm. The 'file' box with its black felt-tip marking 'JR5 Body 6' and in red felt-tip 'Lucy Partington' awaited us on a trolley in the hall. This was my sister's last bureaucratic resting place. I had to reassure the porter that we had already seen the bones.

This society suffers badly from a fear of the reality of death. In Tibet, human thigh bones are lovingly made into exquisite-sounding instruments of great ceremonial importance.

Eventually the porter remembered that there was a chapel of rest next to the hallway. We were shown in, with the reminder that we had to be out by 4pm. The room had obviously been out of use for years. The mantelpiece was shrouded with dust. A blown egg that I had painted at Easter, with an image of a seal poking its nose out of the sea and a starfish sun, that I had placed carefully in the cup of the pelvis socket during our previous ritual had been broken.

But it was time for the final reordering of the bones. We placed sawdust in the bottom of the box, and then a length of Harris tweed that I had bought the previous autumn while exploring the wilderness of that island. We placed the skull at one end of the box and the pelvis at the other. Between these we laid the arm and leg bones. The vertebrae were threaded on a piece of rubber. We unthreaded them and laid them in order with the sacrum and coccyx next to the pelvis. The scapula, collarbone and ribs were arranged as symmetrically as possible in relation to the skull and the vertebrae. Handfuls of wrist and finger and toe bones and the patella were placed under the pelvis. I puzzled about the heel bone because it was quite small and looked as if it needed a socket with its ball-like end. Then I remembered Achilles' heel.

So, bones in order as much as is possible. Now to the gifts. First the book of Lucy's poems that my mother and stepfather had painstakingly collected together and published for family and friends. We proudly tucked a copy behind Lucy's skull after reading a few of the funny poems out loud, particularly one about Felix, our pony. My father had sent a rosary blessed by the Pope. My younger son had sent the crucifix that he had bought from a nun during a holiday in France. My older son's offering was a piece of blue, shiny enamelwork he had made. My daughter gave one of her intricate drawings of a Celtic knot. Nick gave a small jar of honey from our bees. Behind the pelvis I tucked a picture of the Dalai Lama. Chocka and Bunny and the 'soft brown blanket' went in next. Finally Beryl laid one of her most beautiful weavings (a rich maroon Ikat scarf) over our treasure and we screwed down the lid. We carried the box out to the undertaker's car and she drove off to Exeter.

On 16 February 1995, 17 days short of a year since we had found out what had become of Lucy, approximately 21 years and seven weeks after her death, we could have the funeral.

The requiem mass hosted by Exeter University and conducted by Lucy's priest was full of the beauty and love she deserved. Many of the friends and relatives who had attended the memorial gathering the previous July were there, also various friends who had been unable to go to that. Three of the investigation team sped down the M5 to be with us. It was particularly moving to see and hear the choir singing and the musicians playing. They were all present-day students to whom Lucy was a sad but rich legend. I think we all experienced what Joseph Campbell once said: 'Love is the pain of being truly alive.'

The following day our family and a few close friends met at a tiny medieval church near our home. We were about to perform the penultimate ceremony. There had been much discussion within the family about whether to cremate or bury Lucy's bones. My youngest son voiced what became the general consensus: 'Lucy has been buried in a horrible way for 20 years. I think we should bury her in a nice way now.'

I felt very strongly that she should be laid in consecrated ground, that we should have a grave and that her bones be left in peace rather than being ground up (which is what would have happened to them if she had been cremated) and just scattered. It seems that it was the right decision because the grave has indeed become a place where we can go to remember and pay tribute to her, and to grieve. Having lost her for so long, there is some comfort in having finally laid her to rest and in knowing where her bones are buried.

Fortunately, there was room for a grave in the churchyard of a place that was very special to Lucy. It was a place that she used to retreat to when she wanted some time to herself, when she was younger. More recently she had been writing a thesis on the medieval wall paintings that still decorate the interior. The images that oppose each other on the two main walls of the nave are strangely disturbing, because one of them contains echoes of the violence surrounding her death and in the other there is a clear reminder of the strength of her faith. The violent image is of a hunting scene. A hare is cornered and the hounds are about to pounce. Since reading Lucy's unfinished thesis, I realise there are various interpretations for this (what does the hare represent?). My initial reaction was to see the hare as a vulnerable soul about to be pounced upon by the hounds. The hunter brings up the rear of the chase.

On the opposite wall stands a figure of St Christopher, at least eight feet tall, wading through the sea with Christ on his shoulder and a staff in his hand. Even though the church is of Anglican denomination, the vicar was keen to help us fulfil our wishes for Lucy. The Roman Catholic priest kindly travelled from Exeter with the undertaker the day after the requiem mass and blessed the grave.

After a brief service my father, my two brothers and I carried Lucy's box out into the cold wind. It had been raining for at least three months and just at that moment a shaft of sunlight poured down from behind a cloud. The three priests stood in a line in their billowing white robes. Lucy's priest blessed the grave. The sun shone on and we lowered the box into the earth. As we all drew near to gaze into the grave, a bantam cockerel appeared from nowhere and nonchalantly got on with its scratching and pecking. During our childhood we kept bantams. Lucy used to paint them sometimes. There was something deeply reassuring about this moment. As if we had done all that we could to express our love for Lucy and there was a sort of reply going on . . . a real blessing. The undertaker commented later that she had never experienced the length and quality of the silence that held us all in that moment.

. . . .

8 October 1995
Eight months later. I felt very anxious about the trial because I knew how profoundly shocking the details of life in 25 Cromwell Street were. I was deeply concerned about the possibility of children watching the horrors on the news or reading them in the papers. I imagined creating a massive diversion, a national campaign to hang poems in trees in memory of all victims of violence. I wanted to create an opportunity for people to make a positive gesture in the midst of the onslaught of the West trial; to be able to focus on the tragedy of the deaths of the victims rather than on the murderers and their profound sickness.

The idea came from one of Lucy's favourite poems by Yevtushenko called 'I Hung a Poem on a Branch'. The last lines read:

> If we have trouble on the way,
>   we'll remember
>   that somewhere,
>   bathed in light,
>
> a tree
>   is waving
>   a poem
> and smiling we'll say:
>   'We have to go on.'

When most of us were kissing pictures of the Beatles, Lucy was kissing a picture of Yevtushenko! I gave her the book of his poems for Christmas in 1967. She was studying Russian O-level at the time.

Unfortunately, I simply didn't have the time and energy to put my campaign into practice. At that time, though, I was excited to discover Tibetan prayer flags. They hang like rows of bunting, bright-coloured rectangles of cloth printed with spiritual blessings. In an ancient ritual, they are renewed each year to signify hope, transformation and the spreading of compassion. As the year progresses, the wind disperses the energy of the words, which carry the power to pacify and heal everything they touch. A row now charts the wind outside my kitchen window. Filling and emptying, they flap and fray, tracing the invisible.

For the first few weeks of the trial I felt as if I was riding the storm quite well. I relied on DC Russell Williams, our personal policeman from the investigation team, for my information. I avoided any media reporting. I put my energy into my family and my work.

Over the last two years Russell has become 'Russ'. He has kept us informed of the progress of the case and has been there to answer any questions that we had. He always gave us warnings of media releases before they hit the headlines. Throughout the trial he phoned with regular reports from Winchester, so it was unnecessary to read the distortions in the press.

And then the Fred West tapes were played. Someone phoned to commiserate with me about a report by one broadsheet that printed the obscene words verbatim and added to the degradation by including a tabloid subheading. I hadn't been aware of the calumnies, but at that moment I was seized by the need to investigate what had been printed in all of the papers. Russ provided me with a large bundle.

Why was I so incensed by West's fantasies about Lucy and the way they were published? What he did to her was far worse. It was something to do with the crude level of language that was so far from the literary refinements that Lucy was immersed in. It brought out my rage at the inappropriateness of Lucy's death, which just did not seem fitting to her life. It made me aware of the vast gap I needed to cross in order to be able to comprehend and forgive.

It was as if anyone who heard his words or read them became a victim of his pornographic delusions – the print seeped into the air, as insidious as nerve gas. The words were poured out by the skip-full, vile gabblings, an endless rubble of lies. They revealed the completely egotistical, brutish mentality of a human being who was utterly devoid of any sense of truth about himself or anyone else. Not only had he performed these monstrous murders but he had then distorted the truth about them into further pollutions, extending his cruel trademark. It was truly blasphemous.

I had no choice but to crusade.

He said that Lucy was 'just a girl I was knocking off', claiming that after three months of what was 'purely sex, end of story' she had 'come the loving racket and wanted to live with me'. He made out that he was doing her a favour and that it all went wrong because she wanted more than he did. He said: 'I grabbed her by the throat and then I drove back to Gloucester. I brought the van up over the pavement, then I knocked the engine and lights out and let it cruise down to the back.' In his description, Lucy and the van were both subjected to a 'knocking' of one sort or another. He didn't seem to discriminate between the objects of his brutality.

He lumped all his victims into the same category, just bodies that were soon deprived of any individual identity, as their voices were muted and their features were smothered under the masking-tape gags that lasted longer than the flesh they were glued to. During his garbled confessions we could see his total lack of connection with reality in his attempts to justify the killings, as if somehow they weren't really all that much to do with him – as if they were happening in spite of him, like some snuff movie going on in the background. The fantasies were as disarticulated as the bodies by the time he had finished with them. He said about one of the victims: 'I strangled her or held my hands round her neck.' (Meaning she sort of strangled herself because his hands happened to be held around her neck?) Was his repetitive, sadistic behaviour some sort of attempt to get in touch with a feeling of being alive?

I simply couldn't bear the thought that even one person might have believed his words.

We had been warned that the prosecution had chosen this tape, partly because it was easy to prove that West's explanation about why he had to kill Lucy was insane fantasy, because my mother's statement could account for the time that Lucy was supposed to have been involved with him. It could be backed up by Exeter University and the priest who was preparing her for entering the Roman Catholic church in November 1973.

In fact, it was the defence that used the tape because it had a statement about West being the only person involved in the murders. So for three days it hung in the air, unchallenged. I became extremely agitated. Brian Leveson, QC, assured my father that he would make it very clear in his rebuttal that the tape was a cruel lie. However, the press obviously found it less important to print the truth. It wasn't sensational enough.

My next chance was Leveson's summing-up in which he focused even more strongly on just how obscene the fantasy was in relation to Lucy's life.

No, even though I had been in touch with the Press Association asking them to brief the journalists covering the West case to pick up on that point and print it, no words appeared.

The police suggested that we could make a statement after the trial if we still felt it was necessary. I decided to bring the subject up when I met Brian Leveson during the lunch hour at the judge's summing-up in Winchester. I was fighting for the refinement of Lucy's whole being that is so clearly reflected in the carefully chosen words of her poems. Russ gently reminded me that we were dealing with murder, not Lucy's life.

Fortunately, Brian Leveson could understand my feelings, especially when I read him two of Lucy's poems. His last words to me were: 'I'm off to speak to the press about a subject that is dear to your heart.' Apparently, he briefed each journalist individually and that evening the only news on radio and television put the jury's task in a nutshell, using Lucy as a focus. They had to decide between Fred West's version or Lucy's mother's statement. And why would Fred West have felt it necessary to create his story about Lucy if it wasn't to protect someone else (i.e., Rose)? The verdict reflected the truth.

. . . .

19 March 1996
'Hello, Marian, it's Russ. Just to let you know that Rose West's leave for appeal has been turned down this afternoon, despite the fact that it was due to go on until the end of the week. As far as we're concerned, that's the end of the matter. If you want to give me a ring, you can . . . Thanks very much. Message ends.'

It happened in an English city, in an ordinary terraced house, and it wasn't challenged for 20 years. It surpassed the limits of our understanding in its level of cruelty, going way beyond relentless abuse within the family. The Wests pushed sado-masochism to its logical conclusion and needed an influx of live human victims to feed their habit. In hindsight, the symptoms of their profound sickness festered in numerous eruptions. Apparently, life in 25 Cromwell Street didn't seem all that out of order, relatively speaking, so long as one didn't look too closely.

I have recently read these words of His Holiness the Dalai Lama:

> I will learn to cherish beings of bad nature
> And those pressed by strong sins and suffering
> As if I had found a precious
> Treasure very difficult to find.

I know Lucy would have understood their meaning: 'Love thine enemy.' This path offers a way to break the cycle of violence and hatred, to find in danger the opportunity for change. To reach towards the experience of the deepest compassion (empathy with suffering) and humility (from the Latin word *humus*, meaning ground or earth). The earth is common to all forms of life. It is that which connects us and feeds the following generations.

During the judge's summing-up at Winchester I experienced a brief moment of this feeling of unconditional compassion. Anne Marie (Frederick West's daughter and Rosemary West's stepdaughter) was sitting behind me in the gallery, a few feet away. It was her gruelling evidence of continual sexual abuse by both parents that was being dealt with in this session. I felt profoundly sad for her. As we stood up to leave, I found myself reaching out my hand towards hers and saying something inadequate but heartfelt. We both had tears in our eyes. She moved her hand towards mine and touched it lightly. I'm not sure if she knew who I was.

I feel a great need to express my gratitude to Anne Marie, and to all those people who have given of their best throughout this deeply traumatic experience: family, friends, professionals, the jury and the witnesses. But I would especially like to thank the investigation team, who all showed great sensitivity and kindness.

I attended the judge's summing-up at Winchester partly because it was the best opportunity to thank and hug (they are quite cuddly, these policemen!) John Bennett, Terry Moore (who used to go on the same school bus as me) and dear Russ (I miss you already). 'Good on you all,' as we say in Gloucestershire.

Commitment to 'good' seems vital to our survival. It is a journey that each one of us needs to take. It involves looking at the darker side of our human nature as well as the lighter side. As human beings, the Wests have demonstrated how seriously individuals can go wrong. Our society has demonstrated how seriously we can go wrong by not nurturing respect for ourselves and each other. It is time to speak out and learn from this tragedy, even though it is easier to ignore it or write it off as too weird to comprehend. Events like this hold a mirror up to our society. It is time to face ourselves. Every one of us has this responsibility.

So, finally, let me take you on a journey, back to November 1973, when Lucy was received into the Roman Catholic Church. It was a big step to take, coming from an agnostic background (although our great-grandparents were missionaries in China). Her faith was fresh and real. Five weeks later she suffered a death that went way beyond our worst imaginings. The priest who received her into the Church assures me that even though she was murdered, according to her faith she would have died in a state of grace (a divine, strenghtening influence). Fortunately, he was able to perform her requiem mass, 21 years after her death. Later on, I asked the dear priest if he thought that Lucy's faith would have helped her in her terrifying ordeal, one of those unanswerable questions in the league of 'Why did it happen to Lucy? Was it really as random as "she was in the wrong place at the wrong time"?' We have to learn to live with all this. We have to accept that it really did happen. He meditated quietly for a while and said: 'Well, it's just a feeling that I've got, but I do feel that she would have maintained her integrity.' Knowing Lucy's intellectual and spiritual refinement, I can mostly believe that. I pray that her faith gave her strength.

Lucy's suffering ended 22 years ago, when ours began. Four months after her disappearance I had a dream. Lucy came back and I asked her where she had been. She said: 'I've been sitting in a water meadow near Grantham, and *if you sit very still you can hear the sun move.*' This image filled me with a profound feeling of peace, the kind that 'passeth understanding'. I woke up with this feeling. It lasted for a few seconds. I've never forgotten it.

Thank you, Lucy. Your life and your death have deepened my knowledge of love. I will try to pass that on. Each moment that passes is full of significance and the opportunity for change, if we choose to look, if we choose to act.

Maybe we could start with each one of us writing a favourite poem on a small piece of cloth and tying it to the branch of a tree, in memory of all victims of violence and as an act towards hope for a world in which cruelty is replaced by understanding and compassion.

It is time to salvage the sacred. •

....

15 March 1996

Andrew O'Hagan
Scotland's damaged heart

Dunblane's Catholic church, like most others in Scotland, is at the edge of things; it is not like the cathedral, with its tall steeple, at the very centre of town. Scotland is a place where churches still tend to disagree, though backing up your historical claims with violence is not so often the done thing now, certainly not in this place. Yet the country as a whole – anything but alone in this regard – has found other outlets for anger and hatred. It has found new sorts of rage, new ways of capitalising on the madness that can sometimes be found in the atmosphere. Easy violence is there in the culture, on the streets, in places that might not seem part of anything outside of themselves.

There are new heights of terror, new tools of attack, and some, as we know, have found new sorts of victims. Violence breeds violence. Wherever you are in Scotland, you don't have to travel far in any direction to find children whose ambition it is to own a gun or hold a knife. We may be less surprised than we used to be about the number of adults who already do.

Twenty-four hours after the murder of the schoolchildren, the candles in the Catholic chapel at Dunblane were burning themselves out. There were messages written on a pad at the front table. Each child was addressed by their first name; it was hoped, and expected, that each would now be 'with Our Saviour in Heaven'. You want to think this horror has nothing to do with most of our lives, you want to say, hold on, this has to do with nothing but the unexpected craziness of one man. But you might consider it impossible to live in a civilised world, a rational country, without facing the fact that this man is one of our members, and that we have members like this now who might never have existed before.

We will discard this terrible killer now as we must, we will damn him to hell, as we are compelled to do, by ourselves, by each other, in the very name of decency. We will do this, but as we do it we will also, in our way, repress what fears we have about our citizenry, ourselves and the circular nature of modern violence.

Thomas Hamilton's outrage will return to the subculture it emerged from: a place where repression, self-loathing, the need for power through brutality, the taste for oblivion and the sublimation of every important thing to the demands of a mangled libido lie in a well of unknowing too deep for tears. We may be thankful at how very seldom it is that all these parts come together in one man, but it is hard to face the fact that the parts are to be found simmering on our every side.

It is a subculture now taken grip in some parts of Britain. We can deny ourselves just so far (we may need to do so in order not to go out of our minds) but we can't deny everything. There is something up with our way of life, and no amount of repression will quite rub it away.

Scotland has a problem with violence which isn't unique, but it's unique in the manner of its acceleration. In different ways and in quite different places, people are living lives at the very edge of extremity: thousands of Scottish youngsters are killing themselves with drugs; pensioners are being robbed and sometimes murdered for the price of a few Temazepam capsules; random terror and ram-raiding are among the things to get high on if you're a teenager; many more thousands of people are going missing than ever before. You might prefer to see these things as unrelated. They probably are. But they are all happening at the same time, they are all worsening and it is no longer good enough to shrug off the troubles, or madnesses, of people who aren't yourself; it's not so much the corruption of our innocence as the ruination of our experience.

Scotland knows of its damaged heart. Like no one else, in no other place, its more recent sons and daughters have grown up thinking about it, and some of them have begun to write novels and plays about it too. This is the world opened up by films such as *Trainspotting, Shallow Grave* and *Small Faces*; it is the sickening but meaningful centre of Irvine Welsh's *Maribou Stork Nightmares*; it is the reality that props up Duncan McLean's *Bunkerman*, about a weirdo in an anorak who stalks and rapes a young woman in the north of Scotland. It is the dark backing behind Frank Kuppner's *Something Like Murder*; it lingers over much of the work of A L Kennedy; it forms a thread through Alan Warner's debut novel, *Morvern Caller*; and it is partly exposed in Thomas Healy's forthcoming book, *A Hurting Business*

We can't hold down what is under our noses. Dunblane has something behind it, just as the bombing of the infants of Oklahoma had something behind itself. Something crazy, of course, but something real. One's grief at the losses makes it no easier to say it. But in America they spoke of it – or we spoke of it where they could not – and what we spoke of was the sheer extremity of the dislocation a growing number of people exhibited, especially ones who were never very located in the first place. We spoke of a new (we thought American) style of mass killing. The bombing of Oklahoma was the terrible apex of something restless and unacceptable in America. Don't get me wrong: Timothy McVeigh was an isolated figure, just as Hamilton was, but there was a world at their backs, a world of fascists, sexual delinquents, cultists, gun-lovers, idiot extremists, desperadoes, folk who'll do anything to make themselves known.

We can't be expected to explain everything – for most of this will for ever lie beyond our understanding – but we felt the need, and we did well to feel the need, against the grain of our more comfortable instincts, to look at the motivations which brought McVeigh to his own particular spot in hell, to examine the justifications he sought in advance for wreaking such hell on his particular spot of earth. We thought again about America, and what has happened there. We can hate Thomas Hamilton, but we need to know where he comes from. He didn't come from nowhere either: he came from Scotland.

There is, as I said, already a reckoning with violence – which is a sort of return to the reckonings of earlier Scottish writers like Stevenson – but it is hard to swallow, as it always has been. Going through Glasgow on a tram before the last war, the writer Edwin Muir felt the need to isolate time, and look at the state of his people. He chose not to see a Hitler in everyone, but he was worried by the tide of violence he saw rising before him. As he rode through the city on his tram, he noticed a look behind the eyes of his fellow passengers, and with the aid of a mirror he might have noticed it in himself too. He felt the passengers' eyes sat in their respective heads like the eyes of animals. There was a look of imminent violence, of hunger for extremity, or extreme retribution.

I can't say much about this, except to say that I've seen this look myself, and seen it in places quite close to home. I grew up in Scotland, in a small town, and I remember Primary One as if I'd been in it only yesterday. We none of us knew there were Thomas Hamiltons in the world, but random acts of violence of a quite different order were no strangers to us. The need to express yourself in that way was in many of the people we saw and my own generation took it to another place.

It would be some years, though, before violence on the scale we have just witnessed could possibly be imagined, just imagined, and I doubt if there were people then who ever wanted to imagine it. Nowadays of course, in Scotland as elsewhere, there is no shortage of occasions on which one can commune with images of mass violence. There are those who are addicted to it, and it would take someone more confident than I am just now to assert that screen violence, video horrors, and the easy exterminations of arcadia have nothing to do with our increased sense of our time as a time of assassins. If ever there has been such a time it is now.

Waiting at the train station to leave Dunblane, I spoke to a local man. 'It's happening everywhere you look,' he said, 'everywhere, I thought, except here. But now all the head-bangers in this country will be taking up guns.' I told him I hoped that wasn't true. Two German students had come to the town to say prayers at the cathedral. They told me that things had gone crazy, and where could the people of Dunblane look now, to make sense of such a thing? As the train pulled away, I wondered too where they would look. I also found myself wondering where Scotland would look, when it returned to itself, and turned its gaze away from Dunblane.

Stevenson's Mr Hyde is a detestable creature, but he isn't just a crazy manifestation, not just a stranger in the tranquil life of Dr Jekyll. He is more than that. He is part of the doctor's body, a terrible piece of the doctor's mind, of the minds that made his mind, and the bodies that surround it, the places that sustain it. But the science of a century ago would have seen no possible way to be rid of Mr Hyde, nor of those traces of his presence in the most surprising of places. There was Mr Hyde in the culture. It may turn out that Thomas Hamilton is beyond our science too, and has little to do with any other mind or any other body. He may be all the way outside the troubled culture he lived in for 43 years.

He may be a new sort of monster: one with no connection to the land it resides in; one with a body like no other, a mind like no other; one whose habits of violence, whose manner of chaos, have no bearing on our world, one that has taken nothing of its nature from our world. If so, we can try to forget him, and pray that nothing so manifestly evil ever occurs again. But if we doubt it, and think there might be a culture of violence too strong and widespread to be denied or disconnected from our everyday lives, and if we decide to look at the many beginnings and ends of such violence, then perhaps we can begin to look forward to a time when our children, including those survivors of Dunblane, have the chance of a life less threatening than the one that exists right now. •

1 December 1995

Lord Donaldson

Beware this abuse

I was a judge for 26 years. Every morning when I entered my court I knew that whoever else might be on trial, I was too. Neither I nor any other judge would make any complaint about this. Judges are, in a sense, the representatives of society as a whole. It is right that they should carry out their duties in the full gaze of the public and that they should be judged by that public.

That said, there is a difference between informed and uninformed criticism. At one time I believed that if a judge's sentence was criticised, he had failed. Either his sentence was wrong or he had failed to explain the reasons for that sentence. I still think that this is true, but only if those criticising have attended the trial and heard the reasons given by the judge. The problem nowadays is that criticism is so often voiced on the basis of a wholly misleading appreciation of the facts based upon necessarily truncated media reports.

If matters had stopped there I would not be writing this article. Uninformed criticism is irritating and indeed depressing for the individual judges concerned, but nowadays it goes with the territory. However, in recent months we have seen an entirely new development. This is an attack by politicians on the judiciary as a whole. This is without precedent in my professional lifetime and raises very serious constitutional issues.

Our unwritten constitution, like the written constitutions of all other democracies, is based upon a separation of powers. This separation is between the powers of Parliament, those of the government and those of the judiciary. Parliament is supreme. The government governs in the exercise of powers granted to it by Parliament. The judiciary enforces the will of Parliament including the common law in so far as it has not been modified by Parliament. In so doing it administers the criminal law, and adjudicates in disputes between citizen and citizen, and citizen and the state. This is what is meant by the rule of law.

I have said that Parliament is supreme and it is. It can, if it wishes, alter this delicate balance by transferring some of the powers and duties of the judiciary to the executive. Such a course would, however, pose a considerable threat to the freedom of the individual citizens. It is one thing to be governed by the rule of law. It is quite another to be governed by a despotic, albeit no doubt benevolent, government. And any government which seeks to make itself immune to an independent review of whether its actions are lawful or unlawful is potentially despotic.

This concerted attack upon the judiciary is clearly a prelude to an attempt to secure parliamentary authority requiring the judges to pass life sentences, thereby transferring some sentencing powers to the government, curbing the powers of the judges to take full account of the circumstances of individual cases by providing for minimum sentences, and limiting the powers of the courts to decide, by means of judicial review, whether the government is exceeding the powers granted to it by Parliament.

There will be some who will wonder whether such proposed measures are dictated by an objective consideration of the public good, or by electoral imperatives. But let that pass. What could be the objective justification?

First, as to minimum sentences. Human wickedness and frailty know no bounds and every case is different. Judges are trained to evaluate this and to distinguish between wickedness and frailty. This is not to say that their duty is to administer personalised justice. Far from it. Parliament sets maximum sentences and that determines the relative seriousness of different types of offences viewed as a whole. Judges take their cue from this. By contact with other judges, they seek to ensure that offenders of comparable culpability receive similar sentences. In addition they receive and act in accordance with guidance from the criminal division of the Court of Appeal.

No system is perfect and judges will make mistakes. At one time sentences could be altered only if the accused entered an appeal. This left society as a whole with no remedy if the sentence was manifestly too lenient. This has been remedied and now the prosecution too can appeal with the agreement of the Attorney-General.

So what is the need for minimum sentences? There will always be wholly exceptional cases in which an unusually lenient sentence is not only justified but required, if justice is to have any real meaning. If Parliament thinks that the judiciary is identifying too many cases as falling within this category, the remedy lies not in mandatory minimum sentences, but in a statutory direction that judges shall impose lesser sentences only in special circumstances which the judge identifies when passing sentence. If the Attorney-General considers that the circumstances were not sufficiently special, he will be able to appeal. Second, as to mandatory life sentences. At present the only mandatory life sentences are for murder. There are historical reasons for this stemming from the abolition of capital punishment, although many consider that this is an anachronism which should be abolished. Judges, however, can and do in the exercise of their discretion impose life sentences when the law so permits and they are unable to determine when, if ever, the accused will cease to be a danger to the public if left at liberty. It is then for the Home Secretary, acting judicially, to decide when the criminal can safely be released.

I have no problem with the power to impose discretionary life sentences. Indeed, I think that this power is essential. However, this is subject to the vitally important proviso that the Home Secretary can be relied upon to act judicially in deciding whether and when the convicted person can safely be released. This involves, among other things, refusing to be swayed by media and other campaigns in relation to particular cases. On current evidence, I do here have anxieties. Any increase in mandatory life sentences gives the Home Secretary additional scope for exercising the power of release politically.

Third, as to judicial review. Judges exercising this jurisdiction have never been concerned with whether they do or do not agree with the policy which dictates particular action or inaction by government and other authorities. Their sole concern is whether it is or is not lawful. This in turn depends whether it is or is not authorised by Parliament.

All governments believe that their actions are in the public interest and have no difficulty in persuading themselves that they must be lawful. To be told by judges that they are not in fact acting lawfully is an affront which they find hard to accept. Much easier to say, and sometimes believe, that the judges are entering the political arena and are disagreeing on policy grounds.

It is true that in recent times there have been an increasing number of judicial review decisions which have been adverse to the government. Whether this is due to the fact that one political party has been in power for an exceptionally long period and has become unusually convinced of its own rectitude, or to an increasingly careful scrutiny of governmental actions by the judiciary, or to an increasing awareness on the part of the public that they can look to the courts for protection, is not for me to say. Probably all three factors have made a contribution. Suffice to say that if ministers think that they are being treated unjustly, they can appeal. They rarely do so.

As I have said, Parliament is supreme. If, as I think ill-advisedly, it wishes to alter the role and powers of the judiciary, it can do so and the judiciary will, as always, loyally conform. Criticism of individual decisions is the right of everyone, although informed criticism is preferable. What is to my mind unpardonable is to mount a campaign of abuse and criticism of the judiciary as a whole. It can have only one certain result and that is to weaken public confidence in the judicial system. Without that confidence the rule of law no longer works and all our freedoms are at risk. ●

31 August 1996

Jeremy Hardy

Home truths about the Home Office horror show

Sometimes it is impossible to overstate the bleeding obvious. So let me take this opportunity to state that Michael Howard is surely one of the most repellent combinations of DNA ever to wear a dark suit. I do not seek to demonise him in the way the Left once demonised Thatcher, although he is a useful repository for that spare hatred now that she is lost and gone away. Today, Lady Thatcher is like a mad aunt, a person with appalling ideas who manages to be perversely entertaining by saying the wrong thing on family occasions. But in the eighties she was demonised to the extent that she appeared to have unearthly powers, and we lost sight of how eminently defeatable she was. In the end, her own side had to dump her because no one else would.

So I don't want to accord Michael Howard that kind of status. It was only the Falklands War that saved Thatcher from early dismissal; and it was only Jack Straw's utter uselessness that saved Howard from being driven into the sea by the entire nation. There was Howard, having united ramblers, ravers and judges into the most potent opposition force this century. And yet by one of those quirks of history that spawn an eternity of if-onlys, the shadow Home Secretary happened to be Jack Straw. Appointed by Blair to make his own tenure of the position seem like a golden age, Jack Straw squared up to the most reviled man in England and single-handedly rescued his career. Why? Because he was frightened of him.

So there we were, saddled with Howard indefinitely. And he became ever more like Thatcher, utterly brazen. He seems to revel in being hated, in a way that suggests it is all he has ever known. He loves that he can cow civil servants into being his fall-guys. He appears to love the fact that no one believes a word he says. He doesn't even mind that his own side thought for a minute he'd gone soft on hijackers; his record on asylum seekers is so brutal that he has nothing to prove.

And he gets away with it all in a way which is admirable. Even more so than Kenneth Clarke, from whom he inherited the Home Office. Clarke was as despicable in the job as he had been at Health and Education; but at some point, he felt the need to re-invent himself as that amiable, beery jazz-lover for whom the Exchequer is an annoying distraction from appearing on the *Today* programme.

When you listen to Clarke joshing in that silly Chris Tarrant voice, you can almost forget the way he reviled teachers and nurses, that he called ambulance workers 'glorified taxi-drivers', that he denied justice to the Bridgewater Four.

In those days Clarke was still playing the unconscionable bruiser. Then it was decided that he had the potential to replace Major, so he set about becoming what the broadcasters fondly call the 'candidate of the Left'. This title has nothing to do with ideology; it is awarded to whichever Tory has the most convincing resemblance to a human being.

Clearly Howard knows he will never be any good at that, so he doesn't really try. He is one of those men about whom it is said, 'When you meet him, he's the opposite of what you expect' and you know that it's not true. You know he would not be disarmingly funny or self-mocking or tipsy or flirtatious. I suspect he would exhibit a certain vulnerability, but not the kind that is endearing, rather the kind that makes you want to run away lest you become infected by it.

For there is something achingly weak about Michael Howard and he is not very good at disguising it. He does not cope with his refugee parentage at all well. Portillo manages to be both British xenophobe and dashing Spaniard so comfortably and flamboyantly that the shame he brings upon his father is all part of the package. Howard is evasive, furtive. The issue of asylum seems awkward for him, as does the issue of race. So he throws himself whole-heartedly into Law and Order.

The tabloids conspire with him in depicting his court battles as fights between the man in the street and the ulta-left judiciary. And he appears to delight in losing them. Liberal commentators conspire in making the battles seem ever-more perilous for him, so that his survival seems ever-more remarkable.

But the battle over the early release of prisoners was always going to be a cake-walk. The only question is whether he set the whole thing up to his advantage or whether he is incompetent. The latter is suggested by the fact that Richard Tilt's career was spared. Howard is not merciful by nature. He would love to dismiss Tilt and the party would love him for it. But he couldn't, because Tilt would not then have agreed to take the rap.

Similarly, although Howard would love to be like Clarke and deny justice to the Bridgewater Four, he faced a judicial review which he would at the moment have been in the process of losing. And that frightened him so much that he reversed his decision and referred the case to the Court of Appeal.

So let us all take heart. Michael Howard is not as hard as he likes to think he is. ●

18 December 1995

Myra Hindley
My story

When I wrote to the *Guardian* on 4 October to register my objections to being labelled a psychopath, and cited evidence of the combined diagnoses of psychologists and psychiatrists who have examined me over the years, in order to refute the claims made by David Jessel and Ann Moir in *A Mind to Crime*, I was aware that the contents of my letter would beg many questions.

If I wasn't suffering from any kind of mental disorder; if, from what was known of my earlier life, I'd been a 'normal happy girl who got on well with relatives and friends'; if psychopathy had nothing to do with the events which led me to prison – how would I explain what led me to the things I did?

Before I attempt to do this I want to make it quite clear that I make no excuses for my behaviour in the years I spent with my co-defendant; that I take full responsibility for the part I played in the offences, and will not attempt to justify the unjustifiable.

Although on the whole I was a 'normal happy girl', I grew up in what can be described as a tough working-class district where Friday and Saturday nights were known as 'wife-beating' nights; the men worked hard all week and many spent the weekends drinking.

Pub closing times were dreaded, because we all knew what would happen. Women ran out into the street, trying to escape from being beaten. All the kids used to jump out of bed and rush outside to try to stop our fathers hurting our mothers, and we were often turned on too.

My own father – described by Lord Dean of Beswick as being known as 'a hard man' – went off to the pub every night, and being a taciturn, bad-tempered man almost always got into a fight (he'd been a boxer in the Army) and staggered home bruised and bleeding.

I was often sent to the pub to retrieve his jacket, which he'd taken off before fighting; it was the only 'good' one he had. When my mother berated him for the state he was in, he began knocking her about, and when I tried to prevent him, I was hit too.

I disliked him intensely for his violence, drunkenness and the tyrannical way he dominated the household. We were in almost constant conflict, and with hindsight I can see that my sense of family values and relationships were seriously undermined by his influence on me as a child. I have never sought to blame him for anything I did when I was older (it devastated him that his daughter could possibly have done the things I did, and he disowned me) but he was far from being a good role model.

Through witnessing and being on the receiving end of so much violence within my own family, I was given many lessons in dominance and control, which was probably the foundation stone on which I built my own personality.

The clear message was that emotions should not be openly displayed, otherwise I would be vulnerable, and from a very early age I learned to keep them under control, to refuse to cry when being chastised except in the privacy of my bedroom at my gran's house, to never let my feelings show, to build up layers of protective buffers, to tremble, rage, cry and grieve inwardly.

When a much-loved friend drowned at the age of 13, my first experience of the loss of someone I loved, I cried openly and was inconsolable for weeks after his death, until I was told there was something wrong with me: I was abnormal; I'd be ill; I had to pull myself together; I'd become 'soft in the head'. Well-meaning words, no doubt, but they only served my need and ability to bury my emotions as deep as I could.

This – as it turned out to be – fatal ability to control my emotions was probably one of the main ingredients in my relationship with Ian Brady.

I had learned and continued to learn to live on two different levels; to hide my real feelings when necessary and show them only when it was safe to do so – never in front of him or, as with my father, I'd be sorry I had.

From a very early age I developed a strength of character that protected me a lot from emotional harm, but looking back, I realise that this locked out some important feelings that could have provided warning signals in the early days of my relationship with Ian. It also enabled me to lead an apparently normal existence while being actively involved in the offences.

In my letter to the *Guardian* I also said, in reference to those extracts from *A Mind to Crime*, that as a child or teenager I was never cruel to animals or children. I chose those words carefully for two reasons: they were absolutely true, and I was 18½ when I met my co-defendant, and 11 days short of my 21st birthday when the first offence was committed.

In what I am going to say now, I want to stress that I am not seeking to blame Ian Brady for what I am personally responsible for, or even to apportion blame. And whatever mitigating factors there were, my own conscience and acute awareness of my own culpability tell me the unpalatable truth that – excepting God's mercy – I have no excuses or explanations to absolve me for my behaviour after the first offence.

I knew that what I was involved in was indefensible in every respect; I know the difference between right and wrong and I cared deeply about that difference, though I locked these feelings away. I never attempted to justify my actions either to myself or to Ian Brady, and in all these respects I was the more culpable of the two.

I didn't have a grudge against society or a chip on my shoulder. The things I wanted in life were not unusual. I got engaged at 17 to a boy I first met when I was 11 and he pulled the ribbon out of my hair at the pictures.

But when I began to witness many of my friends and neighbours, some of whom 'had to get married', having baby after baby, almost tied to the kitchen sink and struggling to make ends meet while their husbands went out every night, drinking and betting away their wages just as my father had done, I began to feel uncomfortable and restless.

I wanted a career, to better myself, to travel and struggle to break free of the confines of what was expected of me. Although so much was unattainable, I still dreamt and made plans and kept everything to myself. I didn't want to leave home, because I loved my family, but I wanted more scope and space, and they would think I was 'getting above myself' if I confided in them.

My only 'fatal weaknesses' when I met Ian Brady were that I was emotionally immature, relatively unsophisticated and sexually inexperienced – I was still a virgin and intended to be so until I got married.

Before I met Ian, and when I applied for a job as a shorthand typist, a friend who worked in the same small typing pool suggested I phoned Millwards, as a vacancy there had been advertised, and she had worked there herself in the recent past.

She told me something about the firm and mentioned some of the people I'd be working with if I got the job.

She told me about Ian, describing him as tall and good-looking, very quiet and shy, smartly dressed; an 'intriguing man' who had appealed to her. When I was given the job after an interview, I was introduced to the others in the office, and before his name was mentioned, I already knew it was him. I can only describe my reaction to him as an immediate and fatal attraction, although I had no inkling then of just how fatal it would turn out to be.

For almost a year, during which I broke off my engagement, he took virtually no notice of me. When he did, it was either a covert 'come on', which sent my hopes soaring and caused me to write in a diary that I'd begun that I wished he would love me as much as I loved him and begged God to let him ask me to marry him; or an ostentatious antipathy towards me, making cruel and sarcastic remarks or totally ignoring me except when he had to ask me to take dictation and type letters for him.

It was a year of emotional torture which I'd never experienced before. I went from loving him to hating him, and loving and hating him at the same time. When he smiled at or was nice to me, I felt blessed and floated on air.

I often took my baby cousin out in his pram, and when I discovered where Ian lived, I began taking Michael down the long street he lived in, hoping I'd see him and he'd stop to talk to me, but I never did.

I asked one of my friends to come with me to the pub on the corner of his street in the hope that he might be there, but he never was. I'd become utterly obsessed with him, though tried desperately not to show it.

Later on, I began to believe he'd guessed how I felt and had deliberately played his hand in the way he did; drawing me in, loosening the string, then drawing me in until the trap was sprung.

When he asked me, after a Christmas party at the office when he was drunk and I wasn't far from being, if he could walk me home and take me for a drink that evening, I was on cloud nine. I rushed to a phone and cancelled a night out with the girls I always went out with. They were really pleased when I told them I was going out with Ian, for I'd talked about him incessantly.

I don't think Ian was very pleased when I wouldn't let him come into the house with me afterwards – I told him my gran might still be up.

He made a date with me for the Saturday, and for months I became a 'Saturday-night stand'. When he bought a motorbike he came one week night unexpectedly and we went for a ride. After that, because he never made a date, I began staying in every night, terrified that I might be out when – if – he came round.

I became estranged from most of my friends, who had become disgusted with me for 'letting him tread all over me'.

There was friction in my own family because they didn't like him and made disparaging remarks about him, but the more they attacked him, the more I defended him. I'd become totally besotted with him, always trying to fathom out the mystery he'd become to me, the aura that emanated from him.

Whenever I asked him anything about himself, he would only say 'it doesn't matter'. I knew virtually nothing about him or his past, only that he didn't believe in marriage or having children, was a fervent atheist, hated black people and Jews, and had a consuming passion for Nazism.

He argued with me and ridiculed me about my religion, my Catholicism. My faith was strong, but a childhood one, and he gradually demolished my beliefs with theories I genuinely believed couldn't be discounted.

He had a powerful personality, a magnet-like charisma into which my own personality, my whole self, became almost totally subsumed. Almost totally, for I secretly didn't believe or agree with everything he said, but experience had taught me that to question or confront him with anything, to 'fall below standard', resulted in 'silences' when he totally ignored me at work, got my typewriter moved out of the main office into my own, which was less warm, and stayed away for long periods, leaving me wondering where he was, who he was with, would he ever come back. And when he did, I often wished he hadn't.

At the trial, the Crown's picture of my relative role was 'that it plainly acknowledged that the younger Miss Hindley had been indoctrinated by Brady, that he had introduced her as he later introduced David Smith to corrupting literature and to the idea of murder, and that he initiated, planned and committed the crimes in which she participated'.

Later, in a speech to the Medico-Legal Society, from which I quoted a few lines in my letter to the *Guardian*, Mr Mars-Jones [the trial judge] also said: 'There was a clear distinction to be drawn between Brady and Hindley . . . it was not until Brady came into her life that she began to become withdrawn and secretive and changed her whole attitude to life . . . When Brady came on the scene, all was changed.

'There was one letter which she had written to a girlfriend in which she said she was frightened of Brady and was contemplating going abroad after joining the Women's Auxiliary Air Force in order to get away from that man. He had administered a drug to her and she had no idea what he had done to her while she was unconscious.

'When she came to, she found him leaning over her and was frightened. She said in her letter that in the event of her disappearing or in the event of the disappearance of three men, whose names and addresses she gave, the girlfriend was to go to the police with the letter.

'Inquiries were subsequently made to try to trace these three men, but whether by coincidence or not, none of them could be traced . . . There were clear signs that Myra had resisted and at one time had tried to break with Brady. But such was his influence over her that she could not break the chain, and the horrible secret that they later shared bound them together more closely than any ties of affection possibly could bind them.'

None of this was ever mentioned at the trial, and I doubt that the defence team was even aware of it. Nor did the police make my diary available to them. But it wouldn't have made much difference, because by that time I'd become criminally amoral and callous.

When I first met my barrister he told me the only way he could defend me was by prosecuting Ian Brady. I told him I couldn't allow that, and if necessary would have to find another barrister. I couldn't allow it not only because I believed in my heart that of the two of us I was the more culpable, but also because I had never given Ian Brady any inkling of what my real feelings were.

After the first murder, when he'd told me that if I'd shown any signs of backing out I would have ended up in the same grave as Pauline Reade, I felt doubly doomed; first by the crime itself and also because I believed it was impossible to envisage or hope for any other kind of existence.

As Mr Mars-Jones further said, the horrible secret we later shared bound us together more closely than any ties of affection possibly could. There was no going back, and what Ian said shortly after our arrest, that it was he and I against the world, felt very much the case for as long as our relationship lasted.

Mr Mars-Jones also said that by the time we went for trial I was the tougher of the two. This is difficult to explain as it's too easy just to say I'd had a good teacher who had prepared me for every contingency and I'd been a 'blotting paper' pupil who had soaked up and absorbed everything I'd been taught.

I agree that I was tough; I'd had several years in which to become so, and my childhood had been one long toughening up process.

I'll always remember when I was about 16 or 17, my father, who was working on a building site, broke his leg so badly he was made disabled, and quite soon after he had the first of his strokes. For the first time in my life I saw him almost helpless, unable to walk, sitting almost constantly in his, the only, armchair in the house or lying in his bed in the living room, and all my fear of him left me. In spite of all he'd done to make our family life often unbearable, I felt sorry for him, compassionate and even tender towards him.

I could never love him, but seeing this strong brutal man reduced to the helplessness of a baby made me feel strong and almost maternal towards him. I waited on him, fetched and carried for him, because I wanted to and not because I had to in the past.

And in a similar way that is what happened with my feelings for Ian Brady after our arrest. I'll never forget his face when I took the police into the living room the morning after the murder of Edward Evans. It was expressionless, as it often was, but I saw him almost shrink before my eyes, helpless and powerless, just as the victims had been, but now, thank God, there would be no more victims, it was all over. And I felt free.

Arrest and Risley prison symbolised freedom to me. But to Ian it symbolised a living death; something he told me he couldn't endure.

He had a jar of jam brought in with other things on a visit from his mother and he intended killing himself with the glass. I begged him not to, not to leave me, he was all I had lived for. He said I couldn't be found guilty if I went on trial without him; that his influence would pall and I'd be able to rebuild my life. But he said he would wait and see what happened at the trial.

I felt then that he needed me even more than I'd ever needed him and for the first time in the whole of our relationship I knew that he loved me. He deplored what he thought of as sentimentality and had never said he loved me, and afraid of annoying him I'd never told him I loved him.

In his first letter to me on remand he wrote at the end, in German, that he loved me, and I poured all my love for him into my letters to him. I knew he would never be able to come to terms with our arrest, particularly because it was the result of David Smith going to the police, which to Ian was a betrayal of the worst kind.

I vowed to myself that I'd gather all the strength I had to be strong enough for both of us, to nurture him and encourage him and sustain him. I prayed to a God I'd ceased to believe in that I would get a life sentence like I knew Ian would, and when I did and we met briefly with our solicitor after the trial, the first thing I asked him was not to kill himself as he'd said he would do.

When the judge wrote to the then Home Secretary two days after the trial he said: 'Though I believe Brady is wicked beyond belief without hope of redemption (short of a miracle) I cannot feel that the same is necessarily true of Hindley once she is removed from his influence. At present she is as deeply corrupted as Brady but it is not so long ago that she was taking instruction in the Roman Catholic Church and was a communicant and a normal sort of girl.'

And it is true that by then I was corrupt; I was wicked and evil and had behaved monstrously.

Without me, those crimes could probably not have been committed. It was I who was instrumental in procuring the children, children who would more readily accompany strangers if they were a woman and a man than they would a man on his own.

My greatest regret is that Ian Brady and I ever met each other. If we hadn't, speaking for myself, there would have been no murders, no crime at all. I would have probably got married, had children and by now be a grandmother.

Those, however, are 'might have beens'. The reality is that after 30 years in prison and a whole life tariff I'm plastered with labels.

The ironic thing is that when I talked with the senior psychologist with whom I did that extensive series of tests I referred to in my letter, she told me that one of the burdens I'd have to carry was that I couldn't be 'labelled'.

She said if I could be labelled as even one of a number of mental disorders it would mean I could be treated for it and if I responded suitably to treatment it could be said I no longer suffered from whatever it was I'd been diagnosed as and stood a much better chance of eventual release.

But as things turned out, I was labelled as an enigma, someone whom people couldn't comprehend. And it is a fact of human nature that when people do something out of the norm, something incomprehensible, no matter what, we apply labels to help us make sense of whatever it is that's been done.

I had a letter from a lady who had read my letter in the *Guardian* – one of many letters I received – who had spent much of her working life as a neuro-paediatrician. She said I was absolutely right in saying how could those who have never seen me, talked to me or examined me make a medical diagnosis: 'The truth is, there are few cut and dried psychological diagnostic criteria for affective disorders. It really boils down to "by his/her works shall you know him/her".'

Aristotle said much the same thing – forget psychology, forget the inside of men's heads. Read them by their actions. This lady also said, 'In your shoes, I think I would prefer to be labelled "psychotic" rather than "wicked".'

I've so often wished that I had suffered from some affective disorder and been diagnosed accordingly. This would have provided some kind of explanation for my actions. As it is, what I was involved in is indefensible.

I wasn't mad, so I must have been bad, became bad by a slow process of corruption (certainly there was a strong element of fear) which eroded many of the values I'd held and my latent strength of character obviously enabled me to resolutely cast aside my beliefs in order to identify myself completely with a man who had become my god, whom I both feared and worshipped.

By my works, or actions, I was tried, judged and rightly convicted and sentenced. But trial, judgement, sentencing by the tabloids continues to this day, with incessant, emotive articles often accompanied by 'you the jury' polls aimed at their readers.

The *Sun* has described me, amongst thousands of other things, as 'the symbol of the nation's revulsion at all those who prey on innocent children'. In spite of hundreds of other females in the system who have been convicted of quite horrendous crimes against their own and others' children, and thousands of men convicted of unspeakable child offences, the tabloids have turned me into an industry, selecting me as the public icon/evil monster, Medusa-like image which holds the projected hatred, fear and fury of the nation's psyche, which is fed mercilessly by these tabloids which benefit greatly from capitalising on pandering to baser instincts. (Oscar Wilde wrote, almost a century ago, that the public has an insatiable curiosity to know everything except what is worth knowing, and journalism, conscious of this and having tradesman-like habits, supplies the demand.)

None of this has taken account of any ways in which I have changed over those 30 years, of how I've spent thousands of hours peeling off layers of protective insulation, chipping away at bricks behind which I'd hidden my real self for far too many years, reluctantly descending to the 'foul rag-and-bone shop' cellars of my mind and sifting through the refuse.

All the compartments in which I'd locked away so much of what I couldn't bear to think about had to be opened one by one, taking years to gather the courage to examine and attempt to analyse their contents.

To confront and contemplate one's naked self, warts and all, through the eye of truth, unblinkered by deliberate self-deception, and to scrutinise the mind, the memory, purged of selective amnesia and moral cowardice, is the work of a lifetime – for myself, at any rate – and there are many prisoners like myself who don't want to be what they once were, don't want to remain the person who did the things which brought them to prison.

One doesn't just have to confront one's offending behaviour but one's inner self. I found the former impossible to do for an unpardonable length of time, 'publicly' at least, and because I lacked the courage and decency to do so, I could never publicly express remorse and have been labelled for that, too. (I've always been uncomfortable with the word remorse, which so many people – the media, the public, the penal and criminal justice system, hold so much store by. I feel that repentance is a much more positive way of expressing bitter and deep regret. Judas betrayed Christ and filled with remorse compounded the felony by killing himself. Peter denied Christ three times for which he wept bitterly, repented and begged forgiveness.)

This failure to publicly express repentance doesn't mean that I neglected to seek for those traits and shortcomings in my personality or the fatal flaws in my character that contributed to the disintegration of that which was good in me and resulted in my sinking into the depths of depravity.

It was a long, slow process of uprooting poisonous weeds to plant new seeds and encourage new growth of residual ones. To build on experience, life's best teacher, and reach new insights, clearer understanding – this, together with the efforts to deepen one's spirituality, to 'reach out of sight for the ends of being and ideal grace' cannot fail with the help of that ideal grace, to bring about change and transformation in anyone who desires and seeks.

You published a letter on 7 October in response to mine in which the writer said: 'The tone of her letter would seem to indicate her belief that these crimes were committed by another Myra Hindley and that she, the letter-writing Myra Hindley, need bear no responsibility.'

In my letter, I was responding solely to the gratuitous label of psychopath contained in the extracts from *A Mind of Crime*, but in reply to your correspondent I would say that the crimes were committed by the person I was then, between the ages of 20 and 23, for which I bear full responsibility and always will do, but the person I am now, aged 53, bears little resemblance to the creature involved in the crimes.

Your correspondent goes on to say that my salvation must come from within myself by reaching a true understanding of the enormity of those crimes, with no excuses, adding that I seem a million light years away from that stage. That, of course, is her opinion to which she is entitled, but she, like millions of others, knows me only from what has been written and reported by the media, the tabloids in particular.

The truth of this continuing saga-cum-Gothic soap opera is that the majority of people don't want to accept that people like myself can change. They prefer to keep me frozen in time together with that awful mugshot so that their attitudes, beliefs and perceptions can remain intact, to preclude the distasteful necessity of considering causes rather than the effects or the roots of a disease, rather than symptoms which are visible.

And another equally strong resistance to accept change is because I serve the self-interests of so many parties.

The tabloids need me to boost their circulation and sales. They and their readers need me to satisfy their demand for a national scapegoat. Governments need me to enable them to be seen to be enforcing their 'tough stance' on crime and criminals. And the Prison Service needs me in order to retain their own credibility in a time of current criticism.

In a very real sense – and this is not just my own belief – I have become a political prisoner serving the interests of successive Home Secretaries who have placed political expediency and, effectively, a lynch-mob rationale before the dictates of basic human rights.

This reference to human rights will undoubtedly be offensive if not odious to those who believe I have no human rights, but to them I will say, yes, I discarded my humanity and sank to subhuman levels. But that was more than 30 years ago, and contrary to the beliefs of fundamentalists who assert that I am beyond redemption, there is 'that which is of God' in all of us, and I have to say, to make my own position clear, that I will not conform to these myriad perceptions of myself, or remain trapped in the mould I've been forced into by the tabloids.

I will remain true to myself, a real person, not an effigy constructed not just by my actions of three decades ago but by those who want to burn all the facets of their own natures which they can't or won't confront and deal with.

What I have said will be unpalatable and unacceptable to many people and no doubt provoke the customary outraged reactions. But I and many other prisoners, and people outside in their own kinds of prison, have had to face unpalatable truths, take off blinkers and remove cataracts from the mind's eye and attempt to come to terms with faults and failings.

To do so is ultimately cathartic, like lancing an abscess – painful but necessary.

It is too easy for the media to use labels like 'fiend', 'evil monster', 'manipulative', 'cunning and devious' 30 years on, and to transform my role in the offences from a willing accomplice to the instigator and perpetrator of all that took place. But this of course sells newspapers and pays scant, if any, regard to the truth.

For example, because I haven't had the 'decency to go mad' I must therefore be so bad that, as a short article in the *Observer* magazine of 10 December stated, I tortured, sexually abused and killed five young people with Ian Brady. And even worse, added that I strangled Lesley Ann Downey.

It is lamentable that a quality newspaper emulates the tabloids by reversing the roles. I have said that I believe it is a fact of human nature to apply labels to help us make sense of something, anything incomprehensible, and it reinforces my belief that 'broader society' should take care in defining the word psychopath. It can lead to so many misunderstandings and misrepresentations – as in my own case by David Jessel and Ann Moir – when detailed psychiatric reports from several sources have firmly ruled out any forms of psychopathy. •

· ·

16 May 1996
Joanna Coles
A slice of ham with sauce

Drinks are served in the Old Library at 6.30pm; Pimms, Vin Mousseux, red and white wine and ginger ale. OJ wants water and misses his mouth, so it waterfalls down the black and grey silk tie he has bought this morning from Armani. 'How can I miss my lips? They're so prominent,' he chortles, dabbing vigorously at his chest with a handkerchief. He will miss his mouth three more times during the evening and three more times he will give the same excuse with the same, apparently fresh laugh. But then, as I am to discover, O J Simpson repeats himself a lot.

'Do sit down,' invites Paul Kenward, president of the Oxford Union, gesturing to a semicircle of gloriously battered leather chairs. 'If it's all the same to you I'd prefer to stand,' replies OJ, pacing like a famished wolf past deteriorating copies of Diderot, Chateaubriand and Victor Hugo. It is impossible not to watch him. He is blacker and shorter than I recall from TV, his celebrity all the more dazzling in the gloom of this faded Oxford room. His outfit is oddly formal, almost groomish: black Donna Karan jacket ('Donna's a friend of mine'), his now damp tie ('I bought two from Armani this morning'), grey waistcoat, black trousers and black loafers with tassels. 'I'm 10 pounds overweight at the moment,' he says ruefully. 'I put on 20 pounds when I was incarcerated but I've managed to lose 10.'

Did he keep fit in prison? He shakes his head. 'I was in solitary, in a cell of, what was it, seven by eight, or six by nine. Whenever I did exercise I felt like a caged tiiiger!'

'Mr Simpson, can I introduce my girlfriend, Heidi?' begs Kenward, as a tall, rather beautiful blonde, flushed with excitement, slips in. 'Hellooo, Heidi,' says OJ. 'Hello, Mr Simpson,' says Heidi brightly. 'Welcome to England.'

So here we are. Kenward and Heidi, Marina Baker (a former topless model and now diarist on the London *Evening Standard*), Max Clifford, the PR who organised the trip, O J Simpson and me. And then the room goes dark. A hundred photographers, waiting in the gravelled courtyard have suddenly seen him and are swarming *en masse*, lenses pressed against the library windows like wild cyclopian eyes. 'Come on,' cries Kenward, who speaks as if in a permanent state of job interview. 'We'll go to the Poetry Room instead!'

Eliot, Yeats, Pound and now Simpson. The Poetry Room is upstairs and out of sight and again OJ misses his mouth with the glass. His handkerchief is now so wet that someone hands him a beer towel, which he uses for the rest of the evening, constantly folding and refolding it against his upper lip and forehead to absorb a profusion of sweat. Tom, a man with no evidence of surname or humour but with a history of martial arts, murmurs in my ear that he is OJ's bodyguard. Meanwhile, Max Clifford has disappeared to retrieve his daughter, who has gone missing, and OJ wants to talk about the inequities of American justice.

Uh oh. I try to deflect him by asking how he copes with the fact that most people seem to think that he did kill his wife, Nicole, and her friend Ron Goldman.

'I've been convicted of *nothing*,' he cries triumphantly. 'That's not my problem, it's theirs. I'm not here to rehabilitate myself. I don't *need* to rehabilitate myself. I'm here in England because I was asked. The media twists everything. I couldn't believe the trial I saw on TV was my trial! The only people who didn't have access to the media were the 12 people on the jury, the 12 people who acquitted me in record time. The media are . . .' He talks fantastically fast and as he pauses for breath I butt in to try to initiate a change of subject. What, for example, does he do all day?

First he looks annoyed. He doesn't like being interrupted. Then he looks puzzled, as if he genuinely doesn't know. 'Um, I have friends who call and say: "Hey, what are you doin' today? Can I come over at 10am?" And then they stay all day!' But what does he do with them? 'We hang out.' Doing what exactly? 'We play golf. Or sometimes I go out and talk to people who are outside my house, until it gets too crowded, then I go back in. I was in the Bahamas recently. There was so much love and support for me there, Joanna, I coulda been *king* of the Bahamas!'

Outside we can hear the constant rumble of the TV vans, the chirrup of mobile phones and reporters singsonging their pieces to camera. We cross the hall to the dining room, where 12 stuffed avocados are laid in waiting. It is 7.20pm and a single laser of sunlight beams through the window like a natural spotlight and settles on OJ, illuminating him like the finger in the Lottery ad.

The previous night he had supper with his friend, film director Michael Winner. 'Oh,' I say, racking my memory, trying to remember the names of Winner's films, and then, before I can stop myself: 'Which one did you star in? Was it *Death Wish*?'

He ignores this interjection. 'The first time I met Michael was in Antigua. I had heard he could be difficult as a director. So I walked over to his room and I knocked on his door and I said: "Hi, I'm O J Simpson and if you get mad at me I'm gonna kick your ass!" And he slaps the table and lets out a rapid, rattling deep laugh. Frantically jotting notes under the table (OJ does not want to be taped), I laugh too.

Chicken in white sauce with broccoli arrives and on my right Tom the bodyguard is mumbling to Jenny the Union president-elect: 'So you're what, twenny-four, twenny-five, huh?'

'Twenty actually, but lots of people say I look older,' says Jenny.

'Woah, only twenny, huh?'

Back on my left OJ demands to know what other famous people have spoken at the Union. 'Nixon,' I volunteer. 'Nixon? I don't think I wanna be put in the same bracket as Nixon,' he says crossly. 'Mind you, I don't agree with the popular image of him. I mean, I think history will see him as a really great president.' How does OJ vote? 'Well, next time I will vote for Clinton. I loved what he said after my trial – "You've seen the evidence, we've had the verdict, now let's move on." I played golf with him right before my ordeal. I love the way he talks about his wife.'

By contrast, OJ does not talk about his wife. At least not much. The first mention comes at 7.55pm, when he is complaining again about media inaccuracy. 'They say Bo Derek and Nicole were friends but Nicole has never met Bo Derek!' For a second, the use of the present tense jars, but he doesn't seem to notice and I don't say anything. After the trial was over, he declared he'd stop at nothing to find her killer. What has he done?

'I employ two investigators but it's expensive. I mean, one of them called me and said he wanted to follow up a lead and spend a week in San Francisco. Well, I can't afford that. They won't let me earn anything.' Then he grumbles that neither Nicole's parents nor Ron Goldman's are applying sufficient pressure on the Los Angeles police to find the culprit. His heavy gold bangle catches the edge of the chicken plate as it is replaced by chocolate cheese cake and I realise why he seems darker than I'd expected. He is tanned from his trip to the Bahamas.

What about women? Does he have a new girlfriend? 'I'm not going to be too personal, but I don't have energy for a relationship right now.' Does he get lots of offers? 'Oh, I'm more popular with women now than I was before. I mean, some don't like me, like they have all this hate towards me, but a lot want to mother me.' Really? 'Sure. I was kinda pissed with Nicole's parents when they tried to make out I didn't have time to see my kids when I was released. I didn't see my girlfriend for two weeks.' And then he flogged the photos of him and Paula Barbieri together in the Caribbean for a reported $100,000.

On my right, Tom the bodyguard is trying to persuade Jenny to visit LA, and OJ explains that he needs security because people climb into his garden to pinch souvenirs. For example, he has a clay set of Disney's Seven Dwarfs and only last week he caught someone trying to run off with Dopey! And by the way, he wants me to know that he is tremendously popular in his neighbourhood of Brentwood. He goes to the local shops all the time.

'But I thought you couldn't go out,' puts in Max Clifford doubtfully.

'Oh no, I go out and I'm really popular. I always was really popular,' says OJ.

'Do you get a cut from the books your lawyers have written about you?' demands Marina, the former topless model. 'No,' says OJ, shrugging. 'I guess I shoulda insisted but I'm too nice.' We give a collective nod.

I have heard he goes to bed early: is this true? 'I go to bed at 8.30pm and I'm up at 5am, to play golf. I'm asleep by 9pm, unless I'm reading to my kids and then I'm asleep before they are!'

Why don't they live with him? 'Because their grandparents would not surrender temporary guardianship. I was kinda pissed they arranged for shots of them around Nicole's grave.' How are his kids coping? 'They're happy kids. I tried to explain their mom's in heaven, but they seem fine.'

He picks up his glass of water and misses his mouth again. Why didn't he take the stand? 'My lawyers advised me against it.'

Just as it seems things cannot get more bizarre, they promptly do. There is a small kerfuffle at the door and in strolls the former world WBO Super Middle-Weight Boxing Champion, Chris Eubank, resplendent in a green jodhpur suit and brandishing a gold-topped cane. 'I came to have my intellect satisfied,' he declares, somewhat improbably. OJ gets up to greet him.

Meanwhile, Tom is still working on Jenny. 'Hey, do you want to know what I'm thinking right now?' he drawls. 'No, thank you!' giggles Jenny, pouring herself a glass of port. 'I think I know exactly what you're thinking.'

And I am thinking that, strangely, I am bored. That I am tired of OJ moaning about the media and the inequities of American justice. That he has 1,000 well-thumbed paragraphs which he trots out on demand, that he replies to everything but answers nothing. And that he is oddly relaxed for a man who spent 16 months wrongly incarcerated for double murder. Particularly for a man whose wife was murdered but the murderer has not yet been caught.

And of course he is right: the LAPD did manufacture evidence against him. And of course he is right: the media do play to racial stereotypes and we do worship success while rooting for failure. And yet . . . and yet . . . OJ had it all. He was America's dream, a successful black sportsman-cum-actor with lucrative sponsorships and a beautiful wife. What on earth went so terribly, terribly wrong?

I am still pondering on this when OJ rejoins the table.

'I took my kit off once,' says Marina the former model, apropos of nothing. 'Excuse me?' says OJ.

'I used to model, you know, in magazines.'

He twigs. 'You want to audition for me?' And he laughs his deep and rapid rattling laugh again. And, getting up to move next door to the debating chamber, we all laugh with him. ●

Stephen Fry

Cultural matters

· ·

6 October 1995

Blake Morrison
Famous Seamus

The 18 men and women on the Swedish Academy who choose the Nobel Prize for Literature have been known to spring some surprises. Who, in 1983, would have predicted that the prize would go to the American novelist Pearl Buck? Who would have guessed Elias Canetti, a Bulgarian living almost anonymously in London, in 1981? How many of us in the West had ever heard of, let alone read, last year's winner from Japan, Kenzaburo Oe?

The only surprise of this year's award is that it isn't a surprise. Though still, at 56, in his prime, Seamus Heaney has been tipped as a Laureate for some time. His friends Joseph Brodsky and Derek Walcott have both won the award in the past eight years, and as a poet he is at least their equal. He has won most of the honours that it's possible for an English-speaking poet to win. He is highly regarded throughout Europe and in the US, where he teaches for one term a year. He is one of the few living poets British schoolchildren have heard of. He has done time (five years) as Oxford Professor of Poetry. He has even been on *Desert Island Discs*. He is Famous Seamus.

The first time I'd had any appreciation of that fame was in Belfast 15 years ago, when I met Heaney, up from the South for the day, at the railway station. We'd not walked 200 yards before a car screeched to a halt and a taxi driver dashed over, excitedly shouting, 'Mr Heaney, Mr Heaney,' and demanding an autograph. It's hard to imagine this happening when Ted Hughes comes up to London. I was at a dinner for the last Laureate from these islands, William Golding, in a famous London restaurant shortly after his award. No one recognised him.

Heaney's popularity is in part to do with his genial temperament, an odd mix of flickering wit and sturdy rootsiness. Both Prospero and Caliban, he can put a girdle round the world and perform equally well in Harvard seminar rooms, at London publishing parties, in Dublin, Belfast and further afield. Shy but affable, he is his own best ambassador.

Nice men have won the Nobel Literature Prize before (though not often). What in particular was it that commended Heaney to Stockholm? If the Swedish Academy had to suffer from the same time-lag as we do in the translation and appreciation of foreign writers, it would probably still be coming to terms with his early poetry from the late 1960s, which is loud with the slap of spade and earth. The first poem in his first collection, 'Digging' ('Between my finger and thumb/The squat pen rests; snug as a gun') not only established Heaney as a precocious talent, but pointed to the essential themes he has pursued ever since: blood and soil; imminent violence; a deep awareness of, and awkward squaring up to, his taciturn farming ancestors; self-conscious about writing; a need to dig down, through history and language, to unearth the primal sources of the self. The early reviews of Heaney over-emphasised his rusticity and connections to Ted Hughes. One critic, A Alvarez, caricatured him as a lumbering peasant out of touch with the predominantly urban condition of late-20th-century life. His domain was always larger, his demeanour more subtle and his tone more contemporary than that.

In any case, as schoolchildren here know, and as the Swedish Academy (which for its adjudications commissions its own translations where translations of foreign authors are lacking) will also know, Heaney has come a long way since the richly sensuous poems of his first two books. His next two, *Wintering Out* and *North*, turned their attention to the mouth-music of dialect words and place-names, and to the troubled history of Belfast and the North. Under duress to 'respond' to contemporary violence, terrorism and military repression, Heaney proved he could do reportage with the best of them ('Men die at hand. In blasted street and home/The gelignite's a common sound effect'). But he wasn't altogether comfortable with the results, which violated his deeper, instinctual, feminine muse, and at the end he withdrew, 'a wood-kerne escaped from the massacre'. *Field Work*, arguably his finest book, written when he'd moved south to County Wicklow, is a further withdrawal, but meditates beautifully on 'responsibility', and on the conflicting demands of art and nation. Some of its elegies for dead friends and relations are the finest poems he's written.

In recent years, Heaney has turned to quieter, more domestic themes, back to childhood, and also (at the risk, in the allegorical parts of *The Haw Lantern*, of a kind of poetic Esperanto) to more universal themes. His range as a poet, translator (both from the Irish and from Dante) and as a critic is now so wide that it's hard to know which elements of his work the Swedish Academy was drawn to, but in a brief commendation, special mention was made of his ability to 'exalt everyday miracles'. This is an allusion to his most recent book, *Seeing Things*, which, as its title hints, moves beyond literal annotation of the natural world into something more visionary, ecstatic and transcendental. The triumph of this book is that of someone in mid-life, exultant and exalted, casting off the weight of the past – while also honouring what he's learned from it:

> Heaviness of being. And poetry
> Sluggish in the doldrums of what happens.
> Me waiting until I was early fifty
> To credit marvels. Like the tree-clock of tin cans
> The tinkers made. So long for the air to brighten,
> Time to be dazzled and the heart to lighten.

If the Nobel Committee of the Swedish Academy is dazzled by Heaney, it might also be because, alone among 20th-century poets, he has written a love poem which compares his lover to a skunk. The skunk was one he'd seen 'snuffing the boards' of his back porch in California (where he taught for a year), while he was writing love-letters home, and in the poem he connects the creature to Mrs Heaney:

> It all came back to me last night, stirred
> By the sootfall of your things at bedtime, '
> Your head-down, tail-up hunt in a bottom drawer
> For the black plunge-line nightdress.

It takes some effrontery for a poet to use metaphors like that and expect his marriage to survive, but Heaney's marriage, to Marie Devlin, has lasted 30 years and is a very happy one. (They have two sons and a daughter.) It also takes some effrontery to think marital love can be the source for great (and tender) love poetry, but Heaney succeeds.

Cynics will say that — like the awards to Sholokov and Pasternak, Milosz and Seifert — here is another 'political' Laureateship, given to Heaney in the year which has seen the peace process on Northern Ireland begin in earnest. Within an hour of yesterday's announcement, the wires were buzzing with stories of Heaney's alleged keep-everyone-happy chameleon-ism: how, for example, when travelling on the train from Dublin to Belfast he'll switch brands of whiskies at the border. But even supposing the incorruptible Swedes were swayed by extra-literary considerations, the argument is doubtful. In the past, it's seemed that the Nobel Committee has harboured a prejudice against politically clamorous or didactic writers, yet in its brief statement yesterday it commended Heaney for 'speaking out as an Irish Catholic about violence in Northern Ireland'.

This view of Heaney, as a writer who does, when need be, speak out, is much nearer the mark than the popular view of him in this country, which likes to present him as a man who's even-handed, sit-on-the-fence, without affiliations. Certainly, as Heaney himself admits and dramatises in the poems, he was reared on the attitude 'Whatever you say, you say nothing', and is all for the quiet life, if he can get it. But take his open letter to the editors of *The Penguin Book of Contemporary British Poetry* (Andrew Motion and myself) in 1983. Heaney took objection to being categorised as 'British', and, gently biting the hands that had colonised and anthologised him, declared: 'My passport's green.' His letter, all 33 stanzas, is a masterly display of tact, embarrassment, apology and sly wit. But in the end, it firmly insists that names, and nationality, do matter. 'British, no, the name's not right./Yours truly, Seamus.' Heaney, in public, is often a mediator, but no slippery mediator could have written that poem.

Take, too, some lines Heaney wrote in *North*, in 1975, the collection of his which most explicitly addresses the troubles of Northern Ireland. Standing on ground sour with the blood of her faithful, he calls on Tacitus, an early historian of northern Europe's blood-feuds, to

report us fairly,
how we slaughter
for the common good
and shave the heads of the notorious . . .

In a short book about Heaney some years ago, I suggested that those lines can't and shouldn't be read as cultivated liberal irony at the expense of ignorant hard men. Coming from a Catholic family in County Derry, and having an inherited sympathy with Republican aspirations, Heaney understands why members of the Provisional wing of the IRA, carrying out terrorist acts, might indeed believe they were slaughtering for the common good. For this suggestion, I was castigated by several reviewers. Better that, of course, than that Heaney be hounded by Ulster Protestant extremists, as he occasionally was while living and writing in Belfast (when he moved south, the *Protestant Telegraph* celebrated the departure of 'that well-known Papish propagandist'). But I still think I had a point: humanitarian though he is, sceptical of nationalistic fervour and deeply opposed to violence, Heaney understands the gene pool and race-pull, the gnarled roots and ugly blooms of tribal and religious conflict. Though he has moved away into a more personal, religious vision, his poems on such conflict will remain essential reading as long as nations in Europe tear each other apart. It's partly why, deservedly, Heaney is often called the greatest Irish poet since Yeats.

The last time I saw him, four months ago, he charmed a 2,000-strong audience of A-level students in London with readings from his own work. The Nobel Prize money (over £700,000) relieves him of ever again having to give lectures and readings. But he's unlikely to stop: though he needs the private space to write (and will now have even less of it), his work thrives on an intimate, embarrassed awareness of audience. Now that audience, or part of it, has given him the ultimate accolade. It couldn't have happened to a better poet, or a nicer man.

Making Strange

I stood between them,
the one with his travelled intelligence
and tawny containment,
his speech like the twang of a bowstring,

and another, unshorn and bewildered
in the tubs of his wellingtons,
smiling at me for help,
faced with this stranger I'd brought him.

Then a cunning middle voice
came out of the field across the road

saying, 'Be adept and be dialect,
tell of this wind coming past the zinc hut,

call me sweetbriar after the rain
or snowberries cooled in the fog.
But love the cut of this travelled one
and call me also the cornfield of Boaz.

Go beyond what's reliable
in all that keeps pleading and pleading
these eyes and puddles and stones,
and recollect how bold you were

when I visited you first
with departures you cannot go back on.
A chaffinch flicked from an ash and next thing
I find myself driving the stranger

through my own country, adept
at dialect, reciting my pride
in all that I knew, that began to make strange
at that same recitation.

· ·

27 March 1996

Leader

Jane Austen accepts her Oscar

Sirs, please forgive me – I am agitated, nay, I am more than agitated, I am astonished beyond expression, my thoughts are in tumult. Pray do not think me uncivil if my feelings exceed my fluency of expression. For have I not longed, these 200 years, to procure your affection and regard? Yet I could not, in rational expectation, hope to receive any commendation of so fine a nature. I scarce know how to support myself, nor this handsome firedog. How can it be possible that I, who live in a small retired village in the country, could provide such a lively and intelligent company as yourselves with novelty and amusement? How can my poor work compare with the great schemes of Mr Tarantino? I fear that generosity has tempered your discernment. As I once wrote to my dear nephew, Hollywood's medium is the great one of Celluloid; mine is a little bit (two inches wide!), of Ivory, on which I work with so fine a brush, as produces little effect after much labour!

Last evening, as I walked in the higher grounds of Sunset Boulevard I enjoyed a tête-à-tête with Mr Hugh Grant. He had lost none of his civility, and advised me that an acceptance speech should take notice of some unfortunate affair of the day. If this be so: my work is magnified by the fact that the streets of heaven are too crowded with spinsters. They number a thousand for each one of the red ribbons we wear here tonight.

It cannot be proper, nay, it cannot be kind, further to test your patience with my emotions, but I must not retire before expressing my gratitude to my dear brother and agent, Henry Austen, and my sweet Cassandra, dearest and kindest of sisters. Above all, let us remember Miss Emma Thompson. Is she not an angel? Before I quit England, I visited her shrine in the Groucho Club. As I knelt in prayer, I presumed to conjecture her feelings on this most happy day. Would she exclaim, with that violence of expression which habitually followed a night of excess, 'Arseholed again', or would it be, 'Huge spot has appeared on chin'? No, I imagine this great occasion would inspire her most affecting ejaculation: 'I've just ovulated!' Forgive me for taking up so much of your time, and accept my best wishes for your health and happiness. •

∙∙

30 October 1995
Nancy Banks-Smith
See the penguins of Pemberley

O h, I knew it would all come out right in the end!' said Mrs Bennet, who had seen the cover of *Radio Times*.

And so *Pride and Prejudice* (BBC 1) ended with a double wedding, though Lizzie had four greys to her barouche and Jane only two. One hopes sisterly affection will survive these little brushes. Darcy, who naturally had the highest hat of all, kissed Lizzie in her poke bonnet, a manoeuvre which apparently required several takes. I am inclined to think a gentleman should take off his top hat to kiss a lady and I trust he removes his top boots in bed.

But what, gentle viewer, is the real ending? We are in a better position than Jane Austen to say what will happen to large private estates and inherited wealth. As Bingley and Jane toddled off into the sunset like the Start-Rite tots, Mr Bennet warned they would be bankrupt within a generation: 'Each of you is so easy that every servant will cheat you and so generous that you will always exceed your income.'

Mr Darcy will consider himself honour bound to keep Pemberley intact and though, in his fondness for Lizzie, he will allow her to put penguins in the lake ('Come and see the penguins of Pemberley') he will proudly refuse to charge visitors an entrance fee. It will be Lydia who comes storming through. She has already showed a degree of dash wholly lacking in her sisters, who seem able to spin out a little light flower-arranging to fill a lifetime.

When Wickham is lost at Waterloo – the station not the battle – Lydia will be thrown on her own considerable capacity for fun and effrontery. She will go on the stage where, as Frilly Wickers, she will gain great celebrity and many titled admirers. Her rendition of 'There's Something about a Soldier' (and I wish I could put my finger on it) will close several theatres. Her sisters, much reduced in circumstances, will drink the champagne she sends them but they never can forgive.

The Collinses will have innumerable children so hardly miss one, Rosings Collins, a missionary eaten by Fuzzy Wuzzies after describing Lady Catherine's fireplace to them for the tenth time.

I am extremely sorry to see the back of these girls in diaphanous nighties and toffs in tight trousers. The front view is much better.

Jane Austen's interest in 18th-century plumbing has hitherto been overlooked but this was a production where the heroines looked as if they had just stepped fully dressed from the bath and the hero actually had.

I am sorriest of all to lose Jennifer Ehle's Lizzie, the first modern heroine, flickering like St Elmo's fire around the mast of Colin Firth's Darcy. Lizzie reminds me of Lady Mabell Airlie's remark: 'What a comfort it is to be cleverer than one's husband.'

Darcy, like the House of Lords, does nothing in particular but does it very well. As an awed American tourist said after a production of *Julius Caesar*: 'That Brutus! Was he noble!' Darcy has the art of saying nothing thunderously.

I was covering the Olympic Games once when we had to interview a weightlifter. God had been generous with thew and sinew but the glorious gift of human communication had been denied him. We asked how he felt when he won the gold. He rippled. His neck swelled and he drew long shuddering breaths. Sweat stood on his brow. He tore a telephone directory in two. Eventually an old sports reporter stood up warily. 'Well, lads,' he said, 'it's the Strong Silent Hero again then.' And, in the morning, it was. •

....

23 December 1995
Vera Rule
'Last night I dreamt I went to Manderley again'

I n Alan Bennett's play adaptation of *The Wind in the Willows*, when Toad Hall is taken over by weasels, 'taken over' has a contemporary meaning. The weasels are planning visitor throughput, souvenir shops, a marina and very possibly a Toad Hall theme park. Now consider the fates of:

• *Coketown*, Dickens's mid-Victorian cotton-boom borough, which went through

20 years of extreme decay after Bounderby Mills closed (they are now cable-TV studios). But in 1993, the regional authority successfully applied to Brussels for millions in EU grants for revivifying inner urban areas, and spent some of these, to tabloid shock-horror, on gutting warehouses to create cheap hireable multi-media workshops.

• The Prince of Wales recently made 'social investments' in the new development (beyond the edge-of-town Tesco and MFI) at *Casterbridge*, built to 'combine vernacular Wessex architecture with the enclosure patterns of Tuscan hill towns'.

• The great country house *Brideshead* mouldered until the seventies, when it was converted into a recording studio, conveniently within chauffeured distance of the rockocracy. It is now a training school for bodyguards, with a skidpan in the grounds for the defensive driving course. The castle of *Torquilstone* (where Ivanhoe once took refuge), is now administered by English Heritage and open only as a secure international conference facility; the helicopter pad in the courtyard can be used after the drawbridge has been raised.

• Readers of *Hello!* recently enjoyed a photo-spread on the new Jacuzzi and sauna suite added to the master bath/bedroom at *Howards End* by the daytime-TV confession-show presenter who bought the place 'for its wonderful nostalgia value'.

• Barns and stables at *Manderley* not destroyed during the fire were, in the fifties, accommodation for an advanced (and notoriously druggy) fee-paying coed school; but 10 years ago, a Pacific Rim evangelic sect bought the estate and fenced it off. There is a new, if concrete, mansion, and a 30-foot neon cross on the nearby beach.

• *Mansfield Park* was in the fasting-on-lemon-juice and hot-water-and-colonic-irrigation business until last year, when its owners decided that their future was in remedial therapy for bulimia and anorexia. *Locksley Hall* is now a health club and water sports centre, so successful that prospective competitors for *Gladiators* are sent there to beef up. The Barsetshire Regional Health Trust has taken over *Hiram's Hospital*, Barchester, as headquarters for its private finance subsidiary.

• The current tenants of *Wildfell Hall* had a poor start to their mail-order catalogue for sex aids and lingerie, but going online with a home page has increased turnover. *Nightmare Abbey* did murder mystery weekends with bed-and-breakfast until the fad passed, and now takes orders for commemorative porcelain plates through coupons in the more revoltingly sentimental Sunday colour mags. *Dorlcote Mill on the Floss* sold 'stoneground hand-stirred Christmas puddings' through Cranks, but the National Trust's saturation pud output meant a change to marketing aromatherapy oils by post. *Dingley Dell* is, of course, as a restaurant only a little less famous than Le Manoir aux Quat' Saisons, though its chef (a Parisian maniac) despises local produce, except for the riskier sorts of wild fungi, and imports every ingredient directly from France daily on the Eurostar.

• A planning objection was initially lodged to windfarm vanes being installed at *Wuthering Heights*, but the post-privatisation electricity suppliers claim that without many more alternative power sources the region will have to go nuclear, so the campaign concluded. Only one investigative reporter on the *Guardian*'s environment pages noticed the new agri-business at *Cold Comfort Farm* – pig-breeding in laboratory conditions to produce bio-engineered heart and skin transplant material.

• The *Hundred Acre Wood* was taken over by a firm organising paint-gun games for City futures-sellers, while a bungee-jumping crane was erected over Eeyore's boggy place. Both enterprises failed.

• The *Tabard Inn* in Southwark has been relaunched in turn as the Pilgrims' Wine Bar, the Compostella Tapas Bar, the Parson's Port Cellars (very florid on the typography), the Man of Law's Champagne and Oyster Bar, the Clerk's Tavern with 34 beers all from Prague on draught and aggressive stand-up comics, the members-only Monk Club and is now Wifesound, a regular rave venue for the under-17s.

• Despite the protests (63 travellers were arrested), the last motorway constructed under the Government's present programme has cut through *Watership Down*. •

....

22 December 1995
Roy Greenslade
Keep taking the tabloids

They may not agree about much, but the Prince and Princess of Wales do share a deep-seated contempt for the tabloid press. In her *Panorama* interview the Princess criticised 'the media', meaning popular newspapers, on 16 separate occasions. In his biography of the Prince, Jonathan Dimbleby claimed Charles was 'always prone to detect a hostile impulse in the media' and considered the tabloids as 'voyeurs' who persistently distorted the facts.

At face value, this criticism appears justified. Papers were often guilty of exaggeration; on the slimmest of hints they managed to create stories which gave new meaning to hyperbole. They also got details wrong, they sometimes took matters out of context, and they doubtless intruded into the couple's private life.

But to accept this version as the whole truth, even though it is still purveyed as such by Buckingham Palace and its acolytes in the Lords and Commons, would be gross misrepresentation. Yesterday's wholly accurate *Sun* scoop, which revealed that the Queen had ordered the couple to divorce, reminds us that the tabloid press have called this one right all along. They got much more right than they ever got wrong. The divorce announcement therefore represents the final vindication of the veracity of the tabloids' trade in royal tittle-tattle.

Consider their remarkable track record. In 1987, Andrew Morton wrote in the *Daily Star*: 'Separate breakfasts, separate timetables, separate friends . . . These days the Prince and Princess of Wales are leading active, interesting, but totally independent lives.' The *Daily Mirror* had earlier asserted that they were sleeping in separate bedrooms. The *Sun* said she had once driven off alone at night, in great distress, from Highgrove without telling anyone where she was going. It was projected as a 'security alert'.

The tabloids bombarded us with revelations. We were told of Diana's bulimia, of a mysterious 'fall' downstairs, of self-mutilation, of moodiness, of problems with staff, of problems with the royal family, with whom she was said to have little in common. Charles, it was said, showed a 'callous disregard' for her.

Tabloids revealed her visits to a variety of therapists, her 'friendship' with an army officer called James Hewitt, and her falling out with her brother-in-law, the Queen's private secretary Sir Robert Fellowes. There were stories about the couple's 'lack of togetherness' in public, about Camilla Parker Bowles playing hostess at Highgrove and, of course, Camilla sharing Charles's bed. All this before the remarkable tapes – Camillagate and Squidgygate – were also revealed in detail in the tabloids.

Almost every story was dismissed as poppycock or, in officialese, 'wild speculation'. Broadsheet commentators tended to dismiss the increasingly hysterical and intrusive stories about the marriage as fabrication. The general view was that the tabloids only got away with publishing such piffle because members of the royal family could not sue (though this has since been disproved).

Yet there is hardly a story published by the tabloids which has not now been confirmed by either Charles, in his book and TV collaboration with Dimbleby, or by Diana, during her *Panorama* interview.

When the *Sunday Times* serialised Morton's book, it was castigated for publishing untruths. I too raised my eyes at some of the book's tales, especially that melodramatic moment when the Princess was said to have pitched herself downstairs at Sandringham. But I noted that Morton had named sources (a first in this kind of journalism, notorious for its off-the-record quotes) and it was obvious that Diana had allowed her friends to cooperate (how did Morton publish copyright pictures unless he had her permission?).

I also knew that the *Sunday Times* had tested the claims. Now we all know that Morton got it right. As he notes in the preface to his latest edition: 'The book's revelations, initially treated with scorn and scepticism, are now accepted.'

Hold your nose if you must, but this truth-telling has to be seen in retrospect as a tribute to tabloids. They have exercised press freedom to its limits while withstanding assaults and threats from a hostile establishment which believed it better in the national interest (or their own selfish interests) to tell lies and cover up. Even during my brief tenure as editor of the *Daily Mirror* I was aware that the palace press office was a machine built to frustrate the media.

Its routine reply to any inquiry about any story involving any member of the royal family was to say: 'No comment'. If it was true, there was no comment.

If it was wrong, there was no comment. The effect of this kind of response was to encourage newspapers to take a chance and publish. There was also, of course, off-the-record guidance. This usually amounted to the press officer saying something like: 'Look, I don't know for sure. It's not the kind of thing I could put to their royal highnesses, even if I wanted to, which I don't, but it just doesn't ring true with me. I mean, you say it happened on Tuesday. Well, I know for a fact that the Princess of Wales wasn't at Highgrove on Tuesday, if that's any help.'

OK, so the day was wrong, but what about the essential truth of the story? 'No comment.'

It made life extraordinarily difficult for that eccentric band known as the royal rat pack. Their stories could not be verified officially, so they often found themselves at odds with their editors. I still remember my incredulity as far back as 1983 when Judy Wade – then at the *Sun*, now with *Hello!* – said she was convinced that all wasn't right with the marriage. Her 'evidence' appeared to be composed of half-whispers from police with the royal protection squad and unnamed 'courtiers'.

The truth is that we in the tabloids were as overwhelmed as everyone else by the fairytale and were delighted for it to continue. There was no apparent benefit in undermining the marriage; a radiant princess sold papers. Surely Judy, we said, the couple were happily carrying out their duties. 'Look at the pictures,' she said. 'Don't you think she's thin?' We did not. We noticed only a young couple smiling at the crowds and each other. 'You couldn't see the body language unless you were there with me,' she replied with passion. So we shook our heads and wondered at Judy's sanity. I recall it was months before Judy's intuition – backed up, in fairness, by those anonymous sources – became a familiar theme in the tabloids.

After all, most of the royal correspondents were in love with 'Di' and, in their eyes, she could do no wrong. There was no desire to upset her on the part of her faithful followers, who were far from rats: the *Daily Mirror*'s James Whitaker and the *Sun*'s Harry Arnold, along with their photographic side-kicks, Kent Gavin and Arthur Edwards, remained sceptical about genuine problems within the marriage. As did Morton, then with the *Daily Star*.

But the royal correspondents eventually could not ignore what they were hearing from detectives and other members of the entourage. Nor could they overlook the fact that Princess Diana often behaved in a less than regal way. No stiff upper lip for her: she even cried in public. And yes, we sceptics back in the office did begin to think she looked 'too slim'.

Meanwhile, some journalists were building excellent contacts within both Charles's and Diana's camps. Stuart Higgins, for instance, then a *Sun* executive and now its editor, won the confidence of one of Charles's closest friends. They are said to speak as often as three times a week. It is no surprise that it was he who wrote the *Sun*'s 'world exclusive'. The *Sun* may be anathema to many people but Higgins's professionalism is respected by this woman. He is reputed to ensure that every royal story is read to her.

Broadsheet readers might well ask at this point: so what? It was the couple's private life. There is a great deal more to these two being heir to the throne and mother of the future king than their marriage. They have important duties and a constitutional role. Their relationship should have been sacrosanct.

This point was made forcefully by Dimbleby on Prince Charles's behalf. It was also the view of Charles Moore, then the editor of the *Sunday Telegraph*, who argued that newspapers which wished to see the continuance of monarchy had an obligation to be discreet. Similarly, the *Independent* under the guidance of its founder, Andreas Whittam Smith, affected disdain for any story about the royal marriage and refused to publish them.

But this high-mindedness (a.k.a. lack of reality) ignores both newspapers' history and the development of the modern tabloid. Journalists have never forgotten the absurd reticence which allowed Edward VIII to indulge in a liaison which threatened the crown while British papers censored themselves, allowing the foreign press to publish stories they could not.

The papers of the 1990s are very different: the era of deference has long passed. Filtered through the growth of appreciation in the free market, tabloid owners and editors are deeply suspicious of the establishment: old money, old school tie, inherited wealth, inherited privilege. They resent the lack of meritocracy, they no longer revere the institutions which, in their eyes, have held back British society, and they abhor the pervasive culture of secrecy. In this respect, the palace is viewed by the tabloid press as the *sine qua non* of the establishment's failure to move with the times.

It would be easy to point only to Rupert Murdoch, as Moore and his ilk tend to do. They see him as a republican and claim he is solely responsible for the intrusion of the Wales's marriage. Yet Murdoch represents a trend in that he lets the market decide matters of taste and decency. He holds up to public gaze the hypocrisy of that same public which affects to despise the tabloids' preoccupation with royal gossip-mongering while clamouring to read it. Did Diana's TV interview attract 22.7 million viewers because people were worried about the serious matters of the succession and the future of monarchy, or because they wanted to know her side of the marriage story?

However disingenuous it may sound, the tabloids can defend all that they have done as being 'in the public interest', quite apart from it interesting the public. When the future of the monarchy is at stake – and the announcement of the divorce made a specific reference to that concern, along with the damage to Britain's image abroad – then even prurience can be seen as virtuous. Though Charles may view the press as hounds baying for blood at the palace gates, in his exalted position he cannot surely have expected to get away with fooling all of the people all of the time. He made a bad marriage, he got found out, yet he chooses to blame the messenger.

The messenger, confident of its facts, carried out its task to the best of its ability. And it did so relentlessly because the royal marriage is no ordinary marriage. The nation's 'top' family sets the moral climate for its people, and the press was not about to let that family live out a sham behind palace walls. (Nor, indeed, did Princess Diana appear keen to do so either, which is the real reason we know anything at all about this matter.)

Though monarchist apologists are trying to minimise the constitutional impact, the press has always been aware of the consequences. But this country is not at war. There is no need to exercise censorship over royal affairs. If the result of these revelations is to belittle monarchy in the eyes of the people, then it seems wide of the mark to turn on the press. Does this family not bear the brunt of the blame? Does it have rights above those of its subjects? Is it not to be held up to scrutiny?

In a sense, there was tacit support for this point of view from the 30 million or so daily tabloid readers. Their fascination with the breakdown of Charles and Diana's marriage reduced the couple to the level of ordinary people with ordinary problems. Better still, the drama was played out over the years like a TV soap opera. It was at once real and unreal, the perfect combination for a public caught between the mundanity of their own lives and the glamour of celebrity on TV and in newspapers.

There is also no denying that in a competitive and declining market the tabloids were happy to use Diana as circulation fodder. But she played her part. She enjoyed posing for pictures. The Morton book was her choice. She regularly briefs journalists, such as the *Daily Mail*'s royal correspondent Richard Kay, with whom she was twice pictured in a car. The *Panorama* interview, and its content, were under her control.

Then again, this is not a day to apportion blame. For once yellow journalism is exculpated. Next time anyone asks: 'What use are the tabloids?' point to the gradual peeling away of the Great Royal Lie. It has exposed the palace as an untrustworthy institution, imbued with secrecy, unable and unwilling to shed light on the anachronistic world of rulers who don't rule yet who are bound by obsolete rites which force them to act as if they do. Could that explain the Windsor family's succession of failed marriages?

Bagehot, the supreme monarchist, once wrote: 'The mystic reverence, the religious allegiance, which are essential to any true monarchy, are imaginative sentiments that no legislature can manufacture in any people.'

But these 'imaginative sentiments' can vanish too. Where is the mysticism now? Where the religious allegiance from this presumptive head of the Church of England? The tabloid press is more republican than it realises. •

21 August 1996

David McKie

Step forward, all friends of the footnote

We may[1] be about to witness the death of the footnote.[2] Despite its many years of useful and versatile[3] service, publishers in the United States are turning against it.[4] Yet if footnotes disappear, authors will no longer be forced to state their sources, enabling others to check and challenge them. We need an organisation, called perhaps The Friends of the Footnote, to save this unique and valuable art-form[5] from extinction.

Footnotes:

[1] I am indebted[6] for my information on the threat to the footnote to the foreign desk of the *Guardian*, which spotted a piece about it in the *New York Times* News Service.

[2] The origins of the footnote are unknown. The *New York Times* thinks it started with academic critics of Descartes, one of whom, the philosopher Pierre Bayle, published an encyclopaedia in 1697 bursting not just with footnotes but with footnotes of footnotes.

[3] Though footnotes are most extensively deployed in academic works, they also appear in less predictable contexts. The nowadays largely unread Victorian novelist Edward Bulwer Lytton, for instance, peppered his historical adventures with footnotes designed to ward off attacks by real historians who treated such stuff with disdain. Thus in *The Last of the Barons*, the mention of an arras is immediately buttressed by a footnote arguing that the historian Hallam, who had publicly questioned whether such things existed in the reign of Edward IV, was in serious error. (For an instructive account of the use of whirlicotes in Britain before the reign of Richard II, see the footnote on page 427, *op cit*.) A recently published American novel, *Infinite Jest* by David Foster Wallace, has 388 footnotes spanning 96 pages.[7] Footnotes in poems are rarer, but the otherwise deservedly obscure Victorian poet Edward Edwin Foot[8] rarely launched a poem without an accompanying flotilla of footnotes.[9]

[4] The campaign against footnotes, the *New York Times* suggests, gains much of its impetus from marketing people. 'A lot of our authors are aiming at the general reader,' Jennifer Snodgress, marketing director of the Harvard University Press, is quoted as saying, 'and our marketing department tells us that footnotes scare off people.' Though full of appeal for pedants, this kind of academic undergrowth is 'otiose', as Roy Jenkins would say, to the general reader. Does one detect the hands of focus groups here?

[5] The possible disappearance of a whole unique art form is perhaps the most serious cultural danger of all. Like bats in caves, there are words which nowadays live almost entirely in the semi-darkness of footnotes. *Ibid* (short for ibidem) is one, denoting a reference to a work already quoted, a function also performed by *op cit* (work cited) and its cousin *loc cit* (much the same). *Passim* (throughout) is another favourite.

The most lethal, however, is *pace*, a device used for putting down rivals who dare to reach conclusions contrary to one's own. For example: 'as was long ago established, by rigorous investigation, night follows day – *pace* Hessenthaler, who astonishingly in his *Henry VII* and the *Genesis of Blur* appears to believe that day follows night.'

It cannot be said too strongly that one of the principal functions of footnotes is to do down one's academic competitors. Vicious battles are fought in death-dealing small print on these rarefied pages. The wounds are often most savage when the language implies little more than a raising of eyebrows. 'It will perhaps, surprise admirers of Mr Fester to find him asserting . . .' 'Plunge in the poniard politely': that is the watchword.

Footnotes to footnotes:

[6] Authors love to express indebtedness in their footnotes, though only for minor discoveries: the big ones are all their own. They hope it gives the impression of scholarly generosity, though it's often a form of penance. Be wary, for instance, of the academic who says: 'I owe this *aperçu* to my student, Geoffrey Tiddles.' This usually means that Tiddles, who has come to the university for quite other purposes, has been wheedled/ pressurised/blackmailed by his tutor to carry out his more boring bits of research.

[7] Even Wallace's efforts, however, are puny compared to a single footnote in *The History of Northumberland* by John Hodgson, published in 1840, which according to the *New York Times* ran for 165 pages.

[8] See also my 'Taking the doggerel for a long walk' (*Guardian*, 24 July) . . . One huge temptation of footnotes, rarely resisted, is the chance they offer an author to recommend all his other works on this and related subjects.

[9] One of Foot's poems begins: 'The captain scans the ruffled zone . . .'[1] The footnote explains: [1]'A figurative expression, intended by the author to signify the horizon.' Even the Friends of the Footnote, I think I can promise, will draw the line at items like that. ●

4 May 1996

Matthew Engel
Still the one and only

D aily newspapers are not, day by day, much concerned with history. At a rough guess, 90 per cent of journalistic effort goes into producing the next day's paper; 7 or 8 per cent into planning a day or two ahead; and 2 or 3 per cent into bitching about what went wrong the previous day. The ancient past is a matter of concern only if you are delving into the files for historical background.

Most particularly, daily newspapers are not much concerned with their own history. This is especially true of the popular press, but we are all guilty. Very few journalists on this paper will ever have leafed through the bound volumes of old *Manchester Guardian*s. It would be an indulgence, bearing no relation to the job.

When I was the *Guardian*'s cricket correspondent, people would often ask me whether I was not intimidated 'following in the footsteps of Neville Cardus and John Arlott'. The only honest answer was no. The men who intimidated me were my rivals on *The Times* and the *Telegraph.* My concern was to make sure I did not do my job conspicuously worse than they did theirs: you are judged by reference to your peers, not your journalistic ancestors.

And yet a newspaper's business is history, or the first rough draft of it. And its output is its own history. The story of this newspaper is really contained within its 46,544 different issues, not in books recording the machinations about who should succeed C P Scott.

Tomorrow the *Guardian* is exactly 175 years old. By coincidence, this weekend also marks the centenary of the *Daily Mail*. Their achievement is the more resonant; ours by far the more impressive. We are not going to make much of a fuss, because it is not that sort of anniversary (there is not even a word for it) and it is not that sort of newspaper, though maybe the management will give everyone a glass of cheapish Chardonnay and a few nibbles if we make it through to the bicentenary in 2021.

But it is a moment to take stock, and think about what we do and why we do it. There is a difference between the *Mail* and the *Guardian*, aside from all the obvious ones. The *Mail*, started by Lord Northcliffe, was widely mimicked and began what we regard as modern popular journalism. The *Guardian*, started by John Edward Taylor, never has been copied, certainly not successfully. All institutions are unique, but there really is nothing like this one.

There are nine surviving general national daily papers. Two of them (the *Independent* and the *Daily Star*) are less than 20 years old and may yet prove transient, like the ill-fated *Today*, closed by Rupert Murdoch last November – here yesterday, gone tomorrow.

The other six have been participants in the long, historical process whereby papers have captured the public mood for a generation or so, risen to be the top-seller, then fallen away again: in order, *The Times*, *Daily Telegraph*, *Daily Mail*, *Daily Express*, *Daily Mirror* and *Sun*.

The *Guardian* has never been part of that game. It has never been No. 1. It has never even threatened, and heaven help us, all if it did. What it has instead is a special relationship with those who do read it, a relationship no other paper can match.

Any writer who sees someone reading their own paper, especially in unexpected circumstances, naturally feels a little encouraged. What makes the *Guardian* special is that its readers, spotting each other, often feel the same frisson of recognition. We all belong to the same club, less exclusive than White's or Boodle's, but more desirable than either: a sort of fellowship. From the paper's point of view, it enabled our circulation to survive, virtually unscathed, even when Rupert Murdoch, by ruthless cross-subsidisation, temporarily reduced the price of *The Times* to less than half that of the *Guardian*. Do *Times* readers feel uplifted at the sight of one another? I doubt it.

The *Guardian* represents three separate but related traditions. One quite obviously is that of radicalism. Other papers have been protean in their beliefs. The *Telegraph* achieved initial success as a youngish, liberal, almost subversive paper of the mid-Victorian era; the *Mirror* was very Tory in the 1920s; the *Sun* is heir of the old *Daily Herald*, the TUC paper, and was itself pro-Labour, even under Murdoch.

The *Guardian* began as a pro-reform paper in response to the Peterloo massacre; it was a Liberal paper through the 19th century; it achieved intellectual leadership of the left by its opposition to the Boer War; it sustained that into the 20th century, as the Liberal Party faded, by being open, if not slavishly devoted, to the new force of the Labour Party; it denounced Hitler, early and often; it opposed Suez and Thatcherism.

Sometimes the trumpet has given off an uncertain sound; sometimes the paper has simply missed the point. But over 175 years and billions of words, there has been an intellectual consistency that, given the exigencies of newspaper production, remains extraordinary.

The second strand is that of, not provincialism exactly, but non-metropolitanism. The paper began in Manchester. From 1821 to 1959 it was called the *Manchester Guardian*. The weekly edition still keeps the title in the US (the Americans are quite happy to move their football and baseball teams from city to city, but newspapers, they think, have to stick to their roots).

Throughout the 19th century it was competing far more fiercely with a stack of other Mancunian papers, all long forgotten, than with any of the London papers, which sent copies north in the same sort of belated and haphazard way that modern London papers permeate the further reaches of Europe.

Only a handful of provincial morning papers now survive. Outside their own areas, they sell only to the most determined exiles. The *Manchester Guardian* broke its bounds, partly because C P Scott gave the paper a national reputation; partly because it voiced thoughts that were muted in the London papers; and partly because of the quality of its journalism.

Britain, as we all know, is a horribly centralised country. There are very few fields of endeavour in which it is possible to scale the commanding heights without being in London: academe is one – but then Oxford and Cambridge are merely outer suburbs anyway – football is another. Journalism is most emphatically not among them.

It is hard to know what would have happened to the *Guardian* had it taken the soft option and chosen to remain a Manchester paper. Perhaps it would have settled into a cosy local existence like the *Yorkshire Post*; maybe it would have vanished. But I suspect only a Manchester paper could have transformed itself the way the *Guardian* did: the Yorkshire papers were too inward-looking, the Scottish ones too particularist.

A paper that sold largely to cotton traders necessarily gazed out to sea rather than just at its own city and the route south, and thus developed the outlook – *urbi et orbi* – that made it possible for the *Guardian* to match the London papers and then join them.

Curiously, the *Guardian* now has a higher proportion of its sales within the M25 than any other national paper. This is partly because so many of its natural readers gravitate to London, just as the paper itself did. It retains a residual but diminishing strength in the North-West. One of its characteristics over the past quarter-century has been to pay more attention to its branches than its roots, and the decline of the northern base has been one of its failures.

The third distinctive feature is literacy. Anyone who has actually read the turgid and pedantic writing that fills most of the *New York Times* will know that a great newspaper is not necessarily a well-written one. From a very early stage, the *Manchester Guardian* always had a reputation as a writers' paper.

In the 19th century the *Daily Telegraph* believed that good writing had to be verbose; *The Times* thought it had to be pompous. *Guardian* pieces were usually written with far less affectation, and stand the test of time better as a result.

The paper has often been less clever at the simple business of gathering news. C P Scott's most famous dictum, 'Comment is free, but facts are sacred', has often been disrespectfully subedited: delete 'sacred', substitute 'expensive'; and the tradition that *Guardian* accountants have a lower pain threshold than anyone else's is among the most enduring.

These days the news desk works hard to eradicate the perception that the *Guardian*'s news judgements are often whimsical, bordering on the eccentric.

In a way it seems a shame. One change of the past 25 years is that the tabloids (and the royal story is the most spectacular example) have often set the news agenda while the broadsheets struggle like mad to catch up. But another change is that the *Guardian* style and method have begun to spread. The humorous, irreverent, writing that took the paper to its highest-ever circulation in the mid-1980s (before the brief incandescence of the *Independent*) is now more widely accepted elsewhere. In that sense, it is the *Guardian* that is now being mimicked. Lord Rothermere has even been dropping hints that the *Mail* will support the same party as us at the next election.

It is, however, frightfully hard to eradicate people's ideas about newspapers. It is still possible to get a cheap laugh from any audience in the country by making a joke about the 'Grauniad' and mipsrints.

The technical problems were solved a full decade ago (shortly after Ronald Reagan won his second presidential election in what we referred to, in a 72-point headline, as a 'landside') and this paper is now no better or worse than any other. Does anyone give us credit? Do they heck!

Newspapers change and develop. This is a very different product, in its look and tone, from the one that celebrated its 150th birthday in 1971. But it is still recognisably the same old *Guardian*, produced by people with political and journalistic beliefs in line with those of the paper's founders.

'The *Guardian* has changed its mind more because times have changed – and sometimes the *Guardian* has helped to change them – than through instability of character,' wrote the paper's historian David Ayerst. 'The paper's views have developed in a fairly straight line. Admittedly they have sometimes wobbled, but not often.'

When, after four generations of family ownership, Taylor's heirs, the Scotts, handed the paper over to the Scott Trust in 1936, the trustees were given only one instruction: to run the paper 'on the same lines and in the same spirit as heretofore'. When Alan Rusbridger was made editor in January 1995 he was given the same instruction, and no other.

At the time, amid all the conflicting emotions one always feels about one's employers, it made me immensely proud that such a newspaper exists and that I work for it. I think we all share that pride. Yes, it is unique. ●

Pass Notes

8 February 1996   News Bunny

Appearance: Man-sized brown furry rabbit.

Job: Making gestures.

You mean . . . No, not *those* kinds of gestures! Honestly . . . Look, it's very simple. He sits behind the news reader on *L!ve TV* giving a paws-up or a paws-down depending on the nature of the story.

How tasteless. I mean, what if the Queen Mother died? Paws down.

Well, what if Darius Guppy had been freed on the promise of financial help from a newspaper? Both paws up. Funny you should mention that, though. *L!ve TV* is owned by the Mirror Group, which agreed to pay Guppy for his story, then reneged on the deal.

Yes, but isn't *L!ve TV* run by ex-super-soaraway *Sun* man Kelvin MacKenzie? Now you've got it by the ears. The bunny was burrowed out of Kelvin's great warren of ideas.

Cor, bet that impressed his staff? Not really. His reporters have complained that dressing up in a full-sized rabbit costume then being forced to scamper around the newsroom is undignified.

What a load of stuck-up toffs! Exactly. That's just what Kelvin said.

What did he say exactly? 'Bosnia, it ain't.'

So everybody hates News Bunny? No, a researcher is sufficiently enamoured of the furry animal to change his name by deed poll to News Bunny.

Why on earth would anyone want to do that? So he can please Kelvin by standing for Parliament in a Staffordshire by-election next month.

What does Kelvin say about that? 'News Bunny is not standing just for the furry creatures of Staffordshire – he's there for all the little people in life.'

How touching. Does anyone else covet News Bunny? Yes. Channel 4 tried to kidnap . . . er, bunny-nap . . . him by sending along two doe-eyed female bunnies.

I suppose Jon Snow can be a bit dreary. Well, the attempt was foiled. Anyway, Newsy's safely back at Canary Wharf, where he's been promised a mate.

What, a Honey Bunny? Yes.

So there'll soon be more gestures? Yes. Kelvin has suggested they make gestures at each other.

Oh no, you mean . . . 'Fraid so.

Not . . . Oh yes. Lots and lots of Newsy Bunnies.

Not to be confused with: Bugs Bunny, Bunny Girls, Roger, Peter or Brer Rabbit.

Likely gesture: Paws down for Bosnia, Scott report, Harriet Harman, general election, homelessness, cross-media ownership.

Even more likely gesture: Two paws up for topless darts. ●

1 February 1996

Henry Porter
Trivial pursuit

What is happening to Western culture? Harold Bloom's book *The Western Canon* reaches this melancholy conclusion: 'What are now called departments of English will be renamed departments of "Cultural Studies" where Batman comics, Mormon theme parks, television, movies and rock will replace Chaucer, Shakespeare, Milton, Wordsworth and Wallace Stevens.' It reflects a growing anxiety among academics about the sudden descent of Western culture, specifically the literary and historic traditions of Britain and America.

Bloom is not alone. He has lately been joined by the literary critic George Steiner with his book of essays, *No Passion Spent*, and the British sociologist Richard Hoggart, who published his persuasive analysis of decline, *The Way We Live Now*, at the end of last year. All are horrified at the rate at which intellectual values and learning are haemorrhaging from our culture. Where once such decay was accompanied by war or famine, this, they say, is the result of indolence and the institutionalised reduction of anything that is bothersome, too testing or deemed offensive.

The Americans call the process dumbing down, but it is wider than merely playing to the lowest common denominator to find the biggest market. It is the deliberate neglect of history, the trashing of works which do not fit contemporary fads and prejudices, the loss of biblical and poetic memory and the truly remarkable enmity to the idea of standards. In this new world, Hoggart points out, Jane Austen has no value outside the bloodless study of her bourgeois setting, and the Oxford professor Terry Eagleton may assert that there is no qualitative distinction to be made between graffiti and Rembrandt's drawings.

In each of their books you find the overwhelming sense of loss, almost a bereavement for the death of things that averagely well-read people took for granted. They are measured voices – men who have spent a lifetime reading and, crucially, whose education started before the last war. What binds them is not a reactionary political instinct nor even a querulous distaste for modernity, but rather the idea that the interior lives of succeeding generations – not just of scholars – will become gradually impoverished, and that the skills of composition, comprehension and reference will fade.

The following comes from George Steiner's introduction to his collection of essays *No Passion Spent*: 'The great majority of us can no longer identify, let alone quote, even the central biblical or classical passages which are not only the underlying script of Western literature, but have been the alphabet of our laws and public institutions. The most elementary allusions to Greek mythology, to Old and New Testament, to the classics, to ancient and European history have become hermetic. Short bits of text now lead precarious lives on great stilts of footnotes. The identification of fauna and flora, of the principal constellations, of the liturgical hours and seasons on which the barest understanding of Western poetry, drama and romance from Boccaccio to Tennyson intimately depends, is now specialised knowledge. We no longer learn by heart. The inner spaces are mute or jammed with raucous trivia.'

It's interesting that while I transcribed that quotation I began uneasily to measure my own knowledge, but also to feel a dim sense that I should not be making readers suffer pangs of inadequacy. And that perhaps is an important point, because we demand so little of each other these days. We forgive those who are well educated when they good-naturedly confess they have never read Dickens, they cannot recite the Lord's Prayer or do not know the difference between vermilion and indigo. It is a complacency that is either buoyed by a general accord that much of 'old learning' is irrelevant to the modern world, or edgily defended by the argument that the storing of ideas and facts is élitist and calculated to accentuate social distinctions. It is at this intersection of modishness and indolence that the *Sun*'s editor steps forward to grasp the Oxford Professor of Graffiti Studies warmly by the hand.

If ever there was a man more opposed to the idea that learning is élitist, it is the author of *The Uses of Literacy*, Richard Hoggart, who was born into a working-class family and whose whole life has been in celebration of what could be found in the local library. His current book makes the important connection between the mass market and relativism, showing how the intellectual denial of standards has caused a failure of discrimination among consumers.

Relativism holds that knowledge and moral principles have no objective standards: thus there is no intrinsic difference between the novels of George Eliot and Jilly Cooper, the work of Chaucer and the screenplays of Quentin Tarantino, for as the trench structuralist thinkers have insisted, each one is a text where the author's intention has as much importance as the typeface. Relativism, the reckless offspring of liberal democracy, extends beyond literature into every area where objective standards were once applied. Hoggart says: 'It implies levelling, the belief — if belief it is; more likely it is an assumption — that with a few exceptions all are equal in all things and so all views are of equal worth.'

This has all been helpful to the mass marketeer, the tabloid newspaper publisher, the advertiser, the Hollywood studio boss, the television producer, because each may flog his products to the largest possible audience without consideration of standards or ever having to worry about allegations of debasement.

The people who might have known better hesitated in the face of the overwhelming business of the mass market and the power of the supplier. They began to wonder if they should not muster the language to celebrate it all and so the departments of cultural and media studies were born. Even a magazine, the *Modern Review*, was founded to complement the wisdom of the mass market by using traditional techniques of criticism. Before it closed, one contributor – in all seriousness – ended a piece about tabloid newspapers by saying that to condemn the *Sun* was to attack working-class culture. Working-class culture never produced the *Sun*; a graduate of Oxford University did.

In this climate of non-judgement, eventually no one can trust himself. Even the studio bosses may only rely on the response – more spasm – of the audience and must, as in the case of John Cleese's follow-up to *A Fish Called Wanda*, first test the film's end for its optimistic feel before sanctioning release. Cleese has been forced to reshoot the ending to comply with the prejudices of an audience no longer capable of accepting challenge or difference. That is why Hollywood must dumb down.

But perhaps one is being too harsh. After all, Hollywood has just produced *Sense and Sensibility* and *Persuasion*. Are these not good films? Do they not encourage rediscovery of great literature? A qualified yes to both questions, although it must be said that, however good they are as films, they reduce Austen. They also create flash floods of Austenian enthusiasm which die quickly, leaving the abridged versions of the novels high on the shelf, unread. Still, the films, and the recent BBC series of *Pride and Prejudice*, serve to reassure us that we are in touch with high art. Perhaps it is as well that we ignore the fact that a truly literate culture does not have to be prompted by the electronic media. In countries where people still read books (the former Soviet Union) they range over all the literature available, independently finding their own routes, content in their solitude and with their private collections of remembered character, imagery and yes, for goodness' sake, jokes.

This is how Harold Bloom continues the paragraph that I began by quoting: 'Only a few handfuls of students now enter Yale [his own university] with an authentic passion for reading. You cannot teach someone to love great poetry if they come to you without such a love. How can you teach solitude? Real reading is a lonely activity and does not teach anyone to become a better citizen. Perhaps the ages of reading Aristocratic, Democratic, Chaotic – now reach terminus, and the reborn Theocratic era will be almost wholly an oral and visual culture?'

It may be true that reading doesn't teach people to become better citizens, though I happen to think it does. If you read, you generally acquire a sense of history and that makes you a better democrat, a more able voter. But possibly he is referring to the idea that education should be undertaken only with a specific purpose, which echoes the point made in Hoggart's book about vocationalist policies in education that have convinced people that they should learn only what is immediately useful to them. At Cambridge, where Orlando Figes lectures in Russian history, he reports that his students want to know only that what they are reading will give them answers for their exams. 'It's impossible to persuade them to read widely,' he says. 'It does seem that they are a little less intellectually hungry than they were ... What they are interested in is what is in the media, which says something about intellectual shallowness and the people that consume it.'

But it is not just about today's education, it's about the attitudes of the baby-boomers that followed the Steiner–Hoggart–Bloom vintage. As has often been said, it is a privileged and demanding generation with an appetite for novelty, but for some reason not a great sense of the past. The baby-boomers demanded what they learned would be 'relevant' and that the syllabus was updated to embrace modernity and eliminate elements 'offensive' to the ideal of democratric homogeneity.

They also created the technological revolution of the last 20 years and now to a very large degree are running the media and opinion-forming institutions. They live in a world which they have made without Latin or Greek and eagerly appreciate the pace of its advance. Yet individually the members of this genera-tion are consumed by personal schedules and diminishing time. Nearly everyone I talked to before writing this article confessed that they read much less than they felt they should because they had no time: there were simply too many demands on them, too much that they had to read for work, or to keep abreast of developments in their own field. Actually the answer is probably in part Steiner's solution, that we have too little silence, for there are very few sitting rooms these days which do not include a television, a telephone, a stereo, to say nothing of the computer.

Whichever way you have it, our attention is taken hither and thither, which is not at all a good condition for reading, or indeed for the appreciation of art. As far back as 1984 – a long time ago in terms of the developments we are discussing – Gore Vidal wrote: 'The century that began with a golden age in all arts (or at least a golden twilight of one) is ending not so much without art as without the idea of art, while the written word that was at the core of the education system since the 5th century BC is now being replaced by sounds and images electronically transmitted.'

'Without the idea of art': that's a chilling notion, but it may be that finally after 2,500 years, literature in the widest possible sense is surrendering to technology. After all, in just 50 years the study of Latin and Greek has been reduced to a tiny specialist area and now indeed it looks as if departments of English will follow. Can humanity do without literature? I am unable to predict, but it is worth taking note of what is happening. I am sure that these authors are right to protest before we lose it entirely, to stress that literature teaches us to comprehend that which is not immediately visible; to observe minutely; and to compose our thoughts.

Two of the authors end their books with foreboding, Steiner by warning of the 'great emptiness' that will enter our lives and Bloom with an appeal to literate survivors to keep the canon alive. Hoggart is moderately upbeat and concludes with this: 'A fair number of people know how to blow the gaff on the worst of the new and to turn the best to their own purposes.' I hope so. ●

· ·

18 October 1995

Leader

Scandal of toff's lottery jackpot

The following is a composite, cut out 'n' keep, all purpose Sun column for use in the event of lottery money being given to any leading British arts company. Parody? You couldn't make it up:

That's rich! A massive [fill in sum] of lottery cash is to be spent on the posh people's opera house/ballet company/theatre [delete as appropriate]. It's tutu much [if ballet]/it STINKS [all other art forms].

The millions of decent, hard-working people who play the lottery each week want the money to go to causes like medical research – not a bunch of pirouetting pansies/fatbums of the opera. They are just a bunch of Toscas.

The people have had enough of this Lotto nonsense. Handing out lottery dosh to élitist toffs and their minority art forms is a slap in the face for the honest, hard-working Joe Public.

It's time to stop the fat cats taking all the cream. Time for Joe Public to speak – and for the upper-class jackpot twits to listen. These artyfarty types have never bought a jackpot ticket in their lives. Not since Robin Hood has so much money been taken from the poor to give to the rich. Where will your money go next . . . the Old Etonians' Pas de Deux Troupe? Not ballet likely!

No doubt we will be branded philistines. But is it really philistine to object to working-class

money being used to featherbed toffee-nosed luvvies when ordinary decent men and women are dying every day of incurable diseases?

We call for a national boycottery. Stop subsidising the pastimes of the posh and pampered. They'll soon get the message that some of the dosh should go to subsidising some decent English working-class art forms like seaside piers, Jim Bowen and Sky Sports. Tell the fat cats of the opera to stuff their Rigo-Lotto. Where it hurts. ●

7 June 1996

Michael Billington
Bloody barbs

t is clearly meant to shock. R B Kitaj's work, 'The Critic Kills', faces one
accusingly at the opening to the Royal Academy Summer Show. It is a collage
in four panels that both celebrates the artist's late wife, Sandra Fisher, and
forms the opening shot in Kitaj's guerrilla campaign against the art critics
whom he blames for her death.

Like much of Kitaj's work, it is literary, erudite, allusive. It is inspired by
Karl Kraus and ironically quotes Hitler's attack on artists who need to explain
their work: one of the complaints made by the London critics against Kitaj
himself. It is a disturbing, angry work that raises conscience-pricking questions
for anyone in the appraisal business.

But what lies behind it? Kitaj, an American expatriate who has lived in
London since 1959 and who has in the past been highly praised ('Kitaj draws
better than almost anyone else alive,' Robert Hughes once wrote in *Time*), was
in June 1994 given a major retrospective at the Tate. The normally reclusive
Kitaj came out of his Chelsea bolt-hole and gave a number of revealing interviews. Expectations were pitched high. Then came the reviews. They were not
merely bad. They were devastating and called into question Kitaj's whole creative
purpose and artistic talent.

Still shell-shocked, he flew off in September 1994 to visit his 84-year-old
mother in Los Angeles. He no sooner arrived than he got a message that his
wife – who herself had studied painting at the California Institute of the Arts
– was ill. He sped back to London to find that she had had a severe stroke.
Two days later she died, aged 47. For Kitaj, it was the tragic climax to a terrible
year. As he said at the time of the critics: 'They wounded me, they tried to kill
me and they got her instead.'

Only Kitaj himself knows whether that remark is literally true. What is certain
is that the reviews of his exhibition were both savage and highly personalised. It
came as no great shock to find Brian Sewell, that knockabout iconoclast, writing
in the *Evening Standard*: 'A pox on fawning critics and curators for foisting on
us as heroic master, a vain painter puffed with *amour-propre*, unworthy of a
footnote in the history of figurative art.' It was more disturbing to find the
highly respected Andrew Graham-Dixon writing in the *Independent*: 'The careless
manner which Kitaj has lately adopted is a hybrid style of pastiche: a little bit
of fake Beckmann, a little bit of fake Picasso but above all fake . . . The wandering
Jew, the T S Eliot of painting? Kitaj instead turns out to be the Wizard of Oz:
a small man with a megaphone held to his lips.' Criticism often wounds. But

this was something more: a systematic and abusive attempt to cut Kitaj down to size.

The Kitaj affair – and his current retaliation – raises vital questions. What is the relation between critic and artist? Where does one draw the line between responsibility to one's critical conscience and regard for human feeling? Is the critic law-giver or mediator? And is critical reaction these days inevitably distorted by the hype and puffery that precedes any major artistic event?

One thing is clear. Kitaj is not the only person to feel criticism can kill. I was reminded of the extraordinary story told by Robert Brustein, the American director, academic and critic, in his book *Making Scenes*. In the late 1970s Brustein was running the Yale Repertory Theatre and directed his wife, Norma, in a production of *The Seagull*. Richard Eder, then drama critic of the *New York Times*, gave the show a savage review, singling out Mrs B for special obloquy.

'Norma Brustein,' he wrote, 'who is the director's wife, plays the central role of Madame Arkadina but generates none of the oppressive charm that allows this character to rule the play. She is simply oppressive. Mrs Brustein has played important roles in a number of the company's productions and, at least in the ones I have seen, she has tended to sink them.'

What particularly incensed Norma Brustein was the phrase about 'the director's wife', implying that she was cast simply out of uxoriousness. She engaged in a furious exchange of letters with Eder but went on playing in *The Seagull*. Two days after the final performance, however, she died of a heart attack. Brustein doesn't go as far as Kitaj but he leaves the reader in no doubt that Eder's attack on his wife's talent and integrity was a major cause of her death.

It is, of course, the ultimate critical nightmare: that one's words may have a lethal effect. I remember, all too vividly, the tragic end of the actress Mary Ure. In 1975 she appeared in the West End in a play called *The Exorcism*. Her first-night performance was shaky and I remember saying so in no uncertain terms. The next morning I was stunned to see headlines in the early editions of the *Standard* announcing her death.

My instant reaction – and that of unforgotten colleagues – was that my notice may have been partially responsible; only later did I discover that she had died in the night, after a violent domestic row, through a mixture of pills and drink, and couldn't possibly have seen the papers. But, although my notice had nothing to do with her death, my racked conscience was hardly helped by the receipt of letters, one of which suggested I should be horsewhipped.

These are extreme cases. But the history of the arts is filled with examples of hostility between critic and artist. No one likes to be judged. From time immemorial, painters, composers, writers and performers have reacted with fury to the wasp-stings of critics.

To the persecuted artist of today one can offer two consolations. One is that it was much worse in the past. Clement Scott in the *Daily Telegraph* attacked Ibsen's *Hedda Gabler* as 'a bad escape of moral sewage gas'. Ruskin described

Wagner's *Die Meistersinger* as 'clumsy, blundering, boggling, baboon-blooded stuff'. And it was Ruskin who provoked one of the most famous lawsuits of all time by accusing Whistler in 1877 of 'flinging a pot of paint in the public's face': the resulting court case led to Whistler being awarded a farthing in damages.

But, if you think critics are harsh, it strikes me that artists are often tougher on each other. It was Gounod who said of Verdi's *Ernani*: 'It's organ-grinder stuff'; the Austrian dramatist Grillparzer who said of Weber's *Euryanthe* that: 'In the great days of Greece this subversion of all melody, this rape of beauty, would have been punished by the state'; and Tolstoy who announced to Chekhov that 'Shakespeare's plays are very bad but yours are worse.' Critics frequently may make fools of themselves, but it is often the artist himself who delivers the real killer punch.

But must artist and critic always be forced to stare at each other across the barbed wire? A lot depends on the economic context. In any commercialised art form, the critic is inevitably the enemy: a means of stopping people making money. Where art is subsidised, the verdict of the critic is potentially less destructive. But it is my belief that both artists and critics should indulge in more soul-searching. The former should cultivate thicker skins; my own profession, without compromising its integrity, should not substitute ego for evaluation of the work in hand.

The art of deflecting criticism was perfectly illustrated by the great Victorian actor Sir Henry Irving. Shaw, writing in the *Saturday Review*, constantly attacked Irving for his literary judgement and butchery of Shakespeare while still cheekily trying to persuade him to stage one of Shaw's own plays. But when Shaw, in a notice of *Richard III*, was thought to have accused Irving of drunkenness on stage, he wrote to the old man denying any such imputation. Irving replied by saying that he had not had the privilege of reading Shaw's criticism of *Richard III*. He continued: 'I have read lots of your droll, amusing, irrelevant and sometimes impertinent pages but criticism containing judgement and sympathy I have never seen by your pen.' A good example of the biter bit.

Even better is when artist and critic engage in serious public debate. The classic case in modern times was the confrontation betweeen Kenneth Tynan and Eugene Ionesco in the *Observer* in 1958. Tynan attacked the 'anti-humanists' who held up Ionesco's type of Absurdist theatre as the gateway to the future. Back came Ionesco arguing against social and political theatre and claiming that society is 'revealed by our common anxieties, our desires, our secret nostalgias' and that 'no political system can deliver us from the pain of living, from our fear of death'.

The debate went on for weeks, engaging such figures as John Berger, Orson Welles, Philip Toynbee and Lindsay Anderson. This was the genuine stuff of dialectic: far removed from the trading of insults that you often get when artists confront critics.

Of that there have been plenty of examples in recent times. The most famous was John Osborne's formation of the British Playwrights' Mafia – its initial meeting is recorded in Osborne's *Damn You, England* – with the aim of duffing up recalcitrant hacks; all it boiled down to in the end was Osborne sending out mildly insulting, and often quite funny, postcards to selected targets.

Others, however, took Osborne's idea of physical retaliation more seriously. I was once cuffed on the head by David Storey in the Royal Court bar after a fairly bilious review of his play *Mother's Day*. A minor incident was blown out of all proportion and caused a media stir: it may have temporarily relieved Storey's feelings but it did nothing to advance serious argument. Nor, I have to say, did it seriously dent my bonce or my general admiration for Storey and his work.

Wounded artists, I suspect, should either maintain a stoic silence or, if serious matters of principle are involved, should seek redress through the editorial or letter columns of a newspaper. I passionately believe that criticism should not be seen as the last word but as the opening of a public debate.

But critics could also profitably be more self-critical. We should, for example, be able to express honest doubts without indulging in intemperate, personal abuse, as seems to have happened in many of the Kitaj reviews. We should learn to ignore media hype, which, as I know too well, can sometimes create a grating resentment: big musicals are classic examples in that they are so heavily marketed and pre-sold as to create a mood of critical defiance. We should also recognise that a work which aims high and misses is often better than one which aims low and hits its target (of course, some works also aim low and miss). We should not simply ask whether a work is good of its kind but whether the kind is inherently worthwhile.

Robert Brustein, who has been a practising critic as well as a professional director, puts it well in his book *Who Needs Theatre?* when he says that one should resist the temptation to let the criticising self usurp the criticised object. He goes on to argue that opinions should be wedded to passionate convictions. 'If we cannot,' he writes, 'avoid making judgements, then at least we can try to give those judgements meaning by investing our criticism with reference and learning and a transcendent view of the art we have elected to serve.'

What Brustein says about drama can be applied to the visual arts. Indeed the American critic Harold Rosenberg, in his book *Art on the Edge*, believes that the critic should be more than 'a policeman on the lookout for misdemeanours'. He/she should extend the artist's act into a realm of meaningful discourse.

Of course, in an ideal world: one would have space, time and leisure rather than a pressing need to come up with a crisp 500-word verdict by 11pm. But they have a point: that the critic should judge motives as well as achievements and that naked assertions of taste should be reinforced by some larger vision of the art one is writing about.

Artists are fallible. So too are critics. But it would be nice to think that, although temporary opponents, we are sometimes fighting on the same side. The artist and the critic look like natural enemies. In fact – though Kitaj might not agree – we should be united in our detestation of the shoddy, the meretricious and the philistine which surround us on all sides. •

• •

17 October 1995

Nancy Banks-Smith
Bet's off to find the sun

Bet snapped last night with the exhilarating twang of knicker elastic.

The story of *Coronation Street* so far. After working in The Rovers Return for 25 years, Bet the landlady needed £66,000 to buy the pub.

An exciting way to find out who your friends are is to ask them to lend you £66,000. Bet was turned down like a bedspread by her best friend Rita, whose only visible expenditure is on sequined angora sweaters, and by her stepdaughter Vicky, who, as Bet said bitterly, knows when summat's knackered. She sold her 'orse, didn't she?

Now read on. The effect was memorable. Bet's hair boiled over and she ordered everybody out of the pub ('There's not one of you lot I haven't wanted to get rid of in my time!') and threw the Mayoress of Weatherfield out after them ('Out she goes. Out, out, out!').

A bunch of extras shuffled off, very much like the penguins in the John Smith commercial, who mutter in a miffed and muted sort of way that they were going anyway.

It reminded me of *The Bowmans*, one of Hancock's finest half-hours, in which he nonchalantly got shot of the entire cast of an everyday soap of country folk. 'Oh dear, what a shame. They've all fallen down that disused mine shaft.'

You could hear an aitch drop in the Rovers. Silence like a poultice came to heal the blows of sound. Absently, Bet emptied an ashtray, which was odd because no one smokes in the Rovers.

At this spooky moment Alderman Alf Roberts, a grocer (his name, position and profession identical with Mrs Thatcher's father), emerged from a leisurely visit to the gents and found himself the last man left alive. 'What time is it?' he asked wildly. 'Half-past one.' 'Night or day?'

The moral is don't stay too long in the gents. Or in a soap. You may get a shock when you come out.

Bet left *Coronation Street* in a cab, giving no forwarding address. 'A quid says it's a Greek island. Single women they allus go where there's sunshine,' said the cabbie. 'And do they find it?' asked Bet, answering herself: 'Oh, they do you know. They all find it sooner or later.'

An advertisement for beds, timed to coincide with these traumatic events, was less encouraging. ''Ey, Bet,' it said. (Surely 'Ee, Bet? ed.) 'Now you can look forward to an uninterrupted night's sleep.' I don't think that an uninterrupted night's sleep was ever Bet's idea of a good time.

Meanwhile, back in *Coronation Street*, a shop assistant is accusing the manager of sexual harassment. Reg, adjusting his wig nervously, asked sharply: 'You've not been reading the *Guardian*, 'ave yer?' She denied it with spirit. So that's all right then. •

· ·

15 April 1996

Mark Lawson

Lukewarm Lazarus from Potter

There is a famous Hollywood joke about the actress who was so stupid that she slept with a writer to help her career. But this is a gladdening month for those dreamers at keyboards, grumping and glugging about their lowly position in the creative food chain. For Britain has just built a £10 million public memorial to an author. Funded with 40 per cent public cash and 60 per cent finance from the private sector, it is a more substantial monument than has ever been allotted to a politician or scientist, sportsman or economist.

The monument in question is the production of *Karaoke* and *Cold Lazarus*, the two linked four-part television serials scratched out by the playwright Dennis Potter in the months before his death from cancer in 1994. They begin screening in a fortnight's time, shown on both BBC1 and Channel 4 in the unique and sentimental truce which was the writer's dying wish. Three things need to be said at the outset about this project, in descending order of pleasantness. The first is that Potter was responsible for five of the most original and significant programmes in the history of television: the single plays *Blue Remembered Hills* (1979) and *Cream In My Coffee* (1980), the six-part serials *Pennies from Heaven* (1978) and *The Singing Detective* (1987) and the 1994 *Without Walls* interview with Melvyn Bragg, in which the writer spoke about his impending death.

The second observation – arising directly from the last-mentioned programme – is that Potter was a human being of rare courage. People have wondered how someone twisted with pain from cancer of the liver and pancreas could have handwritten 480 pages of dialogue during six of their last nine weeks alive. But the point was that Potter had completed thousands of pages of script with his writing hand jammed into a fist and the bulk of his body skin blistered from the psoriatic arthropathy which was his daily non-fatal condition for the 30 years before the fatal one arrived. If he perhaps lacked the purity of mind and thought required by most churches in candidates for canonisation, he without doubt possessed the forbearance and fortitude.

But. But. But. The five remarkable pieces of Potter television listed above are – and I do not really want to write this – as sure as hell not going to be swelled to seven by *Karaoke* and *Cold Lazarus*. (I have seen some and read the script of all of these last dramas.) Brutally, we are looking at the score going up to five and a half, maybe even five and a quarter.

Karaoke, it is true, holds an appealing irony, signalled by its title, that Potter's favourite metaphorical gimmick – people miming to songs – has become, by the 1990s, a lucrative branch of British popular culture. Beyond that, though, the first serial consists of Albert Finney as Daniel Feeld, a middle-aged television playwright whose characters come to life and who becomes erotically obsessed with a young woman: themes which, rather worryingly, featured in at least half of all Potter's writing projects in the last 10 years of his life, including the creepy *Blackeyes* (1989).

At the end of *Karaoke*, the playwright dies: of pancreatic and liver cancer. However, in *Cold Lazarus* – set in the year 2368 – viewers discover that Feeld had his head cryogenically frozen before death and that a Murdochesque tycoon of the future has developed the technology to access these iced minds and screen their feelings and memories as popular entertainment. It is necessary for the viewer to accept that a vulgar media entrepreneur, having patented this method, would seize on the sub-zero head of a controversial left-wing television playwright rather than, say, a supermodel or actress.

Posthumous work poses a considerable problem for criticism, but, in general, reviewers are faced with only an unrevised play, a bottom-drawer novel, dusted-off juvenilia. Work produced by a writer in the knowledge of impending death is a different proposition. *Karaoke* and *Cold Lazarus* are a message stuffed in a bottle as the ship went down, the longest note and largest receptacle ever known. Because of the scale of their production, the final Potters demand to be considered without sentiment.

Regrettably – on paper, anyway – they confirm the melancholy pattern of most artistic careers, which, represented as a graph, will almost always display a pyramid shape, in which talent accrues and then reduces. (The four greatest Potter dramas listed above were all written in a nine-year, mid-career stretch.)

This creative slippage is all there to be seen in Potter's career. The way that bold original tropes – miming to songs, multi-layered plotting – can become mere habit. The alarming tendency for the minds of middle-aged male writers to become a kind of virtual reality escort agency, fixing them sex with 20-year-old women. And – above all – the gradual refusal of production and editing collaboration, directing their own work, huffing out on one employer in search of another prepared to indulge them absolutely.

Because of a combination of the moral power accorded by the author's condition and the practical difficulty of his unavailability during production, *Karaoke* and *Cold Lazarus* stand as a radical experiment: the first television dramas ever to be produced precisely as written by the author. Much as it pains a writer to say this, it seems unlikely that these productions will make a compelling case for such reverence.

It is the view of many of Potter's contemporaries and collaborators that – for someone who wanted to be a television playwright – he lived and died at precisely the right time, young in television's thrilling infancy, absent from its terminal throes. There is truth in this. It is improbable that a writer as rebarbative and experimental as Potter would ever again, in the newly commercial television environment, command the peak-time slots on mainstream channels which were his regular home.

But the gloomy eulogists of Potter are clearly wrong to say that television no longer takes risks. For *Karaoke* and *Cold Lazarus* stand as perhaps the greatest risk in the history of television drama. Their cost is – by the standards of the hard-eyed accountants who are supposed to run television these days – an obvious commercial folly. Their content and language are a goad to the tabloid and Tory critics of the BBC and Channel 4. They are likely to be trounced in any ratings war.

Cynics will observe that a writer had to die to get such treatment but, if British television really were as it has been depicted by those lamenting the passing of a golden age, there would be no room for such sentimentality. The very existence of this peculiar, expensive, dicey project suggests that the medium is not unrecognisable from the one to which an unknown 30-year-old journalist submitted his first script – for a now-forgotten play called *The Confidence Course* – in 1965. ●

Fond
farewells

· ·

1 November 1995

Ben Okri

Listen to my friend

If you want to know what is happening in an age or in a nation, find out what is happening to the writers, the town criers; for they are the seismographs that calibrate impending earthquakes in the spirits of the times. Are the writers sleeping? Then the age is in a dream. Are the writers celebrating? Then the first flowers of a modest golden age are sending their fragrances across to the shores of future possibilities. Are the writers strangely silent? Then the age is brooding with undeciphered disturbances.

But when you hear that writers have been inexplicably murdered, silenced, that their houses have mysteriously burnt down, that grotesque lies are told about them, that they have fled their countries and dwell in exile, but above all when you hear that writers have been sentenced to death by undemocratic tribunals, then you can be sure that perils and the demons of war and the angels of fragmentation have already begun their dreaded descent into the blood of the millions of people who inhabit that land. Then you know that the air of the land is already rich with corruption and terror, that the air is unbreathable, that the lives are insufferable, that the soil of that land has already begun to deliver its harvest of dead bodies and the bizarre plants of disaster; and that liberty is dead on the fields, that the leaders have placed the nation under the grim sentence of death.

For the writer is the barometer of the age. Elections can be rigged, the results undemocratically annulled and the rightful leaders installed in the presidential quarters of prison houses. The people can be frightened into sullen acceptance, into cynicism even for the sake of their children, for the sake of food; and they can go on living, with the help of their incredible ability to wait for the diseased time to consume itself. And for better seasons eventually to return, when the earth has decomposed the arrogant certainties of tyrants.

But they write, bristling with the unacceptable that grows swollen in their sleeplessness, unable to carry on for the sheer smell of dung in the spirit of the time. The writer cannot help but break cover from the wisdom of silence, cannot help but break faith temporarily with the wisdom of the people who have seen so many monstrosities come and go, so many famines consume themselves to death, and suffered so many wars that devour their children and eventually breathe their last in a landscape devastated, but over which whispers a new wind, bringing the seeds of unexpected regeneration.

The writer breaks cover; the writer cries out at what the oil companies are doing to the air; the writer cries out at the injustice that runneth over and now spills out in floods across the streams and byways of the land; the writer wails at the death of democracy which is the beginning of fragmentation and civil war.

Writers, sometimes, even abandon the pen, out of monumental frustration, and take other routes to warn and draw attention to what can no longer be accepted in the life of ordinary people – they become activists, even soldiers, or they take to politics as an extension of their loving rage.

For, essentially, it is love that we are talking about here: love for the better life that could be real for all the people; love for the greater possibility of the future that has been murdered in the present by short-sighted leaders; love for a greater way, a higher justice that sits in the land like a wise and invisible god; love for better breathing in the beggar and the basket-weaver; love for the women who bear all the suffering and who create such small miracles of survival; love for the children who grow up under a generous sun and who do not know just how distorted and blood-ridden will be the futures that they inherit; love for the regeneration of a people who deserve so much better and who never seem to get any justice or many good days or any hope that gets materialised.

It is love for mankind's better future, that we may all be better, that our mistakes be higher ones, and that the lowest level that can be found in living conditions be at least ones that are adequate; it is love that drives the seed into becoming the future tree; it is love that makes people extend their hands across seas, across race, across creeds to forge links that make the human dream grow into splendid human realities; it is love that drives a mother to protect a child against suffering; it is love that makes the writer weep when the blood tide announces itself just over the horizon.

And when this love has been sentenced to death then those who have hearts that beat with blood, those with flesh that feels the wind and the caress of a lover and life's infinitely great sufferings, anyone who lives life within, should hear this cry – for a writer in Nigeria has just been sentenced to death, sentenced for trying to remind the nation in his own way of something that should be an acknowledged law that governs the rise and fall of nations: that what does not grow dies, what does not face its truth perishes, that those without vision deserve the destruction that will fall upon them, and that whosoever believes that freedom can be suppressed and yet themselves live in freedom is hopelessly deluded.

Either a nation faces its uncomfortable truths or it is overwhelmed by them; for there is a prophetic consequence in the perpetuation of life just as there is an unavoidable fate that refuses to see.

There are some things on Earth that are stronger than death, and one of these is the eternal human quest for justice. A people cannot live without it, and in due course they will die to make it possible for their children. Fables are made of this. Anyone who can listen, hear me: a writer in Nigeria has been sentenced to death in the quest of a better life for his people. The consequence is incalculable. His name is Ken Saro-Wiwa, and he is my friend. ●

· ·

20 January 1996

Roger Omond
Is that it?

The GP looked down at her desk, filling in the form for a scan as she spoke: 'It may be cancer of the brain.' She was a little distracted. Where the form demanded my telephone number, I saw later, she had repeated my date of birth. It was a prognosis, not yet a diagnosis: that was why a scan of the head was needed. 'We want to eliminate the possibility that there are secondary cancers,' she said.

'And if it is brain cancer?'

'It'll be treated by radiotherapy, if we've caught it in time.'

'And if you haven't?'

'Well . . .'

'That's it?'

'That could be.'

I had never even thought of cancer of the brain, despite having had both lung cancer and rib cancer. Much of the literature refers to 'brain tumours' rather than 'brain cancer'. Bacup, the cancer counselling and information service, says that 'the idea of a secondary cancer affecting the brain can be extremely frightening . . . a tremendous shock'. They have a point. A common symptom is headaches. I was in the surgery about an increasing number of migraines, sometimes accompanied by disconcerting loss of vision.

This was why the GP was ordering a scan. 'I'm being ultra-cautious,' she said. 'You fooled us once. I don't want it to happen again.' Nor did I, replaying the conversation in my mind – my cancerous mind? – as I walked home along the Barnes towpath in the Indian summer sunshine. Queen Mary's Hospital in Roehampton, the GP said, would be asked to do the scan as soon as possible.

Next day the hospital phoned: the first available scan appointment was nine days away. It was not an easy time. Two 'ifs' had to be accommodated: if it was a brain tumour . . . if it was untreatable . . . Not for the first time, the prospect of death in the foreseeable future loomed again. And this after two operations for cancer and three for complications arising therefrom. 'It's so unfair!' exclaimed my Alexander Technique teacher when I told her, digging her thumbs into my shoulders indignantly.

The day of the scan finally came. No food or drink after midday, the hospital warned. The man who would shortly know whether he was condemned ate a hearty breakfast, forsaking the usual muesli for a fry-up of bacon, eggs, toast and marmalade, washed down by much coffee. I just resisted the idea of lacing it with whisky, instead taking an extra morphine tablet – used to control the pain that had been with me for 40 long months.

The scan itself was brief, quicker and less uncomfortable than the many chest scans I'd had before and after lung and rib cancer. Could I wait to hear the result? I asked. Sorry, said a doctor briskly, the consultant was not around and the film had to be developed first; it had to go through the GP, probably the following morning.

I had thought that the scan routine was tailing off. Four months before, my surgeon, looking at the negative results of the latest chest scan, said that, after the next one, they would space them out more widely. Medical opinion was that, two and a half years after the last cancer operation, the chances of secondaries appearing had diminished greatly. But the surgeon's words before the first operation kept returning: 'These cancers are devious little chaps.'

Somehow the evening and night after the brain scan passed. This was all getting repetitious, even strangely boring. Surely there must be life besides illness? Next morning came a scheduled session of hydrotherapy, supervised exercise in a heated pool. That, too, passed somehow. When I returned home the answering machine was signalling a message. It took a bit of time to press the buttons. Then came the GP's voice: 'I've just spoken to the hospital: the scan is clear . . .'

Until brain cancer threatened, the worst time had been at four o'clock one Sunday morning when I woke in the darkness, alone on a Greek island, and sniffed the sea air. My back whistled. Disbelievingly, I sniffed again. The whistling noise came once more. It came, I realised, from a hole that had opened near the shoulder blade between my right lung and the outside world – an after-effect of the two bouts of cancer, surgery and radiotherapy. My first coherent thought was: 'I don't want to live like this.' The surgeon back in London later described the hole as a fistula, which is defined as 'an abnormal . . . passage between a hollow organ and the body surface' or a 'natural pipe or spout in whales . . .' The second seemed appropriate. Like a beached whale, I seemed to have only a slim chance of returning to normal life. Is there life after cancer? Was there no end to this spiral of awfulness? It all had a long history. I thought I had no more than a rather irritatingly persistent cough until lung cancer was diagnosed in April 1992. Half my right lung was removed at the Royal Brompton Hospital in London that June, the reward for a quarter-century of smoking. Nine months later, in March 1993, after many weeks of heightening and intolerable pain, and after a number of doctors failed to find anything wrong, a scan showed cancer again. This time it was in ribs on the back, possibly caused when cancerous cells from the lung had been extracted through a needle during a biopsy.

The first operation was bad enough; the second was hell. The early-morning hours after surgery brought pain of an intensity that I would have imagined impossible. But two cancers were about as much as any individual deserved, I thought. That was it. Time to pick up an abruptly interrupted life, both toughened and sensitised by the experience, indebted to family, friends and colleagues for the support most had given unstintingly. One or two friends revealed unexpected crankiness: colonic irrigation, one suggested, might help. A few failed: some people just cannot deal with cancer. Once, in a restaurant, a former colleague and neighbour with whom I'd shared drinks and meals was unable even to greet me. Another publicly fired me from a job I had been appointed to in South Africa without having the courage to tell me beforehand.

But that, I was eventually able to half-convince myself, was part of the deal: cancer is not merely physical. Now I had to recover as much health as possible, to decide what I wanted to do with the rest of my (shortened?) life. Hydrotherapy was prescribed for my back, still painful and weakened by the removal of lung, bone and tissue, the moving of muscle and a month of radiotherapy.

Then one day after hydrotherapy, at the end of January 1994, I noticed a blister on one of the surgical scars. A nurse at my GP's surgery took one look and summoned the doctor. She urged a return to the Brompton chest surgeon: 'He'll have more experience of a stitch sinus like this.'

The surgeon surmised that the plastic plate which he had inserted to replace the cancerous ribs had attracted an infection. Two lots of antibiotics would follow. If they failed, another operation would be necessary. The next hours and day were difficult. As emotions broke at intervals, the suppurating wound provided a focus for, rather than the cause of, new pain. Worse was the fear of another operation, the pain of surgery, the side-effects of morphine, the long days and longer nights in hospital, the mood swings, the slow post-operative recovery, the months wasted. Was this to be the constant spectre for all future years?

After (potentially) bad news the mind tends to create amnesia in self-defence so that one won't say: 'To hell with it.' The feeling was reinforced the next day by a migraine: a not unusual event over the past months, probably exacerbated by the cocktail of morphine and other painkillers, anti-inflammatories, antibiotics, tension and, perhaps even too much alcohol, chocolate and cheese. It wiped out a full 24 hours and left me shaken for another day.

It was also the day for a weekly session with a Jungian analyst who, with others, had been trying to help find meaning in my upside-down life. I returned to a point I had made to my wife, Mary: 'I'm not sure, if I'd known two years ago what was coming, whether I would have gone through with it all.' From his bookshelves he unerringly chose a volume of Jung's letters and read: '. . . If your case were my own, I don't know what could happen to me, but I am rather certain that I would not plan a suicide ahead. I should rather hang on as long as I can stand my fate or until sheer despair forced my hand. The reason for such an "unreasonable" attitude with me is that I am not at all sure what will happen to me after death. I have good reason to assume that things are not finished with death. Life seems to be an interlude in a long story. It has been long before I was, and it will most probably continue after the conscious interval in a three-dimensional existence. I shall therefore hang on as long as it is humanly possible . . .

'Therefore I cannot advise you to commit suicide for so-called reasonable considerations. It is murder and a corpse is left behind, no matter who has killed whom . . . Be sure first whether it is really the will of God to kill yourself or merely your reason. The latter is positively not good enough. If it should be the act of sheer despair, it will not count against you, but a wilfully planned act might weigh heavily against you . . .'

There was much to think about. Just as there was in a letter from Sister Wendy Beckett, the nun and art critic who, some years before, had taught Mary at a convent in the middle of the South African veld. She wrote: 'Roger's affliction seems never-ending and multi-faceted. I pray, pray, pray for him. In a dreadful sort of way he is privileged, in that something within him must be developing, called forth by these extraordinary sufferings. But "dreadful" remains the key word . . .'

In the next weeks, antibiotics did not work, but a scan revealing no trace of new cancer lifted the spirits somewhat. Then the decision was made: another operation would be done on 8 March to remove the infected plate from my back. It would be almost exactly a year since the rib cancer operation. Sufficient fibrous tissue would have grown, said the surgeon, not to warrant inserting a new piece of plastic.

Nurses in the Brompton's Elizabeth Gallery were pleased to see me again, although both sides wished the reunion was not occasioned by medical necessity. There was a long wait before the operation began. As always, the worst moments are just before the anaesthetic mask is put on. Whatever sang-froid you can muster vanishes. The tears of fear appear; you grip the hand of an accompanying nurse in the hope of transmitted strength. After an impossibly long time – at least a few seconds – apprehension fades together with consciousness.

You anticipate, right until the anaesthetic takes effect, the pain with which you will regain post-operative awareness. This time – unlike the two previous operations – the pain was bearable. Cockily confident, I was wheeled back into the High Dependency Unit. A few hours later I was near to that point of despair when Jung might have condoned suicide. The most vicious migraine of my life struck. The nurses could not find any painkiller that had the slighest effect. I was vomiting up even a sip of water. Eventually an overworked senior house officer came. Despite the agony, I could recognise that he had the mysterious ability to make a difference. Not all doctors, one soon realises, have equal expertise or empathy. He also had the skill – which not all share – to replace a drip without major excavation work. An injection to stop the nausea followed; then a painkiller. Jerky sleep came at last.

Six weeks after the operation, I was well enough for a recuperative Easter break in Greece, although still draining noxious fluids from a tube in my right side into a vacuum flask carried at the waist. I grew to hate that drain. It was a constant reminder of ill-being; the fluid that dripped its way through the plastic tubing was repulsive; and the routine of emptying it was nasty. Then a friendly fellow-sufferer said quietly that he had been forced to have a drain for five years. That remark made it seem indulgent to complain about having the tubing and flask for a mere matter of months.

Finally the drain came out. I reduced the painkillers and returned to the office for two days a week, relieved at feeling at least half able-bodied, enjoying the company of colleagues and glad to be back at work after the paper's generosity over the past months.

Then it happened. A small hole opened in my back. A second one appeared, a few inches away. We returned to the Brompton. The surgeon was again reluctant to operate immediately, hoping that, once more, the body would heal itself. The tissue was weak, he said, because of all the surgery and radiotherapy. The spirit, I didn't tell him, was beginning to weaken, too. He prescribed rest and suggested sunshine and sea water. Greece beckoned again. It would be a challenge: the first time I had gone to our house there alone, speaking little Greek, having to fend for myself and having to carry my own physical and mental baggage.

The two holes in my back rapidly grew into one that looked like a volcanic crater. It proved a nuisance trying to swim bandaged to spare others the sight, but no more than that. The sun shone, the locals were helpful, the retsina was good. And then, 10 days into the holiday, I woke at 4am to hear my back whistling. The crater on the surface of my back had now been joined by the fistula into my lung. A couple of days later I flew back to London, trying not to think about a lung collapsing in mid-air. (Later a doctor surmised that scar tissue from the first operation could have helped to keep the lung intact: 'a piece of good luck', he termed it.)

In early August 1994, the Brompton surgeon referred me to the Royal Marsden Hospital, a few doors away, back to a specialist who had moved a quantity of muscle during the second cancer operation. He had joked then: 'I'm just the Irishman filling in the holes.' Now he was to take a chunk of tissue from my stomach to patch over the crater on my back. Yet more hole-filling. A Marsden anaesthetist said I had become something of a professional puzzle among her colleagues. They were used to pumping gases into airtight lungs. Now they had to figure out a way of anaesthetising me so that gas would not immediately escape through the fistula, making the surgical team sleepy and leaving me wide awake midway through it all.

The day of the fourth operation at the end of September came: the same routine, the same fears and tears. It would, I had been told, be long and delicate surgery. They had to remove an expanse of skin, tissue and muscle from the stomach, plug it into the crater, sew it in and (the tricky bit) plumb in the blood supply.

Waking after about four hours, I faced a confusion of voices and faces. There seemed to be half a dozen or more drips and drains and lines, held down by plaster. Every half-hour a nurse would prod the patch on my back to see if the blood supply had taken. To everybody's relief, it had.

My scarred and stitched back now looked like a railway map of the United States: an East Coast line down from under the right arm; the patch formed a big loop from Detroit to Memphis and back up again via Kansas City and Chicago; Memphis itself had an extended line down to Houston; older scars from the lung and rib cancers joined Salt Lake City to El Paso and New Orleans to Minneapolis. Holes where drains had been inserted looked like a series of displaced Great Lakes. On my front, Cecil Rhodes's dream of a pan-African link from Cape to Cairo had reached Sudan, while an old appendicitis scar formed a lateral branch line down south.

The patient's relationship with the body is a strange one. Most people take their bodies for granted. Unconsciously you know to a very accurate degree your physical size. But surgery alters bulk without advising the brain: you keep bumping into walls and doorways, because your perception is no longer accurate. Greater clumsiness results from moved (or absent) muscles and nerves, so conscious thought is sometimes demanded for a few hitherto automatic tasks. Fingers, for example, do not invariably uncurl themselves from tea-mug handles without error.

The inherited baggage of all the operations had its effects: increased irritation with the inability to do ordinary things; wider mood swings and insecurity; greater need for reassurance; resentment at dependency on others; worries about relying on pain-killers like morphine; closer monitoring of their side-effects. How am I holding my body? How much am I slowing down mentally and physically? How much of the damage is visible?

My stomach had gained an immediate four inches after the patch surgery and looked set to stay that way. Back to the Marsden. The registrar expressed sympathy when told I couldn't do up my trousers, but doubted whether the NHS would provide new clothes – even if Labour wins the election. He diagnosed a hernia where they had removed tissue from the stomach. A corset was suggested in the hope that it would push the internal organs back into their accustomed place. If not, possibly more surgery. The prospect did not please. Life seemed to be an interminable treadmill, one damn operation after another. Shifting back and forwards across my mind was a tantalising series of 'ifs'. If I hadn't, as a 15-year-old, been determined to learn to smoke . . . If I had given up tobacco earlier . . . If the biopsy had not been done and cancerous cells had not, as suspected, fallen off the needle . . . If the second cancer had been picked up earlier . . . If there had been no infection on the plate in my back . . . If no crater and fistula had appeared . . . If the stomach wall had been stronger . . .

Later there were two more to add.

Sometimes there was consolation in thoughts that first came to mind when lung cancer was diagnosed. The fatalistic words of Kurt Vonnegut in

Slaughterhouse 5: 'So it goes.' And my own instinct: Take one day at a time. Going on three years later, however, the words of a character in Joseph Heller's latest book, *Closing Time*, find an immediate chord: 'I'm sick of being sick.'

Heller, who suffered from Guillain-Barré Syndrome, which left him paralysed for weeks and muscles weakened for months, wrote about his own illness in an earlier book, *No Laughing Matter*: 'I never once, throughout the whole experience, thought of myself as weak, which to my mind meant sleepy, lethargic, not strong. I was paralysed, not weak. And in truth I wasn't weak. My muscles were weak. I felt just fine . . . It was the rest of me that was lousy and lying down on the job.'

Heller's approach is far from much contemporary thinking, which encompasses a holistic approach: mind and body cannot be separated. 'I' and 'the rest of me' are all involved in this business of cancer, cancer again, infection, tissue weakness, holes into the chest and lung, stomach hernia, depression, constipation, pain, impaired physical stamina and strength . . . It was a painful and long lesson to learn. Heller is typically sardonic on other aspects of illness: 'I had not the character for socialising easily with the strangers in wheelchairs . . .' Nor I. Further: 'Good humour may be one of the few things in a hospital that is not contagious.'

Another writer who suffered ill-health, Damon Runyon, sums up the repetitious question that worries everybody: 'The toughest thing for the victim to overcome is the feeling of resentment that it should have happened to him. "Why me?" he keeps asking himself dazedly. Of all the millions of people around, why me? It becomes like a pulse beat – "Why me? Why me? Why me?"

'Sometimes he reviews his whole life step by step to see if he can put his finger on some circumstance in which he may have been at such grievous fault as to merit disaster . . . "Why not that stinker Smith? Why not that louse Jones? Why not that bum Brown? Why me? Why me? Why me?" '

And you can reduce the question to just one word: Why? That is an even tougher one to try to answer. I have never come even close.

There was a feeling, which came from nowhere one day, and which helped me, that my 47 years until the first cancer was diagnosed somehow had been preparation for all this. The reserves of courage I had not expended; the attempt at stoicism that I had thought desirable as a youth; the one-day-at-a-time, whatever-will-be-will-be fatalism; the feeling that ultimately it was down to me alone to survive and overcome: all came together.

Any idea of medical omniscience has long disappeared. 'We're only on this earth as observers,' the Brompton surgeon had murmured when we had one or another problem. It was a surprising – and welcome – admission of fallibility.

At the end of January 1995, I returned to the Marsden. The surgeon could not guarantee a flat stomach again. But a sense of self-respect made another operation worth the pain. It was. A week later I was home, thinner round the waist and convinced – finally – that all this medical business was now at an end.

Three days later the GP came visiting and I was back in hospital within hours. She was worried about my shortness of breath. She consulted with her fellow GPs and the Brompton surgeon. Together they suspected a pulmonary embolism, a clot that could fatally clog the lungs. It was a pulmonary embolism that killed Maggie Curtin, the cancer patient forced to lie for nine hours on a trolley before treatment in Northwick Park Hospital in March 1995. A bed was found for me within minutes of a tentative diagnosis being made. I survived. She did not. Treatment included injections to thin the blood and orders to get into bed and not to move: movement could make bits of the embolism jam the sieve of the lungs. Days of frustrating, depressing immobility followed.

Three years to the week after the first cancer loomed, I did the round of the doctors. A Charing Cross specialist suggested more drugs and acupuncture for the chronic pain. The Marsden was satisfied with the hernia repair. The Brompton said that a spot on the lung which indicated an embolism had disappeared but the rat poison pills to thin the blood would continue.

More than 40 months of anxiety and pain . . . and now? There is still pain, varying from I-can-just-about-live-with-this to disabling. I am never more than a few yards away from painkillers. There are times during the course of a day when pain is not a constant: I can concentrate on something else. But not often. That is why I was prepared to try anybody, any theory, any practice, any philosophy, any medication, any exercise. A healer to whom I went once managed to make me feel that, although the pain was still present, it was somehow removed. It was like carrying a briefcase filled with pain: you are aware of it, but not part of it. But, unfortunately, that happened only once.

The GP said after the second cancer when I complained about feeling sore: 'Think of it as deconstructing and then reconstructing your back. Then you'll know why you have pain.' The pain specialist put it more bluntly: 'You've come out against the odds.' Mary, who was closest to all the crises that could have been fatal, was equally to the point: 'It's a bloody miracle.'

Mortality was not something that preoccupied me. There were times – regaining consciousness from the two cancer operations, the migraine after the third bout of surgery – when the pain was so bad that death held its attractions. Had I been offered the option, what would I have done? It is a question that cannot be answered easily. But sufferers often echo the words of the song 'Ol' Man River': 'I'm tired of living and scared of dying.'

Jung's words come back: 'If your work now gives you some joy and satisfaction you must cultivate it, just as you should cultivate everything that gives you some joy in being alive.' Much of that joy has come through family, friends and colleagues. Some of the joy is in walking (if not running) in the sun in Richmond Park or along the Thames, being able to ride a bicycle again, swim-ming (rather lopsidedly) in the Greek sea; the pleasure of music, reading, sometimes even talking. The pleasure of being able to work again after so many months.

At one time during these thousand-plus days, a gypsy came to the door. She asked a few open-ended questions, indicating that her palms were to be crossed not with silver, but with banknotes. She looked at the lifelines on one hand, then into my eyes and said: 'God does not want you yet.' It was strangely comforting – but I wish He'd found a simpler way of telling me.

And that should have been that. In mid-December, however, I saw my surgeon after a scheduled scan. 'It shows the right side which we've been concentrating on – site of lung cancer and rib cancer – clear,' he said. 'But there's a spot showing up now on the left lung.' It is lung cancer again. Yet more surgery is due shortly. Was the gypsy right? Watch this space.

Roger Omond lost his fight against cancer in 1996. •

....

3 June 1996
Richard Neville
Tripping the life fantastic

The only drug I shared with Timothy Leary was champagne, when he visited Australia's Blue Mountains on his 69th birthday. I had expected a hell-raiser with iridescent eyes and a headband to materialise, but it was more like meeting a Confederate officer from *Gone With The Wind*.

He strolled among our mauve rhododendrons with easy grace, surprisingly witty, short-haired and self-mocking, cradling his long stemmed glass and our new-born daughter. Admittedly, his minders danced about in cosmic beanies and silver Data Gloves, inhaling constantly, while the former West Point cadet languidly extolled the virtues of his latest frontier – cyberspace. Not so many, I reflected later, would have entrusted a child the world's foremost pusher. For that's what Timothy was, ultimately. He pushed drugs, the establishment's buttons, and the frontiers of human experience as easily as falling off a log.

I still recall the frisson of shock I felt at his first rallying cry: turn on, tune in, drop out. Oh sure, I muttered, penning a headline in response: turn on, tune in, drop dead. But events got the better of my disdain, as they did with hundreds of thousands of others; and we danced beneath the diamond skies, both arms waving free, forgetting about today until tomorrow. Was Tim a sage or the devil?

While it is certain that excessive and careless intake of LSD has wrecked lives – who knows how many? – it is equally certain that a majority of trippers look back on their inner voyages in wonderment and gratitude.

Just about everyone of my generation I've ever met has taken a dose of acid;

and those who never did, for the most part, should have. After the hallucinations wore off and pop culture moved on, the thirst for alternative realities remained. Laugh as you might at the mystic revival in the West in recent decades, the bursts of yoga, meditation, Buddhism, the insights of deep ecology and transpersonal psychology, the shift to holistic health, the shareware philosophy of cyberspace and so much more, the spores of these social changes were carried on the winds of psychedelia.

Leary's first acid trips were a revelation, and he wanted the world to share his cosmic bliss. In the early Harvard 'experiments', he took bigger and bigger doses over extended durations, so he could avoid 'coming down', revealing the role that denial played in his life. (Yes, he was a lousy husband.) In the end we all have to land, even the eagle, and view the world with our feet on the ground. This he could never accept, and thus the allure of the shimmering silicon galaxies.

In my sleepy village, when word spread of Leary's visit, frazzled mums arrived at the door with flowers in their hair, lighting up with memories of hash cookies in the Hindu Kush. There was dancing, laughter and star-gazing; my wife exhumed an embroidered skirt from Rajasthan, flashing with mirrors, people said 'Wow', and we joked about a collective acid flashback. By morning, Mr Tambourine Man was on the plane to California, and I was cutting the school lunches, wishing him well.

Many will rejoice at the death of Timothy Leary, the 'monster who glamorised drugs'. It is true he over-enthused. He was too intent on pushing the horizons to report on the pitfalls for ordinary mortals, and much of today's drug culture is a crucible of tragedy.

But Leary wasn't marketing drugs as a product, he was pushing ecstasy as a political right, and proclaiming chemicals as the key to the kingdom of heaven. If they are, which many doubt, Timothy Leary, tripping out to the end, is fronting up to those pearly gates, where St Peter will launch a new celestial campaign: Just Say No . . . •

....

18 May 1996

Ed Vulliamy
Leader from the front

Admiral Jeremy 'Mike' Boorda, Commander of the United States Navy, took his own life on Thursday, at the age of 57, just when it appeared to have reached its zenith. He had capped an extraordinary military career with the highest office attainable, had been hailed as saviour of the Navy's good name after a sleazy sex scandal and settled back – everyone assumed happily – in America after half a lifetime's voyaging.

But then he took himself to the edge of that life, on a garden bench at home on a rainy afternoon in south-east Washington, and hurled himself over it with a shot to the chest from his son-in-law's .38 handgun.

The surface motive for Boorda's suicide appears to place him among the last victims of the Vietnam War: two reporters from *Newsweek* were due at his home that afternoon, the magazine having reportedly found out that he had carried with him a secret since his war in Vietnam. He had worn, until last year, two 'V-pins' – valour insignia – upon his copious ribbons of decoration, which were not backed up by his service record. The V is meant to accompany medals only if the serviceman is 'exposed to personal hazard due to direct hostile action'. In a suicide note, the admiral is said to have pleaded that it was 'an honest mistake' but was convinced no one would believe him.

Those who knew Boorda talk about a deeper doubt, a trauma that can haunt people who climb from a humble origin, through the ranks to the peaks as Boorda did. He was the only man to start as a common seaman and reach the top. 'Maybe they look into themselves harder than most people,' said one reporter who knew him well.

There was another cruel twist to Admiral Boorda's death concerning a newspaper – this newspaper.

The last years of Boorda's career were marked by his insistence that the US take a robust line and intervene militarily in the carnage of Bosnia-Herzegovina. This opinion became the admiral's anthem, and both isolated and vindicated him within a Pentagon which was stubbornly resistant to intervention. Admiral Boorda's line, in a secret meeting with a senator in spring 1993, was: 'I'm not interested in what cannot be done. I'm interested in what *can* be done.' He had formulated this view during his time as Commander of Nato South, based in Naples, from where he was much more deeply involved in Bosnia's crisis than has been officially admitted.

Boorda had agreed – after detailed negotiation – to give the *Guardian* his first full interview on what he had advocated for Bosnia, where he saw the Pentagon going wrong and how he believed the slaughter could have been stopped soon after its inception. The interview was due for the first week in June and was to conclude a *Guardian* series, 'Bosnia: The Secret War'.

The admiral had asked for an outline memo about the areas we wished to cover, which included highly controversial themes, had agreed to speak out despite his position and had set the date the day before his suicide.

But we are left only with the anecdotes that were to accompany the interview, the secret story of Boorda's bold, sometimes reckless, heresy against the caution which strait-jacketed the West in its response to the war.

In spring 1993, Senator Joe Biden of the Foreign Relations Committee and his then adviser, James Rubin, had been on a visit to Bosnia and Croatia. They were on their way home when an invitation came from Naples, from the commander of Nato South. 'Why not?' said Rubin. 'Let's go and have some pasta with the admiral in Naples.'

'Admiral Boorda,' recalls one of the team, 'said his line: "I'm not interested in what cannot be done, I'm interested in what can be done."' And he proceeded to lay out exactly how he would end the war by force. '"We put a division there, a division there", stuff like that,' recalls Rubin. Senator Biden was anxious to let President Clinton know that 'he may have a lot of no-can-do generals in Washington but he had a can-do admiral in Naples'.

Boorda became far more enmeshed in Bosnia's war than was publicly admitted, or was permitted by the strictures of his command. He became a close friend and comrade-in-arms with General Philippe Morillon of France, UN Commander in Sarajevo and a convert to interventionism after his celebrated entry into besieged Srebrenica. Morillon reveals that the two men opened up a strictly 'unofficial' channel of communication between the UN and Nato, which even involved the admiral dispatching teams of US Marines covertly into Sarajevo. It was he who ordered the first Nato air strikes, against Gorazde, in April 1994.

More dramatically, the admiral's involvement extended to his taking personal flights over the ravaged territory. These sorties were unofficial, unheralded, regarded by some colleagues as reckless but utterly characteristic.

On one occasion early in 1993, he saw from the cockpit of an F-14 the grim fruits of a Serbian 'ethnic-cleansing' spree: burning villages and deportees on the move. The admiral was so incensed that he ordered his pilot, Commander John Stufflebeam (call sign 'Boomer'), to fly down and buzz the Bosnian Serb 'capital' of Pale from a terrifyingly low altitude – so low that the blast from the aircraft smashed every window in Pale's main street. His account recalls that the plane flew at 500 feet but one of his colleagues later let on that this was 'well below 500 feet – more like 100!'

Boorda was promoted to the Washington position of Chief of Naval Operations. He continued to connive with Morillon, who visited him more than 10 times, and to push for intervention in Bosnia. His idea was a precursor to that which, in the event, propelled the conclusion of the war in 1995: to get UN troops out of Serbian-held territory and of harm's way, and to mount serious, damaging air strikes which would cripple the Serbian war machine and bomb them to the negotiating table.

His can-do approach to Bosnia led the admiral into head-on confrontation with the British – there was a showdown at a United Nations lunch in New York. The admiral was telling the US Ambassador to the UN, Madeleine Albright, her French counterpart and British Ambassador Sir David Hannay, how Unprofor troops – many of them British – could be deployed in Bosnia in a way that would not restrict the use of American air power, which could then come in and finish off the war. Sir David objected, saying that he didn't think the admiral would consider putting American soldiers at such risk. 'I'm offended,' said Boorda, 'if you think that I care any less about the lives of British soldiers than Americans.' 'Hannay clammed up pretty fast,' a fellow guest observed.

Admiral Boorda was short (5ft 4in), Jewish, clever, gregarious, astute and knew his own mind. He was hardly the Platonic role model for the man to command the most WASPish and hereditary of the US armed services.

From a Ukrainian immigrant family settled in Indiana, Jeremy Boorda dropped out of high school at 16 and lied about his age in order to join the Navy. He liked to mimic the currently voguish PC parlance and joke about being 'vertically challenged'.

He had married Bettie Moran of Norman, Oklahoma, and acquired four children, one of them handicapped, before he went anywhere near officer-training college. Based in California, he was considering leaving the service for family reasons when his superior, Squadron Chief George Everding, selected him to become what the Navy calls a 'Mustang', a seaman specially earmarked for the officer corps. Boorda was assigned to a scheme called, fittingly, the 'Seaman to Admiral Program', and became a young lieutenant, a weapons officer on the *John Earl* destroyer.

Everding lost track of his protégé, but on finding him again as Admiral Boorda, in a tearful reunion, said: 'Don't you dare screw this up, Boorda.' It had taken Jeremy 'Mike' Boorda 22 years, during which time two of his three sons and a daughter-in-law had become naval officers, and the admiral himself graduated from the Vietnam war to Nato South Command in Naples, a hugely popular 'leader from the front'.

When Boorda moved from Naples to take over the Navy in April 1994, it was in no small measure because he had been well clear of the service's worst-ever public scandal, the so-called Tailhook case. The affair involved an alleged orgy of sexual harassment during a Navy convention in Nevada, with a constellation of senior officers present.

Boorda was now in command of 600,000 men and an annual budget of $78 billion. But it was sexual harassment that continued to be a theme dogging Boorda's command, including the 'retirement' of another admiral after callous remarks about the rape of a 12-year-old Japanese girl by US seamen. 'Each infraction or miscue, and we have had plenty lately, detracts from us and demeans our service,' said Boorda.

Admiral Boorda's leadership of the Navy had come under attack in recent weeks from stalwart opponents of political correctness who felt that he was buckling under to political pressure to deliver up long-serving senior naval officers as a result of what this week's *Navy Times* calls 'overblown' sex scandals.

The admiral salutes when sailors snap to attention as he passes by but inside – he had confided – he is thinking: 'Oh, relax, for God's sakes.' A sailor is presented to his chief and says: 'Sir, you're an inspiration to me.' 'Oh, for heaven's sakes,' retorts the admiral, 'I'm just an old sailor.' •

25 May 1996

Gary Younge

'And when I die, don't send me flowers . . .'

To follow Albert Meltzer, one of the most cherished figureheads of the anarchist movement, to his final resting place yesterday, you need only have followed the black and red stars that lined the roads from the aptly named Celestial Gardens to the local crematorium in Lewisham, south London.

Glistening in the rain, they stood proudly on the lapels and earlobes of the mourners, all in black and with ponytails a plenty, who braved the weather to walk behind the horse-drawn hearse to the sounds of the Bill Stacks Southern Ragga Jazz Band.

They ranged from elderly veterans of the Spanish Civil War in their black berets to the young white Rastas in their 18-hole Doc Martens boots.

During his life, Meltzer's various jobs – fairground promoter, warehouseman and copytaker for the *Daily Telegraph*, to mention but a few – served only as a sideline for his passionate adherence to his own brand of anarcho-syndicalism which he had pursued in a number of guises since the age of 15.

He had fought Mosley's blackshirts in Cable Street, shipped arms to the Republican resistance during the Civil War, and helped anti-Nazi forces in pre-war Germany.

Before his death, at the age of 76, he had made specific plans for the type of send-off he thought would do him justice.

'Personally I want to die in dignity but have my passing celebrated with jollity. I've told my executors that I want a stand-up comedian in the pulpit telling amusing anecdotes, and the coffin to slide into the incinerator to the sound of Marlene Dietrich,' were his last requests, set out in his autobiography, *I Couldn't Paint Golden Angels*.

He would not have been disappointed. After a few gags from the stand-up comedian Noel James, the coffin was whisked away, accompanied by Dietrich singing 'See What the Boys in the Back Room Will Have'.

Then came a powerful song, 'They Called Me Al', by David Campbell, followed by a two-minute video which simply showed Meltzer laughing uncontrollably as someone attempted to interview him.

The congregation followed suit, but by the time they left the crematorium some were reduced to tears, a state of affairs that Meltzer had forbidden.

'Anyone mourning should be denounced as the representative of a credit card company and thrown out on their ear,' he wrote.

In the end that was not necessary as those assembled climbed into two hired coaches and were taken away for an afternoon of 'jovial remembrance'.

But as they left to drink a toast to the man who had been so resolute in all things political, Meltzer had put a question mark over the fate of his soul.

He wrote: 'If I have miscalculated . . . and there really is a God, I'd like to feel if he's got any sense of humour or feeling for humanity, there's nobody he would sooner have in heaven than people like me. And if he hasn't, who wants in?' ●

....

5 April 1996

Peter Preston

Life and death in other worlds

We called it the Zorza salad and I guess my children will remember it for as long as they live. A bit of everything to hand. Diced chunks of cucumber, carrot, apple, cauliflower and orange; radishes, spring onions, grapes, mushrooms, maybe a few dates and nuts, with the lightest of vinaigrette dressings. Victor used to make it himself for lunch, to be eaten with roast chicken on this steep, grassy slope down from Dairy Cottage to the big green pond lying listless on the hottest of summer days.

I was catching a plane to the Middle East a fortnight ago when the news of Victor Zorza's death came through. You paused, and sucked the air a little. The obituarists (here and elsewhere) did splendidly. They told of the young Pole who escaped the Nazis, came to England and became the Journalist of Several Years for his uncanny Kremlinology. They saw him off to America and a syndicated column, then to India to live and write from a peasant village, then to Moscow to found and fund a hospice. They made him seem remarkable. But they only had half the ingredients for a real Zorza salad.

Journalists like to think of themselves as professionals – doctors, lawyers, that sort of thing. Wrong. They're tradesmen and sometimes the trade is rough. Victor, though, was the nearest thing to a professional man I ever encountered on the *Guardian*. He was always unique; he was usually impossible.

The analyses emerged from a tight-packed reference and monitoring library on the sunless side of Dairy Cottage. They were not light reading. Nor could they in any way be subedited, let alone shortened. Cutting meant dispensing with the evidence gleaned day-by-day from *Pravda*, Tass, *Izvestia* and the routine outpourings of the Soviet news machine. Victor dealt in significant half-sentences of facts or chilly adjectives, building a picture of what was happening inside the Kremlin from what those on the outside were told. How could that be *cut*? 'But look,' I said one difficult night, 'it fills the whole bloody page and it's still

20 inches over.' 'What else is there on the page?' he asked. 'Nothing but an ad.' 'Right,' said Zorza, 'you must drop the advertisement.'

He was infinitely stubborn. He played off his politics like a street fighter. He remembered his triumphs of prediction. (Golly, how we heard and we heard again about the day the Red Army rolled into Prague.) He had total amnesia when the prophesies came to dust. In his small, compact, bustling way, he was like some masterful heart surgeon pounding through crowded wards, harassed juniors trailing in his wake.

I never, to be honest, quite believed in the technique. It seemed to rest on the belief that every semicolon in every statement from the Soviet Foreign Ministry had been weighed and balanced by experts to drop plangent clues as though for some international power game. I couldn't credit that anyone – even *Pravda* – could produce a newspaper that way, without chaos or undeliberate mistakes or columns of lead type dropped on the composing-room floor by some vodka-racked timehand as deadlines neared. 'Sure,' said Victor impatiently, 'perhaps that happens sometimes. Perhaps that's when my analyses go wrong.'

The heart-surgeon bit was not without ironies. In the late 1970s after Victor had left the *Guardian* and gone to America, he returned to say the doctors did not give his own heart more than a couple of years. Kremlinology was a dying duck. He didn't wish to spend his last months brooding over its entrails. 'The Third World is the new world. I'm going to move there and work there.' We talked South America. We talked Africa. We settled on India. Not the south, I said, the south is a cauldron. He didn't appear to know that – and, indeed, was reported angry when the car that picked him up at the airport lacked air conditioning.

It was, like most Zorza enterprises, a package of funding – with some mysterious chunks of UN money thrown in at the beginning. The village column came to the *Guardian* (and other clients around the world, then pottered off to *The Times* in one of those mild severances where money was a half-issue. I didn't think it quite worked. Victor's prose (except, magically, in the book he wrote with his wife about the hospice death of their only daughter, Jane) was spare and serviceable. He could not often make the rhythms of peasant life beat with emotion. But as failures go, it was magnificent failure. And then, silence.

He popped up again once the Berlin Wall fell down, of course. He had passed through Moscow. He had seen – because of Jane – the malevolent unconcern for the slowly dying. He was going to start just one, then another, hospice. He was out of journalism for ever as the old heart ticked on.

Last summer he wrote again from Dairy Cottage, offering us a Sunday in the sun. It was not alas, possible; and so the letter in November stood in sharper relief. Victor was looking for funds, hospice cash to keep doctors and nurses paid by the month. When he called, he wanted something: that was usually the way he was. But did I know that I'd been responsible for his finding his lost sister after 50 years? Long ago in Poland, as the family was split in flight,

Zorza had thought he was the only survivor, the last one left. But his sister had come through too and made it eventually to Israel, where one day, nearly half a century later, she read about this Pole who had written newspaper articles from an Indian village. 'If you hadn't sent me,' Victor wrote, 'that would never have happened.' They had been reunited. It was an amazing cap to an amazing life.

What followed seemed almost automatic. Why not write the story of your sister for the *Guardian*? I said. Then you can write about the hospice too and I bet, knowing our readers, that some of them will help to keep the nurses paid. He came back immediately. He was in a wheelchair, as he'd been for a couple of years, and a little tired. But, yes. He would write that piece. It was the natural thing.

Later in February he wrote again. He was feeling stronger. He was turning to the article. Expect it imminently. Instead there was the news of his death, a private funeral for the family, a memorial service later.

That will be time enough to say goodbye to Victor, to remember his angry insistence on the evidence and all the evidence; to recall his head cocked to one side, bantam chest thrust out, foot wedged determinedly in whatever door might be half open – the mixture of charm, courage and sheer chutzpah that took him from the detritus of Poland to awards and scoops and the paraphernalia of a career in journalism that lives in the memory. If he had written that last article about his sister for you, it would have said that contributions to the hospice fund could be sent to the British-Russian Hospice Society, 279 Ivydale Road, London SE15 3DZ. I am sure Victor would have wanted me to mention that. ●

* * *

7 November 1995

Derek Brown

An awesome and agonising farewell to a dead hero

They came from across the world and from the other side of war. Some were friends, others used to be foes. They came from every part of Israel and some, at the core of yesterday's grief, came from a murdered man's home.

The burial of Yitzhak Rabin, Israel's assassinated prime minister, was both awesome and agonising. The vast throng of sovereigns and subjects, power-brokers and presidents, was a stupendous backdrop. But, at the heart of it, a family was weeping.

For 24 hours, the coffin had lain in state on the forecourt of the Knesset. By midday, police estimated that a million mourners – more than a fifth of Israel's population – had paid their respects.

By then Yigal Amir, the Jewish student who confessed to the assassination in the wake of a peace rally in Tel Aviv on Saturday, had appeared before a magistrate in Tel Aviv to be remanded for questioning. He showed no remorse, and even complained about prison conditions: 'Aren't I a human being? I am sure they give Arab prisoners more.'

Back in the sane, sad world, the VIPs had started to flow into Jerusalem. From the United States came President Clinton and former presidents George Bush and Jimmy Carter. From Britain, Prince Charles, John Major, Tony Blair and Paddy Ashdown. From elsewhere in Europe came Chancellor Helmut Kohl, President Jacques Chirac, and Prime Minister Felipe González of Spain.

King Hussein flew in from Jordan, to the city he lost in 1967. The prime minister of Morocco came, and President Hosni Mubarak of Egypt, and ministers from Oman, Qatar and Mauritania. A delegation was there from the Palestinian Authority.

Yasser Arafat did not want to provoke controversy, so he watched the burial on television in Gaza. Yet what was happening would have been unthinkable months earlier: Arabs were coming to Jerusalem to mourn an Israeli general and leader.

Officials reckoned that more than 60 countries were represented, in nearly 50 cases by their head of state or government. There were more than 1,500 VIPs.

Israel's own tribute was even greater. After that huge nightlong procession, it seemed the nation must have exhausted itself. But on the stroke of 2pm, sirens sounded throughout the land and Israelis stopped to stand in silent tribute for two minutes.

At Mount Herzl cemetery the 5,000 mourners stood beneath the pines and cypresses as the eulogies began.

Israel's president, Ezer Weizmann, spoke, and President Mubarak, Mr González for the Europeans, and the Russian Prime Minister, Viktor Chernomyrdin. Mr Clinton was mawkishly sentimental: 'Though we no longer hear his deep and booming voice, it is he who has brought us together again here in word and deed for peace,' he said.

The acting prime minister, Shimon Peres, was warm and generous to the man who was his rival for so long: 'Goodbye, older brother, farewell. We will continue to carry the message of peace to near and far,' he pledged.

King Hussein gave a moving address in which he linked Rabin's legacy with that of his own grandfather, King Abdullah, assassinated in Jerusalem in 1951. 'As long as I live, I will be proud to have known him and worked with him, as a brother and a friend,' he said.

Eitan Haber, who for half Mr Rabin's lifetime was his adviser, speechwriter and trusted aide, came to the lectern last, with words wrenched from his heart.

Sobbing, he reached into his pocket and produced the sheet carrying lyrics to the 'Song of Peace' which was retrieved from Rabin's blood-soaked jacket.

'I want to read some words from this page but it is hard. Your blood, Yitzhak, your blood is covering the words of the "Song of Peace". The blood that ran out of your body in the last moments of your life, is between the lines, between the words,' he said.

But the most poignant words uttered yesterday came from Rabin's granddaughter, Noa Ben-Artzi. They reduced her and many in the huge crowd to tears.

'Grandfather, you were the pillar of fire before the camp and now we are left as only the camp, alone in the dark, and it is so cold and sad for us,' she said.

'I know we are talking in terms of a national tragedy, but how can you try to comfort an entire people or include it in your personal pain, when grandmother does not stop crying, and we are mute?

'People greater than I have already eulogised you, but none of them was fortunate like myself to feel the caress of your warm, soft hands and the warm embrace that was just for us, or your half-smiles which will always say so much; the same smile that is no more, and froze with you. I have no feelings of revenge because my pain and loss are so big, too big . . .'

It was unbearable, yet it had to be borne. Mrs Leah Rabin, who so stoically had received the tributes of the famous, broke down. The family linked arms, leaned upon each other and moved towards the grave.

Swathed in a traditional shroud, the coffin was lowered with merciful swiftness. Soldiers fired three volleys in salute, the cantor raised his voice for the last time and it was over. ●

· ·

29 January 1996

W L Webb

Poet against an empire

Joseph Brodsky, who has died aged 55, was as gifted with words and the power of metaphor as any poet among his contemporaries, but the emergence of his gift at a particular time and place – he was born in Leningrad the year before German invasion – brought him other endowments.

He became the heir to the great tradition of modernism in Russian poetry, rooted in the moment early in the century when, Andrei Sinyavsky believes, this was the finest poetry in the world. Anna Akhmatova in her passionate old age herself anointed him, saying she had heard nothing like his poems since Osip Mandelstam. Nadezhda Mandelstam, characteristically, was more sceptical. Akhmatova, she wrote in her memoir of her martyred husband, Akhmatova's great contemporary, might have overestimated the young Brodsky as a poet because 'she was terribly anxious that the thread of the tradition she represented should not be broken, and imagining she was again surrounded by poets, she thought she could detect a ferment in the air like that of those early years'. Still, Mrs Mandelstam went on: 'He is . . . a remarkable young man who will come to a bad end, I fear' – which points to yet another, still more equivocal, endowment which came with that blessing of Akhmatova's.

In one of his penetrating essays on Mandelstam, Brodsky talks about the older poet's 'growing identification' in the twenties 'with the archetypal predicament of "a poet versus an empire". 'This was also the predicament of the young Pushkin; and, before he was 24, of Joseph Brodsky too.

His career up to that point had not been of the kind that won gold stars or opinions in official Soviet society. For a start, he had been born a Jew ('100 per cent Jew, with a tremendous reservoir of guilt'), the son of a naval officer who had been dismissed when he reached the most senior rank then permitted to Jews; this was in 1949, the year which saw the arrest and execution of the entire Leningrad party leadership. The son dismissed himself from school at the age of 15, read voraciously in the margins of various temporary jobs (one of them as a mortuary assistant at coroners' autopsies), and began writing at the age of 18, a crucial member of that generation and milieu he describes so warmly in one of the autobiographical essays in his prose collection, *Less Than One*:

'Nobody knew literature and history better than these people, nobody could write in Russian better than they, nobody despised our times more profoundly. For these characters civilization meant more than daily bread and a nightly hug. This wasn't, as it might seem, another lost generation. This was the only generation of Russians that had found itself, for whom Giotto and Mandelstam were more imperative than their own personal destinies.'

He was taken up by Akhmatova and by his early twenties, reading at clandestine poets' gatherings, he had become the darling of a milieu where the natural Russian passion for poetry was again being pressure-cooked by censorship and repression. And this in spite of the picture Mrs Mandelstam gives of him at work: 'I have heard Brodsky read his verse. An active part in the process is played by his nose. I have never known anything like it before in all my life: his nostrils expand and contract and do all kinds of funny things, giving a nasal twang to each vowel and consonant. It is like a wind orchestra.' The quality of the writing spoke for itself just as unmistakably, however, in poems like 'The Great Elegy for John Donne', which dreams of a sleeping 17th-century London, a sleeping island, with the poet asleep under the dome of St Paul's, and his poems sleeping too:

> The verses sleep. The stern iambi sleep.
> The trochees sleep like guards, to left, to right
> and in them sleeps a glimpse of Lethe's brook,
> and something else beside it sleeping – fame.'

Another glimpse of the young Brodsky shows him, when the ink was barely dry, reading this poem aloud *con amore* to his friend Anatoly Naiman in a railway station booking hall, to the horror of the stolid ranks of Soviet citizens queuing for tickets.

Inevitably this irregular patronage and fame, unauthorised by membership of the Writers' Union, unauthenticated even by a university degree, meant that he was soon taken up by critics of a different sort. In the days following the fall from grace of Khrushchev and his erratic de-Stalinising, the thought police of one kind and another, literary and administrative, reacted with predictable resentment to Brodsky's far from subdued display of talent and obduracy.

There were several nasty preliminary harassments. In November 1963 he was attacked in the Leningrad press (a piece headed 'A Semi-literate Parasite'), and on a bitter night shortly before Christmas he was surrounded in the street by three men, wrestled into the back of a car and eventually held in the Kashchenko psychiatric hospital in Moscow until 5 January. As soon as he returned to Leningrad he was arrested and finally brought to court on 14 February 1964, charged with social parasitism: since he wasn't a poet licensed by the Writers' Union or any other recognised authority, being a poet couldn't be held to be his gainful occupation, and by failing to take up any other, he was effectively a parasite or vagrant: QED.

By then, however, civil courage among writers and those who cared for literature and freedom, had advanced to the point that a full note of the trial was taken by a woman journalist, and soon got out to the West. It included the famous exchange with the uncomprehending or wilful judge that inscribed Brodsky's name, willy-nilly, in the roll of poet-heroes:

JUDGE: What is your occupation?
BRODSKY: I am a poet.
JUDGE: Who recognised you as a poet? Who gave you the authority to call yourself a poet?
BRODSKY: No one. Who gave me the authority to enter the human race?
JUDGE: Have you studied for it?
BRODSKY: For what?
JUDGE: To become a poet. Why didn't you take further education at school where they prepare you, where you can learn?
BRODSKY: I didn't think poetry was a matter of learning.
JUDGE: What is it then?
BRODSKY: I think it is . . . [with evident embarrassment] . . . a gift from God.

After a further three weeks among the actually mad and 'officially mad' in a psychiatric clinic he was sentenced to exile with five years' hard labour on a remote state farm in Archangel province, but after less than two years, following as much pressure from Russian and foreign writers as could be brought to bear on that system, he was released in November 1965, to return to Leningrad, in poor health but, for the time being at least, in peace. The years that followed he spent partly learning Polish in order to be able to translate Zbigniew Herbert and Czeslaw Milosz, and English so that he could learn deeply from and translate Donne and Andrew Marvell (his poem 'The Butterfly' is an extraordinary reincarnation and translation of the spirit of English metaphysical poetry). He also needed English to be able properly to read Auden, another hero among the older generation of living poets, who during the early years of his coming exile would be important to him in a new literary universe as Akhmatova had been in his native realm.

He was no longer crudely persecuted, though when an invitation was sent to read at the Festival of Two Worlds in Spoleto in 1969, the Union of Soviet Writers replied on his behalf: 'There is no such poet in Soviet Russia.' Compared with the severity with which Sinyavsky and other writers were treated in the late sixties, Brodsky said, he had got off lightly: 'Only two years. By Soviet standards it's positively homoeopathic.' But in 1972 he again was obliged to lead the way in exile – this time out of the Soviet Union altogether, to be followed by Galich, Solzhenitsyn, Zinoviev, Maksimov, Voinovich, Nekrasov and Vladimov.

Two days after Brodsky arrived unwillingly in Vienna, all his manuscripts confiscated and impounded in the airport customs store in Moscow, he was in Auden's house at Kirchstetten. He was already in Auden's debt, not least for helping to focus a notion that would be central to his own aesthetic with those lines about how time 'Worships language and forgives/Everyone by whom it lives'. Now the old poet consoled him and 'looked after my affairs with the diligence of a good mother hen', offering, to Brodsky's embarrassment, to translate him and, more immediately invaluable, fixing a grant from the Academy of American Poets that would tide him over until he arrived at the first of his several American teaching jobs, at the University of Michigan.

Exile and separation from the language Brodsky identified with the deepest spring of the poet's and the nation's soul did not, as the party police may have hoped, silence his troublesome tongue or weaken his spirit. He had understood and declared himself to be an exile in his own land long before he was made to leave it, so he was not now 'beheaded' by physical severance. In any case, passionately though he was attached to the resonant music of his mother speech, his devotion to language was a kind of religious devotion, transcending the sounds and structures of any one tongue. As he put it in his acceptance speech when he was made Nobel Laureate in 1987, it's not that language is the poet's instrument, but that he is its vessel.

If language was something like his god, separation made Mnemosyne Joseph Brodsky's muse and consoling mate in his bereavement. Most literature is an art of memory, and all exiles are also sentenced to be memorialists, but the intensity of the gaze with which he conjured Leningrad's streets and buildings out of its Baltic marshland mists in poem after poem, and page after page of his prose, has more than a touch of the magus about it. In corners of cities everywhere, his sensitised eye found pieces of 'Peter', as its natives were not to be dissuaded from knowing it: a gesture, a mood, a pediment, the limb of a statue. 'I, too, once lived in a city whose cornices used to court/clouds with statues . . .' he writes in a poem for his Italian publisher. And passionately as he loves Venice, in his last prose work, 'Watermark', one often senses behind its celebrations of his love, the presence of that other, northern dreamworld floating not in the Adriatic but the Baltic.

He repeats in 'Watermark' the notion 'water is the image of time', most memorably deployed in a Petersburg essay in *Less Than One*, the earlier prose collection which may prove to be the book by which he is best remembered by readers without Russian. 'Reflected every second by thousands of square feet of running silver amalgam', wrote this son of a sailor-turned-photographer, this wideawake revenant scanning the quays of the Neva, 'it's as if the city were constantly being filmed by its river'.

Like his abiding preoccupation with time itself, it reminds you of his master Mandelstam, whose 'Journey to Armenia', for example, another visit recollected in short 'takes', is as full of metaphors that make your hair stand on end. And like Mandelstam too, with all his power of memory Brodsky is eminently a poet of his present time, and a 'renewer of language', as one of his best critics puts it, wrestling stoically with the bleak existential themes of the late 20th century, but also quickly getting to grips with the second, Anglo-American culture history has required him to take on. (He wrote his first poem in English, an 'Elegy on the Death of Auden', in 1975.) 'Growing old! Good day, my old age!' The poet and his poetry had been fighting the battle with time and death at least since the age of 32.

> Time equals cold. Each body, sooner
> or later, falls prey to the telescope. With the years,
> it moves away from the luminary, grows colder.

But the gift of the Word grants a stay of execution and, if not immortality, an afterlife warmed by the spirit's aspiration:

> . . . to God's least creature is given voice for speech, or
> for song – a sign that it has found a way
> to bind together, and stretch life's limits,
> whether an hour or day.

The way in which the Word most signally defeats time (and other tyrannies, however), is by *remembering*:

'And there was a city,' he wrote in the title piece of *Less Than One*, recalling his route to school along the Neva.

'The most beautiful city on the face of the earth. With an immense grey river that hung over its distant bottom like the immense grey sky over that river. Along that river there stood magnificent palaces with such beautifully elaborated façades that if the little boy was standing on the right bank, the left bank looked like the imprint of a giant mollusc called civilisation. Which ceased to exist.' •

28 June 1996

Leader
A brave foot soldier for truth

More than 20 journalists around the world have been assassinated since 1996 began. They have mostly died in Africa or South America or amid the chaotic detritus of the old Soviet empire. They were doing what they perceived to be their job: reporting, investigating, turning over stones. We salute them, of course; but a touch ritually. They do not report from the democratic comfort of the European Union. They work for papers far away. But Veronica Guerin reported in Dublin, for the *Sunday Independent*. And now she is dead too, murdered in her car – shot for the second time in her short career, and this time over and over again, to kill.

Veronica Guerin was a brilliant reporter. She, more than any other, exposed the brutal subworld of Dublin gangland, a terrain of drugs and terror which the police seem unable to cross. Her stories made Ireland think afresh about the kind of country it is becoming, with dire echoes back across the sea to cities like Liverpool. Her work was necessary. She discovered what nobody else had discovered. She discomforted and shamed authority in so doing. She made terrible enemies.

Veronica Guerin would be the last to see her death as some special horror, inviting special condemnation. She was, ironically, due to speak in London today at an international gathering examining the problems of 'journalists under fire'. She saw herself only as one amongst many. And that is the best way to remember her: as a foot soldier for truth in a battlefield where the troops are too often a rabble. The important thing for Ireland is that her work goes on. And there is an important thing for newspapers too. Sometimes, too often, we forget the core of the work we have to do, the real reason for our existence. Veronica Guerin reminds us of the reason why. •

17 June 1996

John Fordham

The jubilant voice of jazz

Vulnerability has always been a popular quality for jazz musicians to display, and the worse the bruises the better. The media loved Billie Holiday, Chet Baker, Charlie Parker and a raft of others for their haunting eyes, their unpredictability, the sounds of decay in their later music, their bad deaths. Their capacity for spontaneous composition, which helped transform 20th-century music, has often run a poor second in their newsworthiness.

Yet just as suitable a subject for mythology, if it had been deemed as interesting, has been the exact reverse – the apparent indestructibility of many artists, despite being up against the pressures and prejudices that made the jazz life such a tough one for so long. Ella Fitzgerald, who has died aged 79, was the kind of jazz artist who brought that constantly to mind from the 1970s onward.

During the past two decades there have been plenty of opportunities to ponder such situations, involving Fitzgerald and others who grew up with her into an age in which jazz was more widely respected and where they became giants of Western popular music. One such occasion was at the Royal Festival Hall in 1982, when Count Basie's Orchestra was performing, with Ella Fitzgerald as its singer. Basie came on in a wheelchair, by then the age that Ella was at her death, a small, gnomic, humorous-looking figure who could still deliver an inimitably tiptoeing brand of piano introduction that triggered his orchestra into making a sound somewhere between a long drum solo and 100 cats purring at once. Then Ella Fitzgerald came on to whirl through 'Blue Moon', 'I Get a Kick Out of You', 'In a Mellotone' and a headlong 'St Louis Blues' (she introduced it as 'the only blues I know').

The show was a startling display of the Fitzgerald method, which depended on one of the most assured and complete techniques ever possessed by a jazz singer, a blend of driving swing, unswerving accuracy of pitch and instrument-like improvisational skill. But it was fused by a chemistry unusual among jazz artists, an optimistic, even innocent take on the world which gave her interpretation of songs a spirited, jubilant quality. In that 1982 show, even the poignant lyrics of 'God Bless the Child' were caressed into a consoling message of hope, a moving signature of almost all Fitzgerald performances.

The durability of Fitzgerald's spark was apparent with the Basie Orchestra again, at the Albert Hall in 1990. Basie had died and the band was run by his saxophonist Frank Foster. Fitzgerald was physically a different being to the one who had commanded the South Bank stage eight years before. Her sight was poor, she had trouble walking to the spotlight, and sat on a stool for a short set.

But though some of the old gleefully imperious sweep was gone, she still turned the melodies of classic songs around in ways that made them glow all over again, and her timing remained uncanny. Almost as remarkable an achievement as her harmonic sense and ability to swing was Fitzgerald's ability to make all these virtues disappear so she seemed to be just singing in the bath. Sarah Vaughan, one of Fitzgerald's great contemporaries, always sounded like a diva, doing something that you needed to be part angel to do. Ella Fitzgerald made it sound easy, and at one stage this led to criticism that she lacked emotional depth compared to her contemporary Billie Holiday. But Fitzgerald's artless playfulness was part of the secret of the immense affection which she inspired in musicians and the public – jazz buffs and non-buffs alike – for so many years.

Ella Fitzgerald was born in Newport News, Virginia, the daughter of William Fitzgerald and his common-law wife Temperance Williams Fitzgerald. When the couple separated a year later, she moved with her mother and a Portuguese immigrant named Joseph Da Silva to Yonkers, New York. Dancing was her first love in childhood. But, as with Billie Holiday, the transformation of American music that had been wrought by Louis Armstrong and the pioneering jazz improvisers in the 1920s (subversions of predictable rhythm, a broad palette of vocal-like instrumental effects from whistles to growls, strong infusions of the blues) attracted her to a new way of singing. Fitzgerald also liked the close-harmony Boswell Sisters, particularly the lead singer, Connee Boswell, whose emotional depth and timing she tried hard to replicate. Fitzgerald performed as a dancer in the clubs in her district, working a routine with her friend Charles Gulliver.

But when she was 15, her mother died, and Ella went to live in Harlem with an aunt, in the centre of a jazz world on the brink of a roll. The Depression had all but killed the commerciality of the blues, and the New Orleans music of the previous decade sounded dated to an audience that wanted something slicker, quicker and more confident. The big-band boom was about to begin, and an emerging radio network was to launch an era of swing that was as big as rock'n'roll was to be 20 years later.

In November 1934, Ella Fitzgerald sang 'The Object of My Affection' and 'Judy' in the Boswell style, in a talent contest at Harlem's Apollo Theatre. She won first prize. Alto-saxophonist and bandleader Benny Carter spotted her and recommended her to the drummer/band leader Chick Webb, a dynamic and obsessive artist who had shrugged off physical disability and imparted to his band the momentum of a runaway steam engine. Webb thought the homely and unsophisticated Ella didn't have the stage presence for a lead singer, but her popularity at the Apollo convinced him that her vocal skills more than compensated. He had to convince the singer, who doubted her own talents and regarded her singing at the time as 'hollering'.

Chick Webb became Ella's legal guardian as well as her boss. 'He always taught me to follow the beat,' Fitzgerald said of Webb, and they became nationally famous through a string of sensational Savoy Ballroom shows, radio and recordings.

Rehearsing in Boston on a Webb tour, Ella began musing with a children's rhyme, and she and arranger Van Alexander turned it into 'A Tisket, a Tasket', which became a huge hit. She took the lyric, as she said, 'from that old drop-the-handkerchief game I played from six years old on up'.

Chick Webb died in 1939 and the singer took over as nominal leader for the next three years. She recorded prolifically, mostly pop music and novelty songs for the juke-box market. But out of the 150 or so sides she cut in those years, there was enough to remind the jazz world that a singer of massive talent was maturing. From 1935 to 1955 she worked for Decca, often under the direction of producer Milt Gabler, and sang with the Ink Spots on several hits, including the million-seller 'I'm Making Believe' and 'Into Each Life Some Rain Must Fall'.

Bebop, the harmonically advanced and technically demanding jazz revolution that developed out of the musical frustrations of the younger swing-band players and wartime economic pressures towards a self-sufficient small-band style, inevitably affected Fitzgerald. Technically able to handle the melodic convolutions and unpredictable switchbacks of bop phrasing, she adapted elements of the new music to her own style in an influential 1945 recording of the swing tune 'Flying Home'. Scat-singing – the improvisation of wordless, instrument-imitating lyrics – had existed in jazz since Louis Armstrong's amiable 1920s experiments. But no one before Fitzgerald had attempted such ambitious manoeuvres with it, and the method was subsequently adopted and modified by countless singers. A year later, Ella Fitzgerald joined bebop guru Dizzy Gillespie's band for a tour.

In December 1947, Fitzgerald married Gillespie's bassist Ray Brown. It was her second marriage, the first (to shipyard worker Benjamin Kornegay) had lasted two years. Fitzgerald and Brown adopted the son of the singer's half-sister Frances, though work schedules resulted in the child being raised by Fitzgerald's aunt Virginia. The same pressures eventually torpedoed the marriage as well and the couple were divorced in 1953.

Post-war big bands struggled, but Ella's career had transcended them. In 1950 she recorded eight George Gershwin songs (*Ella Sings Gershwin*). They were shrewd and revealing interpretations and she seemed utterly at home. Ira Gershwin remarked: 'I never knew how good our songs were until I heard Ella Fitzgerald sing them.'

In 1954, the imaginative impresario Norman Granz became Fitzgerald's manager, and he drew her away from a solely bop-based repertoire towards the possibilities offered by the Gershwin session. She devoted her gifts increasingly to reinterpretations of works of great songwriters, and Granz recorded them for his Verve label. Fitzgerald's *Songbooks* series, which took in Jerome Kern, Cole Porter, Rodgers and Hart, Irving Berlin, Duke Ellington, Johnny Mercer, Harold

Arlen and Frank Loesser (as well as five Gershwin volumes) became the high point of the singer's career. She attracted Grammy awards like a magnet. But she remained a peerless live performer, as recordings like 'Mack the Knife' from *Ella in Berlin* resoundingly confirmed. From 1955 – with *Pete Kelly's Blues* – she also appeared in movies and reaffirmed her status with events like her own 1957 Hollywood Bowl concert.

Fitzgerald's popularity meant that by the 1960s she was touring up to 45 weeks a year. She collapsed onstage in 1965, and began to develop eyesight problems and diabetes from the early 1970s. The latter led to the amputation of her legs below the knee in 1993. But despite declining health, Fitzgerald continued to perform and record into the early 1990s, broadcasting on occasion with Frank Sinatra, performing with ensembles as different as symphony orchestras and the Basie band. She also worked in her later career in delectably small groups, often with the great pianist-accompanist Tommy Flanagan. But the occasional experiments with rock and soul didn't suit her, and rarely produced enduring music.

Ella Fitzgerald remained shy and abstemious throughout her later life, living in Beverly Hills and seeing only a small circle of friends, most of them musicians and singers, including Carmen McRae and Peggy Lee. She kept the admiration and respect of singers in and out of the jazz world all her life – from Bing Crosby and Frank Sinatra to Elton John and Cassandra Wilson. *Downbeat* magazine named her best female jazz singer for 18 consecutive years, she received awards and doctorates from all over the world ('not bad for someone who only studied music to get that half-credit at high school,' she said in an acceptance speech at Yale) and received a Kennedy Center Award for her work in the performing arts.

The British writer Benny Green maybe put the Fitzgerald magic best, however. He wrote: 'She is the best equipped vocalist ever to grace the jazz scene. There is to her voice a lilting, lullaby quality which renders even commonplace material moving.' As for Fitzgerald herself, she simply said: 'God gave me a voice . . . something with which to make other people happy.'

Football coming home

Sporting life

. . . .

19 June 1996

Richard Williams

Unexpected and unforgettable

By the end of last night's tumultuous match at Wembley, Stuart Pearce was coolly playing a clearance off his right kneecap to Steve McManaman 20 yards away while a man called Cruyff was failing to control the ball when clear in front of goal. Who on earth could have imagined that?

England were, in a word, amazing. Against the best side they have so far met in this competition, they made those of us who have scorned their chances bend the knee to a performance in which they looked thoroughly credible contenders for the Henri Delaunay Trophy. And even if they stumble at the next hurdle, or the one after that, at least Terry Venables and his team have given us a night we never expected, and will never forget.

Actually, we can be very precise about how good England were against Holland. The first half contained the best football the team have played since 28 April 1993, when they were 2–0 up after 45 minutes against the same country in a World Cup qualifying match. But this time fate had arranged a different and much more satisfactory outcome.

This time there was no Jan Wouters to break Paul Gascoigne's cheekbone, nor a Marc Overmars to destroy the career of Des Walker, the most gifted English defender of his generation. And no trench-coated Graham Taylor slinking away into the night.

The difference this time was that England saved their second goal until after half-time, and then sustained the quality of their performance virtually to the end, taking handsome revenge on opponents who had cost them a place in USA '94.

As compensation, Euro '96 will do just fine. In the process of handing the Dutch a beating that will stay on their minds for years to come, a team appeared to discover itself. When Teddy Sheringham slid the fourth goal past Van der Sar, the sound of pure joy was heard all around Wembley. England's fans had found 11 players whose deeds matched their dreams. And you can bet that in the Spanish tent, not to mention those of the Germans, the Italians and the French, new plans were being designed. The England of last week would not have unduly occupied the strategists of the teams who considered themselves favourites. The England of last night will be considered formidable opponents.

From carthorses to thoroughbreds in the space of a few days? Perhaps the confused state of mind in which the Dutch approached this match had something to do with the confidence with which England began it, but the men in orange shirts were undone by Venables's planning, and by the diligence with which his players stuck to their tasks.

For supporting Gascoigne through thick and thin, Venables deserves the admiration of his fellow professionals and a nation's thanks. Last night Gascoigne was in his pomp, a marvellous and majestic sight. In the first half he dedicated himself to the team's cause, running and passing with tactical acumen, immense vigour and never a hint of self-indulgence. After half-time he was able to open his bag of tricks in the knowledge that he had earned the right to express himself.

His and Shearer's goals against the Scots must have raised the whole team's morale. Last night they expanded those cameos into an entire 90-minute show overflowing with creative thinking and fine touches. When Gascoigne gave Aron Winter the slip on the edge of the area and cut the ball back to Sheringham, who angled his boot to redirect it square to Shearer, the Blackburn striker found himself in a position to score a goal which was not an isolated moment of beauty but an expression of the whole. In fact it was the best goal England had scored since, oh, last Saturday.

And what was so nice about it was that each of the three players contributed something characteristic: a Gascoigne shimmy, a selfless Sheringham lay-off, a piece of Shearer smash-and-grab. The whole team was like that all night, each giving the best of himself.

All right, it was only a group match, not a knock-out round (except for the poor Scots, who will be cursing Venables's decision to take off Ince, which loosened the stays of the England defence and let Kluivert in for the goal that allowed the Dutch to remain in the competition). But so much worked well for England that it is hard to envisage their performances sliding back into the old mediocrity.

Any suspicions that this match was going to be a carve-up between the two sides to ensure their continued participation did not survive the first quarter of an hour, which included clattering late tackles by Richard Witschge on McManaman and by Winston Bogarde on Gascoigne. Subsequently Danny Blind's trip on Paul Ince and Ince's own foolish challenge on Jordi Cruyff confirmed the level of commitment to winning the match which ran through both sides.

But Venables's defence held, on a day which proved the continued relevance of the flat back four to England – and to France, for that matter. Faced with only one striker, Dennis Bergkamp for Holland and Stoichkov for Bulgaria, both teams held fast to the supposedly obsolete formation that has served them well in the past, and found that they lost nothing as a result.

But then a lot of received wisdom suddenly came up for reassessment at Wembley last night. •

27 June 1996

Richard Williams

A game no one man deserved to lose

There will be a game of football at Wembley on Sunday night, and they will call it the final of the European Championship, but goodness knows how it can hope to equal, never mind surpass, the drama that played itself out at the old stadium last night, when the footballers of England and Germany gave everything they had, every ounce of skill and thought and effort, to justify a pre-match build-up of almost intolerable intensity.

If ever a game justified the controversial Golden Goal idea this was it. When they entered the unknown territory of sudden-death extra time, with its short history of suffocating timidity, the two sides immediately behaved as though UEFA had paid them a special bonus to demonstrate the potency of the concept. Ignoring the physical effects of the first 90 minutes they tore at each other with renewed vigour and redoubled courage, chances coming by the minute at both ends.

There was no fear, no hesitation, no sense of anything other than a prize there to be won. Mere patriotism dissolved in the spirit of a game played for its own sake.

It seemed as though almost everyone on the field had a chance to go down in history as the first man to decide one of the tournament's matches with a sudden-death goal: first Anderton, then Kuntz, then Möller, Kuntz again, then dear old Gazza, twice in three minutes, then Ziege, then Platt, then McManaman, then Adams. All of them will be seeing those chances again in their dreams; only the Englishmen will wake up sweating.

There was barely a cigarette paper between the two sides all through a night when both these old enemies appeared to have signed a pact to do away with caution. Who would wish to choose between the elegance of Sammer and the wholeheartedness of Adams, between the mad invention of Gascoigne and the chilling deftness of Möller, between the ferocity of Pearce and the athleticism of Ziege? It was a contrast of style but rarely of quality and there must have been many in the stadium who, moved by the sheer generosity of the players, regretted the necessity for either side to lose.

And certainly not to lose through one man's mistake. Well, of course, we can say that penalties are an authentic part of the game, and that it is best to decide such a match by using a legitimate technique. But at the end you just wanted them to draw lots for a place in the final so that luck could be blamed, not a man. No one deserved to be remembered for losing this one by his error, as poor Gareth Southgate will be at the end of a tournament which he entered as an international novice before establishing himself as one of England's most skilful and perceptive players.

It was Stuart Pearce, inevitably, who was first to reach Southgate as the distraught defender made his way back to the centre circle knowing that his failure had ended the nation's hope of an even bigger party than the one we have been enjoying for the past two and a half weeks. Pearce was the only one who knew exactly how Southgate felt, and in the months ahead his example should be of some comfort to a man who will wake up today feeling the entire burden of elimination weighing on his shoulder.

'I am proud of the whole lot of them,' Terry Venables said afterwards, emphatically including Southgate. 'It can be a cruel game, but it can be wonderful.' When he saw how much his players were prepared to give him he could have been forgiven for believing that last night was not going to be one of the cruel ones.

Before the start the big question concerned the true condition of Jürgen Klinsmann's damaged calf muscles. Were they torn, strained or merely bruised? Someone who had seen him the night before said that he could hardly walk but there was suspicion that Berti Vogts might use him in emergency, if only as a talismanic figure warming up on the touchline, to put fear into English hearts. The Germans had spent the night before the match in a hotel a couple of hundred yards away from Madame Tussaud's, which prompted the thought that perhaps Vogts was planning to borrow the wax effigy of the 1995 Footballer of the Year to send out at the head of the team like Charlton Heston in the final scene of *El Cid*.

In Klinsmann's absence, England took the lead after two minutes. Did they think, in that moment, that they had it won? There have been times during this tournament when what they needed to animate their game was a goal; without one they looked anxious and incoherent. Well, they got one last night, with Shearer's devastating swoop, but it had the opposite effect. It put them to sleep.

For the next 13 minutes and for the only time in the match, they sat back on their lead and watched while the Germans pulled themselves together and began to move the ball around. At first tentatively but soon with gathering confidence, Sammer and Möller started to mark out a steady tempo on which a variety of rhythms could be imposed.

England could not have chosen a more dangerous strategy. This German side is not equipped for breakaways. It moved forward as a unit, favouring short passes at damaging angles to men already on the move to accept the ball on the understanding that there would be someone else arriving to receive it in turn. England's unwillingness to force the pace after taking the lead presented the Germans with exactly the opportunity they required to recover from the jolt caused by Shearer's strike, and the move leading to Kuntz's goal, after

Platt's poor control had given the ball away in the centre cirle, unfolded with implacable logic.

Eventually England pulled themselves together, and if there was a player who consistently rose above the throng it was Darren Anderton. Overshadowed by McManaman in the early matches of the tournament, he fulfilled the wing-back's role on the right in the first half last night before relinquishing the task to his Liverpool counterpart and using the consequent freedom to invent most of England's best moves. Had his shot gone in rather than hit the post in the second minute of extra time some sort of justice would have been served. But on we went instead to the unbearable unfairness of the penalties.

No one can deny that the footballers of the Czech Republic have earned the right to their appearance in Sunday's final of Euro '96. And, if they win it, to call themselves champions. But they can count themselves honoured to be facing the winners of a match in which both sides played as if they had nothing to lose, the way it is in dreams. •

....

1 July 1996
Matthew Engel
Spare a thought for the poor workers at the typeface, victims of our success in a new age of uncertainty

A *letter to* Guardian *readers*

Dear [your name cleverly inserted here by word processor so it looks as if I'm an old chum],

I know you probably receive a lot of these letters. Indeed, as a *Guardian* reader and therefore an obviously caring person, you probably answer many of them. You may already be suffering from what is known as 'compassion fatigue'.

Please, don't crumple this up and throw it in the bin. Hear my case. I am writing on behalf of an under-appreciated group of men (and women – don't worry on that score) who are in danger of being left behind in this rapidly changing world of ours. The crisis has happened very quickly.

This group is the Nothing Writers of Great Britain. You probably think of us, if you ever do, merely as sports columnists. Indeed, you may regard us as an idle load of good-for-nothing drunks, getting paid to swan round all the events for which you can't get tickets even after queuing all night. This is a terrible calumny.

Oh, all right, it's more or less true.

Well, anyway, you probably think it's easy. You would probably rather donate your money to retired directors of utility companies. You don't understand. It is tough work, chipping away at the typeface, often far from home, battling against distractions of which most people know little: the constant temptations of room service, mucky films on the hotel telly and the swimming pool.

Until recently little was known about the dangers of the job. Excessive sunshine, we all know now, is a terrible thing. And even close to home there are constant threats to our health. Anyone who has seen a Wimbledon all-day breakfast will be aware that six of them at a sitting could be extremely unhealthy. Ditto six large gins and tonic.

But *we were OK*. We could always find a column somehow. When inspiration failed, there was always a ready-made standby: a subject that could provide 800 words without a pause for breath. We could always take the piss out of the Brits.

Suddenly, without any warning – and certainly no consultation – the world has changed. Oh, there were signs for those who cared to look. Our golfers have been competent, even occasionally brilliant, for more than a decade. The England rugby team started winning at the start of the 1990s (and is guarding against the possibility of that changing by arranging to play in future only before a small audience for vast sums of money).

We could even cope with occasional Olympic gold medals, as long as we didn't have to stay in Glory, Glory mode for more than 24 hours at a time.

Now, within the space of three weeks, the rug has been swept from under our feet. The England cricket team started playing properly. Then the England football team started playing properly. Now the utterly unthinkable has happened: an English tennis player has started playing properly.

Where will it end? I have no faith that our troubles will cease this afternoon. On Saturday I endured extreme privation on Court 13 (well, there was a nasty chill to the wind) to watch Tim Henman's next opponent, Magnus Gustafsson, playing Wayne Ferreira, who had suddenly found himself – in the absence of Boris Becker – seeded to reach the final.

Although Ferreira is South African, he responded to this situation like the traditional Brit and went to pieces. He would have struggled to beat Magnus Magnusson. Then Gustafsson said his ambition was to play on Centre Court rather than to win Wimbledon, compared Henman to Sampras (with a slightly inferior service) and, sounding like a really nice chap himself, said Henman was 'a great guy'.

This is another problem. The tennis players have got likeable. We don't even have the brats and spats of yesteryear to write about.

I have no faith in Gustafsson putting a stop to this nonsense. There are still some hopes that Todd Martin – tall, muscular, powerful, all-American, dull –

will do the business and beat Henman in the quarterfinals. But all the old certainties have gone. It is a traumatic time.

Some columnists are threatening to keep turning out the old jokes about the British No. 1 being beaten by a traffic bollard in Wimbledon High Street for old time's sake. Others need counselling.

Give what you can afford. Five pounds will buy two of us a gin and tonic. A hundred thousand would enable me to retire in reasonable comfort and be replaced by someone who can cope with the new realities. Even a kind word would be something. Please help.

Yours etc.

Matthew ●

10 July 1996
Ian Katz
Friendly fire from Bosnia

Nedzad Fazlija is almost certainly the finest marksman in Bosnia but do not ask him how many enemy soldiers he picked off during his country's ferocious civil war. 'I'm a sportsman, not a sniper,' he says.

The wiry, bespectacled 28-year-old has grown tired of explaining the distinction but over the next few weeks he will have to do it often; by one of those ironies that conjures a smile from the bleakest of circumstances, he is Bosnia's best prospect for a medal at the Olympics.

For the past two weeks Fazlija and seven other Bosnian competitors have been training in this tiny town, a place so sleepy and unremarkable that motel clerks ask not how long you are staying but how long you are stuck.

Desperate for a slice of the Olympic action that will unfold in Atlanta, 100 miles east, the burghers of Pell City subjected their war-weary visitors to a crash course in southern hospitality.

They built an Olympic-standard shooting range for Fazlija and bought a table tennis table for Tarik Hodzic and a competition-quality wrestling mat for Fahrudin Hodzic.

To ease communication they rechristened each athlete with a 'Southern Nickname'. Fazlija became Ned, Tarik Hodzic became Terry and Fahrudin Hodzic was Rhudy. The swimmer Dijana Kvesic will be for ever known here as Lady Di.

Since the penniless Bosnians were able to compete in Atlanta only because of a grant from the International Olympic Committee, local families put them up and every restaurant in town vied to introduce them to fried chicken and grits. 'They said they liked our grease,' said Brenda Hamby, a restaurateur who coordinated the effort to feed the Olympians.

If the arrival of the Bosnian team was the biggest thing to happen to Pell City since the high school girls' basketball team won the state championships in 1989, the Atlanta Olympics hold a monumental significance for those who will compete in the country's blue and white colours.

'To represent Bosnia-Herzegovina after all these tragic years is not only to represent a country but to represent all those people who died for freedom,' says Hodzic.

Although a Bosnian team was spirited to Barcelona in 1992, says Fazlija's coach Dautovic Amir, 'that was important just to see our flag. This time we've had time to chose and take care of our athletes.'

Fazlija represented Yugoslavia 12 times in international shooting events before the country splintered along ethnic lines in 1992. Two weeks before hostilities broke out his Sarajevo club won the national championships. 'Maybe that was the reason the war started in Bosnia,' he suggests with a thin smile.

Within months Sarajevo's sparkling Zetra sports centre, built for the 1984 Winter Olympics, was destroyed by artillery fire and with it went Fazlija's hopes of keeping his skills sharp.

It seems natural to wonder if the embattled Bosnian army sought to harness Fazlija's rare talent but he bridles at the suggestion. He will say only that he served as a reserve policeman in Sarajevo and lost an uncle and a cousin in the fighting.

The Bosnian athletes are similarly reticent about their own ethnicity, stressing only that the team has members from each of Bosnia's three ethnic groups.

Fazlija managed to compete outside Bosnia a handful of times during the war, first escaping Sarajevo by running across the city's airport under the eyes of Serb snipers and later by using the secret tunnel that Sarajevans used to beat the siege of the city.

But he says his skills have been badly blunted by lack of competition and resources. Until last month, when he received three new weapons from a sponsor, he was competing with a 23-year-old rifle. The people here bought him 5,000 bullets, but after the Olympics he has no idea how he will pay for his ammunition.

Despite all this Fazlija finished seventh in one World Cup event last year and near the top of a strong field that competed in Atlanta this year. His best chance of a medal is reckoned to be in the three-position event, he must fire from standing, kneeling and prone positions.

Adding to the emotional baggage the Bosnians will carry into the games, several face competing against former Yugoslav team-mates-turned-enemies.

Fazlija says he has already come up against three Serbian and one Slovenian former team-mates. 'I talk normally with those [Serb] people but I know what they think about me and they know what I think about them. It's not easy to speak with these people if you know that some of them shot in my city and killed 11,000 citizens of Sarajevo, 2,000 of them children.'

No family members of the Bosnian Olympians have got to the games but the athletes can count on support from Pell City residents, so infatuated with their charges that many have promised to shave their heads if a Bosnian wins a medal.

That is more than anyone in the Bosnian delegation dares hope for, says Heda Burdzovic, a 26-year-old student who fled Sarajevo last year and works as a translator for the team. 'I told them the first day I saw them that they won a medal just by showing up.' •

· ·

16 July 1996
Ian Katz
From nightmare to dream

Gilbert Tuhabonye always loved to run. As a child he ran barefoot for miles around the Burundi village where he grew up. As a teenager he toured the country competing in cross-country races. On the night of 21 October 1993, however, he ran for another reason. He ran because his body was on fire.

The 21-year-old middle-distance runner has not yet made any impact on the international athletics scene and may not even compete at the Olympic Games next week. But Tuhabonye's may already be one of the most extraordinary sports stories of the year.

That story is etched for ever across his sinewy body, a trail of shiny, dark scar tissue that climbs his right leg then spreads out across his back like the embossed lettering on a glossy book cover.

Tuhabonye says the scars are the result of appalling burns he sustained when a mob of Hutus rounded up Tutsi students at his high school, locked them in a room, doused them with petrol and set them on fire. There were 250 students in the room, he says. He was the sole survivor.

It is impossible to verify the details of Tuhabonye's account of the incident and perhaps, in the face of his incontrovertibly grotesque injuries, churlish even to try. Suffice to say that in his own country he is known as the Survivor, a hero to Tutsis and a demon possessed of supernatural powers to Hutus.

Tuhabonye says he survived by hiding underneath a pile of his burning classmates. When the bodies above him burned through, he pushed them aside and found others to shield himself from the full heat of the blaze. 'In my mind I'm thinking, I'm not dying. I'm thinking someone could help me, someone could save me.'

After around eight hours, Tuhabonye says, he managed to use bones from one of the bodies to break open a window at the top of the shed. A Hutu militiaman spotted him as he tumbled through it but another man told him not to give chase: 'He say: "He is finished, don't follow him." '

So Tuhabonye ran. 'I tried to run fast. I ran one kilometre and stopped because I was very tired. I tried to breathe and, when I did this, I realised I was burning.'

Tuhabonye lay down in a grassy patch to try to put out the fire and that is where a patrol of Burundian government soldiers found him several hours later.

The soldiers took him to hospital in the Burundian capital, Bujumbura, where he was treated for third-degree burns over much of his body. He spent three months in the hospital, often sleeping on the floor when the beds were allocated to more grievously wounded victims of the ferocious war between the Hutus and the Tutsis.

'I was dreaming about my sport all the time I was in the hospital. One day I tried to move and my leg hurts very bad,' he says, pointing to the ridge of scar tissue running up his right leg.

Before what he refers to as 'the accident' Tuhabonye had been offered a sporting scholarship to Tulane University in the United States. But now his athletic career — and his hopes of escaping his war-ravaged country — appeared to have been buried.

Then in April Jim Minnihan, the director of a Georgia-based programme that trains promising Third World athletes, heard of Tuhabonye's story through the veteran Burundian middle-distance runner Dieudonne Kwizera. 'I said, if you can get this guy an air ticket, I'll get him out,' says Minnihan.

A few weeks later Tuhabonye was training in the salubrious surroundings of La Grange's private Methodist college along with three other Burundian runners and around 40 other Third World athletes on scholarships funded by the International Olympic Committee and the La Grange Sports Authority, a local charity.

A native Swahili and French speaker, Tuhabonye embarked on a crash course in English and plans to study computer science and business administration at the college.

Every morning he and the other African athletes follow the Somalian track star Abdi Bile on a long run through the verdant Georgia countryside around this elegant antebellum town. 'Normally when someone gets an accident they stop running,' he beams through slightly crooked teeth, 'but me, I'm not the same. I have determination.'

Tuhabonye's performances have improved steadily since he began training in the United States but he has yet to post an Olympic-qualifying time for either of his two events, the 800 and the 1500 metres. His hopes of competing in Atlanta lie with the wild cards assigned by the International Olympic Committee to each country.

But as of yesterday they looked slim. Burundi, competing for the first time in an Olympics, has just one wild-card slot which it has allocated to a female athlete training in La Grange. Minnihan plans to petition the IOC president Juan Antonio Samaranch for a special dispensation to allow Tuhabonye to compete.

Tuhabonye insists he will not be too disappointed if his only experience of the 1996 Olympics proves to be the leg of the torch relay he ran delightedly last month. 'If I miss this Olympic Games, the next Olympic Games I will be the star. If 249 persons die and only one survives, I realise that God has something for me. When I run, I say: "God likes me." ' ●

....

29 July 1996

Richard Williams
And then came the bomb

O n the streets of downtown Atlanta, Friday night already felt different. The pavements were crowded. Young people, old people, families, people in town on sponsorship junkets, all wandering, looking, talking, having fun. At last there were queues at the restaurants, the way their owners had anticipated when Billy Payne told them the Games were coming to Atlanta.

But there was an odd feeling to it. Something about the place reminded me of New Orleans: that slightly frenetic edge, an electric buzz, unsettling.

On a normal night, downtown Atlanta is quiet for all the wrong reasons. The better-off inhabitants have retreated to their vanilla suburbs at the close of the working day, leaving a generic American zone that George Clinton (no relation) once christened Chocolate City.

According to Payne, the lawyer who dreamed up the idea of bringing the Olympics to his city, it was to help alleviate this kind of urban blight that he dreamed up the idea of the Centennial Olympic Park.

How much of this was honest, socially responsible intervention and how much window-dressing only Payne and his closest colleagues on the organising committee know. To have left the 20-acre site as it was – an eyesore speckled with derelict low-income housing and abandoned light-industrial buildings – would have invited the world's scorn. But Atlanta is a small town, and such a gesture could have a significant cosmetic effect.

If you look at the plans drawn up by the park's architect, you see sylvan glades and shady groves which appear to offer space for Games-goers to pause and indulge in gentle debate on the relative merits of their favourites. A place, even, to read a book.

But that is for after the Games. During the past 10 days the Centennial Olympic Park has offered perhaps the most highly concentrated 20 acres of high-capitalism in action to be found anywhere on the globe.

'This is America,' a man said to me the other day. 'When people see a crowd, they try to figure out a way to sell them something.' And here was a crowd, all right. And in an age when the signs and language of popular culture – once a living, kicking thing – have been annexed by the forces of Coca-Cola, Nike, Swatch and Budweiser, they were arriving in their tens of thousands.

Look, Billy Payne was able to say in answer to those prissy foreigners who criticised the shortcomings of his small-town Games, look at these people enjoying themselves. This is what the Games are about.

The Park was such a success that for a week it sucked the life out of the old downtown, which had been looking to the Games for a revival of its fortunes. Families snatched hamburgers on the run rather than enter restaurants. They bought their Swatches and commemorative T-shirts from stalls rather than from the shops in the Peachtree Center. Macy's, the town's last old-fashioned department store, was a wasteland.

But on Friday, as the restaurants bulged and the closed-off streets hummed with pedestrian traffic, things seemed to be changing. It wasn't too late, we mused, for these Games to take on the party spirit that made Barcelona a standard for all Olympics to come. And then came the bomb.

The next morning, everything was different. The sky was grey, the temperature had dropped 20 degrees, and periodic rain came to thin the streaks of blood that stained the ground under a wrought-iron bench in the Centennial Olympic Park, ground quartered by the long yellow ribbons placed by agents of the Department of Alcohol, Tobacco and Firearms, who were on their hands and knees around the ruined lighting tower, placing small pink flags wherever they found debris.

And while this work went on, while sirens indicated further alarms, people were returning to the stadiums, putting up with the need to stand in line for two or three hours while bags were opened and binoculars examined.

Like everything about Billy Payne's Games, the security precautions have been haphazard. Before the bomb, examinations of personal effects were good-humoured but usually cursory. In the week before the bomb I was asked only once to switch on my mobile phone and laptop computer. And on the night of the opening ceremony, hopelessly lost while trying to find our way out, three of us simply followed a bunch of VIPs and ended up on a coach ferrying IOC dignitaries and their guests back to their downtown hotel. Virginia Bottomley was three rows ahead. None of us resembled dignitaries, yet nobody once asked to look at our passes.

On Saturday, with the Park cordoned off and even the neighbouring Coca-Cola Olympic City closed down, the tens of thousands who weren't queuing for the athletics or baseball needed somewhere to go. So, at last, they thronged the pavements of the old main street. And the merchants of downtown Atlanta finally had a good day. •

· ·

18 March 1996

Richard Williams

Tyson gets back to basic instincts

Did anyone seriously imagine there could be any other kind of ending? After six minutes and 50 seconds of boxing in the MGM Grand Garden on Saturday night the natural order reasserted itself when Mike Tyson deprived Frank Bruno of the World Boxing Council heavyweight title by a technical knockout following a whirlwind of punches that left the defending champion's senses in disarray.

But in case anyone should think that it was easy pickings for the challenger, Tyson's demeanour at the end of the fight showed the significance he attached to success in the first stage of his attempt to reunify the three heavyweight titles. He fell to his knees, bowing directly at Louis Farrakhan, the leader of the Nation of Islam, who was sitting at ringside. And, when the new champion had the WBC belt safely around his midriff, he came to the edge of the platform to show it off, thrusting it at the world in a display of pure machismo that will have done no good to the morale of whoever his next opponent turns out to be.

Bruno had held the title for 197 days, an achievement of which he can be justifiably proud and which will ensure him a special standing among his fellow countrymen for as long as he lives. This, they will say, was a man who got into a boxing ring with Mike Tyson not once but twice; he will be admired for the dogged courage with which, in the course of a 14-year professional career, he found ways to overcome a complete lack of innate aptitude for the game's techniques.

Tyson, of course, is the most natural of fighters, elemental in his ferocity and his understanding of how to use his limited stature against bigger opponents. Yet it must be said that the Bruno of 1996 could not match the achievement of his younger self, who had lasted five rounds in 1989 and briefly but memorably hurt a man who at the time looked the most invincible fighter since Marciano.

Saturday's opening round must nevertheless have been among the most impressive Bruno has fought, given the quality of the man emerging from the other corner. Tyson rushed at him straight away, looking to get inside his guard. Bruno opened with textbook left jabs and held his own in a series of furious exchanges until, with only 10 seconds left on the clock, Tyson unloaded a long straight right which caught Bruno on the left eye. The value of the blow could be seen as Bruno retreated to his corner and George Francis began working on a deep cut an inch long just beneath the eyebrow.

Effectively the fight ended at that moment. Thereafter Bruno's prime concern was to protect the eye from further injury; he never got a chance to devise a counter-attack. The jab had lost its authority. Now Tyson found a more tentative response every time he walked forward.

Early in the second round, with the two men in a rolling maul, the referee Mills Lane gave them both a lecture. 'I told them, look, you're fighting a hell of a fight, but knock off all this crap, the grabbing and the jerking on the inside,' he said. A couple of minutes later he gave Bruno a further warning and deducted a point. 'He was grabbing and holding. He didn't want to get hit. But it wasn't just defensive grabbing. It was offensive grabbing.'

Tyson missed with a big left hook, as he was to do again early in the third round, but they were the exceptions. When Bruno tried switching to a left lead to protect his cut, it was to no avail. Half a minute into the third, after Bruno had been warned again for holding, Tyson launched the assault that broke the champion.

It began with two big lefts to the jaw, followed by a right and a left to the head which forced Bruno back into the ropes. Bruno's defence was now non-existent. Tyson waited, watched and then unleashed a series of three right-hand uppercuts, the first and third of which detonated in Bruno's face. A further left and right as he went down against the ropes were superfluous. Lane, his shirt splattered with the champion's blood, was already moving in to save Bruno from further punishment.

'He was in real trouble,' Lane said later. 'He was hurt bad, really getting nailed. Tyson's pretty close to being back, I'll tell you that. But it wasn't a dirty fight. It was a pure fight. And he's a pure fighter.'

The winner, unmarked, looked as though he could have fought all night, taking on the champions of the other two governing bodies – the WBA's Bruce Seldon and the IBF's François Botha – if necessary, perhaps with Lennox Lewis thrown in for good measure. 'As you could see,' Tyson said, 'I was throwing punches. I'm doing well but I still have plenty of room for improvement.' Who will his next opponent be? 'I'll fight anyone Don King puts in front of me.'

From Bruno there was an honest admission of failure. 'I was trying to use my weight against him,' he said, 'but he was very fast. He was better than I thought. He beat me fair and square. It's a rough game. Now I'm going to chill out with my family before I make any more decisions.'

The thousands who had travelled from Britain were clearly of a mind to forgive him for failing to extend Tyson further. Not so Floyd Patterson, a great former champion. 'I expected Bruno to box,' he said, 'but he didn't. He fought Tyson's fight. I've seen him box before but he didn't tonight. He just came out and slugged. That made it a lot harder for him to beat Tyson.' Did he think Tyson was back to his best form? 'Based on the way the other guy fought, I could not tell. If Bruno had done all the things I've seen him do before, and Tyson had still won, then I could have told you he's back. But the guy slugged with him. And that's what Tyson is, a slugger.'

Patterson was standing in the hotel casino, patiently signing autographs for a queue of British fans whose aggression had been spent in the hours building up to the fight, when Tyson's admirers had filed into the hall with utter bemusement on their faces as they ran the gauntlet of the hordes in Chelsea and Arsenal shirts chanting: 'There's only one Frankie Bruno' and 'Tyson is a rapist, Tyson is a rapist, la la la la.' But in the end Bruno's supporters appeared to recognise that what they had seen was a thoroughly realistic reflection of the respective abilities of the two, with no discredit to their favourite.

Ten minutes after Tyson had left the ring Bruno was still in there, gathering his wits. The celebrities – Eddie Murphy, Steffi Graf, Ice T, Jack Nicholson, Paul Weller, Kevin Costner, Bill Cosby and many more – were long gone. Only a few hundred British fans were still around to salute what will surely be his last exit from a boxing ring. He picked up a Union Jack and waved it in salute to the last of the faithful. Then he kissed his daughters. It was time to go home. ●

· ·

16 October 1995

John Rodda

The noble art now seems little more than a bloody way of making money

How much longer can boxing hang its head – until the funeral is over or another wheelchair found for a victim of brain damage? The protagonists will soon return to what was once a noble art and now seems little more than a bloody way of making money.

After 49 years of writing about boxing I recoil along with many of my journalistic colleagues when a fighter dies. It is no longer the occasional accident; death in the ring or irreparable damage is happening too often and the drip, drip, drip on my conscience has finally taken me close to the point where I believe it should be banned.

The number of deaths and serious injuries has been rising worldwide for the past 15 years. If the British Boxing Board of Control cannot accept the need to devise measures giving fighters greater protection then it must stop defending the indefensible. Unless it acts before another James Murray, Gerald McLellan or Bradley Stone, the board could be facing a popular protest group which takes the issue into a wider public domain.

The argument that boxing would go underground is hard to support, for it would then not generate the money which makes fighters take the risk they do.

There is unlicensed fighting on a very small scale but that is hardly likely to survive if boxing is made unlawful.

The increasing danger in professional boxing comes from a combination of factors: the decline in amateur boxing; the more sophisticated training methods now used by professionals; and a suspicion that some fighters are using banned substances such as anabolic steroids.

The British Boxing Board of Control has failed to halt the increase in death and damage. Its insistence on ambulances and paramedics at every fight and doctors at the ringside may be seen as no more than a sop to parry critics. Caring for the injured has to be maintained, but preventive measures can no longer be ignored.

What it must do is devise larger gloves filled with substances which inflict less damaging blows, and at the same time revive some of the boxing skills now so badly lacking. The board's counter-argument is likely to be that this would put British boxers at greater risk in international fights, and that overseas boxers would not want to fight in this country with such gloves. But a start has to be made somewhere.

When I reported my first fights in 1946, the training methods used by boxers had hardly changed during this century: the heavy punching bag, the punchball, shadow-boxing in front of a large Victorian mirror and tuition from the trainer and sparring with big gloves and a headguard.

Most of that is still part of the paraphernalia, but in recent years fighters have moved into intensive weight-training with sophisticated equipment; they have added strength and greater speed to their punching. Putting those assets together causes more damage to the opponent's brain.

That danger has been magnified because the skills of boxing have declined. As a local newspaper journalist in London in the 1940s and 1950s my winter nights were filled by reporting amateur boxing tournaments. There were clubs in all kinds of places: church halls, missions, school premises.

In immediate post-war Britain there were no sports halls, no artificial surfaces and little open space, so young boys throughout the country learned to box. They were taught the Noble Art of Self-Defence, in which avoiding being hit had almost the same value as hitting.

In the past 20 years amateur boxing clubs have dwindled and few schools now include the sport on their curriculum. Potential fighters go to a professional gym. The emphasis has shifted to greater aggression, encouraged by promotional interests which know that the crowd – in the hall and those watching on television – want their instincts fed. Most of those who watch want to see the knockout punch.

The first professional fighter I watched was George Daly, of Blackfriars, described as 'the last of the mechanics'. He brought artistry to boxing, through balance, nimble feet and the way he mesmerised opponents with the feint. Daly could not punch and did not have to, for he knew sufficient and applied his skills to have his arm raised as winner at the end.

One extraordinary phenomenon about professional boxing is the camaraderie it generates. All over the country there are ex-boxers' associations which meet fortnightly or monthly to socialise. In this sport which demands such courage the spirit of friendship runs deep. There are many former fighters, into their seventies and eighties, who boxed for a pittance and are now sad to watch their sport decline to the point where the light might be snuffed out. •

. . . .

29 February 1996

Frank Keating

Homely idol from the golden age

Forty years on, possibly to the very day, yesterday was by touching fluke precisely the same sort of blue-bright and bonny late winter's day on the Cotswolds as it had been in 1956. The moment I heard the news I remembered, as wrenchingly as if it was only last week, how the nerves had knotted my stomach and blanked my mind as I pushed my old Raleigh boneshaker up past Bulls Cross and Camp Hill to Miserden, hidden and honeyed and high above Stroud on the Birdlip road.

She'd obviously tell me to clear off. Or, even worse, what if she didn't? What if I can't think of a question? Any road, why should she talk to a berk like me when she's used to being interviewed over lunches and dinners by Fleet Street's finest, my heroes? 'She's shy of the press,' Geoffrey had said when ordering me not to telephone first. 'Don't give her a chance to make excuses, laddie, just get up there and ambush her and bring me back 1,000 words.' *A thousand*. I don't think I even knew that many.

Geoffrey was the belligerent (and to me beloved) former editor of the *Stroud News* and I was his brand-new cub in my first week. The day before he had taken a long slurp of Scotch, wiped his moustache on his sleeve, fixed me with bloodshot gaze and announced he wanted a new column, Personality of the Week, and I could begin it with a bang by going up to see how Stroud's most famous personality was getting on.

Locally famous? After (possibly) Princess Margaret-Rose, in 1956 Pat Smythe was the most utterly famous woman under 30 in all Britain, if not Europe. She was 10 years older than me and she died on Tuesday aged 67.

On that day she was a kindly delight to this tremulous twerp from the moment he leaned his bike on her stable door. She might have giggled at my gormlessness, but she provided her own questions for answers which she dictated to keep pace with my laboured longhand.

Pat really was Britain's first television pin-up. In the early fifties the first mass audience sat by their firesides in front of their fuzzy monochrome screens and, although not knowing a halter from a hind leg, they cheered on this slightly dumpy, apple-cheeked country gel and her string of homely horses – accompanied by Dorian Williams's even more thoroughbred vowels. 'Five to go . . . the water, safely over . . . the wall . . . now the final difficult treble . . . she really stokes him up . . . c'mon, Pat . . . she's over! . . . she's *clear*! Oh, well done, Pat!'

The girl who was so good to me that day was the girl who took on the men, the girl with little money who schooled her own horses to take on the millionaires, and who that same summer became the first woman to ride at an Olympic Games. She came back from Sweden with a bronze in the team event and won an OBE.

Her father, an electrical engineer, had died in the war. In 1952 she lost her mother, who was killed driving to Stroud station on the wickedly steep bend below Slad's Woolpack Inn and Laurie Lee's cottage.

That day of my first-ever interview Pat was still alone in her grief, compensated only by her headstrong athlete Prince Hal, the faithful mottled-grey Tosca and the brave-heart Flanagan, the three names a nation loved and which tripped off the tongue round the rings at Harringay, White City and Wembley. Thanks to Pat (as well as Harry Llewellyn and Foxhunter) showjumping was in its only golden age.

I last saw her about 10 years ago, still commuting for long chunks of each year between the spiky grandeur of her late husband Sam Koechlin's Swiss Alps and her mellow Miserden home. She sat me down, put an old spaniel in my lap and, giggling softly, let me interview her properly. Could she have done it today?

'Not all alone nor, as I had to, on a shoestring. But I think we had more fun. I made my sport my education. I loved art and opera as much as my horses. When they said go and compete somewhere I said: "Oh goodie, Madrid means the Prado" or "Paris means a few more rooms at the Louvre" or "Milan means I can ride Tosca in the afternoons and go and hear it in the evenings". I can't see our Olympic showjumpers thinking like that nowadays. Well, the sponsors wouldn't let them.'

Her autobiography was called *Jumping for Joy*. ●

....

12 July 1996

Lawrence Donegan
Fairway to heaven

24 January: Turnberry, Scotland

Ross and I have a getting-to-know-each-other round at the famous Open championship venue, the course where he started as assistant professional 21 years ago. I'm nervous as hell. Swinging a club in the presence of a pro is like walking into a room full of supermodels, you feel uglier than Quasimodo and twice as clumsy. Thankfully it goes well, though Ross is unhappy at the way he plays and complains about having no rhythm. I have less natural rhythm than Boris Yeltsin, yet play the round of my life. He beats me, but only by 27 shots. We retire to the bar for a chat. I give him the hard sell. We'll be like Don Quixote and Sancho Panza, the great man and his faithful retainer charging round the golf courses of Europe in pursuit of glory. 'You're good enough to win a tournament,' I say. 'All you need is someone upbeat and optimistic like me as a caddie to give you self-belief.'

He's probably heard it a million times before but is polite enough to nod and smile. 'We'll just play it by ear, shall we?' he says.

....

15 February: Johannesburg, SA

The South African PGA championship is staged at Houghton, an elegant tree-lined course in the city's most expensive suburb. Nelson Mandela lives in a white mansion round the corner. I pay a visit. He's out, and armed security guards won't let my taxi stop at the gates, but as we cruise past I spy a basketball hoop in the front garden; is this why the great man always looks so tired?

Half a dozen local caddies are standing outside the clubhouse when I arrive back at the course. 'Fuck off back home,' one says to me. The atmosphere inside is heavy; two other white caddies say they were threatened with knives. Over by the practice putting green another local caddy says he'll dig the course up if nothing is done about 'them' – he points at us, the European caddies.

George Mosheshe, a Sowetan I'd met the week before in Sun City, says the problem is that too many European caddies have flown out to South Africa for the event. In past years the majority of European professionals employed local caddies and paid European tour wages as opposed to South African tour wages (i.e. 50 per cent more). 'The PGA used to be our birthday and Christmas rolled in to one week,' Mosheshe says. 'They are angry that you have taken all the jobs.'

I can't say I blame them. The end of apartheid hasn't ended racism or brought great improvements in pay and conditions. Black caddies say they are routinely paid half of what white caddies get for the same job. Some white pros still call their black caddie 'kaffir' or 'nigger'. In Sun City, Ross and I watched Michael Du Toit, an Afrikaner professional we were playing order his black caddie to wade into filthy waist-high water to look for a ball. For the record, a packet of three balls in South Africa costs the equivalent of nine pounds. Oh yes, and professionals get them for nothing.

....

3 March: Tarragona, Spain

Ross wins his first cheque of the season, £2,313, after finishing joint 31st in the Open Catalonia with nine others. He was fairly sanguine – 'It's a start I suppose' – and I was not. I thought about a lap of honour around the Bonmont-Terres Noves course, but it just wasn't big enough.

....

7 March: Rabat, Morocco

A photograph of King Hassan swinging a seven iron hangs in the reception of Royal Dar es Salam golf club. He is a golf fanatic (keen but hopeless from the look of the picture), which explains why the European tour has detoured into Morocco. Local interest in the Open du Maroc is minimal. I conducted a modest straw poll in Rabat – the receptionist in my fleapit hotel and a man in a leather jacket who tried to sell me drugs outside the train station – and neither knew the tournament was taking place. Officially, anyone can attend. In reality, ordinary Moroccans know they are expected to stay well clear of the tournament. 'If I went there, the police would be very suspicious, they'd take my name and address,' Mr Hotel Receptionist says. I surreptitiously record Ross and myself during the first round: what do a professional and his caddie talk about during a round of golf. The four-hour tape is a mixture of high tension and low comedy.

On hole one Ross relieves the pressure by whistling a tune. 'I wish I hadn't heard that song,' he says.

'What is it?' I say.

'Probably an eight iron.'

'No, no. What's the song?'

'Sorry. It's "I am a Cider Drinker", The Wurzels.'

Neither of us is laughing by the end; he plays well but somehow shoots 79. The second round is much better. We reach the last, a par three, needing a hole-in-one to make the cut. The rain is so heavy it looks like fog. Soaked to the skin, he hits a heroic four-iron but can't quite pull off the miracle. I'm almost in tears as we start packing up in the locker room. This is ridiculous, I haven't cried since May 1987, the night Maggie won her third election. 'I can't believe you played so well and missed the cut,' I explain. Ross looks at me, bemused. 'Don't worry about it, you'll probably get used to it.'

....

24 March: Lisbon, Portugal

Morale is low. Ross keeps a meticulous record of his spending in a hard-backed Boots diary and it reads like Stephen King. So far he's spent £6,391 and 35 pence. He's earned just over £3,000. Ian Woosnam leads the Order of Merit with £226,820. Ross is lying in 144th place. 'To be honest I am getting to the end of my tether,' he says over dinner.

I try to cheer him up. 'Look at the guys we've played with this week, you're a better golfer than all of them but they've just scored a bit better.'

This makes him feel worse. 'I can honestly say over the last few years there has scarcely been a round where I haven't come off the course and not been disappointed, thinking it could have been better,' he says.

'I've got to make things happen in Cannes.'

....

19 April: Cannes, France

Something happens. We miss the cut. To say we are depressed would be to say that Atlantis had a small plumbing problem.

....

28 April: Valencia, Spain

I sign up for the Belgrano, an H-registration Talbot camper van which is the favoured means of transport for a group of Argentinian caddies (hence the nickname). Nine of us squeeze inside for the journey to Milan after a long day in the Spanish sun – if this is not illegal on safety grounds it certainly should be on account of the smell and I'm overcome by jealousy as the luxury coach taking the players to the airport departs the clubhouse.

Caddies, partly by tradition but mostly because of financial necessity, live as cheaply as possible. In the past this meant hitchhiking and sleeping under hedges. These days it means shacking up four to a single room in a Dubai hostel full of Russian prostitutes or £3-a-night fleapits in Rabat or enduring 20-hour road trips from Valencia to Milan in galley-ship conditions.

Did I say 20 hours? We break down in the Pyrenees at 2am and are towed to a garage forecourt in southern France. There are guard dogs outside so having a pee is out of the question. It is only when dawn breaks that we grasp the full enormity of our predicament: 'Does anyone know the French for "Do you have an alternator for an H-reg Talbot camper van?"?'

....

16–18 May: Oxford, England

I confront Ross on the practice green before the first round of the Benson and Hedges International and suggest that 'it is time we got going'.

He doesn't take too kindly to my 'hard man' approach – 'Don't you think I know that. You saying it just puts more pressure on me' – but goes out in a near-gale and plays beautifully to score 73.

He shoots 69 in the second round to finish tied seventh. I wander over to the 18th green and catch my first sight of the huge scoreboard by the closing hole. His name is there in big black type, DRUMMOND, –2, in between FALDO and WOOSNAM.

We are in the fifth last group of the day for the third round, paired with Ryder Cup player Howard Clark. Ross starts with a par four, birdies the second and the fourth to go to four under. He reaches the green on the par-five seventh in two shots and holes a 40-foot, double-breaking putt for an eagle. According to the scoreboard behind the green, the Benson and Hedges International has a new leader: DRUMMOND, –6.

He leads on his own for four holes. I can't keep my eyes off the leader board, partly out of pride and partly out of disbelief. He refuses to look. We talk about the weather and last night's television – anything but the dark, dangerous, exciting fact that he is now leading one of Europe's biggest tournaments. To talk about *that* could break the spell.

It doesn't last. He drops two shots to finish the day on four under par, joint seventh, but still in contention.

· ·

19 May: Oxford, England
The definition of big time golf? The practice range at 12.30 on a Sunday afternoon. Faldo's there, reviewing his last swing on video. Montgomerie, Woosnam, Rocca, Torrance are all warming up. Ross is hitting smooth nine irons into a headwind, I'm drinking tea and trying to look like I've been here before. The banter of the first three days has gone, leaving just distilled concentration and the raw competitiveness of world-class sport. It's exhilarating and frightening. I feel physically sick. What would it be like if I had to hit the shots?

We tee off in a gale at 1.54pm, one group in front of Faldo. He is followed by galleries which are 10-deep. Our gallery is 10, but gradually the crowd thickens. Ross starts steadily, Faldo and others fall away. This is getting serious. We're joined by a BBC camera buggy on the eighth, just as Ross prepares to hit his second into a peninsula green.

He turns to me. 'Nine iron? What do you think?'

I'm paralysed with terror. He waits for an answer, forcing me to say something. 'That's fine,' I mumble. He goes in to a pre-shot routine. 'No, wait, the wind is too strong, I think it's an eight iron.'

Did I say that? He takes the eight iron. The ball is in the air. If it's short it's in water, too long and it's in water. I prepare my apology and ponder a bank loan to repay the money I've just cost him. Applause drifts back on the wind. Cancel the bank loan, we're still in business.

He birdies the 10th, to go two off the lead. This is getting very serious. First prize is £116,000. He bogies the 12th but is still in with a chance. The 13th is tough, a par three into a headwind. He looks over to me.

'Five iron's fine,' I say, this time with conviction.

Five iron is far from fine. He hits a great shot straight at the flag but it's too long and sails straight into a bunker. Mortified, I stride off towards the green. 'Don't worry, it's OK, it's OK,' I say.

The wind is howling but I can still hear him shouting back: 'Yes, it's fuckin' perfect. Plugged in the bunker, bloody perfect.'

Ross finishes his round just after 5.30pm, in seventh place at one-under par for £21,000 prize money. The players still out on the course struggle in the wind and when the tournament ends at 5.50pm he is in fourth place with winnings of £32,000, the biggest cheque of his career.

I figure £11,000 in 20 minutes would make even a privatised utility boss blush but Ross is dreamily happy. 'I can't believe this,' he says.

• •

30 May: Hamburg, Germany

Ross recruits a new member to 'Team Drummond'. Jos Vanstiphout, a Belgian with a Californian vocabulary, teaches 'inner game' techniques, a pseudo-psychological approach to improving a golfer's game. 'In America, they call me Mr Magic,' is his boast.

I stand on the practice range, bemused, as Mr Magic gets down to business. 'We have to silence this motherfucker up here, Self One,' he says, pointing to Ross's head, 'and let this guy, Self Two, take control.' He touches Ross's stomach.

Self One is the destructive part of a player's personality. Self Two is his subconscious, Jos explains. He instructs Ross to 'play one ball', then 'focus my friend' and then 'take in the flowers and the trees'.

Later, he tells me: 'I see this beautiful man standing in front of me. He has so much ability but he is not using it because of his attitude. At the same time it is a beautiful challenge.'

Mr Beautiful Challenge makes two cuts in the next two weeks, finishing 55th in the German Open and 53rd in the English Open.

Mr Magic gives his verdict to Mr Bemused: 'So far, I am happy, but he will still get better. I know Ross will win, my friend.'

• •

17 June: Prestwick, Scotland

Jos was right, almost. Ross breaks the course record, shooting 65 in the last round of the Northumberland Challenge, and finishes second. He picks up a cheque for £33,000. It's almost midnight and we are in Ross's sitting room watching the highlights on EuroSport.

Ross is drunk on excitement. I'm just drunk.

'You're a bloody fairytale,' I slur.

Ross looks 10 years younger than he did in February, 10 years younger and about £80,000 richer. Where did it all go right?

'So often in golf you start thinking, "What if I hit a bad shot here, what if it goes out of bounds?" You play in a state of fear. That's me, I'd been playing in a state of fear for a long, long time,' he explains. I sense an opportunity for some praise. What has brought about the change, I ask; has it been anything to do with your new super-caddie?

'I suppose there's a long list of things that have turned my year around,' he says, 'and to be honest, that one isn't near the top.'

. . . .

10 July: Carnoustie, Scotland
Drummond to win the Scottish Open Championship, 66–1. Every so often an investment opportunity comes along which can't be ignored and this invitation staring down at me from the board of the on-course bookmakers is one.

It's Scotland, he's on home turf, it's windy, he loves the wind, he loves the course, he shot 73 in the first round, he's nicely poised just three shots off the lead . . . need I go on?

Rule One in the unwritten handbook for caddies is never to bet on your own player, but I have £5 each way on Ross. I wonder what price he is for next week's Open. ●

. . . .

21 June 1996
David Hopps
Little Bird in an awful flap

The conviction that Dickie Bird has long been oblivious to the constraints of a normal life, preferring instead to traipse through his own benign fantasy, was strengthened beyond doubt as his 66th and final test began yesterday with a moment of pure theatre.

So much in the first over of his Lord's farewell encapsulated a great and agitated career. The game began half an hour late in fretful light, poor enough for him to fret, and he was unsure whether to use his white hanky to blow his nose or mop up his tears.

'If there's a God, all we need now is a big lbw appeal,' someone said. We laughed, not daring to believe that life would conform so conveniently. With Bird as master of ceremonies, no one should have doubted it. Life rolled over as willingly as a family pet dog begging for a tickle.

Four balls of Javagal Srinath's first over passed by routinely, as if deliberately building the tension. When his fifth ball cut back down the Lord's slope to strike Michael Atherton on the pad, a capacity Lord's crowd turned to stare at the umpire often depicted as the Great Not Outer and held its breath.

It was a desperately marginal decision, of the type that so often over the years has brought a traumatised shake of the head, one hand pressed so firmly into the small of his back that it might drill out the other side, the other hand buried deep into his pocket amid the counters, scissors, sticking plaster and other umpiring accoutrements.

This time, however, Bird's finger was raised with a flourish. Coming only a few minutes after the Lord's crowd had risen to cheer in tribute, there was an overwhelming sense of emotional relief.

Bird had entered the field a good two minutes after a respectful Tannoy announcement, making one wonder whether he had paused for a last visit to the loo. He had walked, back slightly bent, through a guard of honour formed by two applauding teams.

There are some who cling to a vacuous belief that Bird's career has been so delightful that it should be above analysis. There were others who suspected the ball was missing leg stump. After innumerable replays, however, it was possible to draw the most satisfying conclusion that he had got it right. That is some achievement with a mind awash with sentiment and tears still in the eyes.

Atherton is normally the gloomiest of leavers but on this occasion even England's captain could not suppress a rueful smile.

One can imagine Dickie discussing Atherton's dismissal well into the evening, underlining his point by grabbing the odd lapel. 'It were out, you know, it were out,' he will have said to anyone who would listen. 'What could I do? It were out. It were hitting leg. It were first over, too, you know. First over.'

He must have been exhausted after five deliveries. And there are still four days to go. ●

. . . .

7 August 1996

Jim White

'The money won't change me . . .'

She is 63, gets £67 a week state pension; he is 25 and scrapes by on £30,000 a week, or maybe £35,000 or possibly even £42,000 depending on which tabloid you read. Her last pair of shoes cost her £9.99 from a discount warehouse; he gets paid £500,000 a year to wear his.

She lives in a £40,000 house in Denton Burn, a Newcastle suburb with a fashion bypass; he is said to be looking for a place in snazzy Ponteland, something for around £750,000. But the moment Barbara Donaldson heard Alan Shearer was coming to her town, she thought she was the lucky one. 'The morning he signed for us I went to get my pension at the post office,' said Mrs Donaldson. 'Normally, they're a right grumpy lot, but that day everybody in the queue had a smile like a Cheshire cat. If you'd put us in for the Olympic high jump that morning, we'd have set a world record.'

Mrs Donaldson was by no means alone in her reaction to the purchase of Shearer for £15 million. On the day he was presented to his army of new lovers (fans is too slight a word) the entire population of Newcastle appeared to be wrapped in black and white striped nylon.

Everywhere you looked, people in replica Newcastle shirts were heading for St James's Park, Newcastle's ground which stands on top of a hill dominating the town. And Newcastle were not even playing. Fifteen thousand people just wanted to be there, to roar and chant as the new man was paraded.

Mrs Donaldson was luckier than most. While the 15,000 were left in a car park along with the press and 1,400 invitees sent tickets by Newcastle's sponsors, she found herself inside the stadium itself.

'I've been offered £100 for my tickets,' said Brian Bloomfield from Gateshead, sitting next to Mrs Donaldson. 'But I wouldn't take it. It wouldn't be fair on him,' he added, pointing to his son, Dean, aged nine, who was beaming beside him. 'He has to be here on this of all days.'

Now this is an unexpected thing. Shearer cost enough to equip a hospital. He earns more in four days than a teacher will earn in a year. In a town where unemployment is endemic, you might think spending so much on a mere footballer would be regarded as wanton extravagance. But you could find few in Newcastle yesterday who did not think he represented the biggest bargain this side of a Marks & Spencer prawn sandwich.

'I'd have paid the money myself if I had it,' said Brian Bloomfield. 'This is the best thing to happen to this town since I can remember.'

Which is the point about Shearer. On the BBC's *Match of the Seventies* broadcast on Monday night, we saw footage of Malcolm Macdonald, a previous incumbent of the number nine shirt Shearer is about to make his own, signing for Arsenal. That was the way things used to be around these parts: every time someone made good he went down south: Gascoigne, Waddle, Cole, they all migrated. Now the real thing was coming Newcastle's way. Not only that, he is a Geordie coming home. Better still, he was snatched out of the grasp of traditionally bigger, richer rivals.

'There's real pride in that,' said Mrs Donaldson. 'That we are in a position to compete with Man U, who just seem to be able to get whatever they want.'

Thus the very size of Shearer's fee, the weight of his wage, are seen locally as symbolic of a new muscular ambition abroad in the town, the nineties equivalent of the grandiose town halls the Victorians used to build.

'This sends out a signal to the rest of the world,' Kevin Keegan, Shearer's new manager, said.

And the man who provided the funds to bring Shearer back to Newcastle was everywhere yesterday, making sure this point was made. 'Football has always been part of our tradition,' said Sir John Hall, Newcastle United's owner, bouncing around St James's Park in a pair of unexpectedly pointy blue shoes. 'Football has never left the area. It's the talent that's gone away. What we're saying here is you don't have to leave Newcastle.'

And, indeed, there will be economic benefits to the place from buying Shearer. Dozens more staff have been taken on in the club shop to process orders for Shearer shirts. Thousands of extra pounds have flowed through pub tills toasting the new arrival. Hundreds more Scandinavians will flock in for football and shopping weekends.

The cynic might suggest the chief beneficiary of the Shearer boom will be Sir John Hall, owner of Britain's biggest shopping centre, the Metro Centre in Gateshead; in an economy built on retail, to be in possession of a brand as potent as Shearer is to be king.

But there was no place for cynics around St James's Park yesterday. 'Of course, Sir John's making money out of this,' said Dave Trainer, from Darlington, at 25 the same age as Shearer but earning slightly less as one of the area's unemployed. 'But without him, we'd have none of this,' he added. 'Sure, I can't afford to come and watch them, but I'd rather not be able to afford to watch my team with Shearer in it than get in to see rubbish.'

As for the man himself, well, Shearer clearly prefers his venomous right foot to do his talking; his press conference pronouncements were not in the sardines and trawlers class. Blinking modestly in the flashbulb blaze, he limited himself to talking of 'giving 110 per cent' and saying 'For me the season can't come quick enough.'

He also declared: 'If money comes my way, that's fine; I'll deal with that when it comes along. It certainly won't change me. After all, I'm only a sheet metal-worker's son from Newcastle.'

Mrs Donaldson was thrilled by the man. 'He's lovely, everything a mother dreams her son to be,' she said. 'Not one you'd lust over, mind. Not like Sir John. Power, now that's the real aphrodisiac.'

Meanwhile, outside the stadium, the 15,000 fans waited for their new man to appear on the stage. A sense of parochial triumphalism was on their minds as they ignored the rain and sang as one: 'Are you watching, Sunderland?' •